10/14/89

Troubling Biblical Waters

A Gift for ~~The~~ Rev Florence Y Alcorn!

You are a fine example of why our God is bigger than most of us — honor what God has given you to offer to others in your ministry!

Thanks for your support for this 8 yr labor of love!

Cain Hope Felder

The Bishop Henry McNeal Turner Studies
in North American Black Religion

Vol. 1   *For My People*
         by James H. Cone

Vol. 2   *Black and African Theologies*
         by Josiah U. Young

Editor:

James H. Cone,
Union Theological Seminary, New York

Associate Editors:

Charles H. Long,
University of North Carolina, Chapel Hill

C. Shelby Rooks,
United Church Board of Homeland Ministries

Gayraud S. Wilmore,
New York Theological Seminary

The purpose of this series is to encourage the development of biblical, historical, theological, and pastoral works that analyze the role of the churches and other religious movements in the liberation struggles of blacks in the United States and the Third World. What is the relationship between black religion and black peoples' fight for justice in the U. S.? What is the relationship between the black struggle for justice in the U. S. and the liberation struggles of the poor in Asia, Africa, Latin America, and the Caribbean? A critical investigation of these and related questions will define the focus of this series.

The series is named after Bishop Henry McNeal Turner (1834–1915), whose life and work symbolize the black struggle for liberation in the U.S. and the Third World. Bishop Turner was a churchman, a political figure, a missionary, a pan-Africanist—a champion of black freedom and the cultural creativity of black peoples under God.

The Bishop Henry McNeal Turner Studies
in North American Black Religion, Vol. III

Cain Hope Felder

Troubling Biblical Waters

Race, Class, and Family

ORBIS BOOKS

Maryknoll, New York 10545

Third Printing, September 1989

The Catholic Foreign Mission Society of America (Maryknoll) recruits and trains people for overseas missionary service. Through Orbis Books, Maryknoll aims to foster the international dialogue that is essential to mission. The books published, however, reflect the opinions of their authors and are not meant to represent the official position of the society.

Unless otherwise noted, the Bible text contained herein is from the Revised Standard Version Bible, copyright 1946, 1952, 1971 by the Division of Christian Education of the National Council of the Churches of Christ in the USA, and is used by permission.

Manuscript editor and indexer: Toni Sortor

Library of Congress Cataloging-in-Publication Data

Felder, Cain Hope
    Troubling biblical waters: race, class, and family/Cain H.
Felder.
        p.   cm. — (The Bishop Henry McNeal Turner studies in North
American Black religion: vol. 3)
    Bibliography: p.
    Includes indexes.
    ISBN 0-88344-535-2
    1. Blacks in the Bible.   2. Sociology, Biblical.   3. Justice—
Biblical teaching.   4. Afro-Americans—Religion.   5. Family—
Biblical teaching.   I. Title.   II. Series.
BS680.B48F45   1989
220.8'305896—dc19   88-37471
                                                        CIP

This book is dedicated

to the memory of my brothers,
Alvin, Abel and Clayton

to the memory of two of my children,
Ian Russell and Melanie Stacia

to the memory of Dr. Negail R. Riley
and in honor of his wife, Gwendolyn,
whose love sustained him over the years

in honor of my daughter,
Akidah H. Felder

my mother,
Lula Mae Felder

as well as
Don and Evie Hufford

Contents

Introduction   *xi*

PART I
RACE

Introduction   *3*

Chapter One
Biblical Meaning and the Black Religious Experience   *5*
   The Dawn of the Black Religious Experience   8
   Blacks in the Biblical Tradition   12
   Historical Relativism and Cultural Subjectivity in Canon
      Formation   14
   Black Theology, Africa, and a Biblical Revolution   16
   New Testament Radicalism and the Future of the Black
      Religious Experience: Lessons *from* and *for* Africa   17

Chapter Two
Ancient Ethiopia and the Queen of Sheba   *22*
   Ethiopia and Sheba in Antiquity   23
   The Semitic Language and Africa   28
   Interpretations Regarding the Queen of Sheba   30
   The Queen of Sheba as a Black   32

Chapter Three
Racial Motifs in the Biblical Narratives   *37*
   Race and Sacralization in the Old Testament   38
   Election and Sacralization in the Bible   43
   Secularization in the New Testament   46

PART II
CLASS

Introduction 51

Chapter Four
Biblical Mandates on Justice and Social Class 53
    Distributive Justice in Plato and Aristotle 56
    Justice in the Old Testament and Intertestamental Traditions 59
    Justice in the Pentateuchal Traditions 60
    Justice in the Prophetic Literature 63
    Justice in the Psalms and Old Testament Wisdom Literature 64
    New Testament Perspectives on Justice 68
    Love and Justice in the New Testament 69

Chapter Five
Biblical Usage in American Black Churches 79
    An Etymology of Preaching 80
    Historical Notes on Preaching in the Black Church 81
    Biblical Usage and the Negro Spirituals 85
    Biblical Usage in Black Church Art and Education 86
    Guidelines for Biblical Usage 88
    Preaching from the New Testament 96

Chapter Six
Freedom and Class: The Epistle to the Galatians 102
    The American Freedom Crisis 103
    Biblical Images of Freedom 104
    A Divine Call to the Unworthy 106
    The Background and Structure of Galatians 109
    The Politics of Christian Freedom 113

Chapter Seven
Class and God's Law: The Epistle of James 118
    Analysis and Discussion—James 2:1–7 120
    Analysis and Discussion—James 2:8–13 125

PART III
FAMILY

Introduction 137

Chapter Eight
The Bible, Black Women, and Ministry 139
    The Roles of Women in the Bible 140
    Gospel Themes for Black Women in Ministry 142

Sorting Out Paul's Attitude on Women in Ministry   145
The New Testament's Caution and Challenge   148

Chapter Nine
The Bible and Black Families: A Theological Challenge   *150*
The Family as a Patriarchal Household in the Old Testament   151
Moral Action and Blood Kinship in the New Testament   155
Sexual Conduct and the Household of God   160
Listen to the Blood   163

Chapter Ten
The Things That Make for Peace:
New Testament Foundations in the Nuclear Age   *167*
The Church's Confession of Peace and Self-Interest   171
Peacemaking and Apocalyptic Rediscovery   173

Notes   *179*

Bibliography   *209*

General Index   *223*

Scripture Index   *229*

Introduction

The purpose of this book is to provide some sorely needed correctives regarding the Bible in relation to ancient Africa and Black people today. Despite the fact that the Bible has a favorable attitude about Blacks, post-biblical misconstruals of biblical traditions have created the impression that the Bible is primarily the foundational document of "the White Man's religion." The mistaken notion widely persists that the relation of Black people to the Bible is a post-biblical experience. Such historical distortions, created by Eurocentric scholars and missionaries to the detriment of Blacks, have long been one of my concerns. In the course of study and teaching in universities and theological schools, I have encountered little favorable discussion about the presence of Blacks in the Bible or the long, *pre-slavery, pre-Reformation,* and *pre-Islam* association that Africans and those of the Black diaspora have had with the biblical tradition. Under the influence of Western culture and its by-product, racism, too many Blacks themselves believe that they are latecomers in the history of salvation. This book seeks to illuminate the Black story within The Story, so the ancient record of God's Word takes on new meaning for the Black Church today.

Since the seventeenth and eighteenth centuries, successive generations of Bible scholars have examined God's ancient Word in view of biblical traditions. By analyzing the Bible as a product of ancient cultures, scholars have brought new questions to old texts to demonstrate the significance of the Bible beyond the limits imposed by church dogma. Unfortunately, almost all the biblical scholars doing the exegesis have been Europeans or Euro-Americans, among them Ashkenazic Jews. On the whole, the waters of Eurocentric Bible scholarship have been rather calm, with mostly polite disagreements, except for occasional broadsides by such scholars as Walter Wink (biblical hermeneutics), J. A. T. Robinson (redating of the New Testament), Elisabeth Schüssler Fiorenza (feminist reconstruction), William Farmer (dispensing with Q, the Synoptic sayings source), and Jose Miranda (Marxist biblical analysis). Recent insights from studies in the sociology of knowledge[1] help explain the quiet consensus that exists. European/Euro-American biblical scholars have asked questions and shaped answers within the framework of the racial, cultural, and gender presuppositions they hold in common. This quiet consensus has undermined the self-understanding and place in history of other racial and ethnic groups.

During this same post-Enlightenment period, Black people have been enslaved, colonized, and vigorously evangelized by Western Christendom. In light of the biblical themes of liberation, the rich Black heritage in biblical antiquity, or the clear biblical mandates for justice, Bible scholars have scarcely pointed out the ironies and contradictions of such developments. A few Black Bible scholars have produced books and articles attempting to address aspects of the Bible that impinge directly on the lives of Black people. In 1925, the Reverend R. A. Morrisey published *Colored People and Bible History*. Morrisey did not have the benefit of advanced theological training in higher criticism; still, his Foreword is instructive:

> Every foremost race of people in the world today has its history written by its own members. To keep this universal rule, colored people should be no exception. . . . Especially so because the information as well as inspiration will lead their own group toward nobler aspirations and higher ideals in life's activities. . . . The Negro has a history of which he need not be ashamed, but he will wait a long time for a White man to write this history in fairness, for the consumption of the great White public.[2]

Morrisey then proceeds to report, *as objective history,* the biblical genealogies of Genesis 10 and 1 Chronicles 1, arguing that all the descendants of Ham, beginning with Cush, Egypt (*Mizraim*), Put (Punt), and Canaan, were basically Negroes. Much more recently, this romantic appropriation of the genealogies reappeared in Albert Cleage's *The Black Messiah*.[3]

Other books on the Bible by Black authors include Bishop Alfred Dunston's *The Black Man in the Old Testament and Its World*[4] and Latta Thomas's *Biblical Faith and the Black American*.[5] Dunston's work shows a ranging but precritical familiarity with the Old Testament, whereas Thomas's book primarily selects biblical themes congenial with the struggles of Afro-American Christians. The few critical works by Black scholars of the Bible include Dr. Robert Bennett's article, "Africa and the Biblical Period,"[6] Dr. Charles B. Copher's "The Black Man in the Biblical World," and his most recent "3,000 Years of Biblical Interpretation with Reference to Black Peoples."[7] Not long ago, Howard University's *Journal of Religious Thought* published Dr. Vincent Wimbush's "Biblical-Historical Study as Liberation: Toward an Afro-Christian Hermeneutic".[8] As disturbing or shocking as it may be, there is not much more scholarly literature on Blacks in biblical antiquity authored by Blacks, with the exception of the work of Professor Frank Snowden, whose professional expertise is Greco-Roman classical literature.[9]

These observations demonstrate the need for more studies on the significance of the Bible in relation to Black people; these should draw on insights from the "political" theologies of liberation that have come into existence in the last quarter-century. Of course, it is possible to argue that all theology is implicitly "political," that is, a discourse about God in relation to the power and social structures of a given society. Nonetheless, the more recent forms of political theology are distinctive for the explicit manner in which they express a thoroughgoing concern for the socioeconomic and political circumstances of the poor, disenfranchised, and oppressed.

For Afro-Americans, this discourse is Black Liberation Theology, beginning in a formal and systematic way with James H. Cone's *Black Power and Black Theology* in 1969. I welcomed the opportunity to review that book for the *Union Quarterly Review* (Summer 1970), not recognizing at the time how significant the book would be in establishing new foci for future theological discourse about the political implications of the gospel for Blacks and the Third World. Subsequent "political" theology whether Latin American or feminist was able to reassess the significance of the ways our modern context (cultural and/or racial) gives rise to new theological politics of race, class, and gender.[10] The quest for a Black theology of liberation caused others to begin articulating a stunning variety of theologies of liberation, whether African, Asian, Water Buffalo (Japan), or more recently, MinJung Theology (Korea).[11] Modern questions about God's liberating activity in the world inevitably encourage Bible scholars to re-examine ancient biblical texts in view of the unique elements in diverse modern contexts for discerning God's continuing activity.

This volume represents eight years of research on topics that deal with biblical attitudes about or insights into race, class, and family.   I have developed the book in response to the alarming lack of books on the Bible in relation to Blacks.   Yet I could not wait for someone else to provide the study resources needed for this kind of work. Therefore, the chapters that follow represent a collection of articles and papers originally written for a variety of audiences and occasions and subsequently expanded or revised.

The inspiration for the title of this book derives from the words of the Afro-American spiritual "Wade in the Water":

> Wade in the water, wade in the water, children,
> Wade in the water, God's a gonna trouble the water.
>> See that host all dressed in white,
>> God's a gonna trouble the water.
>> The leader looks like an Israelite,
>> God's a gonna trouble the water.
>> See that band all dressed in red,
>> God's a gonna trouble the water;
> It looks like the band that Moses led,
>> God's a gonna trouble the water.
>> Look over yonder, what do I see?
>> God's a gonna trouble the water;

> The Holy Ghost a coming on me,
> God's a gonna trouble the water.
> If you don't believe I've been redeemed,
> God's a gonna trouble the water;
> Just follow me down to Jordan's stream,
> God's a gonna trouble the water.[12]

While the verses combine the Old Testament Exodus motif of liberation (first two) with its provocative understanding of baptism as the New Testament parallel (third and fourth), the refrain states again and again, "God's a gonna trouble the water!" My intent in these chapters is to "trouble" (more precisely, "divide": *schizō*) the waters of the biblical Sea of Reeds (LXX, Exod. 14:21) and clear a new pathway that leads to the Bible as an indispensable tool for liberation — sociopolitical and economic, as well as spiritual. I further intend to trouble (*tarassō*) the placid waters of Eurocentric historiography, exegesis, and hermeneutics on questions of race, class, and family. Those who exhibit a mind and body "paralysis" should be put into biblical waters troubled afresh. While these chapters represent an attempt to "trouble the waters," they also say, "Rise, take up your pallet, and walk" (John 5:8).

In the first three chapters, my purpose is to provide a critical framework for reassessing the status of Blacks and the question of race in biblical antiquity. I try to demonstrate, first of all, that there are numerous mentions of Black people in the Old and New Testaments, despite an unsympathetic attitude on this point by some Bible scholars, ministers, and rabbis today. I give evidence that Blacks, in a modern Western context so often hostile to their interests must continue to participate in what the French philosopher Michel Foucault calls "the insurrection of subjugated knowledges."[13] These chapters also consider the continuity in the Black religious experience, especially when it appeals to, or otherwise derives meaning from, the biblical witness. Finally, Part I confronts the complexities regarding pure racial types and racial motifs in the biblical narratives. I stress important differences within the Old Testament when some "color consciousness" does exist (Num. 12:1-16; Jer. 13:23), but I argue that the problem is not racism based on color, but oppressions based on religion, tribes, nationalism, and imperialism that gave rise in the Old Testament to such notions as an ethnically determined "chosen people." I identify two processes in the Bible — sacralization and secularization. Both seem to clarify aspects of the Bible that do not facilitate the interests of Black people.

To illustrate some of these concerns, chapter one examines the data (biblical and extrabiblical) that indicate a long, ancient history of Blacks in the dynasties of Egypt. No longer is it enough to single out the Twenty-fifth (Ethiopian) Dynasty in Egypt beginning in 730 B.C. and lasting until Taharqa's fall to the Assyrians in 653 B.C. (Isa. 37:9; 2 Kings 19:9).[14] One implication is that now, like never before, we can adduce the truth of Ps. 105:23: "Then Israel came to Egypt; Jacob sojourned in the *land of Ham*" (emphasis mine). Also, such passages as "out of Egypt I called my son" (Hos. 11:1; Matt. 2:15) now take on new meaning.

Chapter two presents the findings of Professor Ephraim Isaac and myself as the result of our collaborative study for a paper he read at the 1984 Congress of Ethiopian Studies in Addis Ababa. The chapter concerns itself with ancient Ethiopia, Arabia, and the Queen of Sheba. We not only explore the Western biases regarding the Queen of Sheba as a Black royal figure (1 Kings 10:1-13; 2 Chron. 9:1-9), but put forth the biblical and extrabiblical evidence that points to her African, or more specifically Ethiopian, identity. In chapter three I amplify the specific matter of racial motifs within the Bible, in order to compare and contrast Old Testament traditions with those of the New Testament, suggesting that the latter has a more authentic universalism.

The four chapters that comprise Part II of this book turn from topics of race to the issue of class. Chapter four takes broad questions of justice and social class in the Bible and attempts a constructive interpretation, especially in view of the vital concerns of the modern context of Black and Third World churches. That chapter offers an extended examination of biblical mandates for justice—a topic somewhat neglected in the published works of biblical scholars. I offer a rejoinder to those New Testament scholars who do not think that any such mandate exists! Then, in chapter five, we discuss the varied but largely precritical/literalist usage of the Bible in churches of the underclass, attesting to the great *chasm* that bedevils us because the guild of biblical scholarship and the seminary stand so far from the Black local church in this regard. I try to show that the problem is critical, heightened by the fact that many of the Black Church laity are more educated and sophisticated than pastors (with or without theological education) who routinely "biblicize" instead of struggling, reading, and studying the text as a vocation.

From these general concerns, I shift to the specific cases of two New Testament communities, represented by the Epistle to the Galatians and the Epistle of James, where the gospel has begun to trouble the waters. Both communities have a problem with class, but Paul and James, in different ways, redress the once faithful to realign their own class consciousness with the biblical ideal that God is "no respecter of persons." Old Testament provisions on this subject take on major significance in light of the Jesus tradition—both in those ancient communities and in modern, capitalistic class-conscious societies evident in our churches today. We adopt a more exegetical procedure in identifying the community concerns of these New Testament epistles.

Chapter six focuses on the ideas of freedom and class consciousness. This chapter is an expanded revision of the manuscript I developed in 1985 as a chapter in George Balla's *Thirteen Divine Calls of the Bible* (Judson Press).

The argument here shows that in Galatians, the problem is an escape from freedom's responsibility and a desire to return to the convenience of a legalistic religion with concise do's and don'ts. When faced with gospel freedom, the Galatians seem to prefer the security of religiosity, so in the end, they are free to do whatever they please! By contrast, those in the Epistle of James want to abandon the requirements of both the Law and the Jesus tradition. For them, worldly pursuits and social intercourse are governed by conventional expediency, not gospel. In either case, class has become a big problem, and it persists in religious settings today, despite the severity of ancient biblical strictures against classism.

The final part of the book contains three chapters that consider the Bible in relation to questions of gender, family, and the Household of God. Chapter eight represents a new version of my article on "The Bible, Black Women and Ministry," which was published almost simultaneously by the *Journal of Religious Thought* and the *Journal of the Interdenominational Theological Center*.[15] I find it rather curious that a number of Black men often seem to allow the woman to be head of the household (more than 50 percent of the Black families in the United States), but have difficulty with the idea of Black women as ordained ministers in the Household of God — the Church. In chapter eight I attempt to identify New Testament evidence that suggests a historical variety of female leadership roles, including ministry in the early house churches. Yet I also caution Black female ministers not to be false prophetesses in light of the ways some of their male counterparts have become false prophets. The biblical waters are being troubled!

In chapter nine, I take up a most important subject: the Bible and family life, with particular application to the Black experience. I presented the original version of this chapter at the 1984 Convocation of the Congress of National Black Churches (CNBC) in Memphis, Tennessee. As that manuscript is now revised, I attempt to show that the Bible does not present a monolithic picture of the nuclear family as the categorical norm. Rather, I contend that the Bible confronts us with diverse family patterns. In the Old Testament, blood relations are very important, but not exclusively so. In the New Testament, blood relations recede in importance as the witness of Jesus Christ on the cross beckons us to listen to the blood in an entirely new way. The New Testament directs us beyond narrow obligations to blood relatives, to broader obligations that proceed from Christ's blood (Rom. 3:25; 5:9). The hurt and needy in society become our family by virtue of spiritual kinship. Thus believers have a new vision of what it means to have membership in the Household of God! The implications are many in terms of ways New Testament people should deal with such modern problems as sexual relations (whether premarital, extramarital, male/female homosexuality, or teenage parenting) or the problems of gossiping, slandering, lying, and stealing. I contend that for New Testament authors, all these problems compromised the vision of wholeness. The theological challenge that presents itself is not merely the nature of the sin, but the nature and quality of the Christian's response to a particular instance of sin. The chapter closes with an appeal to enter into a helping solidarity of *agapē* within and beyond the new Household by virtue of what Christ's blood has done for us all.

In chapter ten we consider the urgent question of peacemaking in an age when the human family stands on the brink of a nuclear Armageddon. The substance of this chapter was developed for testimony during the summer of 1985 before the United Methodist Council of Bishops in their hearings on the nuclear crisis (now published as *In Defense of Creation*). In an expanded format here, my reflections commend the agenda of peacemaking to the Black Church as the corollary to the agenda of justice. We identify several Old and New Testament texts and teachings that establish peacemaking as a blessed task for anyone interested in the survival of the human family. It is important to show that concern for both justice and peace is inherent in the Old Testament concept of Shalom and this double sense is not lost in the New Testament. In the creation narratives, God only rests when the work of creation is completed and perfect. Yet that perfect peace is soon broken by injustices as humans become inhumane to one another, keeping the image of brokenness ever before us—within the Bible and within subsequent Christian history. Luke 19:41, 42 is revealing, for when Jesus finally arrives at the city of wrong—Jerusalem (Zion)—he can only weep, saying, "Would that even today you knew the things that make for peace!" While the New Testament seems to close with images of destruction in the Revelation of St. John, the careful reader will understand that even this last book of the Bible extends the vision of peace and justice to humanity—the vision of a new heaven and earth, the pursuit of a new city, and the symbol of hope in the prayer, "Come, Lord Jesus." New Testament authors never envisioned that God would destroy all life in a nuclear inferno. Thus the prayer that closes the Bible is itself a renewed call to witness and hope in a God who can still trouble the waters for us!

Many have encouraged me in the preparation of this book. I am grateful to several of my Black scholar mentors—Drs. James H. Cone, Gayraud S. Wilmore, Charles H. Long, and Lawrence N. Jones—who favorably reviewed my initial proposal for this book and offered helpful comments. I am especially appreciative of the small but meaningful grant I received from the Foundation for Religious Educational Exchange (FREE) made possible by Dr. J. Deotis Roberts and significantly presented to me at the 1985 Annual Meeting of the Society for the Study of Black Religion (SSBR). I would also like to mention in this regard Dr. John Graebner, Reverends David W. Helms, William R. Porter, Edward D. McGowan, and Mr. David Dix who, over the years as friends, have given much tangible evidence of the confidence that they have in my work. Black female colleagues such as Drs. Jacqueline Grant, Jualynne Dodson, and Clarice Martin, as well as Professor Renita Weems will never know how much they have helped to heighten my sensitivity to the roles and plight of Black women. Beyond these individuals, I am indebted to my other colleagues and students, Black, white, Hispanic, and Asian at Princeton Theological Seminary (1978–1981) and at Howard University's School of Divinity (1981–present). My tutelage by eminent Bible scholars over the years is much more a credit to me than this book perhaps will be to any of them. Perhaps some of them will now understand why I spent so much time during my Union Theological doctoral work "on the other side of the street" at Columbia University, delving into subjects not normally thought appropriate for a Ph.D. candidate in New Testament. For me, it was essential to remove some of the "blinders" that tend to inhibit one from learning about the wider religious experience (especially the history of religions) that can give new meaning to biblical studies.

I firmly believe that Black people need to *trouble the waters* with perspectives and information not usually addressed by discrete theological curricula. This book struggles against becoming lost in "scholarly details" typical of debates between biblical specialists. The general reader will have to bear with me, however, at certain points where technical language is inescapable. Nevertheless, this book constitutes an exploration rather than a definitive study. Although a variety of persons have read separate parts of the manuscript, I alone must take responsibility for its final form—both for possible strengths and weaknesses. I didn't realize how much work re-mained to be done—in terms of arrangement, style, content, and documen-tation—in early 1985, when Orbis Books accepted the articles submitted as the nucleus of a proposed book. I am now somewhat chastened by the task, which I still think is as unfinished as Franz Schubert's famous "Unfinished" Symphony. Yet, it is finished, and I have especially to thank my devoted assistant for *The Journal of Religious Thought,* the Reverend Nancy Jo Floyd, who also serves as my secretary. She has combined a remarkable selflessness, indefatigable style, and a genuine love for the New Testament to provide a rare kind of support. She not only completely retyped and helped to proof the manuscript for this book, but frequently troubled me with queries that proved to be quite invaluable. Because of her, my colleagues and students at Howard Divinity, and my family, I feel truly blessed and offer this book as a token of that blessedness.

Cain Hope Felder
Howard University School of Divinity
Washington, DC

Troubling Biblical Waters

Part I

RACE

Introduction

Today popular Christianity too easily assumes that modern ideas about race are traceable to the Bible or that there is not a significant Black presence in the Bible. Centuries of European and Euro-American scholarship, along with a "save the heathen blacks" missionary approach to Africans, have created these impressions. For this reason, we begin our study with three chapters that focus on biblical ideas of race, Blacks in biblical antiquity, and the subsequent negative racial attitudes against Blacks that have taken many forms in Western historiography and biblical interpretation during the postbiblical period.

Racially biased teachings on Blacks in the Bible have long been and continue to be detrimental, not only to African-Americans or others in the African diaspora, but also to Blacks in Africa. To confirm this observation quickly, one needs only to read portions of the provocative autobiography by Mark Mathabane entitled *Kaffir Boy*. At one point the author depicts surrogate Black African evangelists (trained by white missionaries) expounding the following:

> Our forefathers, who for centuries had lived in utter darkness in the jungles of Africa, worshipping false gods involving human sacrifices, needed Christ bad. That's why God from his sacred seat in heaven one day looked at Africa and said to Himself, "I cannot in all fairness let those black children of mine continue to follow the evil path. They've already suffered enough for the transgressions of their cursed father Ham."[1]

The reader soon finds that not only are Blacks living under the so-called curse of Ham, but the devil himself is a "horned black man with the fork and the pit of fire."[2]

Even in the late nineteenth century, Bishop Henry McNeal Turner, to whom this series of volumes is dedicated, expressed grave concern over misunderstandings of the Bible that cast Blacks in an unfavorable light:

> Yet we are no stickler as to God's color anyway, but if He has any we would prefer to believe that it is nearer symbolized in the blue sky above us and the blue water of the Seas and oceans; but we certainly protest against God being White at all; abstract as this theme must

3

forever remain while we are in the flesh. This is one of the reasons we favor African emigration, or the Negro naturalization, whenever we can find a domain, for, as long as we remain among Whites, the Negro will believe that the devil is black and that he [the Negro] favors the devil, and that God is White and that he [the Negro] bears no resemblance to Him, and the effect of such a sentiment is contemptuous and degrading, and one-half of the Negro race will be trying to get White and the other half will spend their days in trying to be white men's scullions to please the Whites.[3]

CHAPTER ONE

Biblical Meaning and
the Black Religious Experience

In its broadest application, the Black religious experience extends well beyond the parameters of the African-American religious experience. The connotative sense of the Black religious experience is simply the religion of those persons whose parentage, self-understanding, and/or physical features fall within the Black (Negroid/Africoid) race. There is an astonishing diversity of religious beliefs and practices in the history of the world's Black people. This religious experience includes the religions of ancient Africa (Cush, Punt, and to some extent ancient Egypt), Black adaptations of Hebraic, Jewish, Christian, and Islamic beliefs and rituals. We could also mention traditional African religions and numerous derivatives found in the Black diaspora: Candomble (Brazil), Garifuna (Honduras), Shango (Trinidad), and Vodun (Haiti).

Despite this variety, the Black religious experience also has denotative coherence that distinguishes it from the religious experience of other racial groups. On the one hand, the Black religious experience typically considers the supernatural as a mere extension of the natural order.[1] It seeks harmony with (not dominance over) nature, reveres ancestors, rejoices in rhythm, and takes both spirituality and the afterlife seriously.[2] On the other hand, the impact of slavery, colonialism, and racism in the oppression of Black people further clarifies the Black religious experience as a designation for African-Americans, especially those who represent the Black Church tradition in the United States.

It is well-known that the Bible has come to occupy a central place in religions of the Black diaspora. Whether in slave religion or independent Black Churches of the Americas and the Caribbean, biblical stories, themes, personalities, and images have inspired, captivated, given meaning, and served as a basis of hope for a liberated and enhanced material life. They have enriched the prospects for a glorious afterlife, as well. Latta Thomas rightly observes that Blacks identified with daring heroes of the faith and perceived that the God who empowered those heroes would

5

likewise empower them.³ Thomas thinks principally of Black Christians, but his comments could apply to Black Hebrews, Jews, or even many Black Muslims who attach great significance to the Bible, particularly the revealed Law, Old Testament prophetic visions, communal solidarity motifs, and biblical mandates for love, mercy, and justice. Even beyond the confines of African-American religion, Black people are fundamentally people of the Book.

To affirm this centrality is not to suggest, however, that the Bible attains such stature as the result of efforts by Blacks to conduct systematic, critical analysis of biblical texts. In Africa and the Black diaspora, the apparatus of the historical critical methods for biblical analysis and hermeneutics is still in a nascent stage.⁴ Vincent Wimbush reminds us that for well over fifteen hundred years, the Bible, even among Europeans, was not so much analyzed critically as confessed dogmatically through doctrinalist, moralist, and pietistic prisms, and critical analysis of the Bible by trained exegetes is scarcely two centuries old.⁵ He further indicates that the "high" Protestant adoption of critical analysis was a by-product of the new consciousness among the literate bourgeois classes of Europe and America, which usually excluded Blacks.

> Since most of the earliest African-American Christians had been denied, from the beginning of their experience in the Americas, the opportunity to be fully human, including the opportunity to learn to read and write, the "letters" of biblical texts were not crucial in their appropriation and redaction of Christian traditions. What became important was the *telling* and *retelling,* the hearing and re-hearing of biblical stories—stories of perseverance, of strength in weakness and under oppressive burdens, of hope in hopeless situations.⁶

The Black Church and others within Black religious traditions give allegiance to biblical faith and witness primarily because their own experiences seem to be depicted in the Bible. Many of the biblical stories reflect the existential reality of the "Black story" in an environment typically hostile to the interests of Blacks attaining their full sense of human potential. Blacks have become all too familiar with oppression by the socioeconomic forces or political powers—foreign and domestic—arrayed against them. In the Bible they have found ancient symbols of their predicament: the saga of the Egyptian bondage, the devastation of Assyrian invasions, the deportation into Babylonian captivity, and the bedevilment by principalities and powers of the present age. Blacks have consequently developed an "experiential sympathy" with much of the Bible, which in turn receives their reverent attention as quite literally the revealed Word of God.

Mindful of what *has been* the relationship between the Bible and the Black religious experience, we are at the juncture in history where new questions must be posed. We must ask what observations about this relationship have been made by other scholarly disciplines. What is emerging now from those other disciplines, and how do conclusions from such research impinge on what *is, should,* and *shall be* the relationship? Hints at answers have appeared in the literature of Black intellectuals and scholars of religion since the turn of the present century. Many of these hints have gone unnoticed or have remained undeveloped because neither Euro-American academics nor the mainstream publishing world found much that was marketable or acceptable to the dominant racial groups. The irony of this is clear. Too often the results of serious Black scholarship and research have only limited means of mass distribution, and the marks of oppression restrict a Black readership that is scarcely in the position to purchase, study, and otherwise benefit from that kind of research. Nevertheless, Black scholars have offered hints for decades.

In 1900, Henry Sylvester Williams, a Trinidadian lawyer, organized the first Pan-African Conference in London.[7] Later W. E. B. DuBois displayed relentless efforts on behalf of the Pan-African Congress.[8] Researchers have traced other developments in the Black nationalism of Marcus Garvey, the Rastafarian critique of the West, and a renewed focus on the centrality of Africa in clarifying the foundations for African-American cultural consciousness.[9] Then, too, there are the writings of William Leo Hansberry of Howard University, such as *The African Presence in Asia, Africans and Their History, Pillars in Ethiopian History,* and his most recent *Africa and Africans as Seen by Classical Writers.* Other examples include Chancellor Williams's *The Destruction of Black Civilization,* George G. M. James's *Stolen Legacy,* and Cheikh Anta Diop's *The African Origin of Civilization.* Even the extensive, if controversial, research by Yosef Ben-Jochannan, notably *The Black Man's Religion,* belongs to this surprisingly large body of literature, often suppressed and scorned by almost all of American higher education, that points to Africa again and again as the best interpretive framework and the *home* of the Black religious experience.

Within the past few decades, Black theologians and Black scholars of religion have turned their attention again to Africa. Professor Charles Long has repeatedly stressed the importance of aspects of African religions for a proper analysis and understanding of the Black religious experience.[10] Similarly, Gayraud Wilmore, in his provocative volume, *Black Religion and Black Radicalism,* speaks of "the creative residuum of African religions" as contributing "an essential ingredient of Black Christianity prior to the Civil War."[11] I welcome Wilmore's call for more scholarly interest in "the church in ancient Ethiopia and Nubia."[12] James Cone's *For My People* stresses the importance of the relationship between Africa and Black religion in the United States of America. Cone regularly finds himself adopting the term *African-American Churches* as a substitute for "American Black Churches."[13] Professor J. Deotis Roberts, in *Black Theology Today,* goes as far as calling for a new consciousness that would be informed by an African Black metaphysic.[14]

Two things become clear from all this. First, Black writers recognize the total inadequacy and racial bias of the West's intellectual tradition in its endeavors to provide allegedly *universal* conceptual and religious norms. In this respect, Cornel West's *Prophesy Deliverance* is an invaluable resource for tracing the implicit racist tendencies of the European philosophical "giants" since the Englightenment.[15] The implication is that, whatever one may wish to say about the Bible, there is a need for a disciplined *skepticism* regarding its Western appropriations. Second, the many Black writers and scholars of religion who are turning their sights to Africa are demonstrating that what Michel Foucault decries as an "insurrection of subjugated knowledges," may be applied to our quest for the Bible's meaning in relation to the Black religious experience.[16] Evidently, that quest must be conducted in a new dialogue and solidarity with Africa, and this means that Blacks must redouble their efforts in this "insurrection of subjugated knowledges."

Through an exploratory course that I developed in 1980 entitled, "Ethiopia and Arabia in Biblical Antiquity," I was led to confession and a new beginning. The course became as much a learning experience for me as for the students. I began to realize that my own theological training and graduate studies had treated most of ancient Africa as peripheral or insignificant. I also recognized that aspects of European historiography and archeology have been tainted by a self-serving, racialist hermeneutic that sought not objective truth but careful, "scientific" ways of reinforcing the superiority and normative character of Western culture (i.e., white people) as the *sole arbitrator* of the biblical tradition. A challenge presented itself: How does one effectively confront distortions in the sacred story? Rather than ephemeral polemics amid a disinterested guild or theological faculty, the better way to engage this challenge is through research and analysis. The present discussion represents my own initial efforts with respect to much of existing biblical research. As a result, I attempt some realignment with that portion of the subjugated knowledge directly related to the Bible. It is my thesis that determining the meaning of the Bible for the Black religious experience requires the following: 1. an international "African" identity; 2. a new skepticism about prevailing Eurocentric exegesis, hermeneutics, and historiography; 3. a renewed commitment to the New Testament vision of liberation as a self-perpetuating process, continued self-critique, and the establishment of shared power, first for a "beloved Black community," but also for all.

THE DAWN OF THE BLACK RELIGIOUS EXPERIENCE

Recent archaeological discoveries at Cemetery L in Qustul, upper Egypt (ancient Nubia or the present-day border of Egypt and Sudan) indicate that Nubian Pharaohs existed six or seven generations *before* the First Dynasty of Egypt.[17] As Bruce Williams of the Oriental Institute reports, this find revolutionizes our Western perceptions about ancient Egypt and its relation to other parts of Africa:

The place is ancient Nubia at Qustul, where the investigation of archaeological materials recovered during the great 1960's rescue effort [a 1962 international archaeological team effort to save ancient remains threatened by the rising waters of the Aswan Dam] has recently unveiled a birth place of pharaonic civilization several generations before the first historic Egyptian dynasty. This finding is rendered all the more startling by the fact that advanced political organization was not believed to have come to Nubia, or anywhere south of Egypt for another 2,500 years.[18]

The dominant opinion of European scholars has been that the high culture of ancient Egypt derived from cultural sources outside of Africa and that such traces of Egyptian culture found elsewhere in Africa are of Egyptian origin. European and American scholars alike have tended to prefer the Greek geographer Strabo (64 B.C.–A.D. 23), who believed that Egyptians settled ancient Ethiopia, rather than the opposite view taken by the Greek historian Herodotus, who centuries earlier had argued that Egypt derived from the culture of greater Ethiopia. Herodotus's expeditions in Egypt are dated 460–455 B.C..[19]

Professor Robert Bennett calls the belief that the ancient Egyptians originated outside of Black Africa "insidious racism." He attributes the classical formulation of the perspective to C. O. Seligman's *Races of Africa, and Egypt and Negro Africa.*[20] Bennett notes that other Western scholars such as Merrick Posnansky have contested the Seligman thesis and suggested that Nubia and Egypt influenced each other. We may go further and point out that as early as the late eighteenth century, Count Constantin de Volney (1757–1820) insisted that "the ancient Egyptians were true Negroes of the same type as all native-born Africans."[21] Despite Count de Volney and others, most Western Egyptologists have had great difficulty believing that ancient Egypt originated in Black Africa.

With the 1962 archaeological discoveries at Qustul, Upper Nubia, we now have strong evidence that ancient Egyptian civilization was prefigured and shaped by developments to the south, in Nubia. This might shed light on Isa. 11:11, where a threefold division of Egypt is evident in exilic or postexilic times:

In that day the Lord will extend his hand yet a second time to recover the remnant which is left of his people, from Assyria, from Egypt [Misraim = Lower Egypt], from Pathros [Upper Egypt], from Ethiopia [Cush = Nubia], from Elam, from Shinar, from Hamath, and from the coastlands of the sea.[22]

While this cannot be regarded as a scientific geographical fact, it does confirm other more ancient evidence that an integral relationship existed between Black Africa and ancient Egypt, and this was known well after the demise of the Pharaohs.

According to historian William Leo Hansberry, three ancient African territories constitute the geographical contexts for the emergence of the Black religious experience. These are the land of Qevs (Kesh/Cush) or Ethiopia proper, the land of Punt (Greater Ethiopia), and Egypt.[23] Millennia before the earliest Hebrews or Christians, the Black religious experience flourished among the people of Cush and Punt. In fact, a Fourth Dynasty Egyptian text (2620–2480 B.C.) refers to Punt as "the end of the world," beyond which is "the land of the spirits."[24] Many Pharaohs treated Punt as a kind of holy land, considering it the birthplace of the Egyptians and the original homeland of many of the Egyptian gods.[25] The recent discoveries at Cemetery L suggest that cultural *and* religious influence from Black Africa shaped the formative years of ancient Egyptian civilization. Thus, it is likely that the extraordinary variety of local gods associated with independent tribal cults of Egypt over 1500 years before Akhenaton's monotheistic revolution (1379–1362 B.C.) have their antecedents in other parts of Africa.[26]

Of course, it is one thing to argue that Black Africa exerted cultural and religious influence on ancient Egypt disproportionate to influences from other parts of the ancient world. It is an entirely different matter to argue that the ancient Egyptian Pharaohs were for the most part *Black* people. Perhaps the best-known African Egyptologist who argues extensively for the Negroid identity of the Egyptian Pharaohs is Cheikh Anta Diop, who published his dissertation, completed at the University of Paris, on this subject. According to Diop, the Western world has falsified history with respect to the race of the ancient Egyptians. He argues that the West has invented a hypothetical white Pharaonic race that imported Egyptian civilization from Asia.[27] In his view, Egyptian civilization originated in Africa, and the indigenous Pharaohs of Egypt were Black Africans.[28] Diop draws on archaeological, anthropological, linguistic, and other evidence to show parallels between the ancient Egyptians and Blacks from other parts of Africa. Especially striking are the comparative photographic reliefs that indicate the evident similarities between Pharaoh Ramses II and the physical features and hairstyle of a modern Watusi warrior.[29] If the resemblance is more than coincidence, it would mean that this Pharaoh traditionally associated with Moses and the Exodus was a Black African.

At the same time, I hasten to clarify that Blacks were generally regarded rather favorably in the ancient world. Today, we must constantly remind ourselves that *in antiquity, there existed no elaborate ideologies, theories, or definitions of race based on physical features and behavioral patterns* (*see* chapter three). Nevertheless, we must acknowledge, based on available evidence, that far more than the Twenty-fifth Egyptian (Nubian) Dynasty (730–653 B.C.) consisted of *Black* Pharaohs by modern standards of race. This judgment is the result of my visits to Egypt and studies of Egyptian statuary and pictorial reliefs of different ancient dynasties. I find it difficult to believe that Narmer (Menes), the first Pharaoh of unified Egypt, was not Negroid. His broad nose, thick lips, and general facial features would seem to preclude any other objective determination.[30] Other Pharaohs, such as the Menthoteps of the Eleventh Dynasty (2134–1991 B.C.), consisted of a succession of Blacks.[31] Then too, Pharaoh Thutmose III, "the Napoleon of ancient Egypt" who founded the Eighteenth Dynasty by overthrowing Hyksos rule, had a Nubian mother; he was thereby a mulatto.[32] The point is that there is evidence to suggest that, by modern standards of race, the indigenous Pharaohs of the Eighteenth to the Twenty-fifth Dynasties (circa 1500–653 B.C.) were for the most part probably Black.

Whether we call these Pharaohs Black, Afroasiatic, or Negroid does not matter. The substantive point is that they were *not* Caucasians. But none of us can become too sanguine about this, for the probability of the Pharaohs' "blackness" turns out to be a two-edged sword. Suddenly Ramses II, often seen as the Pharaoh of Moses' day and the exodus, becomes a paradigm for reassessing the oppressive "Black Pharaohs" of the Black Church today, giving an expanded meaning to that refrain, "Tell Ole Pharaoh to let my people go!" I have never read or heard a Jewish or Christian scholar, Black or white, address the theological implications of the probable Black identity of ancient Egyptian Pharaohs. The possibility of the existence of oppressive Black Pharaohs influences our perception of the liberation struggle as more than a whites vs. Blacks issue, indeed, there are many ways in which people are and have been oppressed by members of *their own* racial and national groupings. Recent challenges to and critiques of the Black Church by proponents of Black theology may be a progressive and necessary development beyond its earlier uncritical romance with the Exodus saga.[33]

Whether or not we consider the Pharaohs to have been Black, there is considerable information about the ancient Egyptian religious experience, notably in *The Egyptian Book of the Dead, The Pyramid Texts,* and *The Coffin Texts.*[34] These writings provide details about an elaborate henotheistic system of religious belief and practice. Clearly, the ancient Egyptians believed in a Supreme Being, the Creator called *neter.* They also believed in the existence of other gods, including great cosmic powers and finite divine beings with supernatural powers.[35] The Egyptians had a sophisticated doctrine of salvation, concepts of the afterlife, and a long-standing belief in the resurrection. The considerable impact of the Egyptian mystery system on the mystery religions of the Greco-Roman world, though frequently minimized by Eurocentric scholars, is still very clear.[36] Without doubt, the Pharisaic notion of the resurrection derives from Egyptian teachings.

BLACKS IN THE BIBLICAL TRADITION

Millennia before Jesus of Nazareth, there was a sustained intermingling of Cushites and Egyptians. Indeed, as Professor Ephraim Isaac and I attempt to show in the next chapter, there was not just one land of Cush, but two. The first was south of Egypt; the second, across the Red Sea, included the Arabian peninsula and extended toward the Mesopotamian (Tigris and Euphrates) basin.[37] References to two different groups of *Cushites* may be in the table of nations in Genesis 10 and also in writings from the eighth to the second centuries B.C. Such material lends credence to Cheikh Anta Diop's observation that Blacks were established in civilizations from the Nile to the Mesopotamian fertile crescent thousands of years ago.[38]

Despite the reluctance of Euro-American or Ashkenazic Jewish scholars to attribute much significance to explicit references or allusions to Blacks in the Old Testament, such mentions are instructive. There is an impressive array of Black people in the Old Testament, beginning with those in Genesis 9 and 10 or 1 Chronicles 1: Hagar, from Egypt (Gen. 16:1); the Cushite wife of Moses in Numbers 12:1; Jeremiah 38:7 and 39:16; Isaiah 37:9; perhaps even Zephaniah, the son of Cushi (Zeph. 1:1; *see* Zeph. 2:12, 3:10); and the Queen of Sheba (1 Kings 10:1–10).[39] Aaron's grandson, regarded as the progenitor of the Zadokite priesthood (Exod. 6:25; Num. 25:7; Ps. 106:30) and one of the sons of Eli (1 Sam. 1:3; 2:34) had the Egyptian name Phinehas, literally meaning "the Nubian."[40]

Many of these passages attest to the greatness and power of African Blacks participating in the salvation drama of ancient Israel. It has always struck me as incredible that modern scholars have so much difficulty acknowledging the existence of Black Jews before Jesus Christ. The critical point, however, is not that Blacks are an integral part of the Old Testament witness, but that if one considers the Hebrew exodus story as an historical event, we have to reckon with the fact that these liberated Hebrews were most probably a racially mixed stock of people—Afroasiatics. Such observations might seem startling to some, but this long-neglected aspect of the Old Testament is important in tracing the relevance of a new international African identity informed by the New Testament.

Let us now consider how the New Testament mentions or otherwise highlights the Black religious experience. The New Testament presents us with two Black Queens. "The queen of the South" (*Basilissa notou*) is mentioned in the Q source material of Matthew 12:42 and Luke 11:31. We should point out that the title queen of the South is an early New Testament reference to the Queen of Sheba (*see* Matt. 12:42; Luke 11:31). In the New Testament, she has become an eschatological figure who will rise up and condemn the faithlessness of Israel at the final judgment. It is revealing that the New Testament merely called her queen of the South, omitting any reference to the land of Sheba, because the same omission is found in Josephus's extensive account of this person, whom he refers to as "the

Queen of Egypt and Ethiopia."[41] Both Origen and Jerome considered this queen a *Black* African.[42] Such testimonies lend credence to the view that the Queen of Sheba was a Cushite, a Black royal personage whom even Jesus could recast as an eschatological sign against those of his Jewish contemporaries he chastised as being a faithless generation.

The second queen in the New Testament is also a Black Cushite: *Kandakē,* queen of Nubia. Luke refers to her in Acts 8:27 as part of his narrative development depicting the gospel moving away from Jerusalem (cf. Acts 1:8), first to the Samaritan north and then to the Ethiopian south. The pattern is an elaborated re-presentation of Luke 13:29, where Luke amends the Q saying about those who will come and sit at Abraham's table (Matthew 8:11, 12) by adding "north and south." Luke is consciously more inclusive. Consistent with his intentional universalism, he records the expanding witness of the gospel as *definitely* including the south, that is, Ethiopia and Egypt.[43] It may well be that the two queens of the New Testament are quiet reminders of the ancient glory of Africa and also of the way ancient African rulers sought to affirm the wisdom of Solomon in order to become beneficiaries of the Holy Spirit. How appropriate it is to find the Ethiopian God-fearer in Acts 8:32, 33 reading about the suffering servant of Isaiah 53:7, 8: "in his humiliation justice was denied him." In recent centuries his text has become the story of Black people in the West.

A few remarks about the conversion of the Ethiopian finance minister (Acts 8:26–40) are in order at this point. Western New Testament scholars have been perplexed at times by this episode, which may suggest that the Hellenist mission was responsible for bringing Christianity to Ethiopia in the first century. The usual tendency on the part of the exegetes is to deny the historical reliability of this tradition in Acts, despite the fact that the same skepticism is not shown toward the conversion of Cornelius, the Italian, in Acts 10. Ernst Haenchen struggles to be balanced by saying that Luke intentionally leaves the Ethiopian's status as Jew or Gentile God-fearer ambiguous. The Ethiopian is thus "a stepping stone between . . . the Samaritans and the Gentiles."[44] Haenchen does suggest that the story of the Ethiopian chamberlain is the Hellenistic parallel to the Hebrew Christian mission story of Cornelius's conversion by Peter—"its parallel and rival."[45] Martin Hengel asserts without reservation that the Ethiopian minister is a Gentile God-fearer who is not only converted, but takes the gospel to the extreme southern boundary of the known inhabited world—Ethiopia.[46]

Next we consider the flight into Egypt (Matt. 2:13–22), in the midst of which is the often-quoted Old Testament passage of Hosea 11:1: "Out of Egypt I called my son." One could transpose the thought slightly but no less accurately and say, "out of Africa I called my son." Unfortunately, such a change startles many Anglo-Saxons today, since the Eurocentric view creates a Middle East, a non-Black Egypt, even a non-Black Ethiopia. In any case, more so in antiquity than even today, Egypt was intimately (culturally, linguistically, and racially) a part of Black Africa. When one

thinks of the liberated Hebrew slaves as the corporate slave/son called out
of bondage only to reimpose bondage on one another, we have a basis for
contrasting *that son* with the New Testament Son also called out of Africa.
For Matthew at least, it was a suffering servant King whose righteousness
through commitment, suffering, and liberating activity made him also
Messiah, and by theological metaphor, *Black Messiah* and Son of God, as
suggested by James Cone and Allan Boesak.[47] Yet not only does the
Eurocentric domination of biblical interpretation tend to deny the African
identity *of the place* whence the Son was called, but it also shows little
concrete understanding *of what kind* of new suffering slave/servant
(*doulos*) was called and *on what basis* he became King and Liberator.

HISTORICAL RELATIVISM AND CULTURAL SUBJECTIVITY IN CANON FORMATION

While it is important for Black people to adopt rigorously a new critical
stance toward traditional or prevailing exegetical methods and hermeneutical conclusions, more is required. People must seek to liberate themselves from the popular tendency to deify the Bible as *the* definitive and
exclusive Word of God, as if God's entire revelation only exists in the canon
of biblical literature. To be sure, the Bible does represent a foundation for
the Word of God. Moreover, from the faith claims of the biblical tradition,
the Bible does constitute the most important *ancient locus* for the Word of
God. However, even this is not synonymous with the view that the Bible is
categorically *the* Word of God.

One fact that demands a more modest assessment about the Bible as
God's *only* Word is the long, often torturous process whereby Hebrews/
Jews and Christians arrived at their respective canons. Within this mundane
history, we encounter communities of faith struggling for centuries to make
sense out of human existence, or, to be more accurate, their own *particular*
human existence and their specific perceptions about their place in God's
plan of salvation. As historical vicissitudes bring changes, the content of
revelation seems to change. Thus behind the collection of books that
became the Hebrew Bible, Septuagint (Greek Old Testament), and the
Greek New Testament is the very complicated process of canonization.
Many inspired books, "holy writings," gospels, and epistles were ignored
and omitted, often for reasons that were quite arbitrary, dogmatic, and
certainly not scientific.

Space and time preclude a detailed examination of the process and
problems of canon formation, but it is instructive to note that the
Tanak/tripartite Hebrew Bible evolved for at least 1,000 years before it was
accepted by Jews as canon.[48] With respect to the New Testament, the
process of canon formation begins about A.D. 140. We certainly know of the
existence of the Muratorian canon (ca. A.D. 190). The work of Eusebius (A.D.

324) and the influence of Bishop Athanasius's list (A.D. 367) helped the West fix its canon of 27 books over a span of 350 years.[49] However, despite Athanasius's list, parts of the Eastern Church did not agree on all 27 New Testament books until about A.D. 1000.[50] For our immediate discussion, the crucial factor in these long processes is *who* decided which books were to be omitted. More specifically, what kind of worldview, political authority, and cultural/racial self-interest informed their decisions?

Such questions highlight a problem of no small consequence, especially since Western biblical scholars have paid scant attention to the origin and development of Christianity in Greater Ethiopia (including Nubia) and the formation of the ancient Ethiopian canon. Worse still, when we find Western studies on these topics, they are frequently patronizing and negatively biased.[51] Unhappily, one must say that within the very process of canonization of biblical books, there is discernible a narrow cultural and historical subjectivity that reflects sin (cultural and racial bias) almost as much as it reflects God's holy Word. Thus, in a sense, the *Tanak* becomes God's Word for the Jews first and then God's Word for all others who look to Zion. Illustrative texts appear in the Psalms: "Let bronze be brought from Egypt; let Ethiopia hasten to stretch out her hands to God" (Ps. 68:31), and "Among those who know me I mention Rahab and Babylon; behold, Philisita and Tyre, with Ethiopia — 'This one was born there,' they say" (Ps. 87:4). Likewise, the New Testament tends to be construed as God's primary Word by those in the West, who consider it axiomatic that the Greco-Roman world is the beginning of modern civilization. Then the Bible is secondarily presented to others as God's exclusive Word; however reluctantly, they acquiesce unwittingly to such a claim. These considerations aside, I submit that a substantive critique of the process of canonization inescapably leads Blacks "back to Africa."

Furthermore, with reference to Christianity and its New Testament canon, the movement toward canon formation correlates with a growth pattern of "triumphalism" in the churches. Certain victorious Christian groups won and projected themselves as the normative keepers of the tradition; other Christian groups lost and became vanquished sectarians. Indeed, within the New Testament itself, we find early traces of this triumphalism (Colossians, Ephesians, the pastorals). Perhaps beginning with the Edict of Toleration (A.D. 313), we enter a period from Constantine to Justinian where Christianity becomes formally recognized by the state, thus representing an association of "victorious parties." Such writings as the Gospel to the Egyptians or that to the Hebrews, both widely used in Egypt, failed to be accepted into the canon.[52] Various radical Christian groups, both Gnostic and Jewish Christian, become the vanquished parties,[53] whose writings have no canonical status. Echoes of these groups are heard in Arabia at the dawn of Islam.[54] By the fifth century, in both the Latin Vulgate and such Talmudic literature as *Bereshit Rabbah,* we begin to find a few explicit negative attitudes about Blacks.[55]

BLACK THEOLOGY, AFRICA, AND A BIBLICAL REVOLUTION

During the academic year 1984–1985, I was struck by a common theme in four articles that appeared in *The Journal of Religious Thought*. Although phrased differently, the contextualization of religion in Africa seemed uppermost in the minds of J. Omosade Awolalu, Emefie Ikenga-Metuh, Nlenanya Onwu, and Cheryl Townsend Gilkes. Each defended vigorously the integrity of the African worldview, especially as found in West African traditional religions. Awolalu identified four ingredients in this worldview: 1. the Supreme Being (Creator and Sustainer), variously named; 2. divine spirits; 3. ancestral spirits; and, 4. mysterious powers.[56] To these, one could add the village medicine man/priest, who assists local communities as a mediator between the historical and spiritual worlds or between the natural and supernatural realms, the one John Mbiti calls "the priestly specialist."[57] At the same time, I could not avoid being impressed with recent observations by leaders in Black Theology who focus on similarities between aspects of the Black religious experience in North America and Africa. Gayraud Wilmore urges us to appreciate afresh the ways traditional African religion takes seriously the intersection of the spiritual world and that of objective reality in a way that opens the whole person to both the divine and the fullness of human life.[58]

The term *contextualization* would seem to describe precisely the biblical revolution that Professor Onwu of the University of Nigeria sets forth in his survey of biblical studies in parts of Africa today. What he describes is a kind of "insurrection of subjugated knowledge" allowing Western-trained and credentialed Africans to challenge the Eurocentric hegemony in modern biblical exegesis and interpretation on the basis of insights from their traditional worldviews. Unlike the apologetic rationalizations found in John Mbiti's efforts to legitimate the African worldview, Onwu shows that today Africans are presupposing the legitimacy of their traditional worldview and interrogating the Bible and its Western interpreters regarding *their* legitimacy among Africans.[59] Whereas Mbiti wants to show the West the "weaknesses" of African traditional religion in relation to Judaism and Christianity, Onwu, Awolalu, Ikenga-Metuh, Wilmore, Roberts, Cone, and others want to stress its strength and draw implications from that.

I prefer not to speak of contextualization, but to think in terms of "recontextualization." I do not mean an anachronistic and uncritical return to African tribal religion or romanticizing the African worldview and making it normative for Blacks internationally. On the contrary, by *recontextualization* I refer to a process of rediscovering some essential features of the Black religious experience in Africa, including, but not limited to, African traditional religions, and doing this as one enters a new dialogue of liberation and spirituality as found in the Bible. This process might lend unity and new coherence to the future of the Black religious experience in direct relation to the Bible, especially the New Testament.

Apart from the fascinating reports by Diodorus Siculus and Plato about West African civilizations in Minoan times (3400–1200 B.C.) or the results of the archaeological research of Heinrich Schliemann or Sir Arthur Evans, there is even more reason to believe that very ancient migrations took place from the Nile Valley to other remote parts of Africa. The Africanist and historian William Leo Hansberry seems convinced that in ancient times the Sahara was not as dry and forbidding as it is today. He concludes, "hence trade and travel between the African interior and the Mediterranean world took place."[60] The Egyptologist Cheikh Anta Diop devotes an entire chapter to the topic of ancient cross-continental migrations in Africa, documenting his views by listing numerous similarities between the ancient Egyptian language or Egyptian religious concepts and those of diverse tribes in other distant parts of the continent.[61]

Despite the fact that conclusive data are lacking on this point, it is probable that such migrations did occur, and this is exactly why diverse tribes of Africa have systems of rituals, beliefs, sacrifice, and theology with many common features. Indeed, such notions as a Supreme Being/Creator/ Protector God, the multiplicity of spirits (demonic and angelic), a notion of communal solidarity and sharing, and a belief in the afterlife are found in the religious experience of the ancient Black Egyptians, African traditional religions, and the Bible itself. The New Testament world, particularly as reflected in the canonical gospels and Acts of the Apostles, is in many ways congenial to the world of the ancient Black religious experience, despite Bultmannian demythologizing. What we are proposing is that this ancient continuity between the New Testament and the Black religious experience has significant implications for the relationship between the Bible and the Black religious experience in the future.

NEW TESTAMENT RADICALISM AND THE FUTURE OF THE BLACK RELIGIOUS EXPERIENCE: LESSONS *FROM* AND *FOR* AFRICA

It could be instructive to identify the portions of the Bible that Blacks have tended to prefer and have thus become most acquainted with. Because of the enormous impact of slavery and "the middle passage," Blacks have tended to be drawn to the Old Testament. Thus, the story of Joseph sold into slavery by his brothers (Gen. 37:1–36) and the great Exodus saga (Exodus, Deuteronomy) have become focal points in the Pentateuch for Blacks. Because of sustained racial oppression that has translated itself into political and socioeconomic injustices, Blacks have tended to associate themselves with dramatic displays of God's power and the apostrophes against evil in the prophetic literature. The Hagiographa also has taken on special meaning for Blacks because it reflected ancient questions about theodicy and offered poetry of consolation. In the New Testament, apart from the apocalyptic Book of Revelation, Blacks have focused almost singularly on Jesus Christ and the divine, unconventional *agapē* that God refracted through Jesus' ministry and resurrection. Almost universally in the Black religious experience, the apostle Paul is held suspect.[62] This disproportionate assessment of Scripture has created the impression in some quarters that Blacks see themselves as an Old Testament people. In many ways, the Old Testament does project a worldview for which Black people have a natural affinity.

Nevertheless, the distinctive Christian canon is not the Old Testament but the New Testament, determined by the decisive, live-or-die, kerygma and faith claims of the formative Church. One's identity as a Christian presumably stands or falls on this. Many Blacks, disillusioned by the frequent moral ineptitude of the Church in matters of socioeconomic and political policies, have rejected and abandoned the Church, turning to other religions, cults, or cynical atheism. Their responses are not a solution to the problem, but an escape *from* the problem. Those of us left behind to confront the problem may need to give the New Testament and its witnesses — Peter, James, John, and even Paul — another hearing. We must discern afresh what recontextualization can mean to the New Testament.

Two recent books, James H. Cone's *For My People* and Robert McAfee Brown's *Unexpected News: Reading the Bible with Third World Eyes,* remind us of Karl Barth's re-encounter with the biblical text years ago.[63] Barth spoke of "the strange new world within the Bible," and indeed, the privileged and powerful always find a strange world in the Bible. However, for many others the Bible, especially the New Testament, depicts a world that is not strange at all in its radicalism. The process of recontextualization helps us gain access to this brave new world. It is a world that was favorably predisposed to Blacks. As evidence, consider Acts 13:1, where Luke mentions, among the prophets and teachers of Antioch, Simeon who was called Niger (the Black man) in an apparent Latinism. It was a world indebted to the Egyptian doctrine of salvation, taking seriously the glorious afterlife (1 Cor. 15:12–58; Phil. 3:12–16).[64]

Implicit in the glorious afterlife of the New Testament is an invitation to a radical metaphysic that is extended so people of the faith might be *transformed, yoked together,* and *unstained* by gross materialism and false wisdom that subjugates true knowledge (*see* Rom. 12:1, 2; Matt. 11:28–30; James 1:26, 27; 3:13–18). This radical metaphysic is really not an individualistic or internalized spirituality only for the other world. It has to do with the international collective solidarity of the *oikos tou theou* (the Household of God) and the *koinōnia*—understanding in this world that anticipates greater solidarity in the next world.[65]

The glorious afterlife is integral to an apocalyptic metaphysical faith-stance. Moreover, this faith-stance is *always* directed to others, especially the oppressed — the brother or sister in faith, not necessarily related by blood (Matt. 12:50; Gal. 6:10; Phil. 2:5-9; James 2:14-17). In the New Testament, the afterlife/resurrection does not just point to an ethereal new life on the other side; it also points to an empowered new life in *this world,* where one's own self-interest is directly related to the welfare of the socioeconomically and spiritually oppressed other.

In the Greek New Testament, the word *oppress* is rendered *thrauō,* that is, "to break, weaken or beat down" as in Luke 4:18, which derives from LXX Isaiah 58:6. Likewise, there is another Greek word meaning oppress/ press down (*katadunasteuō,* James 2:6). Usually, *thrauō* carries the sense of socioeconomic or political abuse; however, *katadunasteuō* had another usage, in the New Testament referring to being overwhelmed or oppressed by evil spirits/forces (*see* Acts 10:38).

This New Testament intersection between the historical and supra-historical has affinity with an aspect of the ancient African worldview and survives to some extent in African traditional religions. It runs contrary, however, to Western, this-worldly exploitation and the ideologies of racism, capitalism, neocolonialism, and class stratification so often sanctioned by the institutional Church. Clearly, there is a lesson *from* Africa here, but there is also a lesson *for* Africans who lack a metaphysic of international solidarity and often fail to acknowledge an appreciation of the scriptural mandate to place a priority on the welfare of the oppressed not in their midst.

The second part of our conclusion regarding recontextualization centers on the way the brave new world of the New Testament demonstrates an interest in solidarity and power through the *oikoi tou theou,* building on but going beyond the African concern for extended families. Consider, for example, Paul's collection for "the poor among the saints of Jerusalem" (2 Cor. 8:4-14; 9:1; Rom. 15:25-29; Gal. 2:10). Paul gives concrete, practical expression to the principle that the strong should help the weak, not only in matters of faith, but also in economic power (2 Cor. 8, 9; Rom. 14, 15; cf. Acts 20:35). In 2 Corinthians 8:14, Paul is quite explicit about the necessity of those households and communities with an abundance supplying the needs of those that face scarcity. He sees this explicitly as a matter of economic justice (*isotēs*). The redistribution and sharing of economic power is implicit in the traditional African concern for the extended family. Conversely, in modern Western society, the focus is usually on the nuclear family, irrespective of Bible or Church teachings — Protestant, Orthodox, or Roman Catholic. Again there are lessons *from* Africa, even as the new world of the New Testament goes beyond the African perspective. There are also lessons *for* Africa, where today we are appalled by the Western individualism and materialism shown by the African elite hoarding luxury goods and otherwise contributing to the disintegration of solidarity within the extended family.

This leads to a third and final reflection on recontextualization in the brave new world of the New Testament. The aim is to construct an agenda for the future of the Black religious experience. It is at this juncture that one can best speak about Jesus, the suffering slave King whose very *life* was the embodiment of the *agapē* and whose every *action* gave liberation its meaning and practical application. Though he foresaw the cross, he saw beyond it the resurrection that pointed to *new life,* first as it unfolded around him in his ministry and then as a continuous process of training for his disciples and followers, who would be the future leadership of the Church. There, recontextualization means self-perpetuating liberation and the perpetual self-critique of those who would lead in the process.

By contrast, there is the Egyptian Pharaoh of the Old Testament Exodus saga. Though probably Black in skin color, he oppresses the racially mixed Hebrew children of God. In that context of oppression, the Hebrews of Egypt are indeed the children of God. Yet despite their deliverance, a revealed Law, Promised Land, nationhood, and periods of glorious prosperity, the children of God enslaved one another, forgot and neglected the substantive moral dictates of Law, experienced slavery again, were delivered, developed a Temple fixation (an edifice complex), fenced in the compassion inherent in the Torah, and separated themselves — either in ascetic withdrawal (Qumran), militant nationalist death squads (Sicarrii and Zealots), or in the pietism of peaceful coexistence (post A.D. 70 Rabbinic Judaism). Here we have portraits of what can happen to the oppressed once they are liberated. Forgetting their roots, they become condemned to repeat socioeconomically and spiritually their past. So today, Israel appears at times to have become the new Pharaoh for the Palestinians, and history has come full circle. Surely there are lessons *from* and *for* Africans in this.

Lest we be accused of anti-Jewishness or being anti-Israeli, let us remember that today's Palestinians are racially more Semitic than the Ashkenazic Jews of Israel. We must also point out that Christianity, in its Western captivity, also basks in a strange triumphalism that has little or no future. It is not enough for churches to glorify the victory of the cross without a parallel commitment to making the resurrection victory a reality in the global context of suffering and oppression. Jesus Christ, the suffering slave King, and his liberating activity are lost in superficial triumphalism.

Recontextualization suggests primarily an agenda of Black *agapē* within the international African community as the vanguard for "the beloved Black community," which thereby becomes a paradigm for the participation of all. In this regard, it seems crucial to envision liberation as a continual process, like institutionalized revolution, with a perpetual self-critique embodied in its leadership style. It would appear that this is where "the victorious parties" of the Church failed. Their religion became acceptable, even a status symbol. It lost its affinity with the spirit of the times of early New Testament tradition, which then became a "strange world." Its *radicalism* evaporated, and the voice of the ideologically triumphant Church has become, to borrow a New Testament metaphor, "a noisy gong or a clanging cymbal" (1 Cor. 13:1). Yet the Bible still seeks to infuse *new* meaning into the future of a Black religious experience that refuses to be separated from its rich ancient past. Our challenge today is to rediscover how the Bible impels us toward a new international identity, a recontextualization, and a Black *agapē*, all of which represent the future brightness of the Black religious experience.

> What then shall *we* say to this? If God is for us, who is against us? He who did not spare his own Son but gave him up for us all, will he not also give us all things with him? Who shall bring any charge against God's elect? It is God who justifies; who is to condemn? Is it Christ Jesus, who died, yes, who was raised from the dead, who is at the right hand of God, who indeed intercedes for us? Who shall separate us from the love of Christ? Shall tribulation, or distress, or persecution, or famine, or nakedness, or peril, or sword? As it is written,
>
> > "For thy sake we are being killed all the day long;
> > we are regarded as sheep to be slaughtered."
>
> No, in all these things we are more than conquerors through him who loved us. For I am sure that neither death, nor life, nor angels, nor principalities, nor things present, nor things to come, nor powers, nor height, nor depth, nor anything else in all creation, will be able to separate *us* from the love of God in Christ Jesus our Lord [Romans 8:31–39 (emphasis mine)].

CHAPTER TWO

Ancient Ethiopia and the Queen of Sheba

This chapter returns to the biblical accounts of the Queen of Sheba discussed briefly in the preceding chapter. With greater scrutiny of the biblical and cultural background, the ancient elaborations of her identity begin to attain wider significance. For centuries, Western scholarship (whether Jewish, Christian, or Muslim) displayed a tendency to regard this queen as a legendary figure from South Arabia; usually there was also a strong implication that she was not a Black African woman. Those who have taken issue with this implication encountered great difficulty in having their evidence taken seriously by Western scholars. Worse yet, much of the Eurocentric scholarship, particularly in the last two centuries, readily takes offense at any suggestion that the Bible reflects a strong and favorable ancient Black presence. Regrettably, the task of recovering this Black biblical presence is thwarted by the racist or ethnocentric presuppositions of several influential Western scholars.

There is considerable evidence for this claim regarding the Queen of Sheba in the history of interpretation. Not only is it important to provide more support for the contention that she was a Black, but it is necessary to demonstrate how this enhances the prospects for international Black consciousness and solidarity.

The format for this chapter is a four-stage development of our argument. First, we consider the earliest mentionings of the term *Ethiopia* (Hebrew: *Kuš*; Greek: *aithiops*), in an effort to set forth the problem of its geographical location. Second, we present some ways that Western scholars utilize ancient literary references to the Sabaeans as so-called proof of the precedence of South Arabia over Ethiopia. We shall see that claims of ancient tribal migrations from South Arabia to Ethiopia, extant inscriptions (epigraphy), and the respective alphabets of the Ethiopians and Sabaeans must be carefully analyzed. Third, attention turns directly to the Queen of Sheba, whose story begins as an episode in the reign of King Solomon (962–922 B.C.) but continues as a case study for examining Western biases against her Black or African identity. Fourth, we attempt to recontextualize the Queen of Sheba in the history of interpretation.

ETHIOPIA AND SHEBA IN ANTIQUITY

The oldest mention of Ethiopia in the Bible occurs in Genesis 2:13, which is part of the older version of the creation story reported by the author of the "J" (Jahwist/Judah) tradition inclusive of Genesis 2:4–3:24, usually dated around 950 B.C.[1] The Jahwist writer speaks of a river Gihon "which flows around the whole land of Cush/Ethiopia" as part of his description of Eden. Because the river Gihon is not cited anywhere in the Old Testament with greater precision (cf. 1 Kings 1:33, 38, 45; 2 Chron. 32:30; 33:14), biblical scholars have had difficulty deciding on the precise geographical location of this land. Nevertheless, as Claus Westermann points out, "Cush is mainly Ethiopia or Nubia, the land south of Egypt, or more exactly the area between the first and fourth cataracts of the Nile." He adds that scholars such as Hermann Gunkel have connected South Arabia with Ethiopia, while others such as H. Gorapor and W. F. Albright have connected Egypt with Ethiopia.[2] Even though the Old Testament does not give the exact location of the river Gihon, the table of nations in Genesis 10 attributes the name Gihon to one of the sons of Cush (Gen. 10:7; 1 Chron. 1:9; cf. Gen. 10:29; 1 Chron. 1:23).[3] The probability is that the Gihon River refers to the Nile River.

The Old Testament contains numerous references to Cush, or ancient Ethiopia. At times, Ethiopia and Egypt are linked, each being known for its greatness. In Isaiah 20:3–6, the nations of Egypt and Ethiopia are military powers great enough to represent a counterforce for Judah's hopes to avoid an Assyrian invasion. Isaiah 45:14 extols "the wealth of Egypt and the merchandise of Ethiopia," while the Book of Nahum recalls the strength of Ethiopia and Egypt (Nah. 3:8,9): "Are you better than Thebes that sat by the Nile, with water around her, her rampart a sea, and water her wall? Ethiopia was her strength, Egypt too, and that without limit; Put and the Lybians were her helpers."[4] Among the Old Testament citations regarding ancient Ethiopia, few are as important as those found in the famous table of nations (Genesis 10). Here the sons of Noah are listed, particularly those of Ham, who include both Cush and Egypt (Gen. 10:6), whereas the sons of Cush include Seba and Havilah (v. 7).

Literary criticism of the table of nations makes it impossible to construe such biblical genealogies as objective, historical, or scientific evidence. (*See* further evidence in chapter three.) On close inspection, it becomes clear that Genesis 10 is not a single historical report, but a synthesis of an older Jahwist ("J") list and a more recent Priestly ("P") redactor's list.[5] The combination of these two lists may account for the fact that one son of Cush in Genesis 10:7 is named Seba (*sĕbʾā*) and a grandson of Cush is named Sheba (*šĕbʾā*). Furthermore, Sheba is also mentioned in Genesis 10:28 as a descendant of Shem, another son of Noah.

The Genesis 10 citations of Seba and Sheba as descendants of Ham are noteworthy. One scholar identifies the initial Samech in *sĕbʾā* as an old

South Arabic equivalent of sb'.[6] If this is the case, we have in Genesis 10 the curious fact that two persons named Sheba are listed as descendants of Cush, while only one person by the name of Sheba is listed as a descendant of Shem. A further anomaly is encountered by again turning to Deutero-Isaiah. In Isaiah 43:3, God stands prepared to offer the richest and furthest countries, among which are Ethiopia, Egypt, and Seba (Masoretic text [MT]: miṣĕraîm kuš sĕb'ā). As in Isaiah 45:14, we find Seba here spelled with the initial Samech and yet distinguished from Cush. This may attest to the fact that part of Genesis 10 and the Deutero-Isaiah corpus are products of the exilic period, and so the initial Samech represents a South Arabia intrusion.[7]

We can draw a few preliminary conclusions from this. The table of nations presents not so much an objective historical account of genealogies as a theologically motivated collection. The names appear to some extent without regard for consistency of detail that would be of interest to the student of geography and ethnography. Despite this, we may infer that in the midst of the Babylonian exile, Deutero-Isaiah's image of the most remote nations helps us see that wherever Sheba was, it was not the same place as Cush (Ethiopia) or Egypt. Furthermore, Genesis 10 informs us that two of Cush's descendants were called Sheba. This fact seems to show how very close ancient Sheba was to the land of the Cushites. Thus, Sheba was either somewhere in Africa or quite near the African coast. The Bible's ambivalence about the location of the tribes of Sheba is similar to the ambivalence we find in some classical literature about the people called Ethiopians. We must point out, however, that the term *Ethiopians* is used throughout classical literature generally to refer to Black people who inhabited Africa south of Egypt. Occasionally the expression is used to refer to specific African peoples like the Nubians or the Cushites. Nevertheless, in some Greek textual sources, the expression refers to a people who inhabited the two shores of the Red Sea.

By the beginning of the second century B.C., when Strabo lived, the Sabaeans had come to be known as a distinct Arabian people; Strabo identifies them as such without questioning. In this regard, Strabo[8] quotes Eratosthenes (276–194 B.C.), saying that the extreme southern corner of Arabia, facing Ethiopia, is inhabited by four Arabian peoples: the Minaeans on the Red Sea, whose capital is Qarna; the Sabaeans, whose capital is Mariaba; the Qatabanians near the Straits of Bab-el-Mandab, whose capital is Tamma; and the Hadramawti (*Chatramotitae*), whose capital is Sabota. He also gives a description of their trade of myrrh (*Hadramawti*) and frankincense (*Qataban*). Additionally, Strabo quotes Agatharchides (ca. 120 B.C.), who speaks of the Sabaeans in South Arabia.

On the other hand, Strabo comments extensively and revealingly on the location of the people called Ethiopians, a subject that seemed to fascinate him. In Book I, he opens the discussion of the subject by saying, "It is incredible that [Homer] mentioned Ethiopia . . . and the fact that the

Ethiopians are 'sundered in twain' but he did not know what was well-known. . . ."[9] What is the meaning of the Ethiopians being "sundered in twain?" The cynic philosopher Crates (ca. 325 B.C.) had interpreted the phrase from Homer saying that "the Ethiopians stretch along both shores of Oceanus from the rising to the setting of the sun."[10] In agreement with Aristarchus (ca. 270 B.C.), Strabo rejects the hypothesis of Crates. Nonetheless, Aristarchus's own hypothesis — that the Ethiopians being "sundered in twain" may mean the division of Ethiopia into east and west by a river, like Egypt by the Nile — is also rejected by Strabo.

Strabo in this way examines the various interpretations of Homer, including those of Aeschylus (525–456 B.C.), Euripides (480–406 B.C.), and Ephorus (ca. 300 B.C.), then proceeds to investigate the possible ways in which Ethiopia may be said to be "sundered in twain."[11] He finally draws his own conclusions based on various points made by his forerunners and, more importantly, from those who made voyages along the shores of Libya and the Red Sea. Strabo concludes that Oceanus must be understood in a more general sense: "a body of water that extends along the entire southern belt," and Ethiopians, "the people along the same extent." According to Strabo, Ethiopia stretches from the south of Egypt all the way to Asia, from east to west. "Sundered in twain" means divided into two by the Red Sea. So he argues over and over again, saying,

> I contend in the case of the Ethiopians that "sundered in twain" [means] . . . [they] extend along the whole seaboard of Oceanus. . . . For the Ethiopians that are spoken of in this sense are "sundered in twain" naturally by the Arabian Gulf [the Red Sea] . . . as by a river [like Egypt by the Nile].[12]

He goes on to say that the Arabian gulf is a natural boundary of division used by other geographers to divide Africa from Asia. Furthermore, Strabo reports that:

> Homer divides the Ethiopians into two groups . . . not because he knew that the Indians were physically similar to the Ethiopians [for Homer probably did not know of the Indians at all. . .], but rather on the basis of the division of which I have spoken above[13] . . . and that . . . the Ethiopians that border on Egypt are themselves, also, divided into two groups; *for some of them live in Asia, others in Libya* [Africa] *though they differ in no respect from each other*[14] [emphasis mine].

The question of a people who straddle the Red Sea is examined by Strabo with profound interest. The picture he draws of the Ethiopians inhabiting both Africa and Asia reminds us of the biblical genealogies that cite the two Shebas. It is indeed interesting to note that two such diverging witnesses draw an almost identical picture of the location of the Sabaeans and the Ethiopians.

Serious methodological questions can be raised concerning theories that seek to reconstruct the origins of the Ethiopian civilization from South Arabia. In general, any idea of cultural influence should not be taken at face value. In every case where cultural influence is discussed, the complex issues often do not warrant an easy solution. In the present case, it is possible to reverse the argument and demonstrate an Ethiopian influence on South Arabia. Gus Van Beek, while not questioning the old hypothesis of Ethiopia having a South Arabian origin, has nonetheless argued that certain South Arabian pre-Christian pottery, perhaps from as early as the eighth century B.C., shows Ethiopian influence.[15] Moreover, there is hardly any period in Ethiopian history during which South Arabia directly governed or dominated Ethiopia. No evidence has been established for direct South Arabian rule of Ethiopia, despite Conti Rossini's conjectures.

On the other hand, it can be shown that South Arabia was under Ethiopian domination several times during its history, in particular from about A.D. 335–370 and A.D. 525–575. During the first period, some believe that Ethiopia brought Christianity to South Arabia through the missionary work of Tewoflos, even though Haenchen gives an earlier date for the Christianization of South Arabia.[16] During the second period, the Abyssinian governor Abraha extended Christian missionary religious activity in South Arabia and used it as a launching region for the Christianization of the Arabian peninsula.[17] During this latter period, the northern section of the great dam of Marib was constructed with headers protruding beyond the wall face. Gus Van Beek rightly argued that,

> This technique has no construction antecedents in South Arabian architecture. In Ethiopian architecture, on the other hand, the ends of wooden joists frequently protruded beyond the face of the building . . . and often done also in stone. In view of the fact that Ethiopians dominated Sabaeans throughout much of this period, it seems likely that they are also responsible for such architectural forms . . . this technique as cultural influence coming from Ethiopia to South Arabia.[18]

We can now place this matter in its proper historical context. Historians have used ancient literary references to the Sabaeans—in particular the biblical story of the Queen of Sheba—as proof of the precedence of South Arabia over Ethiopia. The origin of the people we call Sabaeans is shrouded in mystery. The earliest known literary source that mentions them is believed to be Genesis 10:7 (cf. 1 Chron. 1:9), where we find Sheba and Seba listed as descendants of Ham through Kush. In this and other biblical sources, Sheba is associated with Egypt and Nubia (cf. Isa. 43:3) and therefore, as one scholar says, "it is possible that Seba was located in Africa."[19] On the other hand, in Genesis 10:28 (cf. 1 Chron. 1:22), Sheba is listed among the sons of Shem. According to another source in Genesis 25:3 (1 Chron. 1:32), Sheba is a descendant of Abraham and a Keturah. In these latter references, the Sabaeans would be related to the peoples of the Fertile Crescent and Arabia. At any rate, "the genealogical references indicate that the Israelites thought the Sabaeans were related to the peoples of the Fertile Crescent — including themselves — on the one hand, *and* to the peoples of Africa on the other"[20] (emphasis mine).

This double identity of Sheba in the literature of the early Israelites brings into focus the enigmatic inquiry concerning the nature and extent of Ethiopian-South Arabian relations. As early as the sixth century, the Greek grammarian Stephanus of Byzantium suggested that the Ethiopians, Sabaeans, and Hadramawti formed three Arabian tribes.[21] Of course, Stephanus was neither an historian nor a geographer; he was simply a linguistic compiler who brought together material from diverse sources. Late in the seventeenth century, however, Ludolphus Hiob posited the formal hypothesis that the founders of Ethiopian culture were foreign immigrants.[22] It was not until the discovery and decipherment of Sabaean inscriptions that Western scholars claimed to have established a firm foundation for the South Arabian origin of the Ethiopian civilization. The subsequent study of Semitic languages and early civilizations began giving Hiob's hypothesis strong credence. In particular, the works of Halevy, Muller, Bent, Glaser, Conti Rossini, and Littmann, who traveled in northern Ethiopia and South Arabia during the nineteenth and early twentieth centuries, sought to confirm definitively a South Arabian-Ethiopian progression.

The first detailed European reconstruction of South Arabian and early Ethiopian histories, by E. Glaser and Conti Rossini respectively, seemed to be conclusive in determining South Arabian influence on Ethiopian culture.[23] Both these scholars attached special significance to the name *hbst* that appeared in a number of Sabaean texts. The obvious similarity between *hbst* and the Arabic *al-habasa* (Abyssinia) was believed to be explicit proof of the Sabaean origins of Ethiopian civilization. In particular, the well-known Italian Ethiopist Conti Rossini worked this view into his historical doctrine. His critic, A. K. Irvine, interprets this theory as follows: "By a process of conquest of absorption [the *habashat*] merged with the local native Hamitic population and became 'Africanized.' From this arose the proto-Ethiopian civilization and the proto-Ethiopic texts of Ethiopia."[24] It thus came to be widely accepted that *hbst* referred to a South Arabian tribe that crossed the Red Sea and settled in northern Ethiopia sometime before the fifth century B.C.

Since the days of Conti Rossini, little, if any, scholarly doubt has been expressed concerning the South Arabian origin and influence on Ethiopian culture. Instead, the theory of large population movements from South Arabia to Ethiopia was accepted by historians as a matter of fact and promoted vigorously. Only recently have serious historians of Ethiopia begun to question the old theory, particularly the view that a large migration had taken place from South Arabia to Ethiopia. But even those like Irvine and Schneider, who doubt the total veracity of the old theory, do not question, as we do here, the concept of the so-called South Arabic cultural influence in Ethiopia.[25]

THE SEMITIC LANGUAGE AND AFRICA

Taken in the context of the past two centuries of Western historiography, the cultural and racist overtones of the Hiob theory cannot be minimized or ignored. As with ancient Egypt, Benin, or Zimbabwe, a clear attempt was made to "Caucasianize" a major African civilization.[26] Ethiopian civilization has been attributed to a core group of superior Semitic colonists. Even those who later came to have doubts about a large population movement from South Arabia to Ethiopia would not think of questioning the superior nature of the non-African founders of the Ethiopian civilization. One author writes explicitly: "numerically the South Arabian leaven was not significant, but its *superior* quality revolutionized life in the Abyssinian highlands and infused into the predominantly Cushite element that peculiarly Semitic ingredient which has throughout the ages given Ethiopian civilization its special character" (emphasis mine).[27]

Based on linguistic, epigraphic, and literary evidence, there is little doubt that a strong tie existed between Ethiopia and South Arabia from the first millennium B.C. until early Christian times. It is also clear that the two shores of the southern end of the Red Sea share a linguistic, literary, religious, and historical tradition. At the same time, there is also an essential difference between historical and cultural ties and direct or indirect cultural *domination*. In the case of Ethiopian-South Arabian relations, the former is a demonstrable fact. The latter, however, is an unproven hypothesis containing erroneous historical, linguistic, and archaeological assumptions that no Semitic language is indigenous to Ethiopia, that proto-Ethiopic inscriptions were brought to Ethiopia from South Arabia, and that no indigenous high culture developed in Africa.

It can no longer be taken for granted that Semitic languages necessarily originated in the Near East. Various attempts at placing the ultimate origin of the Semitic languages in the Fertile Crescent or in Arabia have not proven successful. Contrary to some older assumptions, it cannot be shown that Semitic is a major language family comparable to Indo-European; rather, it is more or less like Slavic or Germanic – a smaller subdivision of a major family of languages. The debate on the origin and scope of Semitic languages or peoples continues. Meanwhile, many serious scholars accept the view that the Semitic language group is a branch of a major family called Hamito-Semitic or *Afro-Asiatic*. A. Murtonen has gone as far as proposing that the Horn of Africa (encompassing Ethiopia) constitutes the original home of proto-Semitic family (Hamito-Semitic).[28] It is possible that some form of the Semitic language is indigenous to ancient Ethiopia. The hypothesis of South Arabian origins for Ethiopian Semitic language(s) is undermined by the lingering problems related to the origin of the larger Semitic language family. No scholar has yet scientifically demonstrated how the first Semitic languages arrived in ancient Ethiopia from South Arabia, or if this ever happened.

There is also a historical problem with the chronology proposed for the migration of South Arabian tribes to Ethiopia. If tribes migrated to Ethiopia as recently as the first millennium B.C., one would expect the people of Ethiopia to speak the linguistic dialect of the dominating colonists, at least up to the third century. However, at least one visitor to this area, the author of the *Periplus of the Erythraean Sea,* does not seem to be aware of any language that was spoken on both sides of the Red Sea.[29] Furthermore, scholars believe that *hbst* is the name of one of the principal South Arabian tribe(s) that migrated to Ethiopia. But A. J. Drewes has pointed out that this name, found in Sabaean inscriptions in South Arabia, does not appear in the Ethiopian ones at least until Esana's time (ca. A.D. 350).[30] It is equally significant that none of the inscriptions on either side had any information about any extensive migrations from South Arabia to Ethiopia.

Clearly, the identification of the *hbst* as the South Arabian precursors of the Ethiopian civilization is at best a guess. At least one scholar has recently suggested that *hbst* refers not to a South Arabian tribe, but to a region around Axum. Using Albert Jamme's more recent contributions to the study of Sabaean inscriptions in South Arabia, A. K. Irvine has cogently argued that the term *hbst* is the name of a geographical region, not of a tribe.[31] He argues that *hbst* is grammatically not a form of a tribe's name, apart from the fact that there is so far no mention of such a tribe in the inscriptions. He concludes:

> There is little or no reason to suppose that any case of *Habasat* or *Habasa* refers to a South Arabian tribe or district. . . . Whenever *Habasat* occurs in a context which permits identification, it is reasonable to suppose that it refers to Abyssinia. . . . It would not, therefore, be legitimate to accord the *Habasat* with certainty the honour of having laid the foundations of a civilization which is at least eight centuries older than their first apparent mention in the country.[32]

Irvine's suggested identification of *hbst* with the Axumite region is far from certain. In particular, his theory fails to explain the reasons the name *hbst* is absent from the earliest Ethiopian inscriptions, opposed to the South Arabian ones. Nevertheless, Irvine is doubtlessly correct in challenging the unsubstantiated theories of earlier scholars.

With respect to ancient inscriptions, most of the earliest Sabaean epigraphy (before 400 B.C.) located in northern Ethiopia closely resemble those found in South Arabia, in both style and content. They are monumental and elegant in character, representing dedication inscriptions. The Ethiopian inscriptions, as Ephraim Isaac indicates, are not merely imitations of South Arabian ones, but manifest various unique features.[33] Many of these Ethiopian inscriptions show independent epigraphic development of indigenous authorship. Cultural ties between Ethiopia and South Arabia should not be used as precedents to suggest that South Arabia in any way dominated Ethiopia. Significant contacts between these two areas clearly existed more than five hundred years prior to Jesus Christ, but existing knowledge of either the Ethiopian or South Arabian epigraphy can do little more than demonstrate a common cultural heritage.

The fact that the earliest Sabaean inscriptions found in Ethiopia are not dated much before the fifth century B.C. does not warrant a conclusion that the alphabet came to Ethiopia through South Arabia. Such a conclusion awaits an exhaustive survey and definitive study of ancient inscriptions in Ethiopia. It should be noted, however, that only in Ethiopia did the Sinaitic-Sabaean script become fully exploited and developed. Not only did the Ethiopians quite early modify the script from the graphic-monumental to a less symmetrical style, but over the centuries, they developed a new order of the letters, one completely different from the Phoenician. Moreover, they became the first to innovate and vocalize the script of a Semitic language, to change and standardize the direction of its writing and use it in manuscripts and literature. It is equally significant that the South Arabians never developed Sabaean much beyond its earliest form, nor were they able to adapt it to literature, as the Ethiopians did. (It was not until after the rise of Islam that they produced local manuscripts in borrowed Arabic script.) The way the Ethiopians used Sabaean with freedom and originality hardly indicates they borrowed the language. We must also recognize that the entire Arabian Peninsula was, millennia ago, part of the African continental shelf.

INTERPRETATIONS REGARDING THE QUEEN OF SHEBA

The foregoing considerations call attention to the racial biases of some Western scholars on the question of South Arabian-Ethiopian relations, providing useful background for tracing a similar tendentiousness in the interpretation of the biblical accounts of the Queen of Sheba. When the Deuteronomic editor decided—sometime between 620 and 610 B.C. in Judea—to insert the short story about the Queen of Sheba into the narrative of 1 Kings, little did he know he was initiating a controversy of no small historical significance.[34] The Queen of Sheba story is actually incidental to the book's editor. A tradition about her was merely pressed into service in 1 Kings 10 in order to aid the writer's own theological design. His primary purpose in using the story about the Queen of Sheba was to dramatize his consistent theological claim that the God of Israel rewards those who obey the Deuteronomic laws (1 Kings 3:12). The writer focuses on the wisdom and glory of Solomon as a loyal, obedient leader of the people of God.[35]

Despite the original intent behind the usage of the earliest account of the Queen of Sheba, a wide variety of interpretations have developed, given certain problematic features within 1 Kings 10:1-10, 13 (essentially repeated nearly three hundred years later by the author of 2 Chron. 9:1-12) indicating that the queen who visited Solomon in Jerusalem arrived from a place called Sheba. She is called *malkat šbʾa,* which in the Septuagint [LXX] becomes *basilissa saba.* This designation causes a major problem for interpreters, since, as we have indicated, much of the biblical evidence about her racial identity or the land of Sheba tends to be confusing. Nevertheless, inherent problems within this Old Testament tradition seek resolution. Do we have here a Cushite/Ethiopian queen of ancient Africa, or is this a queen of South Arabia? For centuries, Ethiopians have insisted on the former and have named her Makeda. Muslims have also claimed this queen as an indigenous Arabian and have renamed her Bilqis.[36] Not surprisingly, European scholars have tended to locate her in South Arabia, not Africa.[37] In accordance with these claims, the story of the Queen of Sheba has undergone extensive Arabian, Ethiopian, Jewish, and other elaborations, becoming one of the most ubiquitous and fertile cycles of legends in the Middle East.[38]

No attempt to resolve the problematic features of the Queen of Sheba story can claim scientific certainty based on available biblical and nonbiblical evidence. The nonbiblical data that would place Sheba in Arabia are drawn from cuneiform (Assyrian) inscriptions which are problematic in themselves. Even so, locating the Queen of Sheba in the southern part of the Arabian peninsula still leaves the issue of her racial stock unresolved, in light of the close relations between Cush and South Arabia.

On the other hand, we encounter the persistent testimonies of Josephus, Origen, Jerome, and the Ethiopians themselves, who all regarded this queen an Ethiopian. Their consensus on this point may offer us an opportunity to discern a *bona fide* historical basis beneath the traditional report about the Queen of Sheba, and also help explain the fascination that the Black Church in America has had with this biblical queen.

Having drawn attention to somewhat limited biblical references to Sheba, let us examine the larger context of 1 Kings 10 in order to discover other clues about the land of Sheba. One need not look beyond 1 Kings 10:15. Following the Queen of Sheba story, the Deuteronomic writer resumes his narrative here. In 10:14, the reader is told about the 666 talents of gold Solomon received in one year. Then, in v. 15 (cf. 2 Chron. 9:14), the reader is told that this wealth was augmented by that brought by all the kings of Arabia (*kāl-malkê hāʿereb*).

A variant of the expression, "all the kings of Arabia" is also found in

Jeremiah 25:24 as a description of one of the groups that is to drink the cup of death.[39] Since Jeremiah's oracles are part of the background for understanding the Deuteronomic reforms of Josiah (621 B.C.) and their aftermath, the use of the phrase, "all the kings of Arabia" appears not to be coincidental. Indeed, Jeremiah and the editor responsible for 1 Kings 10:15 may be informing us that in the land that they understood to be Arabia, kings ruled—not queens.

Just as Sheba has been shown not to be in the land of Cush, the use of the phrase, "all the kings of Arabia" by Jeremiah and the first editor of 1 Kings may demonstrate that Sheba was not considered to be part of Arabia. The most frequently cited nonbiblical evidence appealed to by scholars are the cuneiform inscriptions of Tiglath-pileser III (744–727 B.C.) and Sargon II (721–705 B.C.).[40] While these inscriptions do attest to the fact that there were queens in North Arabia in the eighth century,[41] they tell us nothing about the tenth-century reign of Solomon (962–922 B.C.), or about queens in Arabia during the time 1 Kings 10:1–10, 13 was written. Besides, we have the testimony of Jeremiah and the editor of 1 Kings 10, who explicitly distinguish between the Queen of Sheba and "all the kings of Arabia." Whatever had been the case a century earlier, at the time of the 1 Kings writer and Jeremiah, we may conclude that Sheba was not considered to be part of Arabia, for there is no evidence that indicates Arabia had any queens at that time.

As far as we know, no inscriptions from South Arabia indicate that there ever was a queen of the South Arabian Sabaeans.[42] We apparently have *mukarribs* (priest-kings) before the fifth century B.C. Besides this, all we possess would be silence and conjecture regarding South Arabia of the Solomonic reign.

Regrettably, the situation is scarcely better with Cushite history. The period between the eleventh and eighth centuries B.C. is shrouded in obscurity with regard to Egyptian-Cushite relations.[43] We do find, however, the title *mkrrb* in Ethiopia in post-fifth century B.C. inscriptions. Some have suggested that this word—believed to be the pre-fifth century B.C. title of the king of Saba in South Arabia—indicates a South Arabian origin for early Ethiopian state and royal tradition.[44] This is a meaningless assertion based simply on a secondary inference rather than on tangible evidence. It warrants no conclusion that the title was a loan from outside. At best, it indicates that the early Ethiopians and South Arabians shared a common or similar political structure, perhaps originating from a single earlier civilization on both banks of the Red Sea.

THE QUEEN OF SHEBA AS A BLACK

If we have no biblical or nonbiblical hard data by which the story of the Queen of Sheba can emerge from the realm of legend into the full light of history, why have Josephus, a number of the Church Fathers, and the

Ethiopians themselves claimed that the Queen of Sheba was an African woman? Josephus calls her "the queen of Egypt and Ethiopia" as he amplifies considerably the text of 1 Kings 10:1-10, 13.[45] The most striking feature of the Josephus rendition of the Queen of Sheba story is that it is faithful to the text of 1 Kings 10:1-13, even though it provides much more detail. This raises the issue of the nature of Josephus's source. Does he have a specific source or two, in much the same manner as the first writer of the 1 Kings 10 story, or is Josephus's report otherwise motivated? An answer to this question may help explain why some early Christian writers thought the Queen of Sheba an African.

As a point of departure, let us postulate the thesis that Josephus, who claims to be writing from "his own books," does, in fact, have a version of the Acts of Solomon mentioned as a source for the original story in 1 Kings 11:41.[46] There are a number of factors that catapult such a thesis into the realm of possibility. First, the most significant discrepancy between Josephus's account and that of 1 Kings 10 and 2 Chronicles 9 is that Josephus never refers to the royal visitor as the Queen of Sheba. Rather, Josephus insists that his own books inform him that after Pharaoh, the father-in-law of Solomon, no other king of Egypt was called Pharaoh. Clearly, Josephus has ignored the Old Testament record on this point in favor of his own books.[47] The crucial issue is not that the Old Testament disputes Josephus's source and Josephus is simply wrong. Rather, the central issue is this: Why would Josephus prefer his own source when he was probably aware of Old Testament citations that contradicted his source? One explanation would be that one of his own books was treasured precisely because it was a copy of the very ancient *Acts of Solomon*, a document that may not have used the term *Sheba* at all.

A second factor is that, while Josephus twice describes Solomon's visitor as the queen of Egypt and Ethiopia, his final designation for her is simply the queen of Ethiopia. Josephus may not only have been aware of the Twenty-fifth Egyptian Dynasty, but his source may antedate this period, going back to the time the Nubians exercised a hegemony over Egypt and Ethiopia. A third and most persuasive factor is that Josephus's story may be an indication that, within segments of first-century Jewish communities, there was an awareness of a larger story that focused more on the queen than on Solomon. Ullendorff says, "the way in which he [Josephus] tells the story no doubt reflected the state of contemporary interpretation . . ."[48] If this is true, then—for some first-century Jews—the Queen of Sheba was an African. This may startle some today, but there simply is no evidence that Jews in the biblical and intertestamental period viewed Black skin as a curse. In fact, the reverse seems more likely, as in the Song of Songs 1:5: *melaina eimi kai kalē* (LXX, "I am Black and beautiful").[49] Moreover, we are not surprised to hear Rabbi Akiba (A.D. 135) speak of a Black man as king of the Arabs.[50]

If there is any merit in our thesis that Josephus may have had an ancient source that indicated the existence of a queen of Egypt and Ethiopia instead of a Queen of Sheba, the suspicion of quite a few within the Black Church would be confirmed. Let us briefly consider the pertinent New Testament passages. Matthew 12:42 and Luke 11:31 make mention of a *basilissa notou* ("queen of the South") who has an eschatological function. For some, this image preserved in the Q source of the Synoptics immediately called to mind the Queen of Sheba as a person who knew how to respond to God's initiative among his people. Inasmuch as Luke, in Acts 8:27-39, also provides a story about another queen and specifically refers to her as Candace, queen of the Ethiopians, it was inevitable that not a few would identify the queen of the South with the queen of the Ethiopians. Ullendorff categorically insists that there was no relation between the two.[51] Certainly, any careful student of biblical history would have to discriminate between the vastly different periods of time in which the Queen of Sheba (queen of the South) and the one-eyed Candace were alive.[52] This fact aside, Ullendorff overstates his case by insisting that there is *no* relation between the two queens. If both queens were of African lineage and related to Ethiopia, there certainly would be a relationship, and a most significant one, at that.

Although no scientific certainty can be claimed for the African, or more precisely, the Ethiopian identity of the Queen of Sheba ("the queen of the South"), much evidence exists that leads to this conclusion. Origen and Jerome both believed her to be of African ancestry and built their exegetical opinions on this without expressing any doubt.[53] Therefore, any assertion that the Queen of Sheba was South Arabian and not Ethiopian must construct a defensible criticism of some of the notable historians and biblical scholars of antiquity.

Ethiopians past and present have romantically elaborated this matter. To illustrate, there is their testimony that suggests the Queen of Sheba was the distant ancestor of Haile Selassie. Ullendorff offers an extensive, but unsympathetic examination of this claim. According to him, the *loci classici* on the blending of the Queen of the South and the Meroitic Queen Candace are to be found in the *"Kebra Nagast,"* Ethiopia's national saga.[54] Ullendorff examines the grand contention by the late Emperor Haile Selassie, known as the Lion of Judah. Ullendorff informs us that Article II of the 1955 Ethiopian Constitution underscores this claim that became a part of the official state record. It reads as follows: ". . . the imperial dignity shall remain perpetually attached to the line . . . [which] descends without interruption from the dynasty of Menelik I, son of the Queen of Ethiopia, the Queen of Sheba and King Solomon of Jerusalem."[55] Despite the grandeur of this claim, there may well be some truth in it, once it is conceded that Jews in the biblical period and early Christians found no problem with the idea of Black nobility, dignity, and beauty.

The belief that the Queen of Sheba was a Black woman is also strongly maintained by the Royal Order of Ethiopian Hebrews, an organization of

Black Jews that was incorporated in 1930. The spiritual head of this West Indian group, Rabbi Wentworth A. Matthew, argues that "Negroes are in truth Ethiopian Hebrews; Jacob was a Black man; Blacks are descendants of the union between King Solomon and the Queen of Sheba, which established the royal line down to the present Haile Selassie; and Judaism is their own and the one true religion."[56] A most interesting feature about this claim is that it implies that the ascendancy of the Ethiopian Orthodox Church represents an aberration from the true Hebrew religion of ancient Ethiopia. Also worthy of mention is the fact that the Queen of Sheba is identified as a Black woman by more traditional Falashas of the western hemisphere, Africa, and even Europe. An attestation of this claim in Europe is provided by Dominique Torres in a *Le Monde* article entitled "Les Juifs Noirs de l'Oublie." Mme. Torres suggested that the Falashas, some of whom lived in France, are either ancient Yemenite Jews who crossed the Red Sea or descendants of the tribe of Dan. In any case, she reported that they see the Queen of Sheba as their ancient Black ancestress.[57]

A review of the history of interpretation regarding the Queen of Sheba would be quite incomplete without considering two more constituencies for whom the Queen of Sheba has meant so much. We refer to the Muslims on the one hand and to Afro-Americans on the other. At several points, the Holy Qur'an mentions the Queen of Sheba.[58] In a major commentary on the Qur'an by the Islamic scholar Abdullah Yusuf Ali, one finds the following:

> The Queen of Sheba (by name Bilqis in Arabian tradition) came apparently from Yemen, but she had affinities with Abyssinia and possibly ruled over Abyssinia also. The *Habasha* tribe (after whom Abyssinia was named) came from Yemen. . . . There were frequent invasions of Abyssinia from Arabia. . . .[59]

Certainly, Yusuf Ali is accurate in reporting the close relationship between South Arabia and ancient Abyssinia (Ethiopia, Cush); but he is incorrect when he reports invasions of ancient Abyssinia by tribes from South Arabia. All historic records document the reverse: Ancient Ethiopia dominated South Arabia during several historic periods. Even the year of Muhammad's birth (A.D. 570) is known as the Year of the Elephant, when Abraha the Ethiopian laid siege to Mecca.[60] Furthermore, Muslim traditions about the Queen of Sheba have assigned her the name *Bilqis,* which is not found in the Qur'an. It is a name given to the Queen of Sheba in the post-Quranic popular traditions (the *hadith*). The significance of the Arabian and Muslim treatment of the Queen of Sheba story is that it shows how the image of the Queen of Sheba powerfully influenced diverse traditions—so much so that all have sought to claim her for their own.

A little more than fifty years ago, a Black minister named R. A. Morrisey published a book entitled *Colored People and Bible History.* By the standards of modern literary criticism, Rev. Morrisey's book displays little familiarity with exegetical tools and methods. Perhaps this fact, along with his race, explains why his book, like several others of similar variety, was not widely circulated or taken seriously. Morrisey devoted one of his early chapters to the Queen of Sheba, and, following a remarkably detailed presentation of Josephus's version of the queen of Egypt and Ethiopia, he wrote: "But who was this woman as to race variety? To ascertain the answer we must find out where was Sheba—the country over which she was queen. Sheba was a country in Ethiopia occupied by the descendants of Ham."[61]

Morrisey goes on to describe the Cushites as founders of the Babylonian Empire and locates their true home as "south of Egypt and north of Syrene."[62] Morrisey's earlier question should be posed today: "Who is this woman as to race variety?" From all of the data surveyed thus far, it would appear that the ancient Queen of Sheba was indeed of Negro ancestry. This was the belief of Josephus, Origen, and Jerome. It has been the belief of Ethiopians, whether Christian or Falasha. It has been the belief of the American Black Church. Thus, it is not at all surprising that in her celebrated volume entitled *Beautiful, Also, Are the Souls of My Black Sisters,* Jeanne Noble insists that the Queen of Sheba is also a beautiful Black sister.[63]

CHAPTER THREE

Racial Motifs in the Biblical Narratives

As we have indicated, the Bible contains different, even conflicting, traditions about the precise location of ancient Sheba, although the evidence suggests that Sheba was in or very near Black Africa. The Old Testament may lack details on the race or ethnicity of the celebrated Queen of Sheba, but there are sufficient ancient extrabiblical witnesses that favor her Black identity.

We now take up the larger questions of race and racism — not in relation to a particular biblical figure, but as it pertains to a wide range of biblical narratives. We do not find any elaborate definitions or theories about race in antiquity. This means we must reckon with certain methodological problems in attempting to examine racial motifs in the Bible. Ancient authors of biblical texts did have color and race consciousness (they were aware of certain physiological differences), but this consciousness of color and race was by no means a political or ideological basis for enslaving or otherwise oppressing other peoples. In fact, the Bible contains scarcely any narratives in which the original intent was to negate the humanity of Black people or view Blacks unfavorably.

The specific racial type of the biblical Hebrews is itself quite difficult to determine.[1] Scholars today generally recognize that the biblical Hebrews most probably emerged as an amalgamation of races rather than from any pure racial stock. When they departed from Egypt, they may well have been Afroasiatics. To refer to the earliest Hebrews as "Semites" does not take us very far, since as the eighteenth-century term does not designate a race, but a family of languages embracing Hebrew, Akkadian, Arabic, and Ethiopic (*Ge'ez*).[2] The language of "burnt-face" Africans, for example, is as equally Semitic as the language of the Jews or the Arabs.[3] This reaffirms our earlier contention that sophisticated theories about race and the phenomenon of racism are by-products of the postbiblical era. Consequently part of the task in this chapter is to construct an interpretive framework for a range of biblical attitudes about race and to determine implications for the problem of racism and ethnocentrism that still bedevil both Church and society in many nations today, including those of the Third World.

Although the Bible primarily presents sociopolitical entities that are differentiated as empires, nations, and tribes, there are important ways in which the subject of race acquires particular significance. In the Bible, two broad processes related to racism may be operating. First there is the phenomenon of "sacralization." By this we mean *the transposing of an ideological concept into a tenet of religious faith in order to serve the vested interest of a particular ethnic group*. Second is the process of "secularization" or *the diluting of a rich religious concept under the weighty influence of secular pressures (social or political)*.[4] In secularization, ideas are wrenched from their original religious moorings and fall prey to nationalistic ideologies. These often cultivate patterns of ethnocentrism and even racism, which in turn can have harmful effects on certain racial groups who are scorned and marginalized.

RACE AND SACRALIZATION IN THE OLD TESTAMENT

Several Old Testament passages are quite suitable as illustrations of sacralization, and as such, require a new kind of critical engagement. First, we shall consider the so-called curse of Ham (Gen. 9:18–27), which rabbis of the early Talmudic periods and the Church Fathers at times used to denigrate Black people. Later Europeans adopted the so-called curse of Ham as a justification for slavery and stereotypical aspersions about Blacks. Second, we shall discuss the fascinating narrative about Miriam and Aaron, who object to Moses' Ethiopian wife (Num. 12:1–16). Third, our attention will focus on the Old Testament genealogies that contributed to the Israelite and ancient Jewish perception that they constituted a most divinely favored people ("race"). Fourth, we shall take up the biblical notion of election (chosen people) as it develops as an explicit theme in the Old Testament and changes in the New Testament.

Our first example of sacralization is found in some of the earliest Jahwist ("J") traditions of the Old Testament. It is Genesis 9:18–27, which has achieved notoriety in many quarters because it contains the so-called curse of Ham. Technically, the passage should follow directly after the "J" passage that concludes the flood narrative (Gen. 8:20–22), since critical investigations have shown that Genesis 9:1–17, 28, 29 represent the much later Priestly ("P") exilic tradition.[5] The great significance of Genesis 9:18–27 is not that it contains the so-called curse of Ham, which technically does not take place at all. Rather, these verses make it clear that, to the mind of the ancient Israelite author, "the whole post-diluvial humanity stems from Noah's three sons."[6] On Genesis 9:19, Claus Westermann remarks:

The whole of humankind takes its origin from them [Shem, Ham, Japheth] . . . humanity is conceived here as a unity, in a way different from the creation; humanity in all its variety across the earth, takes its origin from these three who survived the flood. The purpose of the contrast is to underscore the amazing fact that humanity scattered in all its variety throughout the world comes from one family.[7]

Once the passage established this essential aspect of human origin (vv. 18, 19), it continued by providing what appears to be a primeval rationale for differences in the destinies or fortunes of certain groups of persons. Certainly, as one scholar notes, "from a form critical viewpoint Genesis 9:20-27 is an ethnological etiology concerned with the theology of culture and history."[8] This observation alerts us to the theological motives in verses 20-27 that have implications for definite interpretations regarding culture and history. It is this development that most clearly attests to the process of sacralization, where cultural and historical phenomena are recast as theological truths holding the vested interest of particular groups.

A word about the literary form of this narrative is important. In general, the narrative passages of Genesis 1-11 concern themselves with the matter of "crime and punishment; this is particularly evident in the ('J') narratives."[9] Westermann informs us that these narratives have antecedents and parallels in ancient African myths: "It is beyond dispute that African myths about the primeval state and biblical stories of crime and punishment in J correspond both in their leading motifs and in their structure."[10]

With respect to Genesis 9:18-27, the crime is Ham's seeing the nakedness of his drunken father, Noah, without immediately covering him. In error, Ham leaves his father uncovered (an act of great shamelessness and parental disrespect in Hebrew tradition) while he goes to report Noah's condition to Shem and Japheth, his brothers (v. 22). Ham's two brothers display proper respect by discreetly covering their father (v. 23). When Noah awakens (v. 24), the problems begin. Noah pronounces a curse—*not* on Ham, but on Ham's son Canaan, who has not been mentioned before. Noah also blesses Shem and Japheth, presumably as a reward for their sense of respect.

If one attempts to argue for the unity of the passage, inconsistencies and other difficulties abound. To illustrate, Ham commits the shameless act in verse 22, but Canaan is cursed in verse 25. In 9:18, the list of Noah's sons refers to Ham as being second, but in 9:24, the text—presumably referring to Ham—uses the phrase, Noah's "youngest son." Also, the mentioning of Canaan as cursed in verse 25 raises the possibility (albeit untenable) that Noah had a fourth son, named Canaan.

Then too, uncertainties about the precise nature of Ham's error result in a fantastic variety of suggestions, which range from Ham's having possibly castrated his father, attacked his father homosexually, committed incest with his father's wife, or having had sexual relations with his own wife while aboard the ark.[11] The matter was far less complicated: Ham violated a vital rule of respect. Many of the difficulties within this passage find a solution if we allow the possibility that the original version of Genesis 9:18-27 only referred to Ham and his error, and a later version of the story—one motivated by political developments in ancient Palestine—attempted to justify Shem's descendants (Israel) and those of Japheth (Philistines) over the subjugated Canaanites.[12]

While admitting that it is Ham who shows disrespect to Noah but Canaan, Ham's son, who is cursed, Westermann asserts:

> The same person who committed the outrage in v. 22 falls under the curse in v. 25. The Yahwist has preserved, together with the story of Ham's outrage, a curse over Canaan which could be resumed because of the genealogical proximity of Canaan to Ham. Those who heard the story knew the descendants of Ham as identical with those of Canaan.[13]

In Westermann's view, Ham *was* cursed and presumably not just Canaan, but all the other descendants of Ham cited in Genesis 10:6: Cush, Egypt, and Put (Punt).

Although I disagree with Westermann's contention that Ham was, *in effect,* cursed in Genesis 9:18–27, he helps us see that the ambiguity of the text can lead Bible interpreters to justify their particular history, culture, and race by developing self-serving theological constructs. In one instance, the Canaanites "deserve" subjugation; in another instance, the Hamites "deserve" to be hewers of wood and drawers of water.

Whether or not sacralization was actually part of the original narrative, we have much evidence in the Midrashim (fifth century A.D.), where Noah says to Ham: "You have prevented me from doing something in the dark (cohabitation), therefore your seed will be ugly and dark-skinned."[14] Similarly, the Babylonian Talmud (sixth century A.D.) states that "the descendants of Ham are cursed by being Black and are sinful with a degenerate progeny."[15] The idea that the blackness of Africans was due to a curse, and thus reinforced and sanctioned enslaving Blacks, persisted into the seventeenth century.[16] Even today, in such versions of Holy Scripture as *Dake's Annotated Reference Bible,* one finds in Genesis 9:18–27 a so-called "great racial prophecy" with the following racist hermeneutic:

> All colors and types of men came into existence after the flood. All men were white up to this point, for there was only one family line of Christ, being mentioned in Luke 3:36 with his son Shem. . . . prophecy that Shem would be a chosen race and have a peculiar relationship with God. All divine revelation since Shem has come through his line. . . . prophecy that Japheth would be the father of the great and enlarged races. Government, Science and Art are mainly Japhethic. . . . His descendants constitute the leading nations of civilization.[17]

Another instance of sacralization confronts us quite early in the Old Testament, within the genealogies of the descendants of Noah. It is especially useful to consider the so-called table of nations (Genesis 10) in conjunction with the much later genealogical listing of 1 Chronicles 1:1–2:55. On the one hand, these listings purport to be comprehensive catalogs. All too often they have been erroneously taken as reliable sources of ancient ethnography. Critical study of these genealogies illuminates theological motives that inevitably demonstrate a tendency to arrange different groups in priority, thereby attaching the greatest significance to the Israelites as an ethnic and national entity greater than all other peoples of the earth.

At first glance, Genesis 10 appears to be a single listing of ancient nations. However, biblical criticism has for some time demonstrated that Genesis 10 represents a combination of at least two different lists, separated by centuries: Jahwist ("J") and Priestly ("P").[18] In fact, the fusing of different traditions in Genesis 10 doubtlessly accounts for the difficulty in locating the land of Cush, and determining the relationship between Cush and Sheba or the differences between Seba and Sheba. As we said in chapter 2, Genesis 10:7 mentions Seba as a son of Cush, and Sheba is a grandson of Cush. Here the text clearly is identifying the descendants of Ham (ham). Then in Genesis 10:28, the text introduces an anomaly, mentioning Sheba as a direct descendant of Shem, not Ham. Furthermore, since the initial Samech (s) of seb'a is the equivalent of and interchangeable with the Hebrew Shin (s) in old South Arabic,[19] one could argue that Genesis 10 offers us two persons named Sheba as descendants of Cush, but only one person by that name as a descendant of Shem. In any case, it is not clear that the table of nations as it stands does not have the motive of delineating sharp ethnic differences between the ancient peoples of Africa, South Arabia, and Mesopotamia. The true motive lies elsewhere.

Rather than an objective historical account of genealogies, the table of nations in Genesis 10 is a theologically motivated catalog of people. The table not only ends with the descendants of Shem, but does so in a way consciously stylized to accentuate the importance of his descendants.[20] About this, the author of the genealogy in 1 Chronicles 1:17–34 is most explicit; of all the descendants of the sons of Noah, Shem's receive the most elaborate attention. Thus the most primitive "J" listing of the nations is theologically edited centuries later according to the post-exilic Priestly tradition, in order to establish the priority of the descendants of Shem. Centuries later, a further elaboration takes place, as found in the genealogies of 1 Chronicles. In this long progression, the theological presuppositions of a particular ethnic group displace any concern for objective historiography and ethnography. The descendants of Noah not related to Shem become increasingly insignificant and are mentioned only when they serve as foils to demonstrate the priority of the Israelites.

The subtle process being described may consequently be called sacralization, because it represents an attempt on the part of one ethnic

group to construe salvation history in terms that are distinctly favorable to
it, as opposed to others. Here, ethnic particularity evolves with a certain
divine vindication, and the dangers of rank racism lie just beneath the
surface. While the genealogies do not express negative attitudes about
persons of African descent, as my colleague Gene Rice has noted, it is
important to clarify an aspect of his judgment in light of the way in which
sacralization expresses itself in these genealogies. Consider Rice's remarks:

> Genesis 10 has to do with all the peoples of the world known to
> ancient Israel and since this chapter immediately follows the episode
> of Noah's cursing and blessing, it would have been most appropriate
> to express here any prejudicial feelings toward African peoples. Not
> only are such feelings absent, but all peoples are consciously and
> deliberately related to each other as brothers. *No one, not even Israel,*
> *is elevated above anyone else and no disparaging remark is made*
> *about any people, not even the enemies of Israel* [emphasis mine].[21]

Rice's contention that the genealogies do not elevate Israel above anyone
else must be qualified. After all, Genesis 10:21-31 becomes the basis for
amplifying the descendants of Shem and Judah (1 Chronicles 2:1-55) as the
distinctive *laos tou Theou* (LXX "people of God"). Thus the entire
genealogies are construed theologically to enhance the status of a particular
people, and this is sacralization.

Numbers 12 attests all too well to the way individuals can quickly move
from a sacred ethnic stance to racism of the worst sort. In Numbers 12:1,
Moses' brother and sister castigate him for having married a Cushite woman
(*hā ʾišā hacū šiʿt*). Several factors point to the probability that the offensive
aspect of the marriage was the woman's Black identity. In the first place,
this is clearly the view expressed in the wording of the Septuagint *heneken*
tēs gunaikos tēs Aithiopissēs ("on account of the Ethiopian woman").[22]
Secondly, in the selection of the rather odd punishment that God unleashes
on Miriam (v. 10), it can hardly be accidental that leprosy is described
vividly as "leprous, as white as snow." Quite an intentional contrast is
dramatized here: Moses' Black wife, accursed by Miriam and Aaron, is now
contrasted with Miriam, who suddenly becomes "as white as snow" in her
punishment. The contrast is sharpened all the more because only Miriam is
punished for an offense of which Aaron is equally guilty. The LXX witness,
together with these exegetical considerations, point strongly to the probability that more than arrogance is at issue in this text. Also involved is a
rebuke to the racial prejudice characterized by the attitudes of Miriam and
Aaron.

God's stern rebuke of Miriam's and Aaron's incipient racial prejudice is
a perennial reminder of the extraordinarily progressive racial values of the
Bible in comparison to the hostile racial attitudes in the medieval and
modern period.[23] At the same time, however, the Numbers 12 narrative

exposes the inherent difficulties of any quick generality about the racial implications of sacralization that appear when early traditions assume, through years of refinement, an ethnic particularity that marginalizes groups outside the Torah, "The Land of Israel" (ʾereṣ Israēl), and the Covenant.

For theological reasons, the process of sacralization in the Old Testament largely remains racially ambiguous, especially with specific reference to Black people. The distinction the Old Testament makes is not racial. Rather, the Hebrew Scripture distinguishes groups on the basis of national identity and ethnic tribes. All who do not meet the criteria for salvation as defined by the ethnic or national "in-groups" are relegated to an inferior status. It is therefore surprising to many that Black people are not only frequently mentioned in numerous Old Testament texts but are mentioned in ways that acknowledge their actual and potential role in the salvation history of Israel. By no means are Black people excluded from Israel's story, as long as they claim it (however secondarily) and not proclaim their own story apart from the activity of Israel's God.

Extensive lists of Old Testament passages that make favorable reference to Black people are readily accessible.[24] There are many illustrations of such provocative texts. Isaiah 37:9 and 2 Kings 19:9 refer to Tirhaka, king of the Ethiopians. This ancient Black Pharaoh was actually the fourth member of the Twenty-fifth Egyptian Dynasty that ruled all of Egypt (730–653 B.C.).[25] According to the biblical texts, Tirhaka was the object of the desperate hopes of Israel. In the days of Hezekiah, Israel hoped desperately that Tirhaka's armies would intervene and stave off an impending Assyrian assault by Sennacherib. More than a half-century later, another text would refer to "men of Ethiopia and Put who handle the shield" (Jer. 46:9). The Old Testament indicates that Black people were part of the Hebrew army (2 Sam. 18:21–32) and even part of the royal court. Ebedmelech takes action to save Jeremiah's life (Jer. 38:7–13) and thereby becomes the beneficiary of a singular divine blessing (Jer. 39:15–18). The dominant portrait of the Ethiopians in the Old Testament is that of a wealthy people (Job 28:19; Isa. 45:14) who would soon experience conversion (Ps. 68:31; Isa. 11:11, 18:7, Zeph. 3:10). The reference to "Zephaniah the son of Cushi" (Zeph. 1:1) may indicate that one of the books of the Old Testament was authored by a Black African.[26]

ELECTION AND SACRALIZATION IN THE BIBLE

Israel's particularity loses much of its subtlety as the dubious concept of her election (bāḥar) begins to gain a firm footing in the Old Testament. Certainly, traces of the idea of Israel's chosenness and personal, special relationship with her deity were present in "the pre-Jahwistic cult of the ancestors," but the explicit concept of Jahweh's loving preference for the people of Israel develops relatively late.[27] The theologically elaborated belief that Jahweh specifically chose Israel above all other nations does not become a matter of religious ideology—and therefore an instance of sacralization—until the period of Deuteronomistic history toward the end of the seventh century B.C. (Deut. 7:6–8; 10:15; Jer. 2:3; compare: Isa. 43:20; 65:9).[28]

Regardless of the theological structure that attempts to support the Deuteronomistic concept of Israel's election, ambiguities engulf this concept of election. Horst Seebass, for example, insists that even among the Deuteronomistic writers, Israel's election "only rarely stands at the center of what is meant by election."[29] According to him, *bāḥar,* as a technical term for Israel's election, always functions as a symbol of universalism. It represents Israel in the role of "service to the whole."[30] Seebass is representative of those who want to de-emphasize the distinctive ethnic or racial significance of the concept in Israel's self-understanding during the Deuteronomistic period.[31]

The ethnic and racial ambiguities involved in the concept of Israel's election seem to persist. The ambiguity does not result from the fact that a universalistic history is presupposed by the biblical writers who advance the Old Testament concept of Israel's election. Rather, the ambiguities stem from the nature of the presupposed universalism. Gerhard von Rad points out that in the Deuteronomistic circles, the chosenness of Israel attains a radical form and its universal aspect is at best paradoxical.[32] Perhaps the real paradox resides in the notion that Israel's divine election seems to lead inevitably to sacralization, with the people of Israel as an ethnic group at the center. Certainly, the Deuteronomistic authors struggle to demonstrate Jahweh's affirmation of the Davidic monarchy and, more importantly, Jahweh's selection of Jerusalem as the center of any continuing redemptive activity.[33] Although the people of Israel exhibit no extraordinary attributes or values by which they objectively merit Jahweh's election, there later develops an elaborate doctrine of merit, by which those who know and follow the Torah attempt to prove their worthiness as the chosen people.

Despite the absence of any inherent superiority of the people of Israel, the concept of election becomes inextricably bound up with ethnic particularity. Accordingly, the people of Israel claim the status of being preeminently chosen. They thereby claim to possess the Law, the Covenant, and a continuing promise of the land and the city as the "in-group." At the same time, all who stand outside the community or apart from the supporting religious ideology of election are relegated to the margins of Israel's "universal" saving history. Other races and ethnic groups may, of course, subscribe to Israel's religious ideology and derive the commensurate benefits. But the criteria for such subscription always seem to be mediated through the biases of an ethnic group reinforced by elaborate genealogies and the transmission of particular legal religious traditions.

This entire development typifies the process of sacralization, and it is striking to see the different treatment of election in the New Testament.

George Foot Moore provides us with a glimpse of the New Testament conception of election when he asserts that, "Paul and the church substituted an individual election to eternal life, without regard to race or station."[34] However, such an assertion oversimplifies New Testament ideas about election. Rudolf Bultmann provides us with a more helpful understanding of the New Testament in this regard. He argues that in the New Testament, "the Christian Church becomes the true people of God." In Bultmann's view, the New Testament no longer concerns itself with a preeminent ethnic group, that is, *Israēl kata sarka* (1 Cor. 10:18), but with the Israel of God (Gal. 6:16), without any exclusive ethnic or racial coordinates.[35]

In contrast to the Deuteronomistic usage of the Hebrew term *bāḥar,* the New Testament never presents the Greek verb *eklegomai* or its nominal derivatives *eklektos* ("chosen") and *eklogē* ("election") in an ethnically or racially exclusive sense. Paul wants to maintain a certain continuity with aspects of Israel's election, but that continuity is neither ethnic nor cultic (Rom. 9:11; 11:2, 11, 28, 29). For Paul, corporate election can include some Jews, but it must also embrace Gentiles (Rom. 11:25; Gal. 3:28; 1 Cor. 12:13); being "in" and "with" Christ becomes the new *crux interpretum.* In Paul's view, God *chose* the foolish, weak, and low (1 Cor. 1:27, 28). For James, God *chose* the poor who are rich in faith (James 2:5). For Matthew, God calls many, but *chooses* only the few (Matt. 22:14). The new universalism and unity to be found in the Christian Church expresses itself further within the context of "God's chosen ones" in the following sequence of thoughts:

There is neither Jew nor Greek, there is neither slave nor free, there is neither male nor female; for you are all one in Christ Jesus [Gal. 3:28].

For by one Spirit we were all baptized into one body — Jews or Greeks, slaves or free — and all were made to drink of one Spirit [1 Cor. 12:13].

Here there cannot be Greek and Jew, circumcised and uncircumcised, barbarian, Scythian, slave, free man, but Christ is all, and in all [Col. 3:11, 12].

The only New Testament text that refers to Christians as "a chosen race" (*genos eklekton*) is 1 Peter 2:9. Yet, in this text, the phrase is manifestly metaphorical. 1 Peter 2:9 depends very heavily on the wording found in LXX Isaiah 43:20, 21, but the ethnic particularity implied in the Old Testament text has fallen away entirely in 1 Peter.[36] Throughout the New Testament period (which extends well into the second century), "the elect" become the Church as the new Israel. Matthew is even more specific, because the elect represent the faithful few in the Church who accept the call to the higher righteousness and the doing of the will of God. In either case, these New Testament perspectives eliminate all ethnic or racial criteria for determining the elect.[37]

SECULARIZATION IN THE NEW TESTAMENT

Ambiguities with regard to race in the New Testament do not appear within the context of what we have defined as sacralization. The New Testament disapproves of ethnic corporate election, or "Israel according to the flesh." In fact, the New Testament offers no grand genealogies to sacralize the myth of any ethnic or national superiority.

If one is to explore the subject of racialist tendencies in the New Testament, one may turn to a different phenomenon: the process of secularization. How did the expanding Church—in its attempt to survive without the temporary protection she derived from being confused with Judaism—begin to succumb to the dominant symbols and ideologies of the Greco-Roman world? We will see how the universalism of the New Testament diminishes as Athens and Rome substitute for Jerusalem as the alleged new centers of God's redemptive activity.

The early Christian authors' understanding of the world barely included sub-Sahara Africa. They had no idea at all of the Americas or the Far East. These writers referred to Spain as "the limits of the West" (1 Clem. 5:7, Rom. 15:28); they envisioned the perimeter of the world as the outer reaches of the Roman Empire.[38] For New Testament authors, Roman sociopolitical realities, as well as the language and culture of Hellenism, often determined how God was seen as acting in Jesus Christ. Just as Old Testament Jerusalem came to represent the preeminent holy city of the God of Israel (Zion), New Testament authors attached a preeminent status to Rome, the capital city of their world.[39]

It is no coincidence that Mark, the earliest composer of a passion narrative, goes to such great lengths to show that the confession of the Roman centurion brings his whole gospel narrative to its climax.[40] For his part, Luke expends considerable effort to specify the positive qualities of his various centurions.[41] There is even a sense in which their official titles symbolize Rome as the capital of the Gentile world, for their incipient acts of faith or confessions (according to Luke) find their denouement in the Acts 28 portrait of Paul, who relentlessly proclaims the kerygma in Rome. The immediate significance of this New Testament tendency to focus on Rome instead of Jerusalem is that the darker races outside the Roman orbit are for the most part overlooked by New Testament authors.

For lack of more descriptive terminology, this process may be called secularization. Here, sociopolitical realities tend to dilute the New Testament vision of racial inclusiveness and universalism. Early traditions are accordingly adapted at later stages in such a way as to expose an undue compromising of a religious vision and to show how secular sociopolitical realities cause religious texts to be slanted to the detriment of the darker races.

Perhaps one of the best illustrations of this process of secularization is Luke's narrative about the baptism and conversion of the Ethiopian official in Acts 8:26–40. On the surface, this is a highly problematic text. One wonders immediately if the Ethiopian finance minister is a Jew or Gentile. One also wonders about the efficacy of his baptism and whether it constituted or led to a full conversion to Christianity. Probably the best survey of the problems posed by this story is that by Ernst Haenchen, who entitles the story "Philip Converts a Chamberlain."[42] According to Haenchen, Luke is intentionally ambiguous about the Ethiopian's identity as a Gentile or Jew. Luke merely appeals to this conversion story to suggest "that with this new convert the mission has taken a step beyond the conversion of Jews and Samaritans."[43] The story itself derives from Hellenistic circles and represents for Luke (in Haenchen's view) a parallel and rival to Luke's account of Cornelius, the first Gentile convert under the auspices of Peter.[44] Haenchen detects no particularly significant racial difficulties posed by Acts 8:26–40. For him, Luke merely edits this Hellenistic tradition to conform to his own theological design.

Certainly those who tend to exclude Black people from any role in Christian origins need to be reminded that a Nubian was possibly the first Gentile convert.[45] Nonetheless, Luke's awkward use of this story seems to have certain racial implications. Notice that in Acts 8:37, the Ethiopian says, "See, here is water! What is to prevent my being baptized?" A variant reading immediately follows in some ancient versions of the text: "And Phillip said, if you believe with all your heart, you may [be baptized]. And he [the Ethiopian] replied, I believe that Jesus Christ is the son of God."[46] Whether or not one accepts this variant reading as an authentic part of the text, it is clear that the Ethiopian's baptism takes place in the water without reference to a prior or simultaneous descent of the Holy Spirit (*compare* John 3:5; 1 John 5:6–8).

By contrast, Luke provides an elaborate narrative about Cornelius's conversion and baptism (Acts 10:12–48), at the end of which, the Holy Spirit descends and the baptism by water follows. Furthermore, Peter's speech (Acts 10:34–43) indicates a new development in which Gentiles are unambiguously eligible for conversion and baptism. Given the importance of the Holy Spirit's role throughout Luke–Acts as a theological motif, Luke's narrative about Cornelius's baptism gives the distinct impression (perhaps unwittingly) that Cornelius's baptism is more legitimate than that of the Ethiopian.

This by no means suggests that Luke had a negative attitude about Black people. One need only consider the Antioch Church's leadership presented in Acts 13:1 to dispel such notions There Luke mentions one "Symeon who is called the Black man" (*Symeōn ho kaloumenos Niger*). The Latinism "Niger" probably reinforces the idea that Symeon was a dark-skinned person, probably an African.[47] Luke's vision was one of racial pluralism in the leadership of the young Christian Church at Antioch (Acts 11:26). In no way is it important or useful to attempt to show, on the basis of any of the traditions in Acts of the Apostles, that the first Gentile convert was a Nubian rather than an Italian or member of any other ethnic group. This would be absurd, given the confessional nature of the entire Luke–Acts work, which does not come to us as objective history. But Luke's editorializing does result in a circumstantial deemphasis of a Nubian (African) in favor of an Italian (European) and thereby enables some Europeans to claim or imply that Acts demonstrates some divine preference for Europeans.

Luke is not innocent in all of this. His possible apologetics for the Roman official Theophilus, as well as the great significance he attaches to Rome as the center of the world, betrays the subtle way in which Luke's theology fell prey to secular ideological ideas.[48] In the last third of the first century, the Church generally struggled to survive in an increasingly hostile political environment. Luke, not unlike other New Testament writers of this period and after,[49] perhaps seeks to assuage Rome by allowing his theological framework to be determined by the assumption of a Roman-centered world.[50] In this process of secularization, the Lukan vision of universalism is undermined. Fortunately, this is not Luke's only message. We must remember that the New Testament's final vision of the holy remnant (Rev. 7:9) is consistent with Luke's notion of racial pluralism as reflected in the leadership of the church of Antioch (Acts 13:1). Both texts indicate that persons of all nations and races constitute part of the righteous remnant at the consummation of the ages.

Secularization in the New Testament needs much fuller exploration in terms of its racial dimensions. At one level, it highlights a certain ambiguity of race in the New Testament. At another level, it confronts us with a challenge to search for more adequate modes of hermeneutics by which the New Testament can be demonstrated as relevant to Blacks and other people of the Third World, even as it stands locked into the socioreligious framework of the Greco-Roman world. Of all the mandates confronting the Church today, the mandate of world community predicated on a renewed commitment to pluralism and the attendant acknowledgment of the integrity of all racial groups constitutes an urgent agenda for Bible scholars and laity alike. It is an agenda far too long neglected in the vast array of Eurocentric theological and ecclesial traditions that continue to marginalize people of color throughout the world today.

Part II

CLASS

Introduction

This section of our study brings together four essays under the rubric of class. Part I examined Western misconstruals of ancient biblical attitudes about race and Blacks. There is another long tradition in the West that has relegated Blacks to inferior positions of social class—both within society and within many Church denominations. Whether as victims, social prophets, or change agents, Blacks have known the bitter experience of persistently being denied justice. Furthermore, Blacks have not had easy access to scholarship, demonstrating how discrimination translates into patterns of socioeconomic disadvantage that are foreign, even antithetical, to biblical ideals. In support of this thesis, I offer two broad probes in the first half of the section and then two narrower studies on the problem of social class as evident in certain New Testament epistles.

Chapter four begins with a study of various ways of discerning biblical mandates on justice. The related concern of social class is an ancient problem. My aim is to show that Blacks have had a long-standing interest in learning about the Bible's demands for justice. I also wish to demonstrate that Church leaders and Bible scholars alike have not fully appreciated how diverse, changing, and challenging such biblical mandates are.

Whereas chapter four discusses biblical mandates that represent central concerns of the Black Church, chapter five focuses on the centrality of the Bible itself in the Black Church. White racism has historically created the problem of social class for Blacks. Nonetheless, African-Americans have sought ways—at times ingenious—to affirm themselves and their biblical faith. The Black Church reflects a history of creative adaptation and usage of the Bible that is distinctive, but not always favorably regarded by others. Despite the problems of social class that account in part for such distinctive biblical usage, the Black Church, while presenting its historic Bible-centered sobriety, must move from white-imitative, uncritical literalisms to a new level of vigorous biblical criticism. This new criticism would realize that the Black setting in life today is analogous to what it meant to be a minority group in the first century, with only Jesus on your side.

The two chapters that close this section are more detailed analyses of the problem of social class within ancient New Testament communities of faith. My aim is to highlight the mundane character of faith communities in real human crises. Whether in the Epistle to the Galatians or the Epistle of James, nominal Christians show themselves to be all too human. For these

51

New Testament communities, biblical ideals regarding freedom and strictures against class discrimination became little more than pious rhetoric. The author of the Epistle of James, no less than Paul in Galatians, prefigures an agenda that must be taken up afresh in each era. Of course, the Black Church today is by no means exempt from this agenda.

Both Paul and Jesus speak against class discrimination as a social evil and, in so doing, indict modern Church leadership that refuses to do likewise today.

CHAPTER FOUR

Biblical Mandates
on Justice and Social Class

The socioeconomic upheavals and political shifts in many nations since the beginning of the 1960s — the civil rights movement, the war in Vietnam, Communist incursions in the Western Hemisphere, and the independence of many Third World nations — have had their impact on traditional modes of theological reflection and ways for doing theology. The impact has not been as great on presuppositions for reading the Bible. Indeed, the rise and proliferation of liberation theologies (Black, Latin American, or Asian), feminist theologies, and contextual theologies that we have witnessed in the last two decades have come to represent profound impatience with Bible scholars who have been perceived as less than helpful in clarifying important but complex hermeneutical issues.

Many Bible scholars seem to be so preoccupied with what the Bible *meant* in various ancient settings that they have postponed the task of determining what the Bible text means *today,* leaving this topic to others by default. Perhaps nowhere is this as evident as in the area of determining the biblical mandates for justice and social class. Many Bible scholars, especially those whose specialty is the New Testament, have tended to be silent on this topic, although there are exceptions.[1] As a result, professional and lay theologians have found themselves searching the Scriptures to identify topics and themes that help determine what the Bible says about justice and social class.[2]

If Bible scholars have been too silent or obtuse with respect to a biblical hermeneutic of justice, perhaps Eurocentric theologians have been too voluble and impressionistic. The commendable purpose of determining the Bible's relevance for contemporary critical issues should not be the occasion for anachronisms, historical reconstruction, or some fantastic new (revisionist) mythology. The Bible has much to say about justice and righteousness as interrelated concepts; as such, its message is distinctive.

53

The Old Testament is expansive in delineating normative standards for "doing justice." The New Testament, through different theological criteria, also expresses interest that justice is the righteousness (will) of God and was normative for Christian conduct in ancient communities of faith. By no means has the ancient normative character of biblical justice been lost in the history of the Black Church.

Many leaders in the American Black Church have regarded racial justice as second nature to their sense of ministry. The more progressive Black Church leaders have championed broader issues of socioeconomic justice, going beyond the specific agendas of slavery, abolition, or civil rights. In either case, there is an extensive literature by Black historians insisting that African-Americans and persons of African descent in other nations have been victims of all sorts of racial and social injustices.[3]

As a consequence, Blacks have had a certain preoccupation with the question of theodicy (how to account for the justice of God in light of the persistence of blatant social injustices and human suffering). One Black scholar has suggested that theodicy constitutes the central criterion by which the Judeo-Christian tradition has legitimacy for Blacks.[4] For our purpose, we need only to point out that Blacks have long had a vital interest in biblical images, stories, and ethical teachings. These features of the Bible affirm justice as an attribute of God and Jesus, substantially endorsing the Black Church's quest for racial and social justice. Leaders from Richard Allen to Henry McNeal Turner to Martin Luther King, Jr., have made the concern for justice a leading motif in the prayers, songs, sermons, social programs, and public protests of the Black Church.

In recent years, Black Christian ethicists and theologians have renewed the call for the Black Church to appreciate the significance of its historic commitment to racial and social justice. Peter J. Paris takes it as axiomatic that Blacks have been "proscribed historically by structural conditions of societal injustice." Paris undertakes a quest for a constructive "root paradigm" in the heritage of the Black Church that will enable Blacks to recast their image as victims into one as change agents.[5] Paris's study identifies that root paradigm as a prophetic principle in the Black Christian tradition that he describes as the "biblical doctrine of the parenthood of God and the kinship [freedom and equality] of all people."[6] Although Paris seems to sidestep the strong patriarchal emphasis in the Black Church, he isolates in the Black Christian tradition a biblical anthropology that "affirms the equality of all persons under God regardless of race. . . ."[7]

J. Deotis Roberts also recognizes the Black Church's historic interest in racial and social justice. In a recent book, he devotes a chapter to the subject under the title, "Justice in the Service of Love."[8] Unlike those who tend to draw sharp distinctions between love and justice, Roberts prefers to regard the two as "mutually enriching" and " 'interpenetrating' one another as they reinforce each other in personal and social ethics."[9] Nevertheless, even Roberts considers love as a "supplement" to justice, "exalting justice to a higher level."[10] However, the Bible does not offer only one type of love or a single type of justice, but presents varying types of each that bespeak a range of relationships between the two.

The Black Church's general concern for racial equality and justice inescapably has vast implications for social class, because African-Americans and Blacks in other arenas of the African diaspora have found themselves relegated to a second-class (discrimination and disenfranchisement) or even a third-class (slavery) status. James H. Cone not only reminds us of the allure that socialism has had for leaders in the Black Church—like Reverdy C. Ransom in 1896—but renews the call for the Black Church to engage in more vigorous social analysis of the interplay between race and class.[11] Cone puts into fresh perspective the apparent modern romance with Marxist class analysis that typifies Latin American Liberation Theology. He acknowledges the usefulness of Karl Marx's social analysis for some Christians in the United States, where "white American churches have presented the gospel of Jesus as an opium for the oppressed so that they would not challenge unjust conditions in society."[12] Cone is cautious in his recommendations that Blacks utilize aspects of Marxist thought to understand the dynamics of capitalism and the relationship between race and social class. Cone is also mindful of the fact that "the struggle for justice in this world is not the ultimate goal of faith."[13] Yet, even as he affirms faith's ultimate goal as God's final vindication of the righteous and the faithful, he considers the struggle for justice to be not only a social witness but also "a witness to God's eschatological righteousness as defined by Jesus' cross and resurrection."[14]

The writings of these Black theologians and ethicists bring a new urgency to the task of determining how biblical traditions contain specific mandates that justice be done as an activity of great religious and social significance. In this respect, the Bible appears to be a distinctive body of ancient literature with particular regard for the problem of social class as a religious problem, whether in ancient Palestinian Judaism or in the life of the early Church outside Palestine. In these matters, the Bible is progressively self-corrective, presenting a range of attitudes about justice that often seems to be minimized by the powerful and the affluent in the postbiblical period. The task before us is foundational rather than comprehensive, for our principal aim is to explore a different mode of analysis as a basis for interpreting the normative character of biblical holy sentences in matters of justice and social class.

Thus, this chapter develops arguments about justice and social class in ancient texts in stages, as we find differences in literary genres. First, we consider philosophical texts of Plato and Aristotle, for these are widely recognized as the basis for the so-called classical (Greco-Roman) view of social justice. I then show how such philosophical treatments of justice had only limited bearing on religions of Greece and Rome. Second, I discuss groups of Old Testament and intertestamental material, in order to show that changes in community circumstances brought about different points of emphasis regarding justice and social class. Third, I take up such new developments that seem to occur in New Testament teachings regarding justice and social class. Here, I attempt to classify the varying types of justice the New Testament writers may have had in mind. I finally suggest how some features of New Testament teachings on justice and social class are especially important for the Black Church.

DISTRIBUTIVE JUSTICE IN PLATO AND ARISTOTLE

Noting that the term *justice* included more in its original Greek expression than it does today, Robert S. Brumbaugh asserts, "it combines the notion of observing the law, doing the right thing, honesty, respect for the other person's property and rights and fair play [equity]."[15] The pre-Socratics, Socrates, and Plato, while allowing for a modest relationship between religion and morality,[16] stressed that observing the law meant adherence to the civil law far more than to any laws ordained by the gods or God. "Doing the right things" came from understanding moral or natural law, not from a standard of justice that was prescribed by religion, as such. For the moment, let us consider some of the ways Plato and his student Aristotle discussed what has come to be called the Greco-Roman view of social justice.[17]

Philosophical discussions about the foundations of justice in the West often lead with Plato's *The Republic,* citing a single passage at the end of section 433E.[18] The original text reads: "the possession and practice of what belongs to that for which one is naturally suited would be confessed as justice."[19] This text compasses the social element by focusing on the relative inequities between individuals in the city-state, where civic duties or jobs were assigned on the basis of proportional merit. It is evident that this is Plato's meaning, because the text is preceded by a concern that rulers who conduct lawsuits guarantee each person's right to physical property and is followed by a concern for the distribution of functions within the city-state according to one's job as determined by one's natural ability.

The performance of social functions and civic duties in accordance with one's natural temperament constitutes a distributive form of justice. It advances the view that merit is distributed on a proportionate basis as individuals fulfill their natural — but unequal — functions within the society. In *The Republic,* Plato set forth a view of justice (*dikaiosynē*)[20] as a rudimentary form of social justice. His criterion is social equity predicated on a belief in fundamental differences in human worth. For Plato, justice is a social concept, because he considered the well-being of the city-state to be the social goal. Individuals are expected to learn and observe the law, and so do the right thing.

Plato's *The Law* amplifies his discourse on social justice. There, too, the basic assumption is that there are different degrees of human worth. At the top of the hierarchical model in Plato's proposed colony state of Magnesia is the human "law giver" (*nomothetēs*), who "teaches the noble, good, and just, teaching what these are and how those who intend to be happy must practice them."[21] The members of society beneath him are of unequal worth, even among themselves. As John Gould points out, it is the task of the legislator to achieve social justice by distributing "honors" (*timai*) corresponding to the real worth of members of society, and toward this end, he fashions the preamble to his laws.[22] The civil codes and laws of legislators are the criteria for social justice. Only in an indirect way are the gods related to this process.

Plato does not regard justice and religion as mutually exclusive. For him, the laws of the state presuppose the existence of the gods.[23] He often juxtaposes the holy with the just in speaking about the virtuous, noble, and good life.[24] He also calls justice (*dikaiosynē*) a divine quality that comes from wisdom and the rational temperance of the soul before human goods.[25] Plato's description of justice as an attribute of the gods is set forth concisely in the following text:

> What destroys us is injustice [*adikia*] and insolence combined with ignorance, what saves us is justice [*dikaiosynē*] and moderation combined with wisdom in the animate powers of the gods and of which some small trace may be clearly seen here also residing in us.[26]

For Plato, justice is primarily part of "the animate powers of the gods," and as such is only faintly evident among humans.

John Gould, in an otherwise commendable thesis, obscures this point when he argues that there are two criteria for Plato's social ethics: "the moral ideal of the general body of citizens and the ideal of insight beyond the system which the protective element law-givers must gain."[27] Gould does not seem to take seriously enough Plato's view that the gods possess animate powers that are only *faintly* traceable in human beings. We also question Gould's claim that the lawgivers "gain insight from beyond the system," in such a way that they can establish social justice.[28] In Plato's thought, the gods are not the source of social justice. Rather, the lawgivers themselves fashion a distributive type of justice as an expedient social principle.

With the empirical, ethical theories of Aristotle, however, there is a more definite line separating ethics and social justice from the gods. In the *Eudemian Ethics,* he offers a refutation of Plato's idea of the Absolute Good.[29] The notion of "moral insights beyond the system" is out of place in Aristotelian thought, which stresses that politics, economics, and wisdom are "the supreme of all the practical sciences."[30] In *The Nichomachaean Ethics,* he asserts, "Excellence and justice are matters of statecraft [*hē politikē*] but these conceptions involve so much disagreement and uncertainty that they come to be looked on as mere conventions, having no natural foundation."[31] Aristotle asserts that the natural foundations of justice are in the state,[32] because for him, "man is by nature a political/ social animal [*ho anthropos politikon zōon*]."[33] As a consequence, Aristotle assigns justice to practical fields rather than to a transcendent realm of forms or the gods. Although worthy of worship, the gods are in no sense linked to Aristotle's conception of justice as a social virtue; they provide no ultimate standard for it.

Plato and Aristotle differ on the foundations of justice, but they agree in their conceptualizations of the social (distributive) aspect of justice. This explains the tendency of modern philosophers and legal theorists to consider Plato and Aristotle the authors of the classical theory of social justice. Aristotle's principle treatment of the subject is found in Books II and V of *The Nichomachaean Ethics,* and more specifically in Book III of the treatise entitled "On Statecraft" and in various sections of "The Politics." The following selection is typical of Aristotle's argument:

> . . . since those who are equal in one thing only ought not to have equality in all things nor those unequal as regards one thing inequality in all . . . the free and well-born are citizens to a greater degree than those of low birth . . . and we shall admit that virtue also makes an equally just claim, for we hold that justice [*dikaiosynē*] is a social virtue [*koinōnken*]. . . .[34]

This text illustrates Aristotle's conviction that social justice means equity, not equality. Equity involves an *unequal* distribution of human value and legal rights. Equality in terms of *worth* and *rights* was as alien to Aristotle as it was to Plato. Let us now compare this philosophical stance with the nature of Greco-Roman religions.

H. D. F. Kitto[35] and Carl J. Friedrich[36] suggest that in the Greco-Roman world, religion was intimately bound up with the political order. This intimate connection between religion and the political order, however, had little moral content vis-à-vis social justice. Only in Plato's thought do the gods, acting in conformity to the idea of the Absolute Good, provide men with a partial idea of justice. Aristotle's conception of natural law does not even allow this. For him, virtually no relationship exists between the gods and matters of social justice. In their writings, religion is only part of one's duty within the state.

Among scholars of Greco-Roman literature, there are two positions on the relationship between religion and ethics in Western antiquity. One is represented by H. J. Rose, who maintains that the ancient religions indigenous to Greece and Rome were essentially *amoral*, containing no notion of ethics or moral duty.[37] H. D. F. Kitto represents the other perspective that religious and political thinking in the Greco-Roman world were "intimately connected." In Kitto's view, the Olympian pantheon of twelve gods presided over by Zeus protected the tribe, state, or family, taking suppliants under its care.[38] It is, however, possible to reconcile these two perspectives. When Rose speaks about the amoral nature of religion in the Greco-Roman world, he means only that neither the Olympian pantheon nor the mystery cults embodied laws or ethical codes for social behavior. Propitiating the gods was believed to result in divine protection, not in rules for social justice. Kitto seeks only to stress that Zeus was believed to sanction the unalterable moral laws to which the pantheon was subject. Nowhere does Kitto suggest that the gods instituted moral codes for societies. Rose and Kitto are in accord that the gods were not the source of laws governing social conduct.

Even in the pagan religions of ancient Greece, there was a clear notion of retributive justice, mentioned, but not emphasized by Aristotle. The goddess Dikē mentioned by Hesiod[39] was believed in by the masses of the Greco-Roman world in Platonic and even in New Testament times.[40] Hesiod also mentioned another dimension of divine justice that assumed the form of the goddess Themis (*hē Themis*).[41] Again, these goddesses did not provide moral or legal codes for the administration of justice within Greco-Roman society.[42] Thus, Greco-Roman religion did not give rise to notions of social justice. This explains why matters of social justice in these societies were handled by politicians and philosophers rather than by priests, diviners, or "prophets." The matter is very different when one turns to ideas about justice in the Old Testament and intertestamental traditions.

JUSTICE IN THE OLD TESTAMENT AND INTERTESTAMENTAL TRADITIONS

The Bible provides moral codes and extensive provisions for believers to do justice. The earliest traditions of Hebraic thought or ancient Judaism do not separate social ethical obligations and religious observances. George Foot Moore observes, "Obedience to God's law in its entirety is the supreme moral obligation of man [in Judaism]."[43] The element of a divinely ordained law that provides both moral and ceremonial obligations was one of the key features that distinguished Judaism from the indigenous religions of the Greco-Roman world.[44] An appropriate description of the ethics of Judaism would be that "Jewish ethics are in substance and form more exactly described as perceptive morals; they are the morals of a religion and their obligation lies not in the reason and conscience of men but in the authority of the sovereign Lawgiver."[45] Jewish traditions are replete with legislation promoting justice and prohibiting social injustices. Indeed, there appear to be several different types of justice in the Old Testament, including retributive, distributive, and compensatory justice. Also, the Old Testament is clear that the poor, widow, orphan, woman, sojourner, alien/stranger, or slave not only have rights (albeit with subordinate status in relation to the free male members of the community), but also have those rights protected by compensatory statutes that relieve the distributive aspect (Exod. 22:21, 22; Lev. 19:10, 33; Deut. 24:17; 26:12, 13).

David Daube has studied the subject of retributive, distributive, and compensatory justice in biblical traditions in great detail. He argues that some of the legislated morality in the Bible originated in prebiblical civil codes,[46] but he adds that "the priests and prophets who composed the Bible were not deeply interested in private law, they did not bother to create a *Corpus Juris Civilis.*"[47] In his view, these authors created a body of traditions that utilized the principles of retribution, compensation, and redemption in order to see social ethics as coextensive with religious observance. *The just person is now also the righteous person. The vertical piety of the cult that praises and acknowledges the sovereignty of God has a horizontal parallel specifying the believers' social obligations to others.*

Ethical and religious principles illuminate further the unique treatment of social justice in the traditional sources of Judaism. Daube would seem to have an ally in George Foot Moore who, while elsewhere noting the interplay of retributive and distributive principles of justice in Jewish texts, writes: "In all parts of the Bible justice in the broad sense is the fundamental virtue on which human society is based. It is no less fundamental in the idea of God and in the definition of what God requires of [people]."[48]

JUSTICE IN THE PENTATEUCHAL TRADITIONS

The foundation for all Jewish social legislation is the Pentateuch. Within this body of ritual and moral observance,[49] there are criteria for social justice and prescriptions about class distinctions. The Pentateuch (for some, Hexateuch) reflects different approaches to the shaping of Hebrew Law. Again, Daube's study on biblical Law helps. He shows that from the outset, the seemingly strict retributive approaches to law and justice in the Pentateuch represent a progressive tendency to ameliorate harsher prebiblical social legislation. The seemingly harsh law of retribution actually represents an effort to lessen the severity of a provision found in the Hammurabi Code.[50] This provides a positive framework for discerning both the evolutionary nature and the social function of the legal standards for justice within the Pentateuch.

Daube does not wish to expunge the whole notion of retaliation or retributive justice from the Pentateuch.[51] His goal is to interpret passages on retribution in light of compensatory elements that bring out the inherent social function of Hebraic Law. He notes that even such passages as Genesis 9:6 ("Whoever sheds the blood of man, by man shall his blood be shed") are much more than a mere law of retribution. The underlying reason for this text is the idea of atonement.[52] In Hebraic Law, men are interchangeable. A life taken away must be replaced (an atonement made), in the sense that each man's life is of equal value.[53] We must add that Daube's observation refers *exclusively* to the equality of a free Hebrew male. We cannot neglect the following illustrative texts:

"When a man strikes his slave, male or female, with a rod and the slave dies under his hand, he shall be punished. But if the slave survives a day or two, he is not to be punished; for the slave is his money" [Exodus 21:20, 21].

"When a man sells his daughter as a slave, she shall not go out as the male slaves do. If she does not please her master, who has designated her for himself, then he shall let her be redeemed; he shall have no right to sell her to a foreign people, since he has dealt faithlessly with her" [Exodus 21:7, 8].

Both these excerpts from the *Mišpatîm* of Hebraic Law clarify the narrow parameters of equality in an ancient patriarchal society where the lives of slaves and women scarcely equaled the value placed on the lives of free Hebrew males.

Centuries later we find (sixth century B.C.) such Priestly ("P") texts as Genesis 1:26, 27 and 5:1, 2: "When God created man [ʾādam], he made him in the likeness of God. Male [zākār] and female [nĕqēbā] he created them." Implicit in the wording of these Priestly texts is the fundamental equality of those created in God's image. In the evolution of the Pentateuch from the early Hebrew "J" source to the much later "P" tradition, we find clear indications of more equitable humanitarian measures extended to all members of the community or to others within its confines.

Daube's exposition on minute details of Hebraic criminal law has relevance for understanding broader social norms of justice. He shows, for example, that just as compensation underlies criminal law, it is also "prevalent in the domain of peaceful dealings and the settlement of torts causing economic damage only."[54] Daube's analysis of Pentateuchal civil legislation also considers the idea of redemption, primarily the use of gĕʾulā as buying or taking back, with reference to restoring an individual to one's originally intended place.[55] Here, however, Daube draws an unfortunate distinction between gĕʾulā as "social" legislation and its usage in a "metaphorical religious" sense, which dominated its development within the Pentateuch.[56] Such a distinction is problematic, primarily because it creates a polarity between the "social" and "religious" in the Pentateuch that must be challenged. Consider Daube's words, "while priests and prophets evolved the religious notion of redemption, the social laws with the legal notion continued all the time."[57] We must remember, however, that the social and legal provisions in the Pentateuch were *sui generis* religious concepts expounded by the same priests and prophets.

One way to remove any social-religious polarity is to consider the meaning of the Hebrew term ṣĕdāqa (righteousness or justice) in the Pentateuch. This term, perhaps more than any other, combines moral and religious observance.[58] It also combines standard piety with ideals for just social relations. Elizabeth R. Achtemeier argues that the Old Testament concept of righteousness is not strictly moral, legal, religious, or spiritual. "Rather in the Old Testament, righteousness is the fulfillment of the demands of a relationship whether that relationship be with men or with God . . . there are no norms outside of the relationship itself."[59]

Gerhard von Rad states the matter differently. For him, righteousness includes moral, legal, and religious dimensions.[60] The term characterized both the activity of God and socioreligious activity in the community that is pleasing to God. E. G. Hirsch calls attention to the original meaning of *righteous*, which he suggests contained a decided moral intention.[61] The term designates the demands of a relationship, to be sure. But in the Pentateuch, there are discernible norms for the "ought" that should typify the moral relationships (with different nuances) to which *ṣedeq* and its derivatives often refer. In his view, *ṣedeq,* as used in Leviticus 19:15 or Deuteronomy 1:16, refers to a style of public administration of justice by judges or rulers. In Exodus 23:7, the term has a more technical meaning: "the party in the suit who is in the right."[62] Distinctions of this kind are important; others could easily be added.[63]

This suggests that much of the social legislation in the Pentateuch fosters the idea of justice as a social norm. Accordingly, righteousness describes the ideal style of religious and social behavior for judge, plaintiff, witness, defendant, or member of the community. It governs relationships with sojourners, attitudes toward slaves and the poor — in short, everyone in the covenant community. In this regard, G. F. Moore remarks on Exodus 23:2, 3 (". . . so as to pervert justice; nor shall you be partial to a poor man in his suit") and Leviticus 19:15 ("You shall do no injustice in judgment; you shall not be partial to the poor or defer to the great, but in righteousness shall you judge your neighbor") as follows: "Nowhere is the endeavor to develop the highest principles of the Law in ordinances and regulations more conspicuous than in the sphere of judicial procedure."[64]

Any attention to righteousness in the Pentateuch must be balanced with a study of a corresponding Hebrew term, *mišpāṭ*. This word suggests a synthesis between the moral (social) and what is often understood more narrowly as ritual observance. In Genesis 18:25, for example, Abraham inquires, "Shall not the Judge of all the earth do justice?" Here the Hebrew expression *ʿaśa mišpāṭ* (do justice) is used to refer to God's expected behavior.[65] On the other hand, in Deuteronomy 16:18, *mišpāṭ* refers to the behavior of human judges in the public administration of justice: "They shall judge the people with righteous judgment." The phrase "righteous judgment" (*Mišpāṭ/ṣedeq*) denotes social justice based on precepts outlined in religious Law.

Kohler Kaufmann indicates that the original meaning of *šāpāṭ* is "vindicator."[66] God is the judge in the sense of vindicating Israel. God is a just advocate for the covenant community. As far as the Pentateuch is concerned, that vindication takes place on earth.[67] Not explicitly mentioned by Kaufmann, but equally important, is the idea that the vindication is based on a righteousness that is both vertical (exclusive worship of and sacrifices to God) and horizontal (the behavior of individuals and their interaction as the covenant people in accordance with the Pentateuchal social statutes). Kaufmann asserts that Jewish ethics have a more "practical, healthy and mundane character" than what he understands to be the Christian eschatological ethic.[68] Perhaps he should have elaborated or otherwise mentioned the ideal, even Utopian, quality of some Pentateuchal social legislation, such as the Jubilee ordinances (Lev. 25:1-55; 27:16-24).[69] David Daube, for example, agrees with Kaufmann on the *practical* quality of Pentateuchal social legislation, but Daube goes further:

> . . . the prominent part played by this legal–social element, redemption, no doubt is one of the causes and effects, of that constant stressing, in the leading religious literature of Judaism and Christianity, of the tremendous importance attaching to our practical work, here and now, by being merciful to the weak, for the final deliverance of the world. In Judaism and Christianity more than in other religions that I can think of is the idea of salvation combined with that of social justice and charity on earth.[70]

JUSTICE IN THE PROPHETIC LITERATURE

When we turn to the pre-exilic prophets, the data suggest that what Kaufmann calls social justice and charity combine with the idea of salvation to constitute a leading biblical theme. Even a casual survey of the literature produced by the prophets of the eighth through the sixth centuries B.C. shows that these prophets had a deep concern for social justice, expressed in terms of "a peculiar social order" of kinship and solidarity.[71] Despite the differences in points of emphasis, language, and theological orientation, these prophets repeatedly inveigh against cultic excesses and social injustices because of a recurring moral and "religious" malaise into which the covenant people would fall and from which they needed to be extricated.

Consider, for example, that when Homer and Hesiod wrote about the goddess Dikē in the eighth century B.C., the prophet Isaiah was chastising his people on the basis of a different idea of justice. "Learn to do good; seek justice, correct oppression; defend the fatherless, plead for the widow" (Isa. 1:17). In that same century, Amos of Tekoa warned his people of impending wrath for violating covenantal provisions for social legislation:

> "Hear this word, you cows of Bashan, who are in the mountain of Samaria, who oppress the poor, who crush the needy . . ." [Amos 4:1].

> Hear this, you who trample upon the needy, and bring the poor of the land to an end, saying, "When will the new moon be over, that we may sell grain? And the sabbath, that we may offer wheat for sale, that we

may make the ephah small and the shekel great, and deal deceitfully
with false balances, that we may buy the poor for silver and the needy
for a pair of sandals, and sell the refuse of the wheat?" [Amos 8:4–6].

These prophetic apostrophes appeal to Pentateuchal statutes. They are
pronounced in the hope that Israel would amend her ways to stave off
impending disaster. Amos 4:12 exhorts "prepare to meet your God, O
Israel!" while Amos 5:15 offers the appeal that justice (*mišpāṭ*) be established in the gate and 5:24 serves as a poetic litany for justice. It is
noteworthy that Amos 2:4 begins the apostrophe against Judah with the
charge that she has rejected the Law. Prior to this, Amos was speaking to
the northern kingdom, but in 2:4, he redirects his focus to the southern
kingdom. Similarly, the concern for the Law is found in Jeremiah 7:5–7:

"For if you truly amend your ways and your doings, if you truly
execute justice one with another [cf. Exod. 23:2–8; Lev. 6:1–5; Deut.
15:1–18], if you do not oppress the alien, the fatherless or the widow
[Exod. 23:9; Lev. 19:10–15, 33–35; Deut. 14:29, 24:17], or shed
innocent blood in this place [Exod. 20:13; Deut., 5:17], and if you do
not go after other gods to your own hurt [Exod. 20:5; Deut. 5:9], then
I will let you dwell in this place, in the land that I gave of old to your
fathers for ever."

For Isaiah, Amos, and Jeremiah, the presupposition seems to be that the
Law contains sufficient guidelines to enable Israel to avoid impending
destruction. John Donahue's observation is pertinent: "When Israel forgets
the covenant, it is the prophets, most explicitly Amos, Isaiah and Jeremiah,
who proclaim to Israel that their fidelity to the covenant Lord must be
manifest in concern for the poor and the oppressed."[72]

JUSTICE IN THE PSALMS AND OLD TESTAMENT WISDOM LITERATURE

The Psalms and the wisdom literature also allude to certain legal and
social motifs in relation to the idea of justice. The social statutes of the
Pentateuch, however, constitute but a minor theme in the Psalms, as they
appear only in the latest psalms. Sigmund Mowinckel indicates that it was
only "after the development of the typical Jewish law-abidingness, did
'righteousness' come to indicate a definite behavior in accordance with the
Jewish way of life under the Law such as for instance Psalm 1."[73]
Many of the psalms are composites, and in these, references to Law
reflect the period of early Judaism, not pre-exilic times (Psalms 19, 37, 40,
78, 81, 105, or 119).[74] For this reason, we must keep in mind that probably
"the influence of law religion on psalmography is not very discernible."[75]

In addition to the relatively few psalms that focus on Law, one should not neglect justice motifs in early cultic psalms, even if different traditions appear to be contradictory. For example, Psalm 62 serves as a hymn on complete trust in Yahweh, but it ends in verse 12 with the note that Yahweh pays individuals back according to their deeds. We may contrast this flourish on retributive justice with Psalm 103:10, which states that Yahweh does not deal with the congregation according to its iniquities. The conflict may be resolved in several ways from an historical/critical perspective. One possibility is that Psalm 62:12 applies to the individual, whereas Psalm 103:10 applies to the corporate reality. In other words, Yahweh does not deal with the nation according to her sins, but deals with her only according to her election. An alternative is that the end of Psalm 62:12 may be a later change to abrogate an early text and make it conform to a later point of doctrine. This alternative seems to be more plausible, because ideas pertaining to justice that appear in early psalms are frequently repeated or adapted to fit later legal contexts. For example, Yahweh is described as a mighty king, a lover of justice in psalm 99:4 and is likewise described in the much later wisdom psalm (38:28).

It is with the legal references in the relatively late wisdom psalms that the concern for social justice appears most clearly. Here the psalmists begin to question the sufficiency of God's justice in the face of the manifest suffering of the pious. The wicked (*rĕšaˤîm*) seemed to prosper, instead of receiving the punishment due on earth for their injustices (*see* Psalms 49:6, 16).

> When a pious person was affected by personal tribulations and particularly such as had to do with the difference between rulers and ruled, "rich" and "poor," then the problem about the unequal apportionment of the good things of life and about the ungodliness and worldliness of those in power became a big issue. Then the pious person might have reason to "fear," namely that God would fail him, and that the doctrine of retributive justice would not hold good.[76]

In such early texts as Psalms 115 or 22, the expressed anguish of the pious takes the form of laments that sharply pose the problem of theodicy.[77] In Psalms 22:1, the problems of the pious are more explicit: "My God, my God, why has thou forsaken me? Why art thou so far from helping me, from the words of my groaning?" Mowinckel traces the progression in which questions of theodicy give rise to a search for *wisdom,* understood increasingly in terms of obedience to Law. Such Psalms as 37, 112, or 119, composed toward the end of this progression (post-exilic), reflect an accelerated effort to fulfill righteousness/justice in terms of ideal precepts embodied in Pentateuchal social legislation. Righteousness in these psalms becomes eminently legal and social.[78]

The evolution of the Psalms has another important aspect. Obedience to the Law as a norm provides for an increased human role in the covenantal relationship. Under the aegis of incipient Judaism, notably in the wisdom psalms, social legislation again represents the moral norm by which people act in relation to God, while recognizing that everything is still ultimately in the hands of God.[79] Indeed, a linkage exists between the wisdom psalms and the other wisdom texts, since each stresses normative rules for proper social and religious living. We should note, however, that some scholars such as Gerhard von Rad urge caution in the use of the term "morality," even for the parenesis of Proverbs. While morality may be a key in this segment of the wisdom literature, von Rad argues that it does not represent philosophical or theological ethics, but a pragmatic knowledge of rules for correct social behavior.[80] He further maintains that "the sentences in Proverbs speak of the king and how to conduct oneself in his presence as well as the blessing bestowed by an ordered and righteous life."[81] The standards for the ordered and righteous life derive, in this view, from the collective but ever-changing community experience that places demands on individual members of the community.[82] Still, this same tradition displays "an active interest in the poor":

> Here it is particularly clear that, according to the sentences of the teachers, man always and everywhere, stands in a hidden partnership with Yahweh. . . . What, then, is the origin of the harsh judgements on those who despise their parents? It is certainly to be attributed to the experience that they are under the curse of their evil deeds but also surely to the knowledge of Yahweh's desire for justice. The same is true of the active interest in the poor which one encounters again and again in proverbial wisdom.[83]

The different proverbial attitudes about the poor as blameworthy (Prov. 11:16; 2:11, 24; 13:4, 18, 25) and yet deserving honor (Prov. 29:23; Sir. 10:31) demonstrate the complex process by which the discursive wisdom literature was shaped. Furthermore, this varied treatment of the poor and poverty helps to show that a consideration of social justice must acknowledge that Yahweh is always depicted as the creator of rich and poor, the oppressor and the oppressed. The wisdom texts do not try to understand the phenomenon of poverty, but state that the poor are to be respected and shown mercy as creatures of God. Proverbs 29:13 ("The poor man and the oppressor meet together; the Lord gives light to the eyes of both") is not meant to justify the oppressor, but an "ethical world order."[84]

R. B. Y. Scott further clarifies the matter, suggesting that the wisdom writers "addressed themselves to individuals, offering counsel based on social experience and their own reflections about the nature of the world and of the good life for men."[85] Although the canonical wisdom books have little indebtedness to Pentateuchal legal or covenantal motifs, they do exhibit a concern for right relations in the social order. Certain wisdom texts exhort and teach all people to conform to a set of relationships required by a well-ordered and balanced creation.

Wisdom, as a biblical motif, assumes a decidedly theological orientation due to the idea that "all wisdom comes from God" as expressed in Judaism. Wisdom thus took on "the weight of a theological pronouncement" as opposed to the earlier perspectives that wisdom was given by nature.[86] We can trace a progressive development similar to that within the Psalms in the evolution of wisdom literature. Wisdom texts emerged as part of the common stock of ancient Near Eastern folklore and court practices and then came under the influence of Jewish emphases on Law. The authority of these texts, however, was collective practical experience, not Torah. Even the prophetic literature was influenced by early concepts of wisdom.[87] The Jewish influence eventually recast wisdom into the mold of Torah. More specifically, because of Judaism's emphasis on Law, Pentateuchal legal statutes of social responsibility begin to feature prominently in late wisdom documents such as Sirach (Ben Sira).

Sirach achieves a synthesis of Law and social responsibility. As a part of the Old Testament Apocrypha, Sirach is a compendium of diverse ethical instructions[88] preserved by a particular Jewish school (Sir. 50:27; 51:23). Designed to teach second century B.C. diaspora Jews (Sir. Prologue), Sirach shows that its author had a deep social interest in justice. Both Law and covenant are important theological and ethical statements in Sirach. Corporate social practice is important in Sirach. The author gives much attention to the notion of covenant (Sir. 17:12; 23:23; 28:7; 39:8; 41:19; 42:2) than do the authors of earlier wisdom literature.[89]

Professor Jean Laporte stresses the importance of Law and covenant in Sirach, but in doing so, primarily suggests dependence on Greek ethics.[90] This tends to minimize Sirach's Jewish background and the relationship between Law and justice that the author of Sirach makes. The need to establish justice is a prominent theme in Sirach. According to Sirach 35:17, 18 (LXX), it is God who responds to the prayers of the "humble" (*tapeinos*) by executing justice for them. Sirach 27:8 accentuates the parallel human responsibility for seeking justice ("If you seek 'justice' [*to dikaion*], you will attain it and wear it like a robe"). Sirach is equally firm in its stand against injustice (*adikia*) as indicated by such passages as Sirach 7:3; 10:18; 14:9; 40:12, 13. Violations of legal provisions constitute sins. Juxtaposed to this view, however, is the view that by observing such legislation, one can atone for sins. Kindness to one's father, no less than acts of mercy (*eleemosynē*), are for Sirach ways of expiation (Sir. 3:3, 14b, 30; 17:22; 40:17).[91]

Sirach reflects a keen sense of right and wrong, despite some texts that display an almost cynical view of practical expediency (Sir. 8:1, 2, 14; 11:39; 18:21ff; 20:28; 35:25; 39:34). We must remember that Sirach is a composite document that contains diverse borrowings from ancient wisdom traditions.[92] The thematic mandate for social responsibility outweighs those few texts that imply otherwise. Easily discernible in Sirach is a plethora of admonitions about the need to honor social obligations to the poor, needy, hungry, the wronged, and the orphan (Sir. 4:1–10; 7:32ff; 12:4ff; 17:14; 29:1ff; 31:8–11; 34:21–22; 40:12–17; 41:18; 42:1ff). With respect to attitudes on social class, Sirach repeatedly warns against showing partiality (Sir. 4:22, 27b; 7:6; 35:12, 13: 42:1, 2).

Sirach is optimistic about human possibilities being achieved in large measure through obedience to Law. Sirach considers the entire human race worthy of honor, as long as it does not transgress the Law (Sir. 18:3). People, made in God's image (Sir. 18:3), have been left to their own inclinations with full ability to keep the commandments and act faithfully (Sir. 15:14, 15). The didactic material in Sirach urges social responsibility, something fully within the inherent capacity of the individual. The individual's guide is the Law, which provides legal tenets for the continuing social mandate.

Elements of social justice were present in the moral and political philosophies of Plato and Aristotle, who outlined notions of distributive justice. Some modern ethicists have designated this the classical theory of social justice.[93] By contrast, the Old Testament presents a variety of ideas about justice. Compensatory justice, which guides much of the Pentateuchal legislation regulating socioeconomic dealings in community life, is especially significant. Traces of biblical compensatory justice motifs appear in the intertestamental literature, where Law and wisdom represent parallel themes highlighting the continuing influence of Pentateuchal social legislation. As we shall see, Old Testament social legislation is often intensified by New Testament gospel emphases.

NEW TESTAMENT PERSPECTIVES ON JUSTICE

In the New Testament, Jesus preeminently represents the justice of God. For this reason, many New Testament authors associate justice with the Christian love ethic and teachings about the Kingdom of God. The New Testament contains a rich variety of terms relating to justice. These include freedom (*eleutheria*), love (*agapē*), mercy (*eleos*), equality (*isotēs*), integrity (*aphthoria*), commandment (*entolē*), and law (*nomos*).

Nevertheless, both historical and theological developments in the New Testament impose certain restraints on one who might too quickly claim that social justice is self-evident in this part of the canon. New Testament scholars like Martin Dibelius or Rudolf Bultmann point out that the post-Easter faith claims of the early Church and/or early Christian apocalypticism discourage any quest for social reforms or revolutionary justice.[94] On the other hand, J. Arthur Baird offers the following thesis: "the concept of justice is the heart of the prophetic concept of God, the central element in the gospel of Jesus, and the ultimate clue to his mission and message."[95] Given this wide difference of opinion, we must ask several questions. How do Old Testament social values or legislation have continuity with aspects of the New Testament? At which points do we encounter discontinuity between the Old Testament and New Testament, and how is such discontinuity explained? Are there different Christian perspectives on justice in the New Testament?

These questions are formidable for at least two reasons. First, New Testament authors do not define what they mean when they use Greek words for justice (*dikaiosynē, dikē, krisis*) or other expressions normally associated with it. Matthew 1:19 reports that Joseph was just, but there is little effort to be precise, other than explaining that Joseph wanted to avoid bringing shame on Mary and therefore wanted a discreet divorce. Here, as in many other texts, the meaning could be either "just" or "righteous." Luke 2:25 so describes Simeon; Mark 6:20 so refers to John the Baptist. The adjective also applies to Jesus (Matt. 27:19-24), God (John 17:25), Joseph of Arimathea (Luke 23:50), and Cornelius (Acts 10:22). Paul mentions "just/righteous" within varied contexts: as part of the Habakkuk 2:2 quotation (Rom. 1:17; Gal. 3:11; cf. Heb. 10:38); as a Christian virtue (Phil. 4:8; cf. Col. 4:1); and uses the adjecive *dikaios* with reference to commandment/Law (Rom. 2:13; 7:12). Typical of New Testament writers, he does not *define* his meaning. Rather, readers must deduce the probable intent from the literary context or historical/theological setting.

Second, New Testament passages that initially seem to clarify Jesus' attitudes about justice conclude with such enigmatic sayings as "Render to Caesar the things that are Caesar's, and to God the things that are God's" (Mark 12:13-17; cf. Matt. 22:15; Luke 20:20-26).[96] Third, even when explicit vocabulary about justice is absent (1 Cor. 12-14; Rom. 12:1; John 3:11-18), there are issues at stake in New Testament passages that have implications for concepts of justice.

Lacking definitions of justice within the New Testament, we must decide on a possible method for isolating aspects of justice that would help us differentiate between types of justice, while at the same time not distorting the literary or historical setting, or even the shifts in theological nuance that occur in the New Testament authors' varying usage. Our specific interest focuses on "justice" and/or "righteousness," together with related ideas as *"norms for human conduct."*[97] We can engage the task in a *provisional* way, however, in three steps. First, I discuss the relationship between love and justice in the New Testament. Second, I establish categories for distinguishing between possible types of justice in the New Testament that have bearing on the question of socioeconomic class in the New Testament. Third and finally, I address the hermeneutical implications that such biblical ideas about justice and social class may have for the Black Church.

LOVE AND JUSTICE IN THE NEW TESTAMENT

Regardless of variations in New Testament attitudes about justice, the law of love, as derived from a precept in Old Testament social legislation, is central. "You shall love your neighbor as yourself" (Lev. 19:18), while originally referring to other Jews, takes on wider implications in the New Testament, where *neighbor* means another human being, irrespective of the person's race or class.[98]

Of the Synoptic gospels, Luke particularly intends to make this clear. Only Luke presents the Samaritan parable (Luke 10:29–37) that explicitly details the new meaning of "neighbor"; Luke does so as a sequel to his version of the double love commandment (love of God; love of neighbor) in Luke 10:25–28. Although the Samaritan is of different ethnic stock, virtually an enemy to the Jew, he becomes a neighbor to the victim needing help. He extends merciful deeds beyond any legal requirement (*see* Lev. 19:34). Luke's hermeneutic is noteworthy because the clear implication is that *one's neighbor is not necessarily one's fellow Christian.* Such an inference may apply to Paul's citation of the law of love in Galatians 5:14, despite the references to "brethren" in verse 13 and "one another" (Galatian Christians), because of the dictum in 6:10 ("let us do good to all men, and especially to those who are of the household of faith").

Movement toward a broader understanding of one's neighbor is evident in Jewish intertestamental literature. The Old Testament Pseudepigrapha — The Book of Jubilees (ca. 135–105 B.C.), for example — reflects this changing attitude as Jews attempted to be more accommodating in the Hellenistic diaspora, now viewing Gentiles as neighbors:[99] "And he [Abraham] commanded them that they should observe the way of the Lord; that they should work righteousness, and *love each his neighbor,* and act on this manner amongst *all* men; that they should each so walk with regard to them as to do judgment [or justice] and righteousness on the earth" (Jub. 20:2, emphasis mine).

This passage correlates the love of neighbor (now including Gentiles) with a mandate to do justice. This represents a transition from the more narrowly understood application of Leviticus 19:18 to the way some early Christian texts redefined "neighbor" while detailing a righteousness that exceeds the actual practice of certain first-century Jewish groups. Notice that in Luke's parable of the Samaritan, representatives of Jewish groups do not acknowledge the demands of their Law regarding the treatment of strangers (Lev. 19:33, 34; cf. Exod. 22:21). The actions of the Samaritan attest to a higher righteousness that Jesus tells his disciples to emulate: "'Which of these three, do you think, proved neighbor to the man who fell among the robbers?' He said, 'The one who showed mercy on him.' And Jesus said to him, 'Go and do likewise'" (Luke 10:36, 37).

Although the parable mentions showing mercy that exceeds Old Testament Law, Luke 11:42 presents an explicit critique of Pharisees who "neglect justice" and the "love of God" (cf. Matt. 23:23). Thus, the love of the *new* neighbor involves showing mercy, which is both doing justice and witnessing to one's love of God. A similar progression is evident in Matthew's Sermon on the Mount, in which Jesus is explicit about the need to exceed the righteousness/justice of the Pharisees (5:20) as a prerequisite for entrance into the Kingdom of heaven. The antithesis regarding love for one's neighbor follows (5:43); and Jesus returns yet again to the theme of the necessity of seeking God's Kingdom and its righteousness/justice (6:33).

From these observations, we can see that one aspect of New Testament justice is the love of your new "neighbor" as expressed in tangible acts of caring or mercy that *exceed* the requirements of Old Testament social legislation. The implication is that such love affirms the *equal worth* of the recipient of the love. The early Christian adaptation of Leviticus 19:18 presupposes that the Christian cares about himself or herself as a child of God. Because of this, the phrase "as thyself" indicates that one should extend to others the same care that one personally enjoys. Other New Testament passages speak not only about loving one's enemies (Matt. 5:43; Luke 27, 35),[100] but also about an unqualified love (*agapē*) as mentioned in 1 Corinthians 13:1–13, Galatians 5:6, or Ephesians 4:2. Agapaic caring presumes that the beneficiary of the love receives it whether or not it is deserved by conventional standards. Philippians 2:3 ("but in humility count others better than yourselves") may constitute one of the most radical applications of *agapē*. Although Paul may be offering a hyperbole, he intends to accentuate the need for Christians to move beyond their own self-interest, a point stressed in Philippians 2:4 ("Let each of you look not only to his own interests [rights] but also to the interests [rights] of others").[101] The significance of these forms of love in relation to Christian justice is that the interest of others is stressed as a norm for Christian social relations. In our modern world of selfishness, greed, individual competing self-interests, and human exploitation, the New Testament teaching is alien (frequently even in the Church).

We may clarify the interrelatedness of love and justice in the New Testament further by focusing on the specific *types* of early Christian justice. Definitions of classifications for New Testament justice are important, because early Christian literature is so imbued with language and images of salvation—the Kingdom (Reign) of God, New Life in the Spirit (New Covenant, New Birth, New Creation), and prayers, co-mingled with an apocalyptic hope for Jesus' return (*parousia*). These features of New Testament theology, when narrowly understood, become only pious, otherworldly, and/or exclusively mystical preoccupations, unless Christians are mindful of the corresponding ethical mandates for justice. Believers must constantly demonstrate the righteousness of God in an unredeemed world. "For our sake [God] made him to be sin who knew no sin, so that in [Christ] *we might become the righteousness of God*" (2 Cor. 5:21, emphasis mine). Let us now define varying types of New Testament justice and explore New Testament attitudes about them, particularly those that seem to highlight an integral relationship between love and justice.

Reciprocal Justice

Reciprocal justice means that the same love that one claims as a child of God constitutes the criterion of "fairness" in relation to one's treatment of the interest, rights, and welfare of others. As a person receives mercy, compassion, and love, he or she is obliged to show the same in dealing with others. The early Christian adaptation of this Old Testament precept (Lev. 19:18) intensifies it and gives it broader application in the New Testament (Gal. 5:14; Rom. 13:8; James 2:8). Matthew at one point transposes the wording of this law of love, giving us the basis for the now-familiar Golden Rule, which for him is also a summary of "the law and the prophets" (Matt. 7:12).

The reciprocity involved does not necessarily require the direct or immediate response of the new neighbor. Often the socioeconomic circumstances of the needy preclude this, as is evident in Luke 14:14. Rather, the reciprocity is empathetic. The Christian shares the love and grace that he or she has received from God and would like to be treated in such a manner by others (Heb. 13:1-3; 1 Pet. 4:9). Nevertheless, the beneficiary of this type of justice is obliged to become a medium of empathy, mercy, and forgiveness for others.

The parable of the unmerciful servant offers an example (Matt. 18:23-25). The servant whose master had forgiven him a debt of 10,000 talents (today's equivalent of $2.5 million) refused to forgive his debtor the much smaller sum of 100 denarii (today's equivalent of $4,000).[102] Reciprocal justice may be derived from a precept of Law, but in the New Testament, it certainly is not restricted to any legal demand. The Matthean narrative on the great judgment of the nations (*ta ethnē*) illustrates the purely volitional application of reciprocal justice (Matt. 25:31-46). As various ethnic (or racial) groups stand before the Lord, the criterion for their salvation is the extent to which they have reciprocated God's love through deeds of mercy and compassion for the needy, oppressed, and imprisoned.[103]

Eschatological Justice

Eschatological justice refers to the strict reckoning by God at the End Time/Day of Judgment, which is the decisive time for divine rewards or punishments in accordance with the deeds of a person's life. Similar to Old Testament retributive justice (Gen. 9:6; Deut. 19:21), which accentuates punishment in kind, Christian eschatological justice sets forth the specter of a horrible end for oppressors and sinners (1 Cor. 3:13; Rom. 14:10-12; Matt. 12:36). In addition to the extended Christian apocalyptic drama represented by the Book of Revelation, 2 Thessalonians 1:6-9 presents proof of God's righteous justice in this regard:

> God deems it just to repay with affliction those who afflict you, and
> to grant rest with us to you who are afflicted, when the Lord Jesus is
> revealed from heaven with his mighty angels in flaming fire, inflicting

vengeance upon those who do not know God and upon those who do not obey the gospel of our Lord Jesus.[104]

Unlike Old Testament retributive justice, Christian eschatological justice does not emphasize punishment, but a hope for repentance and God's final reward for doers of justice (Matt. 5:12, 10:42; 1 Cor. 9:27; Phil. 3:13, 14). In the thought of some New Testament writings, the prospect of eschatological rewards constitutes a warrant for accepting suffering and injustice, rather than reacting to injustices in ways that would create more harm (see commutative justice below). The Epistle of James warns of God's strict punishment for sins of injustice (2:13), but quickly relieves that possibility by reminding readers that God's dominant tendency is mercy, not strict retribution. "Mercy triumphs over judgment" (James 2:13).[105] In texts like Matthew 25:31–41, dimensions of eschatological justice combine with reciprocal justice.

Compensatory Justice

Compensatory justice is the moral process of correcting past or present injury, dispossession, exploitation, and the violation of rights. It makes restitution, offers reparations, seeks to restore persons to wholeness, and grants them rightful status in the community. Compensatory justice motifs chiefly characterize Jesus' ministry as he fulfills the Law and the prophets, thereby inaugurating the Kingdom of God, not least for marginalized socioeconomic groups (the poor, the sick, the captives, the oppressed). Through healings, acts of mercy and forgiveness, or direct confrontations with the conventional authorities, the ministry of Jesus in each gospel constitutes the paradigm of divine compensations. Consider how Jesus' opening sermon in the synagogue (Luke 4:16–30) focuses upon the poor, captives, and the oppressed as distinct beneficiaries of Jesus' intended compensatory witness on their behalf. Thus, Jesus gives both practical context and substance to the Old Testament prophetic vision (Isa. 56:6; 61:1) and the Old Testament Jubilee ideal (Lev. 25:10).[106] That the Holy Spirit empowers Jesus to articulate this vision of vigorous compensation is scarcely a Lukan literary flourish. The compensatory emphasis enables Jesus to instruct his disciples to report to the imprisoned John the Baptist the following as a sign of the dawning new kingdom of God: "Go and tell John what you hear and see: the blind receive their sight and the lame walk, lepers are cleansed and the deaf hear, and the dead are raised up, and the poor have good news preached to them. And blessed is he who takes no offense at me" (Matt. 11:4–6; cf. Luke 7:22, 23).

Compensations are extended to Gentiles, as well. They gain equal status with the Jews as an expression of God's own compensatory justice. This is illustrated in the parable of the laborers in the vineyard (Matt. 10:1–16) wherein equal pay is given to the latecomers (Gentiles).[107] Other examples include the Lukan "leniency clause" for Gentiles (12:48) and the extended argument by Paul on God's "in-grafting" of the Gentiles as equally eligible participants in the salvation history (Rom. 9–11). Surely, Jesus recognized that the social status (class) of the poor and needy, although guaranteed in some ways by Old Testament social legislation, was frequently abused or ignored in Sadducean and Pharisaic social practice of the first century. Distortions of the love intent behind the Law had become proverbial (Matt. 5:17, 18; Luke 16:17; James 2:8, 9).[108]

By no means is it only Jesus who engages in acts of compensatory justice in the New Testament. The disciples are expected to take Jesus' "yoke" upon them and learn (Matt. 11:29); they are to go and do likewise (Luke 10:37); they are to hear and keep Jesus' sayings (John 12:47), and "bear fruit" (Matt. 7:18; John 15:6; cf. Phil. 1:11; 2 Cor. 2:10). The case of Zacchaeus is instructive, because he is neither a disciple nor one previously predisposed to make restitution as required by the Law. In Luke 19:1–10, Zacchaeus, the rich tax collector, responds first to Jesus' insistence on visiting the home of one whose activities as tax collector automatically made him unclean and "a sinner." So impressed is he by Jesus' compensatory justice that Zacchaeus not only voluntarily decides to distribute half of his possessions among the poor, but he also indicates a willingness to restore fourfold to anyone he has defrauded. Zacchaeus's attitude shows how far beyond the requirements of Law he is willing to go, since Leviticus 6:5 and Numbers 5:6, 7 stipulate that a person who defrauds needs only repay 120 percent, while Exodus 22:1–7 requires 200 percent. By virtue of Jesus' compensation of mercy to him, Zacchaeus offers reparations at a rate of 400 percent. Richard Cassidy suggests that by such actions, Zacchaeus "has joined the ranks of Jesus' faithful disciples, those who have heard Jesus' words and put them into practice."[109]

The New Testament contains evidence that the early Church, as a community of faith, had a compensatory function in arbitrating civil and domestic suits, thereby avoiding pagan courts (1 Cor. 6:1–8; Matt. 18:15–20; 1 Tim. 5:19). James notes a circumstance wherein the rich "drag" poor Christians to pagan courts (2:6). The Old Testament Law offers a formal precedent (Deut. 19:15); however, Christians are expected to exceed the narrow boundaries of mere legal demands. Paul appears to stress forgiveness when he exhorts the highly fragmented and contentious Corinthian congregations to consider enduring an injustice from another member, rather than taking the perpetrator to pagan courts (1 Cor. 6:7). Luke reports that the Jerusalem church reorganized in order to make the compensation of "the daily distribution" more equitable for widows (Acts 6:2), whereas the author of 1 Timothy equates providing for one's relatives (extended family) with claiming the Christian faith (1 Tim. 5:8). We find here an emerging second-century attitude that the Church not be over-burdened with social responsibilities that the individual members should acknowledge.

Commutative Justice

Commutative justice is the prevention and/or reduction of potential injury. This type of justice, in our usage, would include even the strategic voluntary disavowal of one's own rights in order to reduce the possibility of greater future harm. The idea of a type of justice that seeks to commute or avoid harm may be traced back to the writings of Aristotle and St. Thomas Aquinas. Professor Karen Lebacqz attributes the more modern usage of commutative justice to the political-economic theories of Adam Smith, for whom "the root notion in commutative justice is the avoidance of harm . . . by guaranteeing the equivalence of exchange."[110] In 1 Corinthians 9:9, Paul is aware of legal warrant in the Old Testament assuring him of the right to be paid for his work as an apostle. "For it is written in the law of Moses, 'You shall not muzzle an ox when it is treading out the grain.'" By not claiming this right (1 Cor. 9:15, 19), he removes a point of contention that would continue community strife. Later, the author of 1 Timothy appeals to the same Old Testament text to secure the right that Paul had strategically disavowed. James 5:20 presents a different aspect of commutative justice in mentioning the restoration of a sinner to the community of the faithful as an act that "covers a multitude of sins." In this case, the reduction of future harm by the sinner is commutative, but the notion of excusing a multitude of past sins represents the compensatory (cf. 1 Pet. 4:8).

Charismatic Distributive Justice

Charismatic distributive justice, like the other types of New Testament justice, is both a social and a spiritual phenomenon. This type is summed up by the idea that each believer receives his or her "due" in accordance with the manner in which each member claims and uses assigned "spiritual gifts" (*charismata*) in relation to the unity, edification, and mission of the Church. Paul plainly states the distributive aspects in Romans 12: "each according to the measure of faith which God has assigned him" (v. 3); and "gifts that differ according to the grace given to us, let us use them" (v. 6). He is no less clear in 1 Corinthians 12:4–8 (cf. Eph. 4:7): "Now there are varieties of gifts, but the same Spirit; and there are varieties of service, but the same Lord; and there are varieties of working, but it is the same God who inspires them all in every one. To each is given the manifestation of the Spirit for the common good."

Paul's trinitarian language ("the same Spirit . . . the same Lord . . . the same God") underscores the fact that unity is a critical norm for the Church's self-understanding. He says, "For by one Spirit we were all baptized into one body—Jews or Greeks, slaves or free—and all were made to drink of one Spirit" (1 Cor. 12:13). Ernst Käsemann explains the significance of this verse as follows:

> The unity of the body of Christ which according to 1 Cor. 12:13, Gal.
> 3:28, Col. 3:11, comes into existence through baptism, the identity
> with himself of the Christ who reigns in and over all his members, this
> unity and identity is only potential and actual in the multiplicity of
> charismata; . . . it exists only *in actu*—in the act of *agape*—of
> service.[111]

Paul's message is on unity, presupposed by baptism, but reiterated for Corinthians who were tempted by mystery cults and enthusiasts. While caution is necessary in speaking about objective norms for the *charismata,*[112] the distributive aspects of these spiritual gifts appear to provide the basis for a charismatic distributive justice in two ways. First, the spiritual gifts are apportioned differently (1 Cor. 12:11; Rom. 12:6–8; Eph. 4:7; 1 Pet. 4:10) and accordingly have varying functions in the Church community (1 Cor. 12:14–20; Rom. 12:4–8). Second, Paul indicates that each believer has the equal mandate to maximize his or her usage of a spiritual gift (Rom. 12:6–8). The same idea is present in the parable of the talents (Matt. 25:14–20; cf. Luke 19:12–27). Notice Matthew's expression "to each according to his ability" (25:15).[113] This may represent Pauline influence, although the language is somewhat modified.

In any case, Paul urges unity far more than equality with reference to either the comparative value of the spiritual gifts or social class of those who possess these gifts. All are worthy of honor; all are members of the Church; all should suffer, if any member suffers. But there appears to be a hierarchy in status and the respective value of the task that corresponds to *charismata.* In 1 Corinthians 12:28, Paul writes, "And God has appointed in the church *first* apostles, *second* prophets, *third* teachers, *then* workers of miracles, *then* healers, helpers, administrators, [and] speakers in various kinds of tongues" (emphasis mine). Paul seems to single out the spiritual gift of speaking in tongues for his harshest words in 1 Corinthians 13 and 14 and exhibits a strong preference for prophecies over tongues (1 Cor. 14:4, 5, 18, 19). Paul does not mention the charisma of tongues in Romans 12, but leads with prophesy. Rather than seeing this as merely a reflection of the different community issues (abuses in the gift of tongues scarcely being an issue in Romans), different values are assigned to the *charismata,* and they are ranked. Charismatic distributive justice therefore depends on the extent to which one recognizes his or her spiritual gifts and uses them in the service of *agape.*

As far as the New Testament is concerned, *ideas of justice within the context of social relations presuppose that a person should love herself or himself as a child of God, but such self-love must also be the leading criterion for interacting with others, whose interests and welfare are to be regarded as if one's own life were at stake.* (Of course, we are not speaking here of some narcissistic being in love with oneself, but a thoroughly altruistic attitude that reflects a person's own intrinsic worth.) This would apply in matters of race, ethnicity, and class within various ancient communities of the New Testament period.

This does not apply to the status and roles of women, notwithstanding the provocative and brave historical reconstructions by the biblical feminist, Elisabeth Schüssler Fiorenza. While one can easily agree that the New Testament is far less patriarchal in its attitudes about women than the Old Testament, Judaism, or Greco-Roman domestic laws and cultural values, Fiorenza seems excessive in her claims that Jesus' renewal movement was so inclusive as to inaugurate a "discipleship of equals."[114] If Jesus the Jew invited all as equals, why were the twelve disciples entirely men? Passages such as Mark 6:44 and Luke 9:44 report on the feeding of five thousand by counting only the men (*andres*). Matthew's version of Mark's feeding the multitude narratives (the five thousand; the four thousand) reflects even more explicitly the social status of women, as he understood it at the time of Jesus, when both Matthew 14:21 and 15:38 mention "besides women and children." Luke tells us that the resurrection reports by women were regarded by the apostles as "an idle tale." Luke's own attitude is more progressive, for he uses the expression "men and women" in Acts 5:14 when speaking of those added to the believers. John indicates that the Samaritan men quickly clarified for the Samaritan woman missionary that she no longer should take credit for their becoming believers (John 4:42). Jesus' own teachings on marriage and divorce certainly accord greater rights to women,[115] but it would be an exaggeration to say that in these teachings Jesus advocates *full equality* between men and women.

Although a full discussion of women and the New Testament is the subject of chapter eight, we must call attention to another extraordinary observation by Fiorenza that we wish were true with respect to Paul's thinking:

> Gal. 3:28 not only advocates the abolition of religious-cultural divisions and of the domination and exploitation wrought by institutional slavery but also of domination based on sexual divisions. It repeats with different categories and words that within the Christian community no structures of dominance can be tolerated. Gal. 3:28 is therefore best understood as a communal Christian self-definition rather than a statement about the baptized individual. It proclaims that in the Christian community all distinctions of religion, race, class, nationality, and gender are insignificant. All the baptized are equal, they are one in Christ.[116]

Fiorenza's bold assertions gloss over the important tension between Paul's apocalyptic and his attitudes about the status of women (or slaves) in society. At best, Paul tends to encourage a more equitable treatment of women by Christian men and also accords some women leadership roles in the house churches, in a manner untypical of ancient Jewish or Greco-

Roman social mores (excluding early Gnosticism). Fiorenza's claim, none-theless, underscores the need for alternative frameworks for interpreting aspects of early Christian social history. We have offered one such alternative: distinguishing between possible types of justice in the New Testament.

We have now come full circle in our examination of biblical attitudes about justice and social class. The existence of different types of justice in the Bible constitutes a caution for those who would too quickly generalize biblical prescriptions to do justice and then just as quickly proceed to do nothing. By attempting to bring greater specificity to biblical mandates for justice, we acknowledge that some forms of justice in the Bible do not seem fair by conventional standards. Yet the progressive, even self-corrective character of biblical ethics reveals higher criteria for fairness—the love and mercy of God. It is liberating indeed to discern the extraordinary ways later biblical traditions explicitly reinterpret and contemporize earlier holy sentences in the Bible itself. Biblical authors thereby display a wariness with cultures that tend to misconstrue God's original intent to affirm the kinship and equality of persons regardless of race or social class. In this matter, many biblical writers present an uncanny indictment to much of the postbiblical Church tradition that imitates values of secular (sacralized) culture rather than the vision of its own foundational document, the Bible.

In similar ways, representatives of the ancient Black Church and the more modern African American Church have taken seriously the biblical concern for justice and parallel injunctions regarding class discrimination. The Ethiopian finance minister (Acts 8:26–40) perhaps typifies the attitude of the ancient Black Church. This pilgrim from Africa seems intrigued by the suffering servant narrative of Isaiah 53:7, 8, which Luke tells us the Ethiopian is reading on his trip back to Nubia. Under the tutelage of Philip the evangelist, the Ethiopian evidently finds the gospel familiar with the experience of those denied justice (reciprocal and compensatory). As a consequence, the Ethiopian easily accepts Jesus as the *inclusive* suffering servant. Because of this, he knows there is nothing to prevent his being baptized as an equal (Acts 8:36).

Likewise, Blacks in the American slave church and subsequently in the Black Church have identified with biblical justice that has long affirmed the full humanity of Blacks. By contrast, whites who have claimed the Christian tradition have had a long and continuing history of excluding Blacks or otherwise construing their baptism as not being authentic or worthy only of a second-class status in society. Despite this, many Black Christian leaders have relentlessly sought to impart to their communities the Bible's concern for justice. In this they have not only undertaken a quest in their own interests, but have always shown a remarkable concern for the interests of others, even whites who have oppressed them. To explain this somewhat paradoxical aspect of the Black Church, we need to consider the distinctive role the Bible has played in its heritage. It is to that subject that we turn in the next chapter.

CHAPTER 5

Biblical Usage in American Black Churches

In an age when scholars champion the historical-critical ("scientific") method for Bible study, we tend to forget that precritical usages of the Bible are still widespread today. After all, the historical-critical method is only two centuries old[1] and is still the product of bourgeois academics. Observations like these reduce a bit of the alarm caused by many churches who still engage in popular, commercialist, or other precritical (biblicist/ literalist) usages of the Bible.

The Black Church has tended to imitate populist evangelical white churches. Thus it has distorted and misappropriated the text, as have other groups. The Black Church's history of socioeconomic disadvantage has contributed to this problem. Nevertheless, despite the status of the Black Church in society, it is truly striking that Blacks have brought colorful drama and imaginative narrative adaptations to the biblical text by centering on Scripture and tradition. They have achieved no small feat in producing a distinctive, imagistic idiom through sermons, slave narratives, a poetry often created in prayer, rhythmic sorrow songs, spirituals, and gospel songs. From a disadvantaged social class, the Black Church has compensated, often in unique ways, for what her leaders lacked in formal theological education.

This chapter on biblical usage in the Black Church does not, however, excuse the precritical or noncritical study and usage of the Bible. In 1 Corinthians 15:31, Paul says, "I die daily"; and too frequently the biblical usage in churches, whether Black, white, Hispanic, or Asian, gives new meaning to Paul's statement! Indeed, a popular, literalist, and proof-texting approach to the Bible causes many Old and New Testament personalities to die daily—week after week and Sunday after Sunday. The unschooled, like the notorious nineteenth-century Black preacher John Jasper, *boast,* "I don' git my sermuns out uv grammars and reterricks, but de Sperrit uv de Lord puts 'em in my mind an' meks 'em burn in my soul."[2] However that may be, William A. Johnson seems certainly to be correct in characterizing the preaching art as revealing "the soul of a culture."[3]

Even some who have been exposed to theological education still find themselves dealing "on the run" with the Bible and thereby reducing its richness through endless platitudes, quaint anecdotes, sentimentalities, or prepackaged moralisms uninformed by a discipline of regular study. Given this, it is all the more remarkable that the Black Church has fostered a dynamic and distinctive caliber and style of preaching. While some persistent abuses are fairly well-known, what is less known or acknowledged is the apparent correlation between aspects of the Black Church's experience and biblical usage and those of first-century Christians. There may be another correlation, since the earliest proponents of the Christian faith invariably appealed to arbitrary proof-texts to settle complex issues of community life.

AN ETYMOLOGY OF PREACHING

Martin Dibelius has made famous the statement, "In the beginning was the sermon."[4] As in the Black Church today, this suggests that everything begins with the sermon. Clearly, the earliest evangelizing in the New Testament began as the spoken word, a proclamation (Hebrew: *qārʾa;* Greek: *kēryx*) transformed as the sermon. Dibelius tells us that Mark, Matthew, and Luke essentially originated as excerpts from some of the oldest Christian sermons.[5]

The beginning of Mark's gospel presents a brief account of John the Baptist's first public sermon. Mark reports that he "appeared in the wilderness, preaching a baptism of repentance for the forgiveness of sins" (Mark 1:4). It is striking that the first four verses of Mark use two Greek terms designating both preaching and that which is preached. Both *kēryx* and *euangelion* point to the form as well as to the specific content of preaching in the New Testament. Mark uses the Greek participle *kēryssōn* to describe the preaching of John the Baptist. In its two instances within the Greek Old Testament (LXX), *kēryx* simply means a public proclamation.[6] It is easy to make the association with the Hebrew and Aramaic *qārʾa,* which means a proclamation read as a herald's public notice. When Mark adopts this term, more is involved, since he presents John the Baptist as proclaiming a distinctly religious message to which the people respond. It may be that John's preaching is both the Hebrew *qārʾa* and *qāhāl;* it is proclamation and ingathering; it is announcement as well as invitation.[7] Instances of *kērysso* in the prophetic literature of the Greek Old Testament do not normally include both these aspects of preaching.

When Mark reports on the message of John the Baptist, the term *kēryssōn* has a special sense. Although in the wilderness, John's preaching attracts many persons from Judea who felt the need for repentance and forgiveness. We can see the rough contours of a pre-Christian *kērygma* in the content of the Baptist's message. A few verses later, Mark presents another primitive *kērygma,* namely Jesus' inaugural sermon, which differs from that of John the Baptist (Mark 1:14, 15).[8] With the term *kērysso,* one sees that in the New Testament, preaching is a traditional oral form of proclamation. But it also represents a specific invitation to repentance, forgiveness, and a recognition that the power of God may disrupt the prophetic tradition of the Old Testament and cause "all of Judea" to go out into the wilderness.

The second term that Mark uses to characterize a form of preaching is *euangelion* (the good news). In 1 Corinthians 15:1, Paul mentions "the gospel which I preach to you" (similarly, 1 Cor. 9:16). If we translate the Greek literally, Paul's expression would read, "The 'good news' which I 'good newsed' to you." We alleviate this awkward wording by rendering the verb form of "good news" as *preach*. This indicates that the gospel is a speech event designed to propel believers to action. Such an understanding draws on Ernst Fuchs's definition of preaching as a "speech-event."[9] Thus, preaching—in both form and content—directs the hearer to action.

C. H. Dodd confirms this by suggesting that in the New Testament, kerygma and gospel are interrelated. Both represent preaching as different than teaching (*didakē/didaskalia*) or exhortation (*paraklēsis*), and even from "the traditional ethical instructions on Christian conduct" (*parenesis*).[10] One should always bear in mind that the form and content of preaching in the New Testament include the multiple elements of proclamation, ingathering, and action as a reawakening of dormant potential for faith. This seems to be evident in the preaching ministries of John the Baptist, Jesus of Nazareth, and Paul the Apostle.

HISTORICAL NOTES ON PREACHING
IN THE BLACK CHURCH

All who proclaim the gospel in the Black Church today would do well to adhere to Paul's wise advise regarding the preacher's purpose. "Do not lie to one another, seeing that you have put off the old nature with its practices and have put on the new nature, which is being renewed in knowledge after the image of its creator" (Col. 3:9). The preacher stands as the messenger between God and the people of God, in an elevated position (Ezek. 33:1-6), watching and waiting for the coming of the Lord and observing signs of the times and the environment. Then he or she may discern and declare the truth of the gospel as fully adaptable for the needs and conditions of Black life. The Black preacher must plumb the depths of his or her being, in order to discover the continuing mystery of God as the "God with us"— Emmanuel (Matt. 1:23).

The external word proclaimed opens the way for the soul to know God. Before the Incarnate Word can become flesh again, we must seek and find it *within*. Gardner Taylor comments on the central factor of personality in preaching: "The preacher must be willing to look deeply and honestly into himself [or herself], for in those depths, touched by the light and flame of the Gospel, will much of one's preaching find birth and life."[11] The preacher cannot claim that God was in Christ and came down from heaven to save persons from sins unless the preacher has personally discovered this truth in his or her own life.

Preaching therefore begins with a certain *angst* in the depths of one's soul. In this regard, Walter Brueggemann provides an important insight on preaching as a balm and an alternative vision:

> . . . will not be like one-world liberals who view the present world as the only one, nor will he be like the unworldly who yearn for the future with an unconcern about the present. There is grief work to be done in the present that the future may come. There is mourning to be done for those who do not know of the deathliness of their situation. There is mourning to be done with those who know pain and suffering and lack the power or freedom to bring it to speech.[12]

The Black Church has long recognized that, despite the frailties of the human preacher, the Bible as the Word of life can enable him or her to declare a gospel that disturbs and heals. It calls the preacher to mourn and exhort, so the whole creation may know the peace of him who knew suffering and injustice but still conquered demons and death to free the world from the sin of oppression. Through the proclaimed Word, God imparts a dynamic history of salvation to humanity and reminds persons about divine possibilities, if they would but participate.

Africans arrived in the New World before the *Mayflower* (1619) and perhaps even before Christopher Columbus (1492).[13] Although they initially could not participate in their adopted languages, Africans in the Americas did not enter the New World with a religious and cultural *tabula rasa*. They came with remembrances of the past, including their rich oral tradition of the griots' stories of life, death, and rebirth. They came to America with memories of a religion that was the source of life and gave meaning to it through the power of the spoken word. The oral tradition was critical for the African perspective. It often assumed formal expression in rhythmic music, colorful imagery, and poetic force that enriched the more visual Western culture shaped by the printed word.

The first generation of slaves learned the language and religion of their masters, but subsequent generations assumed the responsibility of fusing African oral strengths with Western writing traditions. In some quarters, Blacks overcame their low-class social position by fusing their spirituality and rhythm with disciplined reading and writing in order to "sing the Lord's song in a foreign land" (Ps. 137:4) with power, insight, and effectiveness. In the midst of their sociopolitical plight in the Americas, these pioneers re-enlivened the Bible as the Word of God. Certainly, the gospel proclaimed by Richard Allen and Absalom Jones encompassed a concern for the heavenly, but it also included more mundane concerns about the here and now. They did not avoid forthrightly addressing God's people caught in bondage and a hostile "land of the free."

As a direct result of such ministers as Nat Turner and missionaries like Sojourner Truth in the early nineteenth century, Black uprisings arose in certain instances. Daniel Alexander Payne, an AME minister and bishop, devoted his life's work to the preparation of ministers and the elevation of the race through education. In 1859, Payne demanded, in his speech "The Christian Ministry," that ministers must proclaim the Word as if "the glorious doctrines of the universe were dependent upon his efforts, and his alone." However, he maintained that preaching without intelligence was "like a locomotive without steam—nothing but useless machinery."[14] Listen to Payne, the preacher-educator who established Wilberforce University (America's oldest black college): "To sum up all our ideas in a single sentence, he (the minister) must be holy, studious, instructive and wise."[15] In his 1891 essay on "The Education of the Ministry," Payne continued his crusade and declared:

> Put forth every effort, employ every means, embrace every opportunity to cultivate your minds, and enrich them with holy learning. Be not satisfied with little things, lift your standards to the skies, and your attainment will be great. Swear eternal hatred to ignorance. . . .[16]

Within a century after the arrival of the slaves, Black preachers sought to confess their faith nobly (compare: 1 Tim. 6:21), teaching the truth and refuting errors (2 Tim. 3:16) through the combined force of the spirit's gift and the discipline of the mind.

Although Blacks in the Americas have experienced many disadvantages, the Black Church has always had a tradition that emphasized excellence. In this regard, one should mention such serious stalwarts of the faith and the preaching profession as the AME Bishop Henry McNeal Turner, the AME Zion Bishop James Varick, the Episcopalian Alexander Crummell, the Congregationalist Charles Bennett Ray, the Presbyterian Henry Highland Garnet, the Baptist Leonard A. Grimes, the first Black Episcopalian bishop, James T. Holly, and James Healy, the first Black Catholic bishop in the United States, while in the middle of the seventeenth century, Francisco Xavier de Luna Victoria reigned for eight years as the bishop of Panama.[17] These names are but a part of a larger movement toward Black progress that spanned several theological traditions. Such institutions were committed to training Black ministers to reflect on the Bible in sermons that were theologically more critical. They also took the lead in advancing the Church's effectiveness in the Black community. Not only did they pave the way for the faithful to find the way to Jesus in the more narrow sense of personal piety, but they also found in the gospel a basis for the Black Church to pursue justice and full political rights. Early in the twentieth century, W. E. B. DuBois recognized the talents and influence of these Black religious leaders in his classic studies, *The Souls of Black Folks* and *The Gift of Black Folk.*

The impact of the Bible in the Black preaching tradition was not contained exclusively within the walls of the Church. Reverdy Ransom was a prominent leader in the social gospel movement, and Francis J. Grimke fought racism in the capital of the United States. Bishop Alexander Waters battled nationally for equal rights. During the late 1940s and the 1950s, Adam Clayton Powell, a graduate of Yale Divinity School, led the struggle for justice in Harlem and later in the United States Congress. A century earlier, Hiram R. Revels, an AME minister, became the first Black member of Congress as a senator from Mississippi. At the height of the civil rights movement, Anna Arnold Hedgeman (a lay preacher and church activist noted for her leadership in the Office of Racial Justice for the National Council of Churches and the sole woman on the organizing and planning committee for the March on Washington in 1963); Martin Luther King, Jr.; C. T. Vivian; Wyatt T. Walker; Walter Fauntroy; Andrew Young and other ministers spoke forcefully about the basic rights of Black Americans to participate fully in the nation's social, economic, and political life. Both Young and Fauntroy also served in Congress. Through determined efforts, these leaders elevated their race and demonstrated the power of the Word.

The achievements of such people represent, to some extent, a confluence of the African and Euro-American cultures. The observation of W. E. B. DuBois over half a century ago still holds true:

> Above and beyond all that we have mentioned, perhaps least tangible but just as true, is the peculiar spiritual quality which the Negro has injected into American life and civilization. It is hard to define or characterize it—a certain spiritual joyousness; a sensuous, tropical love of life, in vivid contrast to the cool and cautious New England reason; a slow and dreamful conception of the universe, a drawling and slurring of speech, an intense sensitiveness to spiritual values—all these things and others like to them, tell of the imprint of Africa on Europe in America. There is not gainsaying or explaining away this tremendous influence of the contact of the north and south, of black and white, of Anglo Saxon and Negro.[18]

In effect, they "kept the faith"—not just in their words, but also in their works. For them, Black spirituality encompassed both piety and social practices. The eloquence of the Black preaching tradition integrated political ideals and public-policy matters with the social reality facing Black Americans. Irrespective of alleged failings in some of their personal lives, these leaders, through courageous public stances, achieved a place for the

Black Church as an indispensable institution of Black culture and Black communities. The Bible-centered sermon informed and challenged the communities in sociopolitical crises on crucial issues.

BIBLICAL USAGE AND THE NEGRO SPIRITUALS

One of the earliest and most distinctive forms of rhetoric to be produced by the American Black Church is the Negro spiritual. In many of them, one finds adaptations of biblical ideas, images, and themes. E. Franklin Frazier points out that "the Bible provided the Negro with the rich imagery which has characterized the sermons of Negro preachers and the sacred folk songs of the Negro."[19] Much earlier, James Weldon Johnson suggested that these spiritual slave songs developed a mechanism for coping with the harsh realities of slavery. Accordingly, Johnson argues that they stressed "the cardinal virtues of Christianity," that is, patience, forebearance, love, faith, and hope. They associated the Black American plight with that of Israel in bondage or Daniel in the lion's den and envisioned a similar divine deliverance.[20] The New Testament scholar Amos N. Wilder also makes the observation that the spirituals are "cult songs, fostered and shaped in the recurrent secret assemblies of the slaves, a Christian continuation of the ceremonies they had brought with them from Africa."[21]

A study of the origin and basic ingredient of the Negro spiritual provides a basis for comparing the experience they represent with that of early Christians. The Negro spirituals developed as the enslaved Black's theological adaptation to "a hostile and mean world."[22] A parallel for this is manifested in the spiritual odes or psalmic hymns of the primitive Church. Wayne A. Meeks's book, *The First Urban Christians,* shows that Paul's churches developed spiritual odes that were regularly sung in early Christian meetings, and that such songs were crafted as a means of coping with affliction (*thlipsis*).[23] The New Testament subordination or domestic codes according to which slaves are told to obey their masters,[24] acknowledge the presence of slaves within the primitive churches. Evidently, although these slaves were rarely Blacks, they had a song to sing and fashioned it out of traditional songs of the synagogue that were adapted to Christian beliefs and appeals to Christ's own sufferings.

Opinions differ on the extent to which the Negro spiritual at times represented disguised plans for Negroes to escape from slavery, as perhaps suggested in "Steal Away to Jesus." Benjamin Mays, in *The Negro's God,* argues that while the majority of the spirituals are compensatory (offering compensation for earthly suffering in the hereafter) and otherworldly, not all of them are of that character, for some protested the social ills that Black people suffered.[25] E. Franklin Frazier merely asserts that the Negro spirituals were essentially religious in sentiment and otherworldly in outlook, while Carl Marbury argues that the spirituals simply did not possess the kind of sophistication associated with code songs of escape.[26]

Nevertheless, one cannot overlook the fact that, in one of the earliest churches of the diaspora, Paul advised slaves to gain manumission, if possible (1 Cor. 7:21–24).[27] Such advice came before churches began adopting the codes of subordination (well after A.D. 70). Of course, no one contends that early Christian spiritual odes were songs written to urge slaves to escape. Still, it is striking that in the same epistle, Paul advised escape and instructs the congregations about singing (1 Cor. 14:15). Certainly, a similar circumstance is plausible in the slave church of the Black American.

It seems undeniable that some of the Negro spirituals exhibit an adaptation of biblical themes. The Black slave church rejoiced in its versions of Moses, the prophetic agent of divine liberation from Pharaoh, in "Go Down Moses," just as it vicariously celebrated Joshua's victory and transposed it into a vision of hope for their own liberation in "Joshua Fit de Battle ob Jericho." If the former enjoins a confrontation with Pharaoh, the latter implies that, like Joshua, one desirous of victory must be willing to fight for it with God's help.[28]

By no means is the imagery of the Negro spiritual restricted to the Old Testament. Persons of the New Testament are also prominent in such spirituals as "Give Me Jesu," "Sweet 'lil Jesus Boy," or "Mary Had a Baby." Thus, an early usage of the Bible within American Black churches is manifest in the creative biblical adaptations of the Negro spirituals. On the one hand are the spirituals that somewhat passively express a longing for heaven, to be with Jesus, or for the hastening of judgment day. These sentiments have their parallel in some of the hymns of the first-century Church, in which people also anxiously awaited that "Great Day." On the other hand, Negro spirituals also reflect the biblical theme of deliverance from human bondage. Not only does the Bible itself contain a similar contrasting emphasis, but these contrasting perspectives have long been manifest within the history of the Black Church itself. Beyond noting the variance in worldviews evident in the Negro spirituals, it is important to recognize that they, like their early Christian counterparts, contributed to the formation of solidarity. The biblical associations of the spirituals provide the Black slave with an identity within God's plan that is related to those in the first-century churches who commonly referred to one another as brother and sister.

BIBLICAL USAGE IN BLACK CHURCH ART AND EDUCATION

When our attention turns to the written media of Black churches, we find other types of preoccupation with Scripture. Old and New Testament motifs characterize James Weldon Johnson's *God's Trombones,* which has long established itself as a classic narrative drama within Black churches. The vivid anthropomorphic portrayal of the loving creator God in Johnson's "The Creation" and the movement of the drama depicted in his colorful "The Prodigal Son" attest to the singular way that Johnson preserves the Black Church's tradition of unique biblical narration.[29] Indeed, Johnson's animated narrative conducts the modern reader's attention beyond the Black Church and back to another facet of first-century life.

Amos N. Wilder asserts that the ambience of early Church meetings and testimonies approximates that of the narration of *God's Trombones*.[30] Apparently as Christianity has become the Church of the establishment, its churches have tended to become more quiet, orderly, and sedate. Numerous New Testament passages (1 Cor. 11:13, 14, 22; 1 Tim. 1; 2 Tim. 2; 2 Pet. 2:13; Jude 12) indicate that ancient Christian gatherings were hardly quiet and solemn. In addition to the chanting and hymn singing, Scripture and recent epistles were read aloud; moreover, there were group prayers. A rendition of Johnson's narrative drama captures the ambience of the early Church because in both, the natural style is animated, dynamic, and rather loud.

The poetry of the Black Church also shows an indebtedness to the Bible. Walter L. Brooks, though born a slave, later attended both Lincoln University and Princeton Theological Seminary. He distinguished himself not only as a pastor of the Nineteenth Street Baptist Church in Washington, D.C., but also as a skilled poet attuned to the Bible. Many of Brooks's poems provide a Scripture citation immediately after the title. Illustrative is "Forgiveness," where he cites Matthew 6:15. As one reads, it becomes clear that the biblical passage guides the development of the poem.[31] Similarly, his poem "The Stature of the Fullness of Christ" derives from Ephesians 4:13. By contrast, his poem "Who But God?" draws on a fairly extensive listing of comparative passages from the New Testament.[32] Brooks is particularly interesting because most of his poems seem to be inspired by the New Testament. A variation of Brooks's biblical usage is found in George A. Singleton's historical survey, *The Romance of African Methodism*. Each chapter is organized in relation to events depicted in a biblical passage.[33] In identifying a similar tendency in the early Church, one readily thinks of the manner in which gospel writers, notably Matthew, systematically used Old Testament fulfillment-formula citations.

A third body of Black Church literature frequently ignored is that of the Church school. In 1938, Benjamin Mays published the results of his study of such literature in three denominations. His findings are not comforting, because he discovered that there was little or no attempt made in those church-school materials to differentiate between Old Testament and New Testament. Rather the Bible was treated "like a loaf of bread, all parts of which are equally good."[34] Moreover, he found that every biblical statement about God was accepted without qualification, and often there was no correlation between the Bible lesson and guide questions. He openly questioned the value of such simplistic literature.[35] Naturally, Christian educational resources in the predominately Black denominations have improved in quality and organization in the last several decades. Nevertheless, Mays's discoveries are sobering reminders that in recent times there are instances in which Bible usage in many Black American churches had not attained the level of scriptural reinterpretation and pedagogy seen in first- and second-century instructional materials.

GUIDELINES FOR BIBLICAL USAGE

Given the centrality of preaching in Black Church tradition, we return to this subject, but now our aim is not descriptive but prescriptive. We do well to recall the dictum of Martin Dibelius, "In the beginning was the sermon."[36] It seems at times that, among many Black seminarians and ministers, the beginning as well as the end is the sermon! Within American Black churches, preachers typically have had more power and status relative to their constituents than their white counterparts.[37] As suggested earlier, much of that has derived from the Black American's prowess as a strong, charismatic preacher of the Bible. In several quarters, an acculturated style and technique has governed Black preaching; not infrequently, solid biblical content is crowded out when the Black preacher "preaches himself" and not Jesus Christ as Lord (2 Cor. 4:5). So, while it can be instructive to remember that the Bible begins as sermon and that the sermon is generally the centerpiece in Black Church worship, we must also be mindful of the preacher's temptation to distort or otherwise abuse the potential power of the sermon by questionable usage of the Bible.

In his valuable article, "Biblical Hermeneutics and the Black Preacher," Robert A. Bennett details a threefold challenge directed at the Black pulpit by biblical criticism.[38] He insists that the first challenge is to determine, grasp, and become grasped by God's spirit at work in the biblical passage. The second challenge is to observe what Bennett calls "the divine economy," by which God directs the Black preacher's attention to the need to utilize all the intellectual tools and critical judgments necessary in searching out the Word of God responsibly. He sees the third challenge to the Black pulpit as the mandate to discover the most effective mode of interpreting and transmitting the biblical message for today's Black congregations. This threefold challenge — which focuses on authenticity of the biblical word, its exegetical analysis, and hermeneutical appropriation — is a helpful reminder of the seriousness that should obtain whenever the Black preacher undertakes his or her responsibility as proclaimer of the kerygma. Bennett may be generalizing a bit too uncritically when he suggests that "Black preaching has always been discriminating in its use of Scripture" and that the Black Church has *never* used the Bible uncritically.[39] Presumably, Bennett means that Blacks have brought to the Bible a critical awareness of their own oppressed conditions that has informed their actual historical and contemporary usage of the Bible.

In any case, biblical usage in the Black Church is diverse. We can identify three tendencies within the Black Church tradition: biblical literalism; eisegesis (the process of "leading or reading into" the text our own ideas);

and the Black homily that conscientiously proceeds from exegesis to serious hermeneutical exposition. Whereas biblical literalism and eisegesis depend on proof-texting; the more solidly based Black homily depends on a critical posture that is informed by the historically conditioned features of the Bible. Once aware of such, we can re-engage the text, presupposing its perennial authority in addressing the needs and aspirations of Black people.

Yet we are also familiar with the tendency toward biblical literalism within ultraconservative, fundamentalist, and neo–apocalyptic Christian groups in America in general, and within the Black Church tradition in particular. Certainly, biblical literalism existed in the first century and was at times the source of great disputes between Jews and early Christians, as well as among Christians themselves. The sermons of John Jasper typify the tendency toward biblical literalism. In his celebrated, if not notorious, sermon "The Sun Do Move," Jasper based his argument about the motion of the sun on a very literal understanding of isolated biblical texts. If the Bible in any way mentioned something, then for Jasper, it was automatically and categorically true. Jasper's untutored efforts thus extol the literal reading of Joshua 10:13 ("the sun stayed in the midst of heaven, and did not hasten to go down") or Malachi 1:11 ("From the rising of the sun to its setting . . .").[40] Jasper reasoned that since the Bible says the sun stops, rises, and goes down, it must move. In like manner, Jasper employed Revelation 7:1, where mention is made of the earth's "four corners," to argue that the earth is flat and all scientific evidence to the contrary must be discarded.[41] Before one laughs at Jasper's biblical usage, one should study the extensive literalist approaches of a great number of our preachers today.

The second biblical usage tendency on the part of Black preachers is eisegesis (reading one's opinions into the text). In this way, a person forces the text to say what one wants it to say. Perhaps all of us have fallen prey to this tendency at one time or another. The eisegetical tendency is a temptation to vanity, which, according to Gardner Taylor, is one of "the gravest perils of the preacher."[42] Eisegesis attests to vanity because the culpable preacher uses it to make his or her words more important than those of the text. If, for example, a biblical passage mentions the word *sin* or *freedom,* the eisegete will never stop to inquire what the word actually meant at the time the text was written and placed in its specific original literary context. Rather, the hurried preacher develops a meaning for the text and races on, without reference to disciplined studies or existing bibliographies on the subject. The practice of leading with our subjective intuitions and feelings reduces the Bible to the status of being merely a springboard for one's self-serving predilections.

While literalism and eisegesis represent a preacher's misuse of the Bible, many Black ministers have found the requirements of exegesis are indispensable for effective proclamation in light of the complexities of issues today and the many differences between the ancient world and our modern context. I have in mind the individual who not only has sought the necessary theological training, but also has preserved the discipline for maintaining a constructively critical dialogue with the text.[43] Within the American Black Church tradition, an impressive number of enlightened preachers have examined the text carefully, found God's spirit there, and courageously and effectively translated their feelings into the prophetic word for their people in these latter days. A listing would include those already mentioned and such proclaimers as Howard Thurman, Jupiter Hammon, Willis J. King, William Holmes Borders, Martin Luther King, Jr., and Bishop Leontine T. C. Kelly. Their homilies of high caliber attest to a wrestling with the original meaning of the text and establishing appropriate analogies for contemporary application of the text. Such endeavors show a faithfulness to make the text live in the minds and hearts of their people.

Those who would present themselves as the custodians of the Christian kerygma confront the necessity of doing what the Black preacher, at his or her best, has done. On the one hand, the would-be custodian must accept the invitation to serious dialogue with the text, so the compassion and sufferings of Jesus Christ are always affirmed as the *crux interpretum* that points to the vision of resurrection. At the same time, the custodian of the kerygma must show how the biblical witness becomes adaptable for the enhancement of the human potential and community life of the pilgrims who hurt and struggle, especially in this hostile socioeconomic and political environment. Whenever the Black preacher has observed this twofold obligation, he or she has joined the ranks of the richest strand of first-century Christianity. One should never forget that the early Christians reinterpreted their Scriptures, the Old Testament (invariably the Septuagint), in light of both the Christ-event and the distinctive existential circumstances of faith communities, struggling to make sense out of a seemingly wicked and insane world, either in order to survive in it or to change it completely. Thus, biblical usage is at its finest in Black preaching when the custodian of the text takes seriously the continuities and disjunctures between the daily struggles of life then, and God's contemporary analogies for biblical witness and action.

PREACHING FROM THE NEW TESTAMENT

The danger of seeming to indict preachers about tendencies to be less than responsible in their usage of the Bible is that the critic inevitably hears the rejoinder, "Show me some of your sermons!" Since I welcome serious debate on the substantive issues within the Black Church, I dare to illustrate some of the guidelines I have just offered. I must first confess that I do not consider myself a good preacher. I have never perfected the so-called art of preaching. In fact, I do not even like to preach! Usually whenever I have to prepare a sermon, a certain melancholy and sense of burden come upon me, because I know that to do so effectively requires work (thoughtful meditation, planning, exegesis, reading, outlines, illustrations, and not the least, self-examination). Then, too, only in preaching can one work so hard only to fall short. Even when one has truly presented a "great sermon," one dares not to take too much credit for it. Thus, it has always seemed to me that in many ways, preaching is a losing proposition. One does it best as an obligation rather than a matter of joyous choice (1 Cor. 9:16). Central to my concern about preaching as a teacher and an heir of noble traditions in the Black Church, however, is not so much the goal of becoming a good preacher, but the goal of having preachers probe the Bible more seriously, and especially to utilize the New Testament. My aim in presenting the following examples is to demonstrate the Bible's humanness, this-worldliness, and pertinence for the ongoing struggle for freedom, faith, and courageous visions on the part of God's still exploited and downtrodden people.

Because I have never taught a course in homiletics, I hesitate to offer further guidelines for constructing a good sermon. There is a stunning variety of handbooks on constructing the sermon[44] and an equally diverse array of sermon collections[45] by Black and white preachers who either think they are good in meeting the challenge or have admirers who think they execute their preaching responsibilities with aplomb. The material I now share is only to illustrate the approach I find necessary, given a long-standing sense of being humbled by the awesomeness of trying to preach from the New Testament.

The centrality of the New Testament in our proclamation does not in any way relegate the Old Testament to an inferior status. Rather, the New Testament fulfills the promises of the Old Testament through the birth, life, ministry, and death of Jesus. God's purpose from the beginning is capsuled and completed in Jesus Christ. These sermons are intended to demonstrate the potency of the New Testament within the Black tradition and the continuous struggle for competence in "rightly handling the word of truth" (2 Tim. 2:15). Accordingly, each of us is invited to participate in the proclamation of God's word. Howard Thurman helps us by making the following observation: "For me, the sermon is an act of worship in which the preacher exposes his spirit and mind as they seek to reveal the working of the spirit of the living God upon them. It is a searching moment!"[46]

In the two sermons that follow, one should discern attempts to confront the challenge posed by texts written so long ago and for such different sets of circumstances. Yet, as biblical texts, they carry the imprimatur of the Church, which itself implies they are adaptable for life among successive generations of God's people, however divided as tribes, nations, or subcultures. Neither the Old Testament nor the New Testament tell the preacher how to use the ancient text responsibly. That is the challenge. One is free to abuse the text, ignore it, or wrestle with it for glimpses of a victory that only God — not oneself, not one's fellow ministers, not one's official superiors, not even the congregation — may impart.

Preaching as a searching moment can never be to boast of ourselves but to boast the Lord who recommends us (2 Cor. 10:17, 18). Preaching is a spiritual process that humbles us and empties us of ourselves so the spirit reaches our depths and gives us the esteemed opportunity, by grace of God using us as divine instruments, to proclaim God's glory, truth, and praise. It is following in the way of Jesus, whereby we point others to God so they believe.

"The Tyranny of Endless Excuses"[47]
Proverbs 6:6-11; Luke 9:51-62

Years ago, as a high school senior in Boston, I had an English assignment which was to read a short story entitled, "The Jungle Sloth." I have long since forgotten the author, but I remember vividly the description of this tropical American beast — not quite ape and not quite bear — whose sluggish routine included little more than eating, moving about upside down, or just hanging in trees, always seeking some comfortable place to rest and sleep . . . sleep . . . sleep! Although the portrait of the sloth was somewhat grotesque, I liked him because in many ways, I could see in him traces of myself!

As an undergraduate at Howard, I found much evidence, both on campus and in the larger community, that the jungle sloth was alive and well! Indeed, his image continued to haunt me and increasingly to motivate me to avoid becoming an incarnation of that upside-down unproductive somniac, neither leader nor follower, who eats and sleeps as life passes him by. Nevertheless, surveying the academic and socioeconomic conditions in many Black communities today, some of us cannot but wonder if a whole nation and race of people have not become colonies of jungle sloths — complacent, selfish, toothless, and complaining, whether seeming "masters" or manifest victims of endless excuses at a time when such excuses only foster further socioeconomic, political, and spiritual erosion.

The mood in Black America today may be contrasted with the note of great expectation and pride sounded a half-century ago during the Negro Renaissance. Dr. Alain Lock, Professor of Philosophy at Howard in 1925, offered this commentary on the mood of Afro-America of his day: "The galvanizing shocks and reactions of the last few years are making, by subtle processes of internal reorganization, a race out of its own disunited and apathetic elements."[48] Locke saw hopeful signs in the reawakening of the Negro, but was at the same time careful enough to highlight continuing problems.

> The Negro still has idols of the tribe to smash. If, on the one hand, the white man has erred in making the Negro appear to be that which would excuse . . . his treatment of him, the Negro, in turn, has too often unnecessarily excused himself because of the way he has been treated.[49]

Such observations by Alain Locke more than fifty years ago have a sobering pertinence for our situation in America today, especially as data continue to suggest that, far from a reawakening, many in the Black community have in varied ways fallen back to sleep amid the galvanizing shocks and crises of a modern era. Past visions of creativity, achievement, and solidarity are on the wane, and too many in our time find a woeful kinship with the jungle sloth!

Those today who know that they are asleep may prefer the hedonistic revelry set to verse by Omar Khayyam in his poem *The Rubaiyat*:

> Awake! Awake! For the morning in the Bowl of Night
> Has flung the stone that puts the stars to Flight
> And Lo! The hunter of the East has caught
> The Sultan's Turret in a Shaft of Light.
>
> Dreaming when Dawn's Left Hand was in the Sky
> I heard a voice within the Tavern cry
> Awake my little one and fill the cup
> Before Life's Liquor in its cup be dry![50]

Here in this ancient Persian verse we find the call to wake up—but not to any new level of social responsibility or community solidarity and development; rather to wake up to the revelry of wine in an otherwise empty life of fleeting pleasures. The Bible, my friends, offers more sober alternatives.

We have heard the ancient chastisement from the Old Testament wisdom literature this morning as read from Proverbs 6:6-11.

> Go to the ant, O sluggard; consider her ways, and be
>   wise. . . .
> How long will you lie there, O sluggard? . . .
> A little sleep . . . a little folding of the hands to rest,
> And poverty will come upon you like a vagabond!

This message may seem harsh, but it is also fair. One should realize that this proverb was composed for those in ancient Israel who tended to blame God for their deficiencies and poverty. It was necessary for these people to understand that God had already provided them with potential resources to do something about their own desperate situation.

The call to wake up and stop the tyranny of excuses becomes even more theologically profound in the New Testament. In Ephesians 5:14, we have preserved an early Christian hymn adapted from Isaiah 60:1. The matter is sharply focused and stated succinctly: "Awake, O sleeper, and arise from the dead, and Christ shall give you light." The new theological datum central to the New Testament is that the witness of Jesus Christ can represent light and power for any "sluggish people." All that is needed is a sincere response to God's initiatives of grace and Jesus' own invitations to discipleship in radical new keys. It is within this framework that Luke 9:51-62 bears directly upon our own slothful proclivities to yield to the tyranny of endless excuses.

As my students have heard me say repeatedly, perhaps *ad nauseum,* the theological meaning of a biblical passage cannot be fully apprehended unless attention is given to the larger literary context of the passage. This rule is critical in the case of Luke 9:51-62, for these verses constitute the beginning of the central section of Luke's gospel — Luke 9:51-19:27 — which is called the journey narrative. This entire journey narrative seems to be carefully edited tradition that Luke has arranged in a unique manner in order to dramatize the second phase of Jesus' ministry. Significantly, it begins with 9:51: "When the days drew near for him to be received up (*analēmpsis*), he set his face to go to Jerusalem." Luke wants to show that Jesus' ministry discloses no exclusive preoccupation with the salvation of the Jews, as we have to some extent in Mark and Matthew, but rather that Jesus' ministry has a second phase that involves a sojourning among the Samaritan villages and among the despised and the lowly, in short, among those whom the Jews have rejected or otherwise excluded from their history of salvation scheme.[51] The journey narrative thus confirms for us Luke's conception of Jesus not just as the suffering Messiah, but as the one who, en route to his destined appointment in Jerusalem, is determined to call those "outside" the Jewish nation who may be sleeping and sluggish, in order to wake up those groups to a bold invitation by God.

Our passage, Luke 9:51-62, though introducing the journey narrative, stands between two different formal commissionings of disciples. Earlier in Chapter 9, Luke reports on the commissioning of the twelve Jewish apostles, but following our passage, seventy "others" (*heterous*) are sent out. They are to minister in pairs, a fact which, as Hans Conzelmann points out, undergirds the way in which the seventy other disciples are to protect one another in the new mission field.[52] Even though it is frequently suggested that these are two separate bits of tradition in Luke 9:51-62 — 9:52-56, which is a story about the Samaritan's rejection of Jesus, and 9:57-62, which is generally seen as a narrative on the cost of discipleship — it is possible to discern a common theme throughout all these verses.

Notice how anxious Jesus is to include the hated Samaritans in his ministry (9:52) and yet how reluctant the Samaritans are to receive Jesus! Like many in the Black community today, the Samaritans were, in effect, oblivious to the rich opportunity being extended to them. They were so governed by historical shabby treatment from the Jews that they failed to grasp the opportunity to march forward with the Christ who was sending special messengers to them. For this, Jesus' disciples, like too many Bible-thumping, self-righteous Christians today, were ready to destroy the Samaritans in an act of vengeance analogous to Elijah's in the Old Testament (2 Kings 1:9-16).

Jesus, however, was more gracious! Luke tells us that Jesus rebukes his disciples for their lack of comprehending the way that God's graciousness and forgiveness are vehicles for an eventual triumph of Gospel power. Other Lukan passages show that though the Samaritans initially reject Jesus the Jew, some come to accept him as the true Son of God (Luke 10:25–27; 17:11–19; Acts 8:9–25). The first lesson is clear: A people may let a past stigma of shame serve as an excuse for not taking advantage of the present moment of opportunity and deliverance. The Roman poet Ovid gives us a dictum for guidance: *Ad Astra per aspera* ("to the stars through difficulty"). These are the words of the successful Daedalus in his flight from Crete to Sicily.[53]

The ensuing narrative, verses 57–62, is also partially reported in Matthew 8:19–22 in a rather different context. In Matthew, the context involves Jesus' deeds within the unfolding drama of his identity as the Jewish Messiah. The Matthean version of the three invitations to discipleship are to a Jewish scribe and the disciples. By contrast, Luke's version suggests that the three persons who now entertain the idea of discipleship may be Samaritans, or even Gentiles.

It is important to notice the way in which Luke exposes the empty rhetoric of persons who claim to be serious about their future. If the Samaritans used the excuse of past and continuing Jewish injustices against them as an excuse to reject a new future, the man in Luke 9:57 who says, "I will follow you wherever you go," is immediately exposed as an unthoughtful opportunist, one who thinks only of the possible advantages, by way of conventional wisdom, in his being associated with Jesus. Without thinking through the actual costs of discipleship, this would-be disciple says what he believes Jesus wants to hear! Jesus quickly exposes the man's superficiality: "Foxes have holes, and birds of the air have nests; but the Son of Man has nowhere to lay his head" (Luke 9:58). The opportunist uses rhetoric to mask his selfish agenda. What the opportunist does not admit is that his gods are individual security and comfort. These are his hidden excuses for not being able to respond to discipleship with integrity. The Samaritans attest to the first excuse—their treatment by the Jews past and present (vv. 57, 58).

The third excuse is especially deceptive, because it has the appearance of being a good excuse. In 9:59–60, Jesus asks another man to follow him. The response is an implied yes, but there is an expressed proviso: "Lord, let me first go and bury my father." Not only in Judaism but also in Samaritan thought, filial piety was recognized as an important duty. Under normal circumstances, this would-be disciple would have a good excuse, and Jesus would seem strident by saying "Leave the dead to bury their own dead!" Are we to apply Molière's statement in the French comedy *Tartuffe* to Jesus: "He loves to preach an ethic so sublime That anything we do becomes a crime!"[54] Cannot one observe the traditional duty to one's family without being judged unfit for discipleship? Jesus confronts us with our penchant for devising even "good" excuses to avoid a priority quality encounter with him! There are, Luke suggests, a million rationalizations for not turning the core of your life over to God. More often than not, these are excuses to maintain one's own status quo as opposed to engaging the future.

The fourth excuse is so petty when compared to Jesus' own radical determination to empower persons to help themselves that it is followed by a jolting pronouncement. In verse 61, another would-be disciple agrees to be a follower but asks that he at least be allowed to say farewell to those family and friends at home. The pronouncement that follows in 9:62 shows that Jesus was not likely to grant such permission: "No one who puts his hand to the plow and looks back is fit for the kingdom," Jesus says. The analogy is clear. One who claims to want to progress, to go forward under the light and power of God, who does not want to be a sluggard, sloth, or slave is a person who, in effect, places his/her hand on the plow to dig up furrows. If such a person begins making excuses—like the Samaritans, like the opportunist who seeks "security", like the convenient "I've got family responsibilities" that take precedence, like the sentimentalist who knows nothing of uninterrupted attention, discipline, and determination—such a person is already becoming his or her own worst enemy and shall not plow anything but zig-zagged furrows!

Awake this morning from slumber and excuses, realizing that you have a dynamic role to play in helping this larger community. Let ours not be a tyranny of endless excuses but an acceptance of new marching orders.

> We have tomorrow bright before us like a flame
> Yesterday's but a sundown's name
> Resolutely toward our bold new future
> We march.[55]

                                                            Amen.

Lessons from Jesus' Own Family
Micah 7:2-6; Mark 6:1-5

In most ecclesiastical calendars, we regularly observe a Mother's Day, a Father's Day, and a Children's Day, but it is the exception, not the rule, for a church to designate a Sunday as Family Day. This, in one sense, may seem strange, since it would appear to be quite natural for churches today to set aside a special day to honor the family, which, after all, must be considered the core social unit within any society, providing support and enhancing one's prospects for survival and stability.

Among the Ten Commandments (Decalogue) of the Old Testament, we recognize the presence of that fifth commandment to honor one's father and mother (Exod. 20:12; 21:17; Lev. 19:3; Deut 5:16). Jesus himself acknowledged this commandment as still binding on his audiences (Mark 10:19; Matt. 19:19; Luke 18:20). Despite the fact that the fifth commandment is thereby part of early Christian teaching, the larger reality is that the New Testament does not place an emphasis on the family as such! Of course, Paul talks about the expediency of being married (1 Cor. 7:9, 29–31) and other New Testament authors give various instructions on the duties of husbands, wives, and children (Col., Eph., pastorals, and 1 Peter). These teachings scarcely offer any major guidance for family life and together represent only a slim corpus of redundant formulae. The fact is that, on the whole, particularly in Jesus' teaching, the family does not receive much attention; and Jesus' words about the family, when they do occur, often seem insensitive and even harsh.

Consider, for example, Jesus' words in Matthew 10:34–36: "I have not come to bring peace, but a sword . . . to set a man against his father, and a daughter against her mother, and a daugher-in-law against her mother-in-law; and a man's foes will be those of his own household." On the face of them, these words are hardly consoling. Jesus' words are even stronger in Mark 13:12 and Luke 21:16: "You will be delivered up even by parents and brothers and kinsmen and friends, and some of you they will put to death." What a gloomy forecast Jesus makes about the signs of the last days, the apocalypse, when utter chaos and bitter strife shall destroy households from within!

Perhaps, when we consider the frightening state of affairs in so much of modern family life in America today, we should realize that not only did Jesus know what he was saying, but we, in our time, may be unwittingly helping his predictions to come true in our households, neighborhoods, and larger communities. Although few want to admit it, in many instances, our family life is a nightmare, in shambles, and the source of great anxiety, tension, and quarreling. The stress that results accounts for our unprecedented high divorce rates, marriage-avoidance patterns, runaway children, child abuse and yes, even murder within the households of our communities! In the last days, "a man's foes will be those of his own household" (Mic. 7:6; Matt. 10:36)!

Without a doubt, people in America today are under extreme stress as the result of many new pressures of coping and surviving in our impersonal dog-eat-dog world, in a period that even Billy Graham (whom I seldom quote) has called "the decade of the me-generation." That is, I'm only concerned about myself, my own survival as an individual, 'getting-over' the best way with no regard for anyone who might get hurt in the process." Such attitudes are woefully evident in much of modern family life. It is hardly acceptable to excuse ourselves because Blacks are so consistently under much greater stress than our counterparts in America as the result of continued racial harassment, economic disadvantage, and persistent subtle insensitivities.

The cover story of *Time* magazine a few months ago was captioned "Stress: Can We Cope?" The author at one point made the following observation that the relentless stresses of poverty and ghetto life for black

Americans have also been associated with higher health risks. Studies of poor black neighborhoods in Detroit and Boston show that hypertension among blacks is double the rate for Whites as the result of over-crowded housing, high unemployment, and crime with even a 37% higher rate of cancer and fatal heart attacks in some areas.[57]

In his major but controversial study, the black urban sociologist Dr. William Julius Wilson demonstrates that three times the percentage of Blacks, as compared to whites in 1974, were actually below the low-income level.[58] Worse still, Wilson points out that nearly one-fourth of all Black men between the ages of 19 and 34 had become, in 1976, part of a nonlabor force, an underclass of persons not merely unemployed but unemployable.[59] One consequence of this is the sad reality that more and more poor Black families have women as the sole head of the household, while the erstwhile Black "fathers" are, for complex reasons, increasingly found idle on the corners, on drugs, in mental hospitals, in jails, in disproportionate numbers as economically forced volunteers in the military, or as nameless casualties in the quiet war against them, which, when lost, grants the strange peace of the city morgue! Oh my friends, we may be in the last days, for, at alarming rates, strong supportive Black families are becoming extinct due to modern anxieties, pressures, and stresses often satanic in nature. Such crises threaten to destroy all sense of stability, meaning, and human worth or achievement in our families today!

Given this sad set of circumstances which illustrate that family life today is in crisis, let us examine the New Testament, or more specifically the family life of Jesus, in order to see if Jesus' own family relations have anything to teach us today. What does the Bible tell us about the characteristics of Jesus' family? Well, first of all, it tells us that Jesus was one of at least eight children. He had four brothers (James, Joseph, Jude, and Simon) and at least three sisters, although they are never named in the New Testament (Mark 6:1-5; Matt. 13:56). Therefore, by today's standards, Jesus was from a large family. We also know that his father, Joseph, was a carpenter. He had a job and could apparently pay taxes (Luke 2:5), but carpentry was then equivalent to what today one might call blue-collar work, low middle class, struggling-to-make-ends-meet type of work. The next point of information is that Jesus' parents insisted on solid religious training for him (Luke 2:39, 41). From these observations, we can see that Jesus' family was a big one, somewhat religious by traditional Jewish standards, with a working-class blue-collar income. One that obeyed the civil law as imposed by Rome. In other words, with the possible exception that Jesus was reared by both parents, in many respects Jesus' family resembles many Black American families today—lots of kids, hard work under oppressive conditions, law-abiding churchgoers!

Yet, also like so many Black families today, Jesus' famly was under great anxiety and stress! The problems, of course, started even before his unusual birth. Many neighbors had thought that his mother, Mary, had become pregnant by a man other than Joseph, to whom she was betrothed. Jesus was therefore illegitimate in their narrow view. Evidently, Joseph, too, had his doubts (Matt. 1:19). No sooner had his parents worked out this peculiar embarrassment than they found out that Herod wanted to kill their child! Not able to fight the king, they fled to Egypt for refuge (Matt. 2:13–23). Their stress continued to mount when Jesus, the extraordinary youth, became typically a source of anxiety—as for example, at the Passover in Jerusalem (Luke 2:41–49). Jesus' parents, we are told, believed he had been lost for three days. That text tells us vividly how his parents rushed back to Jerusalem, anxiously searching for him. Oh, what a precocious child was Jesus! When his parents found him there, baffling the rabbinic elders, only he would say, "Did you not know that I must be in my Father's house?" He must have worried Mary and Joseph to no end!

Later, when Jesus' public ministry was in full-swing, he was still a manifest problem for his family, as Mark 6:1–5 makes clear. In this New Testament lesson, we find Jesus having returned to his old community in Nazareth, the locale of his "hidden years." Doubtless, he thought that he would preach, heal, and teach in his old neighborhood, as he had been doing in other parts of Palestine, but the "home folks" were hardly prepared to receive him! True to the adage, "familiarity often breeds contempt," his kinfolks rejected him, causing Jesus to utter those fateful words that haunt us still: "A prophet is not without honor, except in his own county." Shall we read here Paul Robeson, W. E. B. DuBois, or Martin Luther King, Jr.? To former acquaintances and his family members, it appeared that Jesus had lost his mind! Again, he had become the source for great anxiety; the neighbors were talking, again! He had become a public embarrassment into whom they just could not talk any sense. And what does Scripture say then? Well, it says that, as a result of the family's failure to understand or appreciate Jesus' uniqueness as a servant of God who happened to be actually related to them, Jesus could do no mighty work there! Oh, how much more good could Jesus have done in Nazareth, had he received the support and blessings of his own family?

But *no*! His family was in some ways rather ordinary, and as such, probably like not a few of our families today. Where they could support, protect, and help, they opposed bitterly what they neither understood or cared to understand. His family failed to allow for the possibility that what they were opposing might, in fact, have been a bona fide work of God for the good of others. Families of the nonsupportive, uncompromising variety have tendencies to remain utterly selfish, closed, unloving, and spiteful— invariably when they are needed most. My own family is something of a mixed bag. Some are consistently supportive, others do not care, others display a cold competitiveness or a jealous and mean spirit! We must remember that Jesus was no easy person to understand. So much of his ministry had been a challenge to old, traditional ways of assessing matters or relating to God. No doubt, he simply scared many close relatives who could not believe that someone they knew was truly gifted by God.

Now to the lesson's real punch! Look at the manner in which Jesus dealt with his family's opposition, misunderstanding, mistrust, and doubts! He forgave them their trespasses even as they did not forgive him for what they perceived were his trespasses. He actually went beyond the dictates of the Lord's Prayer! He could have borne a grudge or cursed out his family. He could have stopped his ministry right there, conceding to the presumed wishes of his kinfolk. But, no! Jesus took their criticisms and used them to strengthen his ministry.

Why? Well, I suspect that he realized his whole life was no longer his or his family's. He was flowing with a spiritual energy, purpose, and awareness directed by none other than God. How could he do otherwise but lay hands on a few of the sick and move on? Unlike some of the homefolks, he did not merely give lip service to his religion: He loved it; he was the embodiment of it; and in so doing, he offers families a paradigm.

There's a sweet old story translated for us
  But written long, long ago
The Gospel according to Matthew, Luke and John
  Of Christ and his mission below.

We read and admire that Gospel of Christ
  With its love so unfailing and true
But what do they say and what do they think
  Of the Gospel according to you?

'Tis a wonderful story that gospel of love,
  As it shines in the Christ life divine
And Oh that its truth might be told over again
  In the story of your life and mine.

Unselfishness mirrors in every scene
  Love blossoms on every sod
And back from its vision the heart comes to tell
  The wonderful goodness of God.

You are writing each day a letter to others
  Take care that the writing is true
Tis the only gospel that some will ever read
  That gospel according to you![60]

In the *Time* magazine article not long ago, some rules were offered for coping with stress: 1. Don't sweat the small stuff. 2. It's all small stuff. 3. If you can't fight and you can't flee, then just flow! In a sense, Jesus' response to his family proves the wisdom of these rules. He didn't "sweat the small stuff." In relation to God's great purposes for him, all the opposition, the give-me-give-me demands, the misunderstandings, the frustrations were nothing — absolutely all "small stuff," — merely folks caught in smallness. But most of all, Jesus, through the discipline of prayer and thanksgiving, nurtured a spiritual flow that sustained him throughout life.

Yes, there are so many stresses upon us as a people, upon our families in America today! A recent issue of *Life* magazine featured an article on the hundreds of thousands of runaway children — mean, dangerous, and dying in the streets.[61] The Reagan administration has successfully managed to make our lives more desperate with all the cutbacks, layoffs, "riffs," discriminatory policies against Blacks. Hard drugs abound; crime is matched by police brutality against minorities. Unstable people poison products in stores, corporations contaminate our water supplies with industrial chemicals. And if that were not enough, there are old and new health scares, the mental pressures from natural disasters or accidents, and, of course, the perennial nightmare of a devastating nuclear accident or nuclear war that could mean the end of the planet through the instrumentality of sinful hands.

Is there any wonder why our society is so unhealthy, with such mental illness, cancer, suicides, and the like plaguing family life and all life? But thanks be to God, an answer comes in our moments of crisis. We can't flee, because there is scarcely anywhere to go and little money to get there. So we are left exactly where Jesus was. We are left to flow with a gounding in God — a flow that pointed him to the cross so others might have new life. A deep spiritual reservoir can be ours and our family's that can help us, like Jesus, embody that gospel written by each of us every day of our lives. Amen.

CHAPTER SIX

Freedom and Class:
The Epistle to the Galatians

The preceding two chapters have provided a framework for appreciating the Bible's concern for justice and how that concern and the Bible itself have occupied central positions in the life of the Black Church. It is no exaggeration to say that the Black Church of the Americas was born out of the inability of whites to accept the full humanity and equality of Blacks. Over the centuries, the New Testament has affirmed the desirability of freedom for all persons and highlighted the impropriety of discriminating against people because of outward appearance and social standing. Nevertheless, especially since the African slave trade, Western churches have had great difficulty allowing themselves to be guided by the biblical visions of freedom and human equality. Even whites who are Christians have often had little difficulty denying basic freedoms to Blacks and relegating them to inferior positions in society. As a consequence, the Black Church has always had a certain preoccupation with the idea of freedom and a clear yearning to see its members free from discrimination based on race and class, which for most Blacks are overlapping realities.

This chapter explores the ideas of freedom and class consciousness as problems in the Epistle to the Galatians. Paul's passionate appeal, rebuke, and exhortations to the ancient church at Galatia reflect his perception that the Galatians abused their freedom and fell prey to the improprieties of class consciousness. His concerns are instructive for Western churches that not only abuse freedom, but deny others its benefits. Galatians also seems to speak to realities within the Black Church, where the historic quest for freedom, once the hallmark of the Black Church, seems to be on the wane. Instead, there are indications, even within the Black Church, of a resurgence of a class consciousness that imitates patterns of the dominant culture. Such social-class differentiation has not only caused some Blacks to vaunt themselves as better than others, but it has obscured the erstwhile solidarity that Blacks have had in giving priority to their common freedom struggle.

The discussion in this chapter unfolds in five steps. First we identify elements in what appears to be a modern American freedom crisis. Stunning ironies are evident within this crisis, particularly as one applies the rhetoric of freedom to the socioeconomic conditions of most Blacks. Next, we explore the biblical images and language of freedom which, unlike our modern Western context, seem rather clear about freedom. On the one hand, the Old Testament serves as a commentary on an ancient quest for freedom; on the other hand, aspects of the lives of Jesus and the apostle Paul epitomize both freedom and their strong stances against class discrimination. Third, we trace the contours of the divine call to freedom that comes to Paul, who at first seems unworthy of this high calling. Fourth, we take up the Galatian church's structure and the interplay of concerns associated with freedom and class consciousness. Finally, we consider the hermeneutical application for the Black Church.

THE AMERICAN FREEDOM CRISIS

Freedom is one of those abstract words that everyone seems to use rather blithely, as if its meaning were self-evident. Few ever try defining it with any precision. In the United States of America, people often assume that freedom is such a basic part of the national heritage that the equation, America equals "the land of the free" has become axiomatic. The Declaration of Independence proclaims that liberty (freedom) is one of the inalienable rights of human beings, despite the fact that all the white Anglo-Saxon Protestant men who wrote the document scarcely believed in any comprehensive application of freedom as an inalienable right. They obviously did not subscribe to the view that women, native Americans, or Blacks were fully human or equal to them. In newly emancipated America, Blacks were given the value of only three-fifths of a human being. Furthermore, nearly a century after the Declaration of Independence, there was need of an Emancipation Proclamation (January 1, 1863) that formally abolished the American institution of enslaving Blacks.

Throughout the history of the Western Hemisphere, profound tensions have existed regarding the meaning of freedom. Such tensions have reached crisis proportions. Political freedom from Europe meant dominance over native Americans, who were partially exterminated, deprived of their ancient lands, and confined to Indian reservations or offered halting opportunities to assimilate into the American mainstream. A similar pattern is evident in the history of Central and South America, where the descendants of the Spanish and Portuguese presented equivalent options to the indigenous aboriginal peoples. Freedom in the Americas has also meant the enslavement, socioeconomic deprivation, incarceration of and/or "equal opportunities" for Blacks. As Charles H. Long has remarked ". . . my native land has always been for me a strange place . . . a constant enigma."[1] On the occasion of Karl Barth's lectures at the University of

Chicago during the late 1960s, Long could not resist exploring this strangeness with Barth, whose last lecture perhaps contained the key to his response. Long provides us with Barth's concluding remarks:

> Now a concluding word: If I myself were an American citizen and a Christian and a theologian, then I would try to elaborate a theology of freedom—a theology of freedom, let us say, from any inferiority complex over against good old Europe. . . . You may also have freedom from a superiority complex, let us say, over against Asia and Africa. That's a complex without reason. Then may I add—your theology should also be marked by a freedom from fear of Communism, Russia, nuclear warfare and generally speaking, from all the afore-mentioned principalities and powers.[2]

Barth's appeal is for nothing less than a "freedom for humanity."[3] It is precisely the lack of this form of freedom that troubles Long, who envisions much of Western history as a parochial and self-interested redefinition of what constitutes "authenic human existence":

> During the period of Western modernity the conquest and exploitation of the world by the West created a geographical context in which the white races formed the centers from which the exploitation and exercise of hegemonous power took place. These centers defined the structures of authentic human existence. The distances from these centers were adjudicated by varying degrees of humanity, so that at the outermost periphery, where color or blackness coincided with distance, the centrist held that these were lesser human beings.[4]

BIBLICAL IMAGES OF FREEDOM

The Bible often presents us with images of freedom by contrasting them with images of bondage or forced servitude. To be sure, the Bible also mentions freedom in relative terms that at times are difficult to reconcile. Let me illustrate this. On the one hand, the Old Testament shows the cruelty of the Egyptians in their captivity and oppression of the ancient Hebrews (Exod. 3:7–9; 5:10–21). On the other hand, once they are emancipated from Egyptian bondage, the Old Testament sanctions the institution of slavery among the Hebrews (Exod. 21; Deut. 15). The paradox is not relieved by the fact that the Hebrews probably treated their slaves better than the Egyptians or the fact that the Hebrew Law contained provisions guiding slave owners in their treatment of slaves, even providing for their release under various circumstances. The fact remains that the apparent Old Testament emphasis on freedom is little more than a sociopolitical or religious ideal, rather than a practical daily reality.

Similarly, New Testament authors insist on the importance of freedom and the need for believers to free themselves from materialism, conformity to conventional values, or certain practices of the Jewish religious establishment. However, some New Testament authors seem willing to sanction the institution of slavery and the forced physical bondage so prevalent in Greco-Roman society (Eph. 6:5–8; Col. 3:22–25; 1 Pet. 2:18–25). Even in the Bible, freedom is a complicated social, political, and religious issue that always requires careful clarification of its varied manifestations and degrees of purity.

In the New Testament, Jesus epitomizes a life of freedom. Here, the temptation narratives of the Synoptic gospels are instructive. First Matthew and then Luke have amplified in narrative form the terse mentioning of Jesus' temptation in Mark 1:12, 13. The content of the extended temptation narratives is noticeably similar. Nonetheless, Matthew and Luke do include elements (language, order of temptations, style of Old Testament citations) that are unique to each writer. It is significant that these temptation narratives occur between Jesus' baptism and the beginning of his public ministry, because they represent "a quasi-rabbinic debate" between Jesus and the devil[5] on whether or not Jesus is the Son of God (Matt. 3:17; Luke 3:22). In this debate where both Jesus and the devil quote and allude to Scripture, Jesus begins to show that he is truly free as the Son of God. He exercises not only his *freedom from* the three assaults by the devil, but also his *freedom for* service in behalf of God.

The temptation episodes of Matthew and Luke have captured, in a symbolic form, different aspects of evil that perennially undermine human aspirations. Whether the need is for food (daily sustenance and material possessions), magical powers (including "black" magic), or political power, a person should always be aware of potential enslavement by evil. Believers must vigorously inquire whether the motives for acquiring material possessions, magical solutions, or power emanate from God or Satan. G. B. Caird offers a sober reflection by fashioning five truths as safeguards against believing in the "devil":

1. Evil is real and potent. It is not just the sum total of individual bad deeds, but a power which gets a grip on human life and society.
2. Evil is personal. The very distinction between good and evil can arise only where there is *free choice* [emphasis mine] to obey God or to rebel against him.
3. Evil is distorted good. In a world which God has created good, evil exists only by perverting the good gifts of God. The devil himself is a fallen angel.
4. Evil masquerades as good. The devil is the "slanderer" who misleads men [people] by telling them lies about God.
5. Evil is the enemy. . . .[6]

In the temptation narratives, Jesus does not surrender the freedom granted him by God at his baptism. He had ready rejoinders for the devil, showing himself ready to stand against the forces of evil. The Jesus in these narratives is free from external authorities that do not proceed from God. He is free to make responsible choices by trusting and waiting to obey the voice of God. He is even free to accept the full consequences of having made the hard but correct decisions.[7] Such freedom characterizes the Son of God's ministry, and in this sense, Jesus means freedom. He epitomizes grace; he is not the individual whom Martin Luther describes as *"homo in se incurvatus,"* one who is "inescapably imprisoned and entangled in himself."[8]

Jesus of Nazareth has many opportunities to set himself above others or otherwise relegate others to an inferior class. He tends to do the opposite in his ministry by freely identifying with the poor, the women, and the outcasts. As the selection following Luke's temptation narrative shows, Jesus exercises true freedom when faced with evil (Luke 4:16-30). Luke stresses this by indicating that the Holy Spirit empowers him to proclaim freedom on behalf of those who are seldom heard or seen: the poor, the captives, and those oppressed by the social and religious elite. We should not be surprised that Jesus was known as one who did not discriminate against persons on the basis of their appearance or social standing (Mark 12:14; Matt. 22:16; Luke 20:21). Even the crucifixion represents Jesus' freedom to accept the full consequences of his divine love for others of low estate in a world too full of unforgiveness and hate (Luke 23:39-43).

Likewise, the life and writings of the apostle Paul provide evidence that he became a free man when he received God's call and decided to answer responsibly (Gal. 1:11-24; 1 Tim. 1:12-17; Acts 9:1-22). As in the case of Jesus, Paul cultivated a personal sense of freedom in its highest sense. As such, he became a worthy human instrument for God's message of freedom, which he felt compelled to proclaim to others (1 Cor. 9:16). Nowhere is this as plain in Paul's writings as in that famous passage within the Epistle to the Galatians: "For freedom [*elytheria*] Christ has set us free; stand fast therefore, and do not submit again to a yoke of slavery" (Gal. 5:1). Exactly what Paul means by his use of the word *freedom* has been debated for some time. There are many who would argue, as did Martin Luther, that Paul merely refers to our inner spirituality made possible by Christian faith.[9] This interpretation suggests that Paul does not have in view a freedom with direct implications for sociopolitical realities. It is more accurate to take Paul's use of the word *freedom* in a comprehensive or holistic manner, for a "free spirit" inescapably guides the body toward freedom.[10] Thus for Paul, no less than for Jesus himself, the good news was a full rejection of discriminating against persons or deferring to the wealthy or powerful by virtue of their social position or outward appearance (Rom. 2:11).

A DIVINE CALL TO THE UNWORTHY

The New Testament makes it clear that anyone—irrespective of ethnicity, religious background, or social position—is eligible to receive freedom's call. In fact, it often comes to persons not normally thought to be worthy of such a high calling. Several New Testament passages inform us about Saul's zealous Pharisaic life before he became Paul, the tireless Christian missionary and pastor (Acts 9; Gal. 1; 1 Tim. 1). By all accounts, Paul's past career had many blemishes. He had not been one of Jesus' disciples. He was not even a member of a Christian church. In fact, he had bitterly opposed the Jewish Christian movement (a fact that perhaps made many radical Jewish Christians unable to forgive him later) and had done all within his power to annihilate it. These are hardly the kinds of credentials to qualify one worthy of a distinctive apostleship to the Gentiles. Nevertheless Saul became the apostle Paul, who emerged as a distinct beneficiary of God's grace, forgiveness, and compassion. Moreover, we are told in Paul's own words that the divine call (*klēsis*), like the spiritual gifts (*charismata*), is irrevocable, once given (Rom. 11:29).

Paul became convinced that once God imparts special favor on an individual, irrespective of that person's presumed or manifest worthlessness by conventional values and standards, the divine call will not be annulled or otherwise taken away by God. That it does not matter how worthy a person may seem to be in relation to a divine call is crucial to understanding what Paul writes to the Galatian church about freedom. Once we understand Paul's utter seriousness about the irrevocable nature of the divine call, we begin to comprehend Paul's passionate argumentation throughout Galatians, and elsewhere. Since the Galatians had previously accepted the divine call to freedom, they could not revoke it. In a sense, Paul sees the Galatian tendency to backslide into old practices (Jewish or pagan) and conventional class attitudes as unworthy of their call to freedom. Yet, Paul seems relentless in reminding the Galatians about their call to freedom as the better way.

The Galatians act as though they do not truly want to be free. After Paul's departure, they quickly fell prey to Judaizers and others, discovering that Paul's freedom was not as desirable or needed as alternatives to that freedom. It was difficult for the Galatians to withstand new external pressures to conform and assimilate old, conventional values. They began desiring the security of a regularized cultic calendar (Gal. 4:10) and the comforts of an existence strictly mediated by the Law. Matters must have seemed easier to cope with, when presented in the uncomplicated guise of being either black or white. The Galatians found that perhaps they were merely simple folks for whom freedom meant too much risk of being different, too much fear of being alienated from (or isolated in) the crowd, or too much courage to discover the creative individuality known only by one who is called to freedom by God and who remains steadfast in that freedom.

Jacques Ellul makes the important observation that freedom is not an inherent need, since most people seem to prefer security, conformity, adaptation, or economy of effort (taking shortcuts irrespective of how much quality is sacrificed).[11] Erich Fromm puts the matter even more forcefully when he notes that human beings have the tendency to submit uncritically to external, often anonymous, power, and that by so doing, people lose power, freedom, reason, morality, and revert to prejudice, superstition, and fear.[12] Even though Fromm writes about the plight of modern men and women, we can apply his description to persons within the ancient Galatian church. Paul issues again the divine call to freedom, but the Galatians are obviously fearful of the personal and social responsibility that comes with this freedom.

Like so many within the Black Church today, the Galatians were experiencing a value crisis, a sense of powerlessness, and a loss of identity. Despite their Christian baptisms, the Galatians still did not know who they were. They had fallen prey to the class presumptions of Jewish Christian missionaries. As a result, they tended to become whatever the new external authority told them they were supposed to be.[13]

The Epistle to the Galatians presents a very modern problem in an ancient historical context. Paul cares so much about the Galatians' welfare that he chooses to start all over again by making his struggle their struggle, by making his response to this call a possible basis for the Galatians to respond again to the call to freedom. The Galatians are showing themselves to be as unworthy as Paul once was; still, Paul the Apostle invites them to reclaim and remain steadfast in the freedom that God would have them know. There seems to be a message in the Epistle to the Galatians that is of singular importance for the Black Church today as it struggles with the problem of class amidst its yearning for freedom that seems so elusive today.

A recent example of adducing the significance of Paul's thought for the Black Church appears in a book by Amos Jones that rejects the views of Black theologians suggesting that Paul seems to support slavery.[14] Jones also repudiates white scholars of the New Testament who restrict Paul's views about freedom to such matters as spirituality, sin, and the Law.[15] Instead, Jones adopts the thesis that Paul was "a rather militant opponent of slavery."[16] He construes the ancient churches of Paul's ministry as elements of an underground movement, a secret religious society patterned after the *collegia,* in which slaves and women were "totally free."[17] By attempting to recast the apostle Paul as a first-century abolitionist and social egalitarian, Jones seems excessive in his efforts to contemporize Paul. Whatever else may be said of Paul, he certainly was shrewd and practical enough not to advance ideas of social revolution, which would not only bring him into disfavor with the Jerusalem church but cause the Roman obliteration of the very churches he worked so hard to establish.

Nevertheless, an aspect of Jones' book is quite helpful: the twofold challenge of freedom that he detects in Paul's writings. On the one hand, he suggests that Paul invites all persons (including women and slaves) to claim the freedom that God makes possible through Jesus Christ. On the other hand, Paul insists that believers maintain vigilantly an allegiance to this freedom. In Jones' view, the Corinthian correspondence emphasizes the claim of freedom, whereas Galatians stresses the corollary, which is to *maintain* one's stance of freedom.[18] Perhaps one could go further and suggest that in the interplay between the claiming and maintaining of freedom, Paul alerts his readers to the social implications of freedom's call. He thereby urges them to avail themselves of opportunities to be free and to free persons in the Church and in the larger society. This would apply to 1 Corinthians 7:21, the Epistle to Philemon, and certainly to Galatians.

THE BACKGROUND AND STRUCTURE OF GALATIANS

The Epistle to the Galatians represents the earliest Christian treatise on freedom, in relation to Old Testament Law, that is presented in terms of a sustained theological argument. Paul was the first evangelist to bring the Christian gospel to the territory of Galatia in the northern part of Asia Minor. Despite the silence of Luke in the Acts of the Apostles regarding the actual founding of the Galatian church, we know that Paul brought the gospel to the Galatians as he passed through Phrygia and Galatia strengthening all the disciples there (Acts 16:6). The Epistle to the Galatians was therefore written at the beginning of Paul's third missionary journey in A.D. 54. Word has come to him that Judaizers have entered the largely Gentile territory of Galatia and are undermining the precepts of Paul's gospel, questioning the legitimacy of his apostleship, persuading the Galatians to adopt Jewish cultic practices (including circumcision), and insisting on strict adherence to the yoke of the Torah, or Jewish Law.

The news of this was most disturbing to Paul. More than once, he had difficulty controlling his temper (Gal. 1:9; 3:1; 5:12). Perhaps nothing hurts as much as hearing about abuses of or blatant attempts to escape from the irrevocable divine call to freedom. Clearly, Paul is hurt, but he is also indignant. His language is occasionally so strong and passionate that some scholars have wondered whether he correctly understood the situation among the Galatians. Did he have accurate reports? Were his opponents in Galatia Judaizers, recent Gentile converts to Jewish Christianity, or gnostic syncretists? Almost certainly, we must answer by pointing to both the formal structure of the epistle and the careful ways Paul presents biblical (Old Testament) texts, interpreting them with considerable skill and care for detail. The reasoning throughout is that of one who goes to great lengths to show that he knows what is at stake in the Galatian church crisis.

Gerd Leudemann calls attention to the consensus among most New Testament scholars that four points characterize Paul's opponents, who are the interlopers in Galatia:

   (a) the opponents' preach a gospel that differs from Paul's (Gal. 1:7);

   (b) the opponents have introduced legal observances that are described more precisely in Gal. 4:10: observation of days, months, and years;

(c) the opponents are promoting circumcision for the Galatians (Gal.
     6:12);
(d) the opponents have attacked Paul's apostleship (Gal. 1:1, 12).[19]

Most probably, Paul's opponents are representatives of the radical Pharisaic wing of Jewish Christianity in Palestine who have entered the territory
of Galatia with a sense of self-importance. They apparently become aghast
at Paul's so-called gospel of freedom, because to them it seemed to dispense
with the Law and traditional Jewish calendar observances. As Leudemann
remarks, "in their opinion, Paul had diverged from this true gospel [one
that included full observation of Law] in an inadmissible way, even though
he had received his gospel from those in Jerusalem."[20]

From the outset of the Epistle, Paul shows himself to be very upset with
the results produced by these opponents. Their arrogance as Jewish
Christian missionaries has led them to present themselves as a higher class
of representative of the Jerusalem church. They discredit Paul's apostleship
and gospel, as well as substitute their gospel, which included Law-
abidingness. This they did without any effort to contact Paul himself to sort
out the matter *before* launching their formal attacks against him in Galatia
during his absence. Notice the strident manner in which Paul speaks about
his opponents. In Galatians 1:9, he says, "If any one is preaching to you a
gospel contrary to that which you received [from me], let him be accursed
[anathema]." In Galatians 3:1, Paul suggests that his opponents have
bewitched the Galatians. Then in Galatians 3:10, he engages in a counter-
attack through Scripture. Paul's midrash of Deuteronomy 27:26 is a firm
redress of his opponents: "For all who rely on works of the law are under
a curse; for it is written, 'Cursed be every one who does not abide by all
things written in the book of law, and do them' " (cf. Gal. 5:3).

In Galatians 5:12, his irony has an acrimonious edge: "I wish those who
unsettle you would mutilate themselves!" Hans Betz may be too casual in
referring to Galatians 5:12 as a " 'bloody' joke that conforms with the
practice of diatribe preachers and that Paul thereby intends to caricaturize
and thus discredit the opponents."[21] Paul's indignant remark in Galatians
5:12 must be aligned with other similar ones which, when taken together, do
not merely indicate that Paul engages in jokes or caricatures. Rather, they
convey the apostle's outrage over the *class presumptions* of his opponents
and the ways in which the Galatians themselves have deferred to this *class
consciousness* that Paul vigorously contests.

The first two chapters of Galatians set forth the elements of the crisis in
the community and provide the historical background for it. C. K. Barrett
finds it helpful to see these initial two chapters as history. He then classifies
Galatians 3–4 as theology, whereas he considers Galatians 5–6 as representing ethics (parenesis).[22] (Such a typology can even help one to grasp the
importance of Galatians in terms of three segments of a theological

curriculum!) In effect, Paul takes the backsliding and class-conscious Galatian congregation back to school.

The history segment of the epistle begins with a vigorous defense of the bona fide nature of Paul's own call to freedom. He simultaneously confronts class distinctions in the larger Church. Whenever he does so, he reinterprets the Old Testament juridical principle that judges are not to be partial to litigants by basing their decisions on the economic status and/or social class of the litigants (Deut. 16:18–20; Lev. 19:15). Even in the Old Testament, it is evident that the stricture against partiality in legal proceedings derives from the idea that such practice does not reflect God's own attribute (2 Chron. 19:7). Nevertheless, when Paul says "God shows no partiality" (Rom. 2:11), he gives the Old Testament principle a new meaning and appears to radicalize that principle as he applies it to God's dealings with the Jews and Gentiles.[23] The new application of the Old Testament principle of impartiality that Paul makes in Romans qualifies everything, despite the simple concession of the historical priority of the Jews in God's redemptive activity (cf. Deut. 14:2). Paul argues against any class superiority of Jews and/or Jewish Christians in Romans. He expresses the same concern even more forcefully in Galatians.

Hans Betz provides a seven-fold outline for the literary structure of Galatians which I modify as follows for non-specialists:[24]

1. Epistolary Prescript (Proem) 1:1–5
2. Introduction 1:6–11
3. Narration of the crisis 1:12–2:14
4. Christological significance of issues at stake 2:15–21
5. Statement of proof/theological exposition 3:1–4:31
6. parenesis (ethical discourse) 5:1–6:10
7. *Peroratio* (Conclusion)

Betz wants to show the possible affinities between the literary form (structure and style) of Galatians and that of formal rhetorical argumentation in Greco-Roman literature. He pursues this aim so vigorously that he does not adduce the possible significance of Galatians 2:6 as more than a parenthetical aside related to earlier ideas in the epistle.[25]

We must remember, however, that Paul's citation of the principle of God's impartiality in Galatians 2:6 is an extension of a concern he raised in Galatians 1:10, 11 ("Am I now seeking the favor of men, or of God? Or am I trying to please men? . . . the gospel which was preached by me is not man's gospel"). Here Paul gives notice that he is not motivated to curry the favor of a higher class of Christian leaders. Rather, Paul only seeks the favor of an impartial God who has made the Christ-event possible and inaugurated in him an extraordinary service for Christ. Whatever else Paul says about his acknowledgment of Jerusalem authorities in Galatians 1:11–2:14 should not obscure this fact. In Galatians, Paul's recognition of "the priority" of Jewish Christian leaders is equivalent to his acknowledging the so-called priority of the Jews in Romans 2:9-11. Consider Galatians 2:6: "And from those who were reputed to be something (what they were makes no difference to me; God shows no partiality)—those, I say, who were of repute added nothing to me."

This suggests that Paul does not recognize any higher class of Christian leader with a more authentic call than his own apostolic office. It is enough for Paul that his own story or self-defense has integrity and that his call was verified sufficiently by James, the brother of Jesus, who had become the chief elder of the Jerusalem church. Indeed, Paul indicates twice that his call had been confirmed by "Cephas," that is, Peter (Gal. 1:18; 2:9). Now Paul confidently shows that both he and his gospel are independent of what other Judaizing opponents or enthusiasts might think about him, his credentials, or the integrity of his ministry. Unlike Peter, Paul will not allow himself to be intimidated by those Jewish Christians who insist that their new converts must be circumcised (Gal. 2:2). Then Paul reminds the Galatians that not even the new convert Titus, a Greek, had been required to be circumcised in Jerusalem (Gal. 2:3, cf. Acts 16:3). Paul demands consistency, but also established himself as a courageous leader who is not easily intimidated by the posturing of "superlative apostles," the Pharisaic Jewish Christians (Acts 15:5). As elsewhere in his writings (1 Cor. 11:1), Paul offers himself as a model of perseverance for his congregation that has allowed itself to be intimidated by the credentials of self-styled "higher" Jewish Christian authorities (Gal. 2:18-21). Paul encourages the Galatians to join him in opposing such oppressive external "authority" by repudiating class distinctions. He wants them to turn back to the new universal story occasioned by the Christ-event. By realigning themselves with this story as originally preached by Paul in Galatia, backsliding members of that congregation can rewrite their story (*see* Gal. 3:28).

The central section of the epistle is Galatians 3:1-4:31. Here Paul documents the view that the Christ-event (death and resurrection) automatically makes possible new levels of freedom. These two chapters take up the ways in which Jesus Christ has set the believer free from works of the Law (3:18), from elemental spirits or superstitious powers (3:19-29), as well as from any form of a slavery covenant (4:21-31).

Galatians 5 begins the ethical discourse of the epistle by presenting the positive content of freedom—not a freedom *from,* but a freedom *for* responsible faith working through love (Gal. 5:6). At the beginning and end of Galatians 5 are single sentences that capture both the indicative and imperative of salvation. In Galatians 5:1, the indicative proposition is "For freedom Christ has set us free," while the imperative sequel is "stand fast" in that freedom. In other words, claim your freedom and persevere in that claim. These propositions are restated more simply in 5:25: "we [in Christ] live by the Spirit" [of freedom], and following this indicative statement is the imperative "let us also walk by the Spirit."

Taken together, Galatians 3-5 constitute what may be referred to as the freedom chapters of the epistle. In a sense, these chapters are foundational for the freedom chapters in the Epistle to the Romans (Romans 5-8) which, with more refinement, expand on the ways that Christ frees the believer from sin, death, and law (Romans 5-7), while freeing the believer for a new life in the Spirit (Romans 8). Of course, the freedom chapters of Galatians are less theoretical and more governed by the actual community crisis that confronted a particular church. For this reason, the divine call to freedom as contained in Galatians is particularly striking, because it stresses the fact that such a call really comes to a people amid the *struggles* of their daily lives. Jürgen Moltmann captures this truth when he makes the observation that "in history freedom came always and only in struggle."[26] We might add that the struggle on the part of the Galatians was complicated by their inability to liberate themselves from a class consciousness that allowed them so quickly to discredit Paul, who was the first evangelist to labor among them.

Paul knows that part of God's own righteousness expresses itself in the fact that God is "no respecter of persons." Paul recognizes that the Jewish Scriptures have long considered this aspect of God as normative for the believing community. There can be no preference to those of high social and economic-class status in Paul's teachings, and he carefully applies the principle in Galatians when dealing with the Jewish Christian leadership in Palestine. It would have been easy for Paul to attack the character of his opponents in the same way they attempted to discredit him—his message and his apostolic credentials. Yet the apostle does not betray his own commitment to the law of love; he does not let himself become un-Christian. His desire is that the Galatians reembrace the joy of Christian freedom and the new life in the Spirit that is the result of such freedom.

THE POLITICS OF CHRISTIAN FREEDOM

The call to freedom that Paul reextends to the Galatians has a political dimension, and although it is made possible by an act of grace, it does have a cost. It appears that the imagery Paul uses in Galatians 5:1 draws on the words of Moses in Exodus 14:13. Consider the following:

And Moses said to the people, "Fear not, stand firm, and see the salvation of the Lord which [God] will work for you today; for the Egyptians whom you see today, you shall never see again" [Exodus 14:13].

For freedom Christ has set us free; stand fast therefore, and do not submit again to a yoke of slavery [Galatians 5:1].

Paul, no less than Moses, would have his congregation liberate themselves from *any* slave covenant. He envisions active resistance to any form of human bondage as part of the cost of freedom. Certainly, Galatians 3:28, "There is neither Jew nor Greek, there is neither slave nor free, there is neither male nor female; for you are all one in Christ Jesus" represents a spiritual ideal within the Church, but it also represents Paul's recommendation that believers avail themselves of opportunities to make this spiritual ideal an everyday social reality in the world. This is part of paying freedom's price; it is essential to the proper exercise of Christian freedom.

Freedom always costs. But, when great religious and social value is to be derived, one should not mind trying to pay freedom's price! In a recent collection of essays dedicated to the memory of the Black American mystic theologian Howard Thurman, Luther E. Smith contributes a chapter entitled "Community: Partnership of Freedom and Responsibility." At one point, Smith asserts that freedom is "experienced, nurtured and preserved through responsible involvement in the community."[27] In this case, the *cost* of freedom is being "response-able" to the needs and hurts of others in the community. The idea is quite congenial with Paul's thoughts in Galatians 5:14, 15: "For the whole law is fulfilled in one word, 'You shall love your neighbor as yourself.' But if you bite and devour one another take heed that you are not consumed by one another."

But how can members of society become truly "response-able" when the white dominant classes subtly restrict the parameters for "equal opportunities" and deny Blacks and others access to economic and political power? In modern societies such as the United States, we find too many instances of "biting and devouring one another" or destroying those on the margins of society. If we hear Paul's message correctly, today there should be clear efforts to empower them with genuine applications of the law of love. C. Eric Lincoln notes the hypocrisy evident in modern multiracial societies in which certain groups are denied the power to be responsible:

> In short, a society in which large numbers of people find life to be solitary, nasty, mean, brutish and short is already in reversion toward a state of nature, however it may be styled. When the power that belongs to the people is by whatever artifice arrogated and manipulated in the preservation and extension of selective interests, what stake have the distressed and the oppressed in the responsible maintenance of that society? They have all of the responsibilities of citizens and none of the power to fulfill those responsibilities.[28]

The danger of abusing freedom (that is, seeing it apart from God's divine call) is that whites, Blacks, Asians, Hispanics, and native Americans turn in mindless patterns of devouring one another or in the kind of self-destruction that expresses itself in an alienating class consciousness. Paul's ancient vision of loving concern for one another is completely lost in all of this (Gal. 6:10).

We may well ask what freedom meant to that Black American slave woman who, on April 9, 1865, witnessed the Confederate flag suddenly being lowered in the surrender of Richmond, Virginia. Vincent Harding presents her sheer ecstasy:

> Run to de kitchen an' shout in de winder:
> > Mammy don't you crow no mo'
> > You's free! You's free!
>
> Run to de henhouse an' shout:
> > Rooster don't you crow no mo'
> > You's free! You's free!
>
> Go to de pig pen an' tell de pig:
> > Ol' pig don't you grunt no mo'
> > You's free!
>
> No no!
> You's free!
> Praising Father God,
> Praising Mother Earth
> Running and loving all their creatures,
> You's free! You's free![29]

Perhaps in the broken speech of this slave two years after the Emancipation Proclamation, we come closest to an understanding of the utter joy and excitement that freedom brings when one, under God, believes that she or he is on its threshold! The restrictions, limits of choice, chains of bondage, and prescribed no's from external authority disappear, and the natural instinct for the believer is to become, like Paul, a messenger to all creation for the divine call to freedom.

Not long ago, James H. Cone wrote that the central message of the Black Church over the years has been *freedom* and hope. He argued that these themes of the Black Church are primarily responsible for the emphasis they received in the life and work of Dr. Martin Luther King, Jr.[30] We may ask: How seriously does the Black Church continue to address its historic quest for freedom? Furthermore, doesn't the call to freedom come with equal force to *all* Christian churches, and shouldn't all churches resist overly spiritualizing the New Testament's call to freedom? If our understanding of the historical context of Galatians is correct, it would seem that Christians everywhere would rekindle a zeal for the unique freedom under God made possible by Christ Jesus. This freedom is an irrevocable call, an inalienable right, enabling all persons to let Christ mediate conventional loyalties to oppressive external authorities. Paul needed to reinvoke "the call to freedom" in strong terms for the Galatians. The turmoil of the Galatian church was in part due to a class conflict they created between Paul and the self-aggrandizing Judaizers. The Galatians were too impressed with the credentials and presumed status of the Jewish Christian missionaries who sought to impose their own perceptions about Law on the infant Gentile Galatian church. In that circumstance, we found that Paul had to clarify the limits of Jewish *cultic* law. In this way, we begin to make life-affirming choices that put us in touch with one another and ourselves as inheritors of the new life in the Spirit.

For many, church attendance has become either a bourgeois force of habit or an exercise in public socialization. In particular, young people who participate in church activities often do so with a quiet resentment. Frequently, this later becomes a church-avoidance syndrome. The perception is that religion—especially certain forms of Christianity—is a sanctimonious enslavement of the human body and spirit rather than a call to freedom. It is not unusual to hear the complaint that the Church is often a system of "don'ts." Regardless of such perceptions and complaints, it is helpful to study the Galatian divine call to freedom *from* a religion of "don'ts" as well as the divine call *to* a constructive program of freedom to care about human needs, hurts, and development. In this epistle, freedom is not a matter of legalisms, but a courageous disavowal of class differentiation, a commitment to voluntary service, and loving concern on behalf of our neighbor's welfare and destiny—irrespective of race, class, or ethnic background.

Ours is an age of too much cynicism and skepticism regarding the human potential for decency and altruism. We live in a world—from Cambodia to India, from South Africa to Brazil, from the United States to the Soviet Union, from Northern Ireland to Lybia, and from Israel to Syria—that is filled with far too much greed, envy, hatred, strife, and war! Unfortunately, many Christians today do not pay enough attention to New Testament mandates for justice, sharing, and acts of loving kindness. This does not, however, mean that these mandates are any less divine. The apostle Paul found himself reminding the Galatians about their divine call to freedom as an antidote to their deteriorating community circumstances. Similarly, this epistle can easily be directed to the Black Church, for it serves as a reminder of the need on the part of Blacks to reclaim the call to freedom. In still another ancient community, Paul had occasion to write his summary commentary on the divine call to freedom. In 2 Corinthians 3:17, he says simply but profoundly, "where the Spirit of the Lord is, there is freedom." As in the past, the Black Church must open herself afresh to God's Spirit in our midst and reclaim what Howard Thurman called "the inner religious experience of God." This way, the Black Church can provide the necessary leadership to help Blacks become a truly free people with the ability to respond to life with courage, discipline, and vision. The Black Church thereby establishes the fruit of the Spirit, not as an externally imposed authority, but as an extension of God's own grace inherent in the divine call to freedom.

The Spirit, however, produces in human life fruits such as these: love, joy, peace, patience, kindness, generosity, fidelity, tolerance, and self-control—and no law exists against any of them.

Those who belong to Christ have crucified their old nature with all that it loved and lusted for. If our lives are centered in the Spirit, let us be guided by the Spirit. Let us not be ambitious for our own reputations, for that only means making one another jealous.

Even if a man should be detected in some sin, my brothers, the spiritual ones among you should quietly set him back on the right path, not with any feeling of superiority but being yourselves on guard against temptation. Carry one another's burdens and so live out the law of Christ [Galatians 5:22–6:6 (PHILLIPS)[31]].

CHAPTER 7

Class and God's Law:
The Epistle of James

It is useful to study Galatians and the Epistle of James in sequence. Like Galatians, James addressed Christians who were experiencing community conflict that had reached crisis proportions. The root cause of this crisis seems to have been the community's adoption of questionable social values derived from the world rather than from God's law or the Jesus tradition. James's response is as strident as Paul's in the Epistle to the Galatians, providing what is perhaps the New Testament's strongest castigation of class discrimination. By inference, James castigates *any* discrimination based on outward appearance; in so doing, he accentuates a principle basic to the social legislation of the Old Testament and important in the teachings of Jesus. Groups that are victimized by the wanton disregard of such precepts will usually take more serious notice of the Bible's teaching on this subject than their oppressors. Such an assertion seems well-founded and illustrated by Black history in America.

From the pages of Black history, we need only excerpt an account of the role of religion in the American Black slave revolts. Gayraud Wilmore's *Black Religion and Black Radicalism* suggests that on December 6, 1831, Governor John Floyd of Virginia blamed the revolt by the slave Nat Turner on more than the Negroes' general reading the Bible. Wilmore reports as follows:

> Governor John Floyd in his message to the Virginia legislature . . . expressed the opinion that the spirit of insubordination and insurrection among slaves had its origin in "Yankee pedlars and traders" who taught that "God *was no respecter of persons* [emphasis mine] — the black man was as good as the white" and "that the white people rebelled against England to obtain freedom, so have blacks a right to do so."[1]

Whether for antebellum slaves or for Blacks in America subsequent to the Civil War, biblical injunctions prohibiting discrimination against persons

118

because of color or social class have been taken very seriously and have exposed the continuing hypocrisy of so-called Christian nations that disregard the Bible's authority on this subject.

Therefore, James's teachings chiding ancient Christians about their class attitudes that cause them to discriminate against the poor have particular pertinence for Blacks who still experience such discrimination daily. No other phenomena in modern history have exerted as great an impact on Blacks globally as European colonialism, Euro-American neocolonialism (economic), the forced servitude of Blacks, and persistent forms of subtle and overt racism. These practices have produced patterns of severe socio-economic injustice and have relegated Blacks in many "Christian" nations to the lower classes.[2] Whether on the basis of race or class, disrespect for groups or individuals has become, in some nations, the rule of law (official and unofficial). Worse still is the fact that, beyond secular, modern-day legal practices, we find evidence of strong biases against Blacks within more than a few churches and synagogues. These biases are frequently the product of fraudulent appeals to Scripture, even though historical or literary features of the Bible bear little or no relation to the ways many so-called devout persons treat Blacks or the poor. In such practice, God's law appears to be filtered through the dictates of sociocultural privilege. James H. Cone offers the following remarks on the subject: ". . . it is unquestionably clear that the dominant representatives of the Christian Tradition, both Protestant and Catholic, have contributed to the political oppression of humanity by defending the economic interests of the rich against the poor."[3]

Tragically enough, many racial and ethnic minority churches have themselves tended to become class-conscious and oppressive in relation to members of their group whom they perceive as socially inferior. In generation after generation, socioeconomic advance has spawned attitudes of superiority toward less well-off neighbors and fellow Christians. This social process is not at all new. What is forgotten today is what many of James's readers also had forgotten: God's law always stands in judgment over abuses of law, whether such discriminatory law is secular or makes a pretense of being sacred.

One of the most important biblical passages that mentions class discrimination within the community is James 2:1-13. The explicit social strictures against acts of class discrmination given in this pericope are directly related to God's law. Although the author of James addresses the issue of discrimination based on socioeconomic class, his teachings may also be applied to discrimination on the basis of color, since James, not unlike the Matthean Jesus (Matt. 23:27, 28), castigates the human tendency to judge people on outward appearances.[4] It is unfortunate that Christians today who wish to accentuate grace to the exclusion of law find themselves avoiding James or otherwise chiding this epistle for its so-called lack of theological depth. An analysis of this passage can show its richness of thought as its two unifying motifs — class discrimination and God's law — are brought to the center.

The legal aspect of the Epistle of James poses difficulties that have caused scholarly debate. This stems as much from possible ambiguities in James's usage of the term "law" (*nomos*) in 1:25, 2:8–12, and 4:11, 12 as from allusions to precepts of Old Testament Law that exist elsewhere in the document.[5] In either case, it is not self-evident what James considers the primary datum for his idea of law. J. H. Ropes, A. T. Cadoux, and O. J. F. Seitz, for example, maintain that the Mosaic moral law stands in the foreground of James's thought.[6] Philip Carrington construes the law in James to be a part of "baptismal torah";[7] whereas Rudolf Obermüller considers the legal element within James to be *"christlicher Halacha."*[8] Martin Dibelius argues that the Mosaic Law is much further in the background, since law for James is "a norm of Christian piety."[9] As our analysis develops, we need to determine which of these views seems most tenable.

James 1:26, 27 serves as a fitting transition from the initial reference to law in 1:19–25 and the amplification of the need for adherence to such law in 2:1–13. Verses 26, 27 contain an antithesis between false and true, that is, "pure and undefiled," religion; we also find the idea of social caring for the traditionally less fortunate in the community as the first obligation of true religion. Verses 26, 27 follow James's initial reference to law in 1:25. Thus James sees a close relationship between precepts of Old Testament Law and the gospel. He then amplifies this relationship, especially in 2:1–13.

The discourse on acts of class discrimination provides a basis for considering James 2:1–13 as a unit. He introduces the idea of class discrimination (*prosōpolēmpsia*), that is, "disrespect for persons," literally "receiving the face" (Hebrew: *nas'a pānîm*) in 2:1 and returns to "discrimination" by mentioning *prosōpolēmteo* ("show discrimination") in 2:9. The word "discriminate" *(diakrinō)* in 2:4 adds to the internal unity of these verses. While James 2:1–13 constitutes a unified body of thought,[10] this pericope appears to be arranged into two large subdivisions: verses 1–7 and 8–13, each amenable to further subdivision. The first unit considers acts of social class discrimination among those who profess Christian faith. The second unit continues to discuss discrimination, but now in direct relation to *nomos*. Our analysis begins with the first unit and its further subdivision: verse 1, the general admonition; verses 2–4, a pertinent but hypothetical example; verses 5–7, the treatment of the poor. In the detailed analysis that follows, I shall use my own translation from the Greek text rather than that of the revised standard version.

ANALYSIS AND DISCUSSION — JAMES 2:1–7

James 2:1 mentions Christian faith with a particular view toward acts of discrimination: "Do not hold the faith of our Lord Jesus Christ, the Lord of glory, in acts of discrimination." The phrase *"in* acts of partiality" has the comprehensive sense of "in/through *any* act of discrimination," as Sophie Laws argues.[11] In this verse, James does not say what constitutes acts of discrimination. He only introduces the general subject that he will later amplify.

James 2:2–4 contains both a formal example of acts of discrimination (vv. 2, 3) and the lesson drawn from it (v. 4). The example may not represent an existing historical circumstance among his readers. It is probably a generalization based on a report or his own experience.[12] The scene illustrates both an instance of deference toward a person based on his outward appearance and an instance of discrimination against a person whose outward appearance suggests he is of wretched circumstances. Dibelius observes that here: "James simply wants to use an example in support of his argument and for this purpose, he selects not a petty but rather a flagrant demonstration of discrimination; moreover, in 2:3 he depicts this example in quite unrealistic terms."[13] On the contrary, the discriminatory practice in the instructions to the poor man and the wealthy person are neither petty nor "implausible as an actual exchange," as Dibelius suggests.[14]

The example presents a situation where a man described as having a gold ring on his finger and lavish clothing enters the assembly (*synagogē*) and receives one set of seating instructions. A poor man (*ptōchos*) enters to receive a demeaning set of instructions. The apparent criterion for these instructions is the outward appearance of the respective individuals. When James completes the formal example in verses 2, 3, he immediately offers his own interpretation of the scene. In verse 4, he asks, "have you not made distinctions among yourselves, and become judges with evil motives?" James intends a relationship between *prosōpolēmpsia* in 2:1 and the ideas of 2:4. James's concerns in 2:4 are not merely with attitudes, as Franz Mussner postulates.[15] To suggest that only attitudes are involved is misleading, drawing attention away from the actual acts of discrimination that James sets forth in his example.

The strongest indication that a scriptural legal precept on discrimination in judgment influences James 2:2–4 appears in the wording of 2:4b. In her study of v. 4b, Sophie Laws argues that James shows an indebtedness to Leviticus 19:15 and that *kritai dialogismōn ponērōn* should be translated as "judges who give corrupt decision."[16] But it is unlikely that James was thinking exclusively of any one Old Testament injunction against discrimination. Rather, 2:4b reflects a general familiarity with the standing of impartiality in the Jewish legal tradition, as opposed to any specific biblical text.

This position finds support in the two examples of discrimination. The assembly not only defers to the lavishly dressed person (cf. Lev. 19:15c; Job 34:19; Sir. 4:27b; 7:6), but it also discriminates against the poor man (cf. Mal. 2:9b; Sir. 42:1b). In comparing Old Testament injunctions on discrimination and the poor, we find an anomaly. Leviticus 19:15b (cf. Sir.

35:13) mentions the poor (*ptōkos*) in relation to discrimination, but the injunction is *against* preferential treatment that would *favor* the poor man ("do not receive the face of the poor man"). James deals with the opposite issue in 2:2, 3: discrimination against the poor man. If James has considered Leviticus 19:15b, he evidently changed and enlarged this biblical text. Irrespective of James's use of any specific Old Testament passage, it is clear that he considers acts of discrimination to be violations of Law, matters of sin, and instances of injustice.

James 2:2, 3 has primarily a parenetic rather than an historical purpose.[17] Despite this, some scholars have taken James's example as a source for reliable historical data. Bo Reicke illustrates this tendency when he suggests that the lavishly clothed individual was a rich non-Christian politician.[18] Similarly, Sophie Laws explores the possibility that this same individual may have been a member of the equestrian order in the Roman aristocracy.[19] Ward adduces parallels between James's example and rabbinic proceedings that he maintains are traceable to "early Tannaitic times."[20] Such conjectures would seem to press James's parenesis too far.

If one could demonstrate that James portrays the two characters of his example as members of the assembly in question, perhaps we would have a clearer sense of their identities or circumstances. Then we could speak more confidently about similarities between them and litigants in a Jewish judicial setting. It is doubtful, however, that verses 2, 3 resolve the membership question, or even that this question figured prominently in James's mind. The text offers only the slightest hints, and these suggest that the two individuals are guests or visitors. In James 2:2 the author says "in your synagogue." If the two were members, wouldn't it be more natural for James to delete the pronoun "your" and simply say "the synagogue"? Again, while it is true that James 2:4a speaks about discriminating "among yourselves" (*en heautois*), the author could merely mean "within the assembly," leaving aside any resolution of the actual status of those who enter the assembly.

Distinctions in seating arrangements within the Jewish synagogue were known to have existed.[21] A possible allusion to the practice of giving preferences is found in Matthew 23:6 (the Pharisees who love "the best seats in the synagogues"), although in James 2:2, 3, we are dealing with a Christian assembly.[22] We cannot be certain about the extent of seating preferences in ancient Christian gatherings. Rather than strain James's example, it is more feasible to examine the implications of James's rhetorical images. By contrasting the apparel and treatment accorded the two characters in verses 2, 3, James dramatizes the fraudulent actions of the assembly. He sees these as violations of biblical injunctions in the Old Testament Law and contrary to the gospel of Jesus Christ.

The absence of the term "rich" (*plousios*) in 2:2, 3 merits consideration. James mentions the gold ring and lavish clothing of one of the characters, but does not call him a rich man. This is odd, when one considers that elsewhere James speaks of the rich (1:10; 2:6; 5:1). We would also expect James to refer to the rich in 2:2, because he describes the other character as a poor man, which is confirmed by his outward appearance ("in shabby clothing"). James portrays the poor man as a victim of discrimination, and in so doing, he shows his concern for the poor man. Furthermore, by not describing the lavishly clad man as rich, James may have something other than a "rich versus poor" theme in mind. He focuses on the fraudulent *criteria* of the assembly's judgments and their acts of discrimination, especially their shabby treatment of the ill-clad man. James thus sketches two acts of discrimination against the background of scriptural injunctions about class discrimination.

The status of the poor comes into view in verses 5, 7. Here James appears to speak directly to the experience of his readers, extending his commentary in verse 4.[23] The example in verses 2, 3 prompts Ward to ask: "How effective would this example be if it were completely unrelated to the experience of the readers?"[24] As the second segment of 2:1-7, verses 5, 7 apply lessons from the example and the commentary in verse 4. The new sequence of thought begins with the reappearance of the formulaic "Listen, my beloved brethren" (v. 5). Then James offers a graphic contrast of God's promise for the poor (v. 5b) and their evident status and treatment among James's readers (v. 6). The author begins with the rhetorical question in 2:5: "Has not God chosen the poor with respect to the world[25] [to be] rich in faith and heirs of the kingdom which he promised to those who love him?" Ward regards this as one of the strongest New Testament statements about the poor, comparing favorably with Lukan and Qumran attitudes (4QpPs 37).[26] Sophie Laws thinks that James depicts the poor as "the natural members of the community."[27] These assessments also may indicate the multiple elements within and the extensive biblical background for James 2:5.

The election of the poor is first to be understood within the framework of the Old Testament tradition. The Old Testament attitudes about the poor do not represent a monolithic perspective. At times the Old Testament conveys sympathy for the poor; at other times, it presents the poor as blameworthy for their condition. Provisions for improving the lot of the poor are in the Mosaic Law (Exod. 23:6, 11; Lev. 19:9, 10; Deut. 15:7-11). At no point in the Pentateuch, however, are the poor depicted as *the elect* who are heirs to the Kingdom of God. Scholars have shown that the idea of the poor as God's elect enters the literature of early Judaism through different streams of thought.[28] A special concern for the poor as victims of society is found in the pre-exilic prophets (Isa. 29:19; Amos 2:7; 4:1). This concern about the social status of the poor is then translated into the religious concept of the "pious poor" ('*ānawîm*) who represent the people of fallen Israel in captivity (Isa. 58:7; 61:1) as well as the suffering righteous within Israel. It is the suffering righteous who, in raising the issue of theodicy, see God as the deliverer of the poor (Septuagint [LXX]: Ps. 9:19;

71:4; 81:4; 85:1, 2).[29] In the discursive wisdom literature of the Old Testament, both the traditional social obligations to the poor and the view that God is the ultimate vindicator of the poor receive attention (Sir. 4:11; 7:32, 35:17).

To the extent that the Old Testament details certain rights of and obligations to the poor within the legal community, James 2:5 owes some debt to this aspect of the biblical tradition. Even traces of the religious nuance that attaches itself to the idea of the collective "pious poor" (*'ānawîm*) in the Old Testament bears on the faithful poor concept found in verse 5. Nonetheless, the Old Testament itself does not refer to "the poor with respect to the world" as the distinctive heirs of the Kingdom of God. Among the Jewish apocalyptic writers, the author of Jubilees affirms the election of Israel without reference to poor (Jub. 15:30). On the other hand, the author of 1 Enoch mentions "the elect of the world" as a parallel idea with "the righteous" (1 Enoch 93:1, 2). Since 1 Enoch expresses the view that oppression, blasphemy, and riches stand opposed to righteousness, there is a possible basis for adducing similarities between this view and those found in James 2:5-7.[30]

The distinctiveness of James's commentary on the poor must be evaluated in terms of New Testament references to the poor. In turning to other New Testament literature, we find terminology for the special status of the poor that resembles James. In the Beatitudes of Matthew and Luke, the poor (*ptōchoi*) are blessed as those who inherit the Kingdom of God (cf. Matt. 5:3; Luke 6:20). Matthew 5:3 refers to the poor with respect to their spiritual status in terms reminiscent of the traditional *'ānawîm* (the collective pious poor of the Babylonian captivity). James 2:5b, however, uses the dative of respect differently. Here the expression *to kosmō* ("with respect to the world") specifically means socioeconomic poverty. Luke 6:20 refers to *hoi ptōchoi* ("the poor ones") without qualifications, but some suspect that the biblical *'ānawîm* motif still governs.[31] According to Sophie Laws, James 2:5b represents a middle position between Matthew and Luke on the status of the poor: "There is a promise for the poor, but inasmuch as their poverty is accompanied by faith and the love of God, and as they are chosen in order that it should be so."[32] The affinities that Matthew 5:3 and Luke 6:20 have with James 2:5b tend to affirm the *Christian* character of James's divine election of the poor. James 2:5b implies that because of God's choice and promise for the poor, they are worthy of honorable treatment within the Christian community.

The warrant for this inference appears in 2:6a: "But you yourselves dishonored the poor man." The Greek word *hymeis* ("yourselves") gives an intensive force, heightening the possibility that James was thinking of some experience among his own readers that was an act of dishonoring the poor. Ropes argues that James indicts those Christians who cater to the rich.[33] Another possibility is that verse 6a returns to the charge "have you not discriminated among yourselves" that James leveled in verse 4. James does not mention the rich as a group in 2:1-6a, but he does refer to "the poor man" in verses 2,3; to "the poor" as an elect group in verse 5b; and to "the poor man" again in verse 6a. In these references, the rich are those who discriminate against the poor on the basis of class. His attitude in verse 6a is summed up nicely by Irénée Fransen: "James strives to show that the social divisions and especially the contempt concerning the poor threaten communal unity and the unity of Christian faith."[34]

The explicit mentioning of the rich in verses 6, 7 seems to heighten the paradox of any Christian deference to them: "Do not the rich oppress you and drag you into courts?" The verb *katadynasteuō* ("oppress") in verse 6b only appears once more in the New Testament. In Acts 10:38, it is used in connection with the devil ("Those who are oppressed by the devil"). In the Septuagint [LXX], however, *katadynasteuō* occurs more than twenty-five times. There, too, its meaning is to oppress in the socioeconomic sense (Deut. 24:7; Amos 4:1; 8:4; Jer. 7:6; Zech. 7:10; Ezek. 18:7, 12, 16; Mal. 3:5; Wisd. of Sol. 2:10).[35] James illustrates this by juxtaposing to *katadynasteuō* the idea of persecuting lawsuits in verse 6b. Furthermore, the rhetorical question in verse 7 contains a reference to blaspheming, which suggests the oppressive actions of the rich are tantamount to blasphemy (*see* 1 Tim. 6:1; Rom. 2:24; 2 Clem. 13:2-4), not just their formal pronouncements (Mark 3:28-30; Matt. 12:32).[36]

Another indictment of James's readers seems to be an important feature of verses 6b, 7. The author recites the questionable practice of the rich, but he places emphasis on the series of personal pronouns initiated in verse 6a and continued through verse 7: *hymeis* ("yourselves"), *hymōn* ("your"), *hymas* ("you"). This series of pronouns may well indicate that James is addressing actual experiences of his readers. The rhetorical questions in verses 6-7 do not specify any deference shown to the rich, unless somehow the example in verses 2, 3 is still in view. Since that example is probably hypothetical, James would have had in mind similar instances of deference toward the rich in verses 6, 7. *These verses expose the underlying paradox that Christians show deference to the rich. At the same time, it is precisely the oppressions by the rich that prove them not worthy of honor.* Thus, James 2:5-7 involves an antithesis between the poor, who are shown to be worthy of honor but are victims of class discrimination, and the rich, whose own actions disqualify them for honor but who are nevertheless beneficiaries of deferential treatment by Christians. This peculiar and paradoxical situation has become a familiar pattern in the life of the Black Church over the years.

ANALYSIS AND DISCUSSION—JAMES 2:8-13

Despite allusions to Old Testament ideas in 2:1-7, the word *law* is absent from the first half of the pericope. The matter strikingly changes when we examine verses 8-13 and encounter the term more frequently than in any other section of James. For this reason, it is not surprising that Seitz

believes the most important passage in James to be 2:8–14.[37] I do not agree
with Seitz, however, when he maintains that the preceding context is "quite
unrelated" to the idea that James now introduces as the unity of the Law.[38]
Sophie Laws, who divides the pericope into verses 1–9 and 10–13, entitles
her first unit "The Sin of Discrimination" and her second unit "The Whole
Law."[39] In my view, the entire pericope is an exposition on matters of law,
namely, *class discrimination*. First, James appears to treat this subject in
terms of Christian faith and community social behavior (vv. 1–7), then he
relates it to law and shows the eschatological consequence.

The formula for scriptural quotations, *kata tēn graphēn* ("according to
Scripture") in James 2:8 demonstrates explicitly that James acknowledges
an Old Testament legal precept. Verse 8 reads: "If you really fulfil the royal
law, according to the scripture, 'You shall love your neighbor as yourself,'
you do well." The particle *mentoi* ("really"), in Dibelius' judgment, assures
us that James mentions Leviticus 19:18c as a result of the content in verses
6, 7.[40] Dibelius thinks mainly about the readers' "favoritism" toward the
rich in verse 6, 7, but we must not discount James's particular concern for
the poor (vv. 2–6a). The particle *mentoi* in verse 8 heightens the irony that
James sees in his readers' behavior, for verse 6a shows that his readers
obviously do not conform to the love commandment.

The scriptural formula, as well as the wording of the Old Testament
precept in verse 8, indicate that James quotes Leviticus 19:18c, the only
mentioning in the Septuagint [LXX] of what Christians began to call the
love commandment. Still, James's usage of the quotation is somewhat
ambiguous. Sanders, for example, contends that James refers to the love
commandment because he knows "that it belonged to the bedrock of
Christian tradition."[41] Dibelius thinks that here James shows indebtedness
to a Jewish parenesis that dealt with partiality in the context of its treatment
of the commandment of love on the basis of Leviticus 19. Part of the
difficulty in taking James's citation of the love commandment as a direct
Old Testament quotation results from his description of this commandment
as "the royal law," which seems to attach a pre-eminence to the commandment beyond its status in Leviticus 19.

The expression *nomos basilikos* ("royal law"), though lacking in the Old
Testament, exists in such divergent ancient literature as a poem by
Pseudo-Phocylides that draws on Leviticus 19 and the writings of Plato,
Pindar, and the Stoics.[42] Adolph Deissmann reports that the expression—
also found in a Pergamum inscription that probably predates the Christian
era—refers to the law of a Pergamum king. Deissmann believes that James
likewise uses the expression to mean the law of a king.[43] For Dibelius, the
"royal law" in James 2:8 means " 'the law with authority' as well as 'the law
which is set for kings'," but not the love commandment of Jesus.[44] In my
view, Sophie Laws adopts the most balanced approach:

It is reasonable to suppose that the prominence of a command to love
in many of the New Testament documents is due to its prominence in

the teaching of Jesus, even when this is not explicitly acknowledged. If so, it is probable that when James quotes Lev. XIX.18 as "scripture" he does so in the knowledge that this scripture has received the added authority of Jesus' use . . . Lev. XIX.18 is for James the "royal law" because it is the law of the kingdom of God. . . .[45]

This position has value because it offers an explanation for the differences between the pre-eminent status of the love commandment in the Jesus tradition and the modifications found in James's exposition on the law in verses that follow 2:8.[46] In 2:9, James applies the law of neighborly love to the specific issue of discrimination: "but if you show discrimination, you bring about sin and are counted by the law as transgressors." At first glance, verse 9 has features that suggest an Old Testament quotation. There are thought parallels between verse 9 and Exodus 22:24, with affinities in later rabbinic texts.[47] Both Leviticus 19:15 and Sirach 42:1b deal with discrimination. The latter passage even classifies it as a sin. The Old Testament does provide a general basis for James's concern about discrimination and, given this, verse 9 may be an allusion to the Old Testament idea. Yet, the range of James's indictments regarding discrimination precludes construing verse 9 as a direct Old Testament quotation.

James does equate discrimination, sin, and a transgressor (v. 9) in a manner compatible with some Old Testament legal provisions that deal with discrimination. But James's concern for the poor [who are not to be discriminated against (v. 4), who are God's elect (v. 5), and who are worthy of honor (v. 6a)] appears to go beyond Old Testament injunctions for impartiality in the Old Testament legal community. In verse 8, James reveals the Christian "Kingdom" that is, the "royal kingdom" (*basilikos*) as the context for the scriptural (*kata tēn graphēn*) provenance of the love commandment. Then, in verse 9, he applies that commandment directly to discrimination for the purpose of calling attention to improving the treatment of the poor (vv. 4–6a; vv. 14–17). He associates the love commandment with an injunction against partiality in verses 8, 9 in a unique fashion within the Old Testament and New Testament. Indeed, he accomplishes this by utilizing the motif of law.

The next two verses offer a midrash on the second table of the Decalogue:

For whoever keeps the whole law, but stumbles in one [commandment], has sinned against all [the commandments] [James 2:10].

For he who said, do not commit adultery also do not murder, and if you do not commit adultery but you commit murder, you have become a transgressor of law [James 2:11].

The resemblances between verse 10 and the Rabbinic law of solidarity ("But if a man does all things, but omits one, he is guilty of all") are persuasive for Kelly, who considers James to be primarily Jewish.[48] Because it is doubtful that James's expression "the whole law" (*holos ho nomos*) refers to the entire 613 prohibitions the rabbis counted in the Law, caution is advisable when adducing rabbinic parallels for James 2:10. We must remember that Paul also mentions "the whole law" (Gal. 5:3, 14), and he seems to think comprehensively about the Law in other contexts, as well. For example, in his exposition on circumcision and the Law in Romans 3:25-29, it is clear that Paul sees the Law as a unity, even though he does not mention the expression "the whole law." Even when he does mention "the whole law" in Galatians 5:3, as Hans Betz notes, he may be reminding recent converts to Judaism "what they are getting themselves into," that is, the awesome task of attempting to conform to the full complement of Torah regulations.[49] More important is Betz's view that "the whole law" in Galatians 5:14 indicates that Paul thinks of "a principle which sums up and contains the whole Torah."[50] Such observations help us to see that the meaning of *law* in Paul's thought often varies with its context.

The expression "the whole law" is not in Romans 13:8-10, but there are other similarities with James 2:8-11. Paul and James both mention the thought of love for the neighbor (an allusion in Rom. 13:8; a scriptural citation in James 2:8) and then call attention to the second table of the Decalogue. Käsemann suggests that Paul is speaking in a global fashion, "referring only to the ethical portions of the Torah."[51] I believe that Käsemann is correct, for we see that Paul can refer to "fulfilling the Law" without necessarily meaning the whole Torah. Moreover, the second table of the Decalogue and the love commandment provide a basis of law for Christians.[52] It should prove instructive to examine further the word *law* in James 2:9-12.

The word *law* occurs five times in James 2:8-12: royal law (v. 8), counted by law as a transgressor (v. 9), the whole law (v. 10), transgressor of law (v. 11), and the law of freedom (v. 12). Each instance involves Old Testament moral law. James cites Leviticus 19:18c as the chief commandment, as elsewhere in the New Testament.[53] As such, he calls it the "royal law," but this royal law is not a summary of the Torah in general or of the second table of the Decalogue (Gal. 5:14; Rom. 13:9).[54] *The royal law is a symbol of unity that coheres in God's moral law. For James, class discrimination breaks the essential unity of this law.* It is as if James thinks of the "rabbinic solidarity of Law," but now within a Christian framework.[55] Notice the clause in 2:10b: "but stumbles in one [commandment] has sinned against all." Clearly James envisions a fundamental unity of the law, not just isolated commandments. In fact, the explicit reference to the second table of the Decalogue in verse 11 leads me to think that *law* certainly includes the Old Testament moral law. In verse 11, two commandments from the Decalogue receive attention as legal entities within an interrelated whole. The verse mentions "do not commit adultery" and "do not commit murder." (cf. LXX Exod. 20:13-15; Deut. 5:17-19; 20:13-15; Deut. 5:17-19).

Various lists of the Decalogue exist in early Christian literature, as well. Frequently, modifications are made on the Old Testament lists. For example, Matthew 19:18 mentions four commandments from the second table of the Decalogue (murder, adultery, theft, false witness), and Matthew 19:19 joins the fifth commandment of the Decalogue (honoring parents) with Leviticus 19:18c in a series of other Old Testament commandments. The closest wording, grammar, and sequence to James 2:11 is Luke 18:20, as the following list shows:

James 2:11	"do not commit adultery"	"do not murder"
Luke 18:20	"do not commit adultery"	"do not murder"
Mark 10:19	"do not murder"	"do not commit adultery"
Matt. 19:18	"do not murder"	"do not commit adultery"
Rom. 13:9	"do not commit adultery"	"do not murder"
Did. 2:2	"do not commit adultery"	"do not murder"

It is possible that James relies on a version of the Septuagint [LXX] in which the commandment on adultery precedes the one on murder.[56] Another possibility is that Luke and James show a dependence on a common parenesis that dealt with the Decalogue. In this case, the important factor would be the identical phraseology of the commandments in James 2:11 and Luke 18:20, not necessarily the sequence of the commandments. Worthy of further study is the fact that the commandment on adultery occurs before the one on murder in the Old Testament, James 2:11, Luke 18:20, and Romans 13:9.

O. J. F. Seitz points out that Romans 13 and Matthew 19 cite the Decalogue more fully than James.[57] In Seitz's view, Leviticus 19:18c has a "climactic prominence" in Matthew 19:16–22.[58] This claim is open to question. The fact that Matthew mentions the love commandment at the end of a list of Old Testament moral precepts does not attribute a "climactic prominence" to the last element in such a listing, unless the prominence that Matthew attaches to the love commandment in Matthew 22:39 is read back into Matthew 19:19b. Our alternative to Seitz's assessment of Matthew 19:18, 19 is to recognize that Matthew 19:19b mentions Leviticus 19:18c as one among several Old Testament commandments that some Christians regarded as Old Testament moral law. The tendency to juxtapose the love commandment with precepts found in the Decalogue appears in 2 Clement 4:3: "So brethren, let us confess him in our deeds, by loving one another, by not committing adultery, nor speaking against one another, nor being jealous. . . ."[59] Although 2 Clement 4:33 generalizes on the love commandment and ideas that roughly conform to the second table of the Decalogue, it shows that, *well into the second century, Christians prescribed precepts based on Old Testament moral law, because such precepts had been affirmed in the Jesus tradition. It is our contention that James 2:11 also displays this tendency, as it insists on the unity of moral law.*

Having argued for the unity of "the law" in verses 10, 11, James 2:12 returns to the initial characterization of *nomos* (1:25) by referring to it as "the law of freedom." Dan O. Via finds a conflict in James's theological vocabulary. He suggests that on the one hand, James speaks about "freedom," but on the other, he mentions a "system of commands (2:10, 11)."[60] The supposed confusion of ideas in 2:10–12 is difficult to substantiate. Freedom always implies certain obligations. James, no less than Paul, acknowledged faith as resulting in responsible action to enhance community life (*see* James 2:14–17). Accordingly, "the perfect law of freedom" inevitably means accountability for the welfare of others and accountability before God: "So speak and thus do as persons about to be judged by means of[61] the [law] of freedom." The verbs "speak" (*laleō*) and "do/act" (*poieō*) are partially analogous to the "doer" (*poiētēs*) and "hearer" (*akroatēs*) imagery central in James 1:22–25.[62] In James 1:22–25, the progression of the words *doers, doer, doer,* and *doing* underscores the concern for Christian action beyond mere hearing, rhetoric of verbal confessions of God's Word. The Greek term *poiēsis* ("doing") found in 1:25a occurs only here in the New Testament. This same emphasis is in 2:12, for verse 12 begins by calling attention to the *unity* or consistency that should exist in word and deed. Like God's moral law itself, the community, in James's perspective, should represent the unity of word and deed, and as such, would disavow any class discrimination.

"The law of freedom" (v. 12), seems to be both the basis for determining sin and transgression and the criterion for determining one's status in the coming judgment. Some scholars would not make this claim, however. Via discerns traces of a thematic pattern of development on the "law of freedom" in James, but finds a certain awkwardness:

Since the idea of the law of freedom occurs in three different discourses (1:25, 2:12, 4:11–12), we may conclude that James is consciously trying to develop this concept. He wants to maintain that Christian faith calls for an attitude of love and for concrete deeds, and he also wants to break through legalism. But he does not do the latter consistently or successfully.[63]

If our argument is correct that by *law* James means the Old Testament moral law as mediated in the Jesus tradition, then we must qualify Via's remarks about James's inability to break through "legalisms" consistently. James's primary aim is to expose the hypocrisy of his readers who call themselves Christian but violate legal traditions that even the Jewish tradition affirmed as principles of accountability. There is a profound difference between "legalism" (rigid adherence to religious regulations of the cultus to gain merit and guarantees) and moral obligations by which persons of faith are held accountable to God's law and purposes for humanity. James concerns himself with the latter, not the former. *Christian faith, no less than God's moral law, for James, necessarily involves criteria for Christian social behavior.*

This is why the progression of James's teachings on class discrimination in verses 8–11 associates law with sin and transgression. In verse 12, James solicits from his readers a unity between word and deed (apparently conforming to the unified *nomos*). The remainder of verse 12 reintroduces the expression "the law of freedom," but there is no evidence that James thereby introduces a new legal idea. On the contrary, we have shown that the use of *nomos* in 1:25 differs from that in verses 8–11 only in the sense that the latter verses provide a rationale for observing law. Verse 12 continues this rationale, but *nomos* in verse 12 refers to the same moral law. The new aspect in verse 12 is the assertion that *nomos* also pertains to "the coming judgment" (*mellontes krinesthai*).

The pericope concludes with verse 13, containing elements that do not make the relationship between this verse and the rest of the pericope immediately self-evident. Between verse 13 and verses 1–12, Dibelius, for example, detects "no material connection" beyond the catchwords *krinesthai* ("to be judged") . . . *krisis* in verses 12, 13.[64] I propose that we modify Dibelius's position, in order to resolve some of the problems of verse 13. In my view, verse 13 bears equally upon the issue of discrimination (vv. 1, 9) and the eschatological aspect of *nomos* observance (v. 12). James 2:13 contains two grammatically separate clauses: "For the judgment is without mercy for the one who does not perform mercy; mercy boasts over judgment."

Several factors indicate that the idea of judgment in verse 13a is a reference to God's final judgment, rather than "justice" in the sense of Matthew 12:18 (cf. Isa. 42:1), 23:23; Luke 11:42; John 7:24; or of "the court" (Matt. 5:21, 22).[65] The relationship between "about to be judged" (v. 12) and "judgment" (v. 13) increase the likelihood that James refers to God's final judgment. Furthermore, the wording in James resembles that found in noncanonical Christian texts of the second century, which suggests that we have more present than a mere "catchword association." The Greek term *hē krisis* occurs as an explicit reference to "the coming judgment" (*hē krisis mellousa*) in both 2 Clement 18:2 and Martyrdom of Polycarp 11:2 (cf. Hermas Vision 3, 5, 9). In comparison to biblical ideas about the day of judgment (Isa. 34:8, Ps. 1:5, cf. 1 Enoch 10:6, 63:8), these Christian texts seem to offer the closest parallels for the wording and thought of James 2:12, 13.

Another factor in assessing the meaning of *hē krisis* in verse 13 is James's understanding of God's eschatological role in other passages in the epistle. Both Ropes and Dibelius agree that when James mentions "the one lawgiver and judge" in 4:12a, he refers to God.[66] Because James does consider God to be the authoritative judge, we have an imminent eschatological metaphor in James 5:9c ("the judge stands at the door") with God as the central figure in the final judgment. The idea would thus differ from such texts as Barnabas 4:12 or Matthew 16:27, wherein "the Lord (Jesus)" or "Son of Man" appears respectively to be the agent of final judgment. When considered in this light, *hē krisis* (2:13) serves well as a reference to God's final judgment. It is the specter of that judgment that James poses as an apparent motive for persons to honor the less fortunate and otherwise perform acts of mercy. The content of verse 13a is a principle on the reciprocity of mercy: God's mercy in the coming judgment will be shown on the basis of demonstrated acts of mercy that Christians have shown. The principle is a derivative of the Jewish idea illustrated in the Septuagint by Psalms 61:13: "Mercy belongs to you, O Lord, for you will pay back to each according to his deeds" (cf. Sir. 35:22; Tob. 4:10). Similarities exist within the Jesus tradition (Matt. 5:7; 6:12, 14; 16:27; 18:23–35; Luke 14:14) and in such texts as Barnabus 4:2 and 2 Clement 10:6. James seems to employ the principle of reciprocity in terms of a threat of ultimate accountability, in order to underscore the significance of showing mercy and disavowing class discrimination.

The Greek expression *poiein eleos* ("show mercy"), the equivalent of the Hebrew *lĕ 'ăśot ḥeṣed,* means to perform acts of mercy and loving kindness. It is for this reason that I translate *mē poiēsanti eleos* in verse 13a as "who does not show mercy."[67] Just as James 1:19–27 closes with a stress on doing, the last part of 2:1–13 has a similar emphasis.[68] Whereas 1:27 calls attention to the plight of orphans and widows, the idea of showing mercy in 2:13a appears to relate directly to James's admonitions in 2:1–12, including not "lifting the face against the poor" (discriminating against persons of low social class), dishonoring them (and the implied corollary of improving the treatment of the poor [2:4–6a]), along with other precepts within the moral law (2:8–12). The finale to all of this is James's conclusion in 2:13a that infractions of God's law involving class discrimination have eschatological consequences.

James 2:13b complements rather than contradicts the principle of the reciprocity of mercy as stated in verse 13a. The use of the Greek verb *katakauchaomai* ("boast over") is rare in the Septuagint ([LXX] Zech. 10:12; Jer. 27:12, 38). In the New Testament outside of James, it only occurs in Romans 11:18 (*see* James 3:14; cf. 4:16).[69] Used in relation to the Greek word *eleos* ("mercy"), the term is puzzling, since James's subject "mercy" involves figurative speech that has various interpretations. There are at least two possible meanings of *eleos*. If the term describes human conduct, the phrase *eleos katakauchatai kriseōs* may mean that acts of mercy "boast over" (are better than) judgment, whether *kriseōs* is understood as judgment in the congregation (2:4) or judgment of one's neighbor (2:8; 4:12b). This interpretation has the advantage of continuing in verse 13b the emphasis on "doing" that we indentified in verse 13a, but it has the disadvantage of eliminating the eschatological motif in verses 12, 13a.

Sophie Laws offers another possibility. She thinks that the saying means that showing mercy enables one to "stand with confidence" before judgment.[70]

The interpretation by Sophie Laws retains both the emphasis on doing and the idea of eschatological judgment that we have detected in verse 13a, but against her interpretation is the fact that *eleos* refers to God's mercy — not the merciful deeds of Christians. Dibelius asserts that the correct sense of verse 13b "has already been captured by the Scholion: 'For mercy rescues from punishment those who in purity practice mercy, since at the time of judgment it stands by the royal throne'."[71] Dibelius' judgment seems to make verse 13b redundant, for James already states in verse 13a the principle of the eschatological reciprocity of mercy. Yet, a case can be made that *eleos* in verse 13b involves God's mercy as its subject.

James 2:13a accentuated "doing" merciful deeds and continues from verse 12 the eschatological significance from Christian demonstrations of mercy, but in verse 13b, God's mercy becomes the new subject. The final saying of the pericope provides, as the corollary for verse 13a, the notion that mercy is ultimately descriptive of God. In this case, verse 13b introduces another motive for "doing" beyond that of the moral law. It is the idea that perhaps gives substance to the moral law in the first place, namely, an implicit *imitatio Dei*. Even eschatological reciprocity becomes subject to God's mercy (cf. 5:11).

James 2:13a presents the idea of reciprocity in terms of a standard of fairness, along with Old Testament lines of retributive or reciprocal justice, whereas verse 13b relieves such traditional Jewish standards by indicating that ultimately the issue is working of the "righteousness of God"; mercy becomes a paradigm, because as with righteousness, it, in James' view, describes God's nature.[72] Thus James concludes the pericope in a manner similar to the development of the legal motif in the preceding pericope (James 1:19b, 20). He indicates that anterior to law is "doing" motivated by an *imitatio Dei* (righteousness and mercy), and so offers paradigms for Christians to stand against class (or color) discrimination. For the author of the Epistle of James, such class discrimination is irreconcilable with claims that one holds faith in Jesus Christ and repudiates the perfect law of freedom.

The Epistle of James offers each generation of the Christian Church a sobering message, especially since the Western Church has such a long history of differentiating social classes and arraying clergy and the laity in hierarchies. In modern times, the Black Church has often imitated the behavior of those whom James passionately seeks to correct. Having in recent centuries held second-class membership in churches of the dominant culture, some Black Church traditions have fallen prey to social stratification of the worst sort. It was not so long ago that the Black Church routinely honored the poor and disenfranchised through benevolent societies and outreach programs lacking in the larger society. In recent years, this historic sense of mission has been less evident. Surely, the retrenchment and "benign neglect" domestic social policies of the government and private sources reflect a refusal by whites to abandon their racism or to share economic and political power more equitably. But, irrespective of the continuing insensitivities of whites, the Black Church must do more than imitate the values and alienating discriminatory practices of the larger society. Like those in James 2:6 who were dragged to courts and oppressed by the rich, many Blacks today tragically still imitate and defer to their white oppressors. Yet, James, much like the author of Luke–Acts, Paul, and the author of the Revelation, shares an ancient vision of the Church as a socially concerned paradigmatic "family." One can only be troubled today when comparing this vision and social ideal with the socioeconomic realities that make such a New Testament vision and social ideal still so elusive.

Part 3

FAMILY

Introduction

The third and final part of this book consists of three chapters collected under the rubric of family. Our concern, however, extends beyond the conventional understanding of family as a distinct association of blood relatives. Throughout these essays, *family* constitutes a biblical metaphor of kinship patterns and obligations that characterize the Household of God in general and the specific mission and outreach of the Black Church. Existing literature on the Bible in relation to women, the family, or the very survivability of the human family pays insufficient attention to the significance of these important topics for the Black Church. Each chapter in this section represents an effort to correct this imbalance, for Blacks have to wrestle with these topics to shape a coherent future that includes more than suffering and struggle.

Chapter eight is an appeal to the Black Church to redouble her efforts in affirming and enhancing the roles and rights of Black women as leaders with full biblical warrant within the family called the Church. The patriarchal conservative tradition so evident over the centuries must give way to leadership patterns that are gender inclusive and thus more representative of the progressive movement within the Bible generally, but especially within the New Testament. Too often being a Black woman with ministerial aspirations has meant a triple-jeopardy experience, for racism, white feminism, and male chauvinism have all resisted efforts by Black women to be accepted fully as ordained ministers with the Household of God. For this reason, we identify throughout the Bible personalities, images, and themes that affirm the distinctive kinds of leadership that can be offered by Black women ministers. Without an appreciation of their unique contribution, the Church becomes far less meaningful as family.

Chapter nine directs attention to the varied household and family patterns in the Bible and contemporary society. Despite the litany of recent calls to strengthen and revitalize families and "family values," the Bible often confounds the modern mind on this subject. An astonishing variety of household arrangements are found in the Bible. The gospels in particular show Jesus' teachings to be almost hostile to some of the traditional matters of family obligations or familial piety. Our aim is to show the unique, if troubling, theological challenge posed by the New Testament, which focuses not only on traditional family values, but also on the spiritual demands of the fictive kinship made possible by the blood of Jesus Christ.

This chapter's aim is to expand the notion of "family" obligations in an age when the Black Church may need to recall her fine heritage of having once been a *family* to those in the community who hurt.

In the last chapter of the book, I extend the image of family to its widest limits, in order to address the role of the Black Church in helping the human family survive. For too long, the Black Church has languished on the margins of society, bedeviled by white racism and reticent about the concerns of nuclear war. Nevertheless, the Bible's concern for preserving and transforming creation calls the Black Church to witness for peace. Indeed, the matter is all the more urgent for Blacks, since in America and elsewhere, they are concentrated in urban areas that would be the primary targets in any nuclear war. Our intention is to conclude this book with an emphasis on hope—both for the human family and the Black Church. We therefore stress the need to appreciate the apocalyptic hope of New Testament authors as a life-affirming reality rather than a doomsday message. Perhaps the Black Church, so often rejected and regarded as "the least of these," may claim and exercise a leadership role and thereby be a cornerstone in the witness of peacemaking that seeks to save the human family from nuclear devastation.

CHAPTER 8

The Bible, Black Women, and Ministry

The family begins with the woman when she gives birth to the child. This is no less true of the Church as family, for, while Joseph's caring and protective role is important, everything begins with Mary, who gives birth to the Christ Child. This is often minimized as a motive for giving attention to the roles, rights, and status of women in the Church. Of course, we have seen a recent marked increase in studies on this topic.[1] Before then, this subject received sustained attention in only a few books published in Europe and the United States. By no means does the scope or variety of recent volumes about women compare with the paucity of similar works that began to appear shortly after the turn of the century.[2] The current preoccupation with this subject is a barometer of the perception that women have a number of legitimate grievances to set before the Church. In fact, some have even suspected that modern society has not accorded women anything that approaches what the Bible itself at times seems to demand, or at least imply strongly, in terms of equality.

However, most, if not all of this literature purporting to study the roles and status of women (presumably *all* women) in the Bible appears to have been written for the specific benefit of Anglo-Saxon or Ashkenazic Jewish women of today. Seldom does this literature give public notice about the particular plights of Black and other women of the Third World, who find themselves in far more wretched circumstances than their more privileged white female counterparts. For this reason, the present chapter examines the Bible in an effort to identify possible images and themes for the uplifting, liberation, and recognition of the divinely inspired leadership of women in general and Black women in particular.[3]

Our task would be more difficult if we restricted our discussion to those few women in the Bible who were unquestionably Black Africans: the Cushite (Nubian) wife of Moses (Numbers 12); the Queen of Sheba (1 Kings 10; 2 Chronicles 9) to whom New Testament writers later refer as "The Queen of the South" (Matt. 12:4–21; Luke 11:31) or the *Kandakē,* Queen of the Nubians of Meroë (Acts 8:27). A number of other biblical women

139

could be classified as Afroasiatics, which by modern standards of race would mean they could be identified as Black.[4] Although I discussed some of the Black women of the Bible in Part I of this book, I now do so as paradigms for Black women in positions of ministerial leadership today. While one might construct a larger hypothetical list of biblical women who could be classified as Black, such a procedure might lead to unproductive and unnecessary squabbling, given the difficulties in bringing precision to criteria for pure racial types in the Bible. On the other hand, many of the female personalities in the Bible are progenitors of so many Black women today, in terms of their "low estate" in ancient society (Jewish and Greco-Roman), their enormous faith, and their responses to opportunities to exercise ministerial leadership. In some instances, men, despite a patriarchal tradition, accepted such leadership willingly. In other cases, they accepted it begrudgingly. In still other cases, the male response was marked by disbelief or a refusal to accept female leadership.

THE ROLES OF WOMEN IN THE BIBLE

Phyllis A. Bird has pointed out that one needs only to scan the genealogies of the Old Testament (Gen. 5, 10; Num. 16, 26; 1 Chron. 1, 2) to see that "the biblical world is a man's world, for the genealogies are fundamentally lists of males, in which women do not normally appear."[5] As is well-known, ancient Hebraic/Jewish society, as well as that of the Greco-Roman world, was essentially male dominated. It was certainly the exception rather than the rule for women to possess prestige and economic, political, or social power. The Old Testament especially reflects a decidedly patriarchal hierarchy, despite the mention of exceptional women such as Miriam the prophetess and sister of Moses (Exod. 15:20), "chosen" women like Hannah (1 Sam. 1:5ff.), Sarah (Gen. 17:16–19), Rebekah (Gen. 25:21–26), Rachel (Gen. 29:31), Hagar (Gen. 16, 21, 25), and Bathsheba (2 Sam. 11; cf. Matt. 1:6). Political figures such as Jezebel, Queen of Samaria (1 Kings 21:1–5) or the Hasmonean queen, Salome Alexandra, held major political power for brief periods in ancient Jewish history.

Whatever the racial type of these women, there was no ideology of racism that affected their circumstances. Nevertheless, the genealogies of the Old Testament make it clear that the principal images associated with God tended to be those of dominant males. In the Old Testament and Greco-Roman society, the world was mediated through cultures controlled by men.[6] In such societies, the typical role of the women was domestic, and her status was subordinated. Indeed, it was frequently seen as inferior to that of the man.

To put the matter into sharper focus, the female in the Old Testament was most often cast in the role of Eve, who deceived and caused Adam to fall (Gen. 3:4–6); or the crafty and vindictive Jezebel; the harlot Rahab; the adulteress Bathsheba; or the seductress Tamar. These are, in conventional wisdom, hardly favorable descriptions. In fact, of the thirty-nine books that constitute the Old Testament, only two are named for women: Ruth, who is a foreigner, and Esther, a book whose canonical status has long been a matter of dispute. Despite these observations, it must be pointed out that some of these Old Testament women come to play a vital role as instruments of God in the history of salvation. Irrespective of their social position, some Old Testament women who at first appear to be of a very low estate later attain great theological significance by liberating themselves from their circumstances and participating dramatically in God's redemptive plan.

It is within this context that we should recall our earlier discussion about certain Black women in the Old Testament. In Numbers 12, there is an interesting combination of a Jahwist and an Elohist tradition that presents a controversy between Moses and his sister and brother, Miriam and Aaron, who evidently have disapproved of Moses' marriage. They see their brother's Black wife (Hebrew: *hāʾiša hakušit;* Greek: *gunaika Aithiopissan*) as evidence that Moses has compromised his distinctive relationship with Jahweh.[7] The narrative does not elaborate on the Black woman's reaction to these recriminations. Nevertheless, the fact remains that her racial identity caused her to be scorned by Miriam and Aaron. What is seldom emphasized is that the severest punishment was reserved for Miriam, whom God strikes with leprosy, making her "as white as snow" (Numbers 12:10). The erstwhile prophetess is severely punished for her acrimony regarding the African.

The parallel Old Testament accounts of the Queen of Sheba (1 Kings 10; 2 Chron. 9) have spawned a rich proliferation of tradition in Jewish, Ethiopian, Christian, and Muslim histories.[8] Both Origen and Jerome considered her to be of African ancestry.[9] This should not surprise us, for 1 Kings 3:1 reports on the marriage between Solomon and Pharaoh's daughter, who by modern standards of race was probably a Black woman. In Ethiopian tradition, the Queen of Sheba is known as "Makeda" (meaning "not thus"), since she is thought to have turned her people away from worshiping the sun to the worship of God.[10] Conversely, among Muslims she is called "Bilqis," and believed to have been a Yemenite.[11] Although not a Hebrew, this woman traveled a great distance (1 Kings 10) to discover the extent to which Solomon was worthy of the Lord's name. Not only does the story tell us that she came to believe the reports she had heard, but she praises the God of Israel (1 Kings 10:9) and exchanges many precious gifts with Solomon. This narrative is a poignant portrayal of a Black female leader who, regardless of her position outside the covenant community of faith, hears and responds to God in faith and is not the least disappointed, for her faith was handsomely rewarded.[12]

Then there is the other black queen in the New Testament, the *Kandakē* referred to in Acts 8:27. Unlike the Queen of Sheba in the Old Testament, the *Kandakē* does not traverse great distances to seek verification of events taking place in Jerusalem. Rather, she commissions her finance minister to worship in Jerusalem and presumably to bring back to her some holy words from Zion! In all the modern tension evident in some male ministerial circles that resist commissioning female ministers, it is instructive to be reminded of this Nubian precedent: A Nubian queen *commissioned* and *sent* the man. Thus, Acts 8:26–40 may have greater significance than merely serving as an episode in the gradual transition of the gospel message from the Jews to the Gentiles.[13]

GOSPEL THEMES FOR BLACK WOMEN IN MINISTRY

By the prevailing standards of Palestinian society in the time of Jesus Christ, the woman was to take no part in public life. She was to remain as unobtrusive as possible, confining her duties to domestic responsibilities.[14] Accordingly, women of the ancient Near East enjoyed minimal civil and religious rights. The Torah itself seems to presuppose that the woman is inferior to the man and that the wife is largely the property of her husband.[15]

When Matthew amplifies Mark's narratives about the feeding of the five thousand (Mark 6:30–44) and the four thousand (Mark 8:1–10), he includes a significant editorial note that helps us understand the prevalent attitude about women: "And those who ate were about five thousand men, besides women and children" (Matt. 14:21 and 15:38). To be sure, Matthew's editorial note involves a hyperbole designed to dramatize the extraordinary nature of Jesus' power and authority. But Matthew also tells us that women, like children, simply *did not count* as bona fide members of the community. Within such a milieu, the increased visibility of women — sometimes even in leadership roles — as reported by the writers of the four gospels (particularly in their presentations of Jesus' stance) is all the more remarkable.

We must advise caution, however, when anyone attempts to suggest that certain groups of passages in the New Testament gospels present the pristine perspective of the historical Jesus of Nazareth. Would that the challenge of New Testament study were so easy or simple as numerous Bible Belt fundamentalists and electronic mass-media evangelists seem to insist. No, the discernment of Jesus' probable attitudes or those to be attributed to the respective editors of gospel traditions requires careful, critical study. The biblical witness suffers enormously when everyone disregards such guidelines and becomes a self-styled expert. We should note that persons concerned about the propriety of women in ministry often use the same biblical passage as a basis for arguing in favor or in disapproval of women's leadership in the ordained ministry. It becomes imperative to establish guidelines and principles, and for biblical hermeneutics based on exegetical and objective (not merely dogmatic or confessional) considerations of a given set of biblical texts.[16]

Mindful of the foregoing admonitions, we note that the advent of Jesus' ministry provides evidence that women began to be viewed as entitled to greater rights as human beings. They also began to assume larger responsibilities and more significance in the primitive Church than was customary. We find an instructive example of this in Matthew 1:3, 5, 6, where four women—Tamar, Rahab, Ruth, and Uriah's wife (Bathsheba)—are listed in the opening genealogy. It is clear that Matthew includes these women in order to make a distinctive theological statement. In his seminal study of the Matthean and Lukan Infancy Narratives, Raymond E. Brown makes an important observation about Matthew's genealogy. "These women were held up as examples of how God uses the unexpected to triumph over human obstacles and intervenes on behalf of his planned Messiah."[17] Regardless of the social or ethnic stigmas originally attached to the identities of these four Old Testament women, Matthew demonstrates that they exercised leadership by performing a service for God important enough to entitle them a place in a genealogy of Jesus. By appealing to the examples of these women, Matthew also underscores the point that instead of attaching a social stigma to Jesus' mother, one should recognize in her giving birth to Jesus the fulfillment of Isaiah 7:14 and 26:9.[18]

Although Luke's genealogy (Luke 4:23–38) follows the traditional patriarchal pattern, he deliberately attributes the *Magnificat,* that is, the prayer of Hannah (1 Sam. 2:1–10) to her, so that Mary now expresses "definite sympathies for the poor and oppressed."[19] Accordingly, Mary is not merely the domestic mother; she is also a paradigm for the socially concerned female. Luke–Acts displays, in a way disproportionate to the other gospels, a prominent interest in the witness made by women. Notice how many other women Luke names or mentions: Elizabeth (Luke 1:36); Anna the prophetess (Luke 2:36); the women who provided for Jesus "out of their means" (Mary Magdalene, Joanna, and Susanna [Luke 8:2]); the persistent widow who demands justice as one of God's elect (Luke 18:1–8); Dorcas (Tabitha) of Joppa, known for her good works and merciful deeds (Acts 10:36); Lydia (Acts 16:14, 40); Mary and Rhoda (Acts 21:8, 9).

Another illustration in the gospels that depicts the new public access of women as a result of Jesus' ministry is the narrative concerning the Syrophoenician woman in Mark 7:26–30 (but the Canaanite woman in Matt. 15:21–28). Courageously, this individual, who is both a *Gentile* and a *woman* (double jeopardy) approaches Jesus in public on behalf of her *female* child. According to the story, even Jesus refers to the Gentile woman and her daughter as "dogs." Still, the woman persists in her petitioning with an utterly disarming measure of faith that Jesus cannot but honor. Like the relentless widow in Luke 18, the Syrophoenician woman's bold faith helps her gain full access, recognition, and direct assistance from Jesus, despite traditional biases against her full humanity. Luke's omission of this story undoubtedly results from the story's anti-Gentile and anti-female nuances, which were not consistent with his theological and hermeneutical preferences. Luke emphasizes that the Holy Spirit is the grace and mercy of God that guides both Jesus and the primitive Church in their efforts to include within God's plan of salvation Gentiles, women, the poor, and other excluded or scandalized people.

There probably is little need to belabor the observation frequently made by feminists within the last decade that women were the first to discover Jesus' empty tomb and to report what an angel at the site had told them about Jesus' resurrection. Certainly, the Matthean and Lukan accounts confirm this, despite the fact that the original text of Mark closes with the matter-of-fact comment, "The women told no one, for they were afraid" (*see* Mark 16:8), and also despite the fact that the events in the fourth gospel are altered by that evangelist's concern to stress the primacy of the beloved disciple's status (John 20:4, 5). It is clear, at least in three of the gospels (Matthew, Luke, and John), that angels first explained aspects of the significance of Jesus' resurrection to women. It seems inescapable that women, not the male disciples, were chosen as the initial instruments for spreading the news of the resurrection. The women evidently tended to believe, whereas the men tended to be much slower in believing. Luke establishes this tendency rather clearly, it seems: "O foolish men, and slow of heart to believe all that the prophets have spoken!" (Luke 24:25).

Few gospel passages are as amenable to themes for Black women in ministry as John 4:4–42, which describes Jesus' encounter with a Samaritan woman and the immediate consequences of that encounter. In the opening dialogue between Jesus and this woman at Mt. Gerizim (4:9), the woman reminds Jesus of the poor relations between Jew and Samaritan, especially since events of the second century, B.C.[20] The Luke-Acts corpus and the fourth gospel mention the Samaritans in sympathetic ways, but Matthew and Mark, writing earlier, in climates of less polemics and tension with Judaism, are silent about the Samaritans and the Jewish disputes or difficulties with them. In the Johannine tradition reporting Jesus' encounter with a Samaritan woman, there are multiple ingredients for today's Black women in general and the Black woman contemplating or actually engaged in ministry within American society.

As one reads through John 4:4–42, serious notice needs to be made of the way this story contrasts with the story of Nicodemus in the preceding chapter (3:1–23). The Samaritan woman seems to lack everything that the respectable Pharisaic member of the Sanhedrin possesses. In fact, the woman stands in triple jeopardy, for she is a Samaritan, a woman, and one who not only has been married five times (Jewish law permits only three marriages), but is also living with a man who is not her husband (4:18). Each aspect of her condition has its parallel among many Black women in America today. Like the Samaritan, they often find themselves in a state of quiet domestic chaos, with all the societal stigmas attached to such circumstances.[21] Given standards of conventional values, the Samaritan woman, like her Black counterpart today, brings great liabilities to her encounter with Jesus. Yet Jesus, as the Black gospel song goes, saw beyond her *faults* and found her *needs*!

The truly instructive segments of this extended pericope are threefold. First, Jesus' disciples were shocked (*ethaumazon*) to discover him deep in conversation with such a woman (4:27).[22] The gospels seem consistent in their portrayal of the limited perspectives or theological narrowness of the men who were Jesus' first disciples. In some quarters today, Black women, transformed and strengthened by faith, have to contend with similar narrowness on the part of a male-dominated clergy. Second, the Samaritan woman did not let the disapproval of the disciples stop her. Instead, she rushed back to her city to beckon her people to come and see the one who might be the fulfillment of their messianic expectations (4:28). Third, this Samaritan woman became the cause of many other Samaritans coming to believe in Jesus (4:39), despite the fact that some Samaritans later seized the opportunity to indicate that the woman could only have partial credit for their newfound belief (4:42). In any case, in this story we have what at the very least could be a report about the first woman missionary to the Samaritans.[23] Although there is neither a laying on of hands nor other formal sign of commissioning, this woman volunteers and functions as a minister to her people, despite some hesitancy on the part of her own people to accept her as such.

SORTING OUT PAUL'S ATTITUDE ON WOMEN IN MINISTRY

Because some of the most conservative-seeming New Testament passages about women are found in writings attributed to the apostle Paul, the tools of critical scholarship are indispensable in deciding what Paul wrote and what his later disciples wrote in his name. Of first order of importance is to recognize that only seven epistles in the New Testament are written by the historical Paul. These seven undisputed epistles are 1 Thessalonians, Galatians, 1 and 2 Corinthians, Philemon, Philippians, and Romans. Even within these authentic epistles of Paul, we find strong evidence of textual glosses and interpolations. In writings like 2 Corinthians and Philippians, we do not have a single unified epistle, but a composite of several fragmentary epistles. As much as we might wish that Paul's writings were a bit more tidy, the reality is that they are a complex literary mosaic.

The task of sorting out Paul's attitudes about women, particularly in relation to the questions of ministry and ordination, is much less onerous today, due to the contributions made in several lucid studies within the last few years.[24] These studies help us either to appreciate the limitations imposed on Paul by his ancient historical-cultural context or weigh the substantial evidence that passages like 1 Corinthians 11:7 or 14:34, 35 are interpolations that reflect Church circumstances well after Paul had been martyred.[25] Most of the New Testament passages calling for the subordination or subservience of women are found in the "Deutero-Pauline" material—Colossians, Ephesians, or First and Second Timothy and Titus (the Pastorals)—and does not reflect Paul's own stance.

Where does one look to ascertain Paul's stance about the status of women and their suitability for ministerial leadership? Two crucial places provide some answers: Galatians 3:28 and Romans 16:1-16. The Galatians text is often cited, as well it should be, for the observation has been made that Galatians 3:28 is "the first occurrence of a doctrine openly propagating the abolition of sex distinctions" within Judaism or the Greco-Roman world.[26] Of course, one could cite the segment of this pre-Pauline baptismal formula that says "in Christ . . . there is neither male nor female," to argue that on a metaphysical plane Paul wishes to obliterate *all* distinctions between men and women. One would be on stronger ground to focus on the radical *social* implications of Galatians 3:28 in what is, in effect, a call for the emancipation of women within the life of the *Church* (not necessarily society in general).

The opening verses of the appendix to Romans shows just how seriously Paul regarded the social implications of Galatians 3:28. In Romans 16:1, Phoebe is identified as a deacon (*diakonon*) of the church in the port city of Cenchreae. Even though one usually finds English translations of her function as "deaconess," the Greek word here for her function is the masculine "deacon." We are not told what her specific duties were, other than that she had been a helper of Paul and many others (16:2). It may be quite incidental that Paul first mentions the word *ekklēsia* (church) at this point in the epistle. That he does so while calling attention to a female by identifying her formal function cannot be purely coincidental. The text does not say that she is *the* deacon of the church; the definite article is absent. Nevertheless, she is clearly described as a leader of a given congregation, and it appears that we have some indication of "an early stage of what later became the ecclesiastical office [minister]."[27] It would seem that Paul was not nearly so reluctant to acknowledge female "ministerial" leadership within his churches as were his male devotees of another generation and a subsequent ecclesiastical tradition that adopted (and indeed adapted) him as its champion.

Beyond the references to Phoebe in Romans 16:1-16, Paul acknowledges other female leaders in a variety of ways. He expresses extreme gratitude, for example, to Prisca (Priscilla of Acts 18:2, 18; cf. 2 Tim. 4:19), who evidently is one half of an effective wife-and-husband team ministry in their house church (Rom. 16:3-5; 1 Cor. 16:19).[28] Paul mentions a Junias in Romans 16:7, but the preferred reading should probably be "Junia," in which case Paul includes this woman among the *apostles*.[29] Consider further how impressive is the list of women missionaries and leaders cited in Romans 16: Mary (16:6); Tryphaena, Tryphosa, and Persis (16:12); the mother of Rufus (16:13); Julia, and the sister of Nereus (16:15). In this closing segment of Romans, one gathers considerable evidence that Paul took seriously the social implications of his dictum regarding the full recognition of male and female leadership within the life of the Church. To say this should occasion no surprise if one recognizes that Paul's own views, which acknowledge and enhance the ministerial leadership of women, proceed as a natural consequence from a theology so fundamentally governed by an apocalyptic perspective that fully envisions a transformation of the created order.[30]

Does this mean that we simply ignore today those many New Testament passages that are patently conservative or, by modern standards, repressive on the status of women? Does the Christian in our time seek only to ascertain the probable stance of Jesus and Paul, discarding the rest of the New Testament? To both questions, the response must be in the negative. Otherwise we would be contributing to the tendency of creating "a canon within the canon." We would also be hopelessly lost in understanding how the entire New Testament witness confronts us with the great range of problems associated with the early Christian movement's development from its status as an apocalyptic reform movement within Judaism to a separate religious institution within the Greco-Roman world. The most substantive challenge offered by the New Testament is to take full cognizance of its rich diversity and simultaneously develop the kind of hermeneutic that recognizes the mundane or human character of the struggles on the part of ancient communities of faith in transition as preserved in the New Testament.[31]

A couple of illustrations may substantiate the case. First, when I said earlier that texts such as 1 Corinthians 11:7, "[Man] is the image and glory of God; but woman is the glory of man," or 1 Corinthians 14:34, 35, "women should keep silence in the churches" are interpolations, I mean that the tone and content of such passages are inconsistent with dominant ideas in Paul. These texts are more consistent with ideas found in early second-century New Testament texts such as 1 Timothy 2:11, 12: "Let a woman learn in silence with all submissiveness. I permit no woman to teach or to have authority over men," or 1 Peter 3:7, "the woman as the weaker sex." As the primitive, unstructured house churches expanded, attracting more women who claimed the *charismata,* greater attention had to be given to order and stability. The institutionalizing process was partly achieved by the Church's pattern of accommodating itself to a world in which the Church as an institution could exist, given both the "delayed Parousia" and gnostic as well as other external threats. We must keep in mind also that certain gnostic groups sought especially to convert women (2 Tim. 3:6, 7).

Second, although many New Testament scholars still insist that Paul was the author of Colossians and Ephesians, the arguments for such a view are far from convincing. Usually, proponents of that stance must postulate an elaborate developmental scheme distinguishing phrases through which Paul's theological teachings shifted in focus, emphasis, and content. Several factors are against this line of reasoning, however, including the fact that in Colossians and Ephesians, we begin to find Christological and ecclesiological elements stated in terms not easily reconcilable with those of Paul. Furthermore, it is precisely in Colossians and Ephesians that we first encounter the formulaic "domestic tables" or codes of subordination: "Wives, be subject to your husbands" (Col. 3:18; Eph. 5:22). This phenomenon indicates that the Church itself is in a different (later) phase of institutionalization, adapting itself to some of the institutional mores of other forms of institutional life in the Greco-Roman world. We do not have here the historical Paul's teaching—for these codes are absent in his writings—as much as an index of an accommodation pattern by a religious minority group trying not to give unnecessary offense to the larger, often hostile, environment.

THE NEW TESTAMENT'S CAUTION AND CHALLENGE

American society seems to be remarkably susceptible to "causes" and ephemeral "fads," rather than long-term commitments to major social issues. When critical issues are raised in our society, the tendency on the part of the political and corporate establishment is often to give the issue an initial hearing, to make a series of immediate but minor and superficial adjustments, and to wait until both the rhetoric and passionate concerns taper off or, more cynically, to shift the media's attention away from the old cause to some new one. Certainly, Black people have enough firsthand evidence about this syndrome in America. Black women in particular cannot forget how little they were featured in the so-called women's suffrage movement at the turn of the century. Therefore, considerable care must be exercised in assuring that the questions of Black liberation and Black female ministerial leadership do not pass off the scene as causes that have had their hearing.

A safeguard against that possibility is provided by a biblical caution implicit in Relevation 2:18–29, the fourth of seven "letters" to the churches. In this passage, we find a sobering message to the church in Thyatira, where a woman called Jezebel was evidently causing havoc by claiming to be a prophetess and leading many within the church astray (Rev. 2:20). The graphic image is that of an influential, charismatic woman whose activities in the area of religion aggrandize her, and not the church of God. This text is a disturbing reminder that just as there have been and are charlatans of the false-prophet variety, there have also been false prophetesses capable of arrogance, guile, and utter deception. The caution comes within this framework: "And all the churches shall know that I am he who searches mind and heart, and I will give to each of you as your works deserve" (Rev. 2:23). This caution and promise is followed finally by the sublime challenge of Revelation 2:26–28:

He who conquers and who keeps my works until the end, I will give him power over the nations, and he shall rule them with a rod of iron . . . even as I myself have received power from my Father; and I will give him [or her] the morning star.

Male church leadership has no exclusive right to this challenge that Revelation also extends to female church leadership. Women are part of the family. Indeed, they give rise to the Church family and sustain it sometimes even when men disbelieve or otherwise falter. The Bible shows a remarkable, progressive spirit in improving the social position of women and securing them greater recognition, expanded leadership roles, and more human rights. Perhaps today we are only catching up with the first-century attitudes of Jesus and the earliest Christians in accepting the unique leadership that Black women ministers can exert in God's family, the Church.

CHAPTER 9

The Bible and Black Families:
A Theological Challenge

The perception that families are in crisis has increased greatly in recent years. This no doubt explains the proclamation by the late Pope Paul IV that the 1980s should be regarded as the Decade of the Family. Almost simultaneously, President Ronald Reagan declared 1980 the Year of the Bible. The family and the Bible, once meaningfully yoked in sacred trust, are being invoked like magical incantations to produce instant cures and realignments for complex modern problems. *De facto* secularism, materialism, moral confusion, and chaotic public policies have endangered the stability of all types of families. Sadly, however, some social commentators single out Black families and households to highlight the so-called pathology of Black life without any mention of the political decisions, socioeconomic policies, and biblical distortions that contribute to the Black condition. In a climate of right-wing capitalism amid the rhetoric of freedom and power, "modernity has emptied things of divinity and emptied them of meaning."[1] On the one hand, today we find a yearning to return to pristine biblical teachings and "traditional family values," but on the other hand, too many either see the Bible as irrelevant to the modern family crisis or, worse still, refuse to be shaken from their parochial, dogmatic usage of it.

This chapter examines the Bible's many words about family life and its significant silences on the subject. In fact, the Bible may *not* be suitable as a rule for traditional family values. It surprises us in its profound messages on blood kinship and the need to recognize and appreciate kinships beyond blood relations. The simple fact is that the nuclear family model (father, mother, and children) no longer represents the household pattern of most American families.[2] At the same time, the extended family typical in traditional African societies is receiving new attention.[3] In significant ways, the Bible endorses the extended family model and even supplements it with a kind of fictive kinship.[4]

The burgeoning concern about family life and the Bible has spawned many new volumes.[5] However, scarcely any of this literature treats the

150

condition, needs, or predicaments of diverse Black families and households. Of course, John Mbiti's book, *African Religions and Philosophy,* helps distinguish the African household, which traditionally includes grandparents and other blood relatives, from the European nuclear family paradigm.[6] Also, there are many studies on Black American families written from the perspective of sociology, the allied health sciences, or political science. Very few of these, however, have emerged from Black academies of religion or the Black Church.

There are two exceptions. In *Roots of a Black Future: Family and Church,* J. Deotis Roberts acknowledges that in many quarters, the Black family in America is in trouble. He goes on to examine the causes and implications in light of the Black family's African background.[7] In an earlier book, Roberts suggests that the Black community needs to view the family as "the domestic church."[8] Charles Wallace Smith, in *The Church in the Life of the Black Family,* explores the Black Church's potential as an "extended family" and outlines elements for Black family theology.[9] We still lack a study on the possible ways in which the Bible provides insights and challenges for the doing of theology through a *revitalized ministry* to families in general and, given the complexities that beset them today, Black families and households in particular.[10] We must ask how to discern the relevance of the Bible for a modern social milieu that differs so dramatically from that of ancient Palestine, Africa, or the Greco-Roman environment.

Within the Bible, we do not find a monolithic, static view of family life. Rather, we find changing attitudes, values, and practices as God's Word seeks expression in diverse ancient cultural settings. I will suggest that while the nuclear family is commendable in some respects, neither in biblical times nor today can discussions of family life be restricted to the nuclear family model. Furthermore, we will show that the New Testament has a distinct concern for greater priority on quality relationships in the household (Greek: *oikos/okia*), which emerges as a theological paradigm for membership in the Household of God. We shall also encounter some of the limitations—indeed, dangers—of popularizing simplistic and literalist usages of the Bible, which is so much in vogue today in electronic media religion and American churches, whether they are Black, Hispanic, white, or Asian. I will then suggest a creative agenda for the ministry of the Black Church—a challenge for today and the years ahead.

THE FAMILY AS A PATRIARCHAL HOUSEHOLD
IN THE OLD TESTAMENT

There is a long-standing tendency on the part of many to romanticize Old Testament portrayals of family life as either uniformly monogamous or harmonious. Actually, early Hebraic society showed less interest in monogamy than it did in variations of polygamy (Abraham, Sarah, and Hagar of Gen. 16; Jacob, Rachel, Bilhah, Leah, and Zilpah of Gen. 30).[11] Likewise,

Hebraic family life frequently reflected tensions between brothers (Cain and Abel in Gen. 4; Jacob and Esau in Gen. 27; Joseph and his brothers in Gen. 37) and between sisters (Gen. 30). Even incest was not excluded, for Hebraic life depicts daughters, such as those of Lot, who engage in sexual relations with their fathers (Gen. 19:36). It sanctions Tamar's seduction of her father-in-law, Judah (Gen. 38; cf. Matt. 1:3). Here again, the purpose is to continue the blood line of God's people through successive covenants. By contrast, when there is no honorable theological motive, as in the case of the man who has intimate relations with his mother-in-law (1 Cor. 5), there is a strong biblical rebuke. These examples demonstrate that God uses a range of possibilities in forming families and households, often as the result of preexisting tensions and social pressures. One could say that the Old Testament appears to display a *divine flexibility* in advancing God's purposes through diverse patterns of family and household life.

Irrespective of the diverse structure of Old Testament households, the Bible consistently places emphasis on the need to honor one's father and mother. This is the fifth commandment of the Decalogue (Exod. 20:5; 21:12; Deut. 5:16; Lev. 19:3).[12] Some might construe this bestowal of honor on one's parents to mean that the early Hebrews envisioned social equality between men and women in Hebraic society. The honor to be given to one's mother derived from the love and care that she was expected to exhibit toward her children, but she herself remained in a subordinate position as wife/concubine to the father of the household. Throughout the Old Testament, the dominant authority figure is consistently the father; his sons were next in prominence in the social hierarchy. The Hebrew father had authority to regard other members of his household (Hebrew: *bet ʾāb* or *baît,* which is also a Hebrew term for "temple") as his property. He even had authority to offer his son as a blood sacrifice (Gen. 22).[13] This circumstance has led modern feminist Bible scholars to observe routinely that the Old Testament presents a rigid patriarchal system. Elisabeth Schüssler Fiorenza sees this system as one of patriarchal oppression, "a social-political system and societal structure of graded subjugation and oppressions."[14]

Part of the father's dominance and control of the ancient Hebraic households manifests itself in the liberal legal privileges extended to the husband, who could divorce his wife almost at will. The governing text is Deuteronomy 24:1-4, which says a husband may divorce his wife if he finds some "indecency in her." In such cases, he need only write a bill of divorce and place it in her hand.[15] Postexilic Jewish husbands did not have the power to rid themselves of their wives so easily, since Malachi 2:13-16 sternly rebukes those who not only divorce their wives but also those who physically abuse them and fail to raise up "Godly offspring."

This passage in Malachi is important because its attitude is consistent with the *changed perspective* in the Priestly version ("P") of the creation story in Genesis 1:1-2:4, which postulates the *imago dei* for male and female and also implies greater equality between the sexes. Centuries earlier, the Jahwist ("J") version of the creation story in Genesis 2:4–3:24 had projected woman as mere helper of man. She was subjugated to man, the one who led man astray, and not one to be heeded. One can see the conceptual similarity between this older Jahwist creation story and the severe restrictions on the rights of wives and women. Later biblical traditions often are more equitable and humanizing, as the Old Testament later demonstrates changed perspectives in the matter of divorce. In this shift in attitude, we speak of an evolutionary progression within the Bible, which shows itself *adaptable for life.* By contrast, too many "religiou>" people today find themselves only able to be rigidly unadaptable.

Another dimension of the patriarchal household in the Old Testament is the development of class stratification by tribes and families. The Old Testament places heavy emphasis on the primacy of blood relatives and the purity of ethnic stock. As the land of Canaan was settled and the pastoral Hebrews became more of an agricultural people, they began intermarrying with the indigenous "people of the land" (Hebrew: *'ām ha'āres*). This phenomenon eventually led to a rigid social stratification of families and households based on the degree of blood purity. Mixed marriages were discredited as the Jews developed the concept of "the holy race" (Ezra 9:2; "the holy race has mixed itself with the peoples of the lands"). Wholesale divorces became the order of the day (Ezra 6:21; Neh. 10:28–30) in order to purge the presumed scourge of miscegenation. This development in postexilic Judaism occurred over a century before Alexander the Great instituted the policy of miscegenation (Greeks cohabitating with diverse subjugated peoples of the "known world," *oikoumenē*) to facilitate the growth and resilience of Hellenism.

Joachim Jeremias extensively documents that Judaism, at the time of Jesus Christ and later, carefully distinguishes among the importance of its families/households. First, there were families of legitimate descent (priests, Levites, and full Israelites); second, families of illegitimate descent with only a slight blemish; last were families with grave blemishes of ancestry.[16] Illegitimacy included proselytes, illegitimate children of priests, freed men, temple slaves, and illegitimate children of the laity. Categorizations and distinctions of this type in early Judaism are significant because they show that the early Jewish religious community was fully stratified in social classes, with damaging stigmas being attached to "illegitimate" families. Such class stratification also helps us understand why a controversy developed between the early Church and the synagogue regarding Jesus' birth. It helps to explain why Matthew and Luke, somewhat apologetically, go to extraordinary lengths to establish Jesus' bona fide lineage through Joseph (Matt. 1:16; Luke 3:23).[17]

The foregoing remarks on the patriarchal household of the Old Testament have included scarcely any mention of God, whom Hans Küng refers to as the pre-eminent "patriarchal symbol," even though Küng does qualify the assertion by saying that God also has "matriarchal features."[18] If one surveys the actual references in the Old Testament, one discovers that God is rarely referred to as "our Father" (Isa. 64:8).[19] The usual designation for God is "God of Abraham," "God of your father Jacob," or "God of David."[20] Naturally, the Old Testament offers passages that imply the image of God as the parent of humanity, of the covenants, of Israel, or of her King (Exod. 4:22; Isa. 64:16; Jer. 21:9; Ps. 2:7). Despite our tendency to cast God in a masculine image, it cannot be demonstrated that the image of God in the Old Testament is in any consistent way gender specific. Although God has traditionally been called "He," the Priestly version of the creation story provides the corrective: "Let *us* make human kind in *our* image, after *our* likeness" (*see* Gen. 1:26).[21] How fitting it is that God cannot be too closely identified with human fathers or mothers who are subject to a higher reign that is not gender specific.

Despite the popular tendency to do so, it is quite inadequate to resort to simplistic, literalist approaches to the Old Testament, as if it provides us with ready-made guidelines for addressing the needs of today's Black families and households. In Black communities and others, Church leaders and the laity alike have allowed themselves to imitate the popular biblicist and proof-texting tendencies of street-corner evangelists, insensitive missionaries, and electronic-media preachers. Many people in the Church, including church-school teachers and pastors, tend to pick and choose biblical texts that suit their own tastes and personal values, without making much attempt to reflect critically on how these values often only mirror their own narrow socialization. Furthermore, Church leaders barely study the ancient historical and cultural background that gave rise to this Word of God. What is forgotten is that the Bible confronts us with a series of theologically motivated histories of ancient communities (including families and households) in crisis or struggle, trying to make sense out of constantly changing socioeconomic and political circumstances. Biblical authors were both *creative* and *flexible* as they adapted successive divine revelations. Too often today, we neglect this fact and are not instructed by it.

In Hebraic or Jewish society of biblical times, and only slightly less in the socioreligious environments of Greece and Rome, the human household was male dominated, with women and children regarded as property, much the same as slaves. With the possible exception of those teachings in Stoicism, the Cult of Isis, and among some Gnostics, this was the situation during the Hellenistic diaspora, when the earliest missionary churches emerged.[22] Whereas membership in the patriarchal household of the Old Testament was determined on the basis of blood kinship, the evidence from Hellenistic culture suggests that such was not the case in the Greek household (*oikos/oikaikos*) which, like its Roman counterpart (Latin: *domus,* perhaps even *familia*), included slaves as members of the household, and in some instances as members of the family.[23]

The sociocultural background of the Old Testament is an indispensable factor for determining the meaning of household practices and values *then* as a basis for determining their usefulness or relevance *now.* By now, certain disjunctures between then and now should be clear. Still other illustrations may help. It would hardly be acceptable today to enslave a person or offer one's child as a blood sacrifice. Furthermore, in our time, notions of a "holy, pure race/nation" bring to mind the horrors of the Jewish Holocaust and crimes still seen in the South Afrikaners' policy of apartheid. Conversely, the Old Testament idea of corporate solidarity lends itself to a modern-day revitalization of Black *agapē* in the Black community.

There are ways we can appreciate both the perennial relevance and adaptability of Old Testament traditions as part of God's ancient Word. It may be that too many churches today have allowed *selfishness, individualization, snappy condemnations,* and the scramble for *ecclesiastic power* to retard their ability to discover new life from the Scripture. Nevertheless, a decisive challenge still confronts the Black Church: to break down the dividing walls of its own imitative socialization and acculturated, institutional self-understanding. These elements separate the Church from the needs and aspirations of her oppressed people who have been relegated to the margins of an affluent but often hostile larger society. That the oppressed languish so is a continuing symbol of our collective brokenness.

MORAL ACTION AND BLOOD KINSHIP
IN THE NEW TESTAMENT

Many who consider themselves to be Christians and strive for family stability and moral decency derive much comfort from the categorical ways in which the New Testament seems to provide clear-cut guidelines on aspects of family life and human sexuality. Rather than struggling with the complexities or ambiguities of the text, such individuals devise quick formulae for simple daily living "above reproach." In some ways, these practices are well-intentioned and even admirable. What responsible person could question the goals of family stability or moral decency? Indeed, our churches have long taught that the New Testament has a normative or prescriptive function for Christian living, despite the fact that people at times appeal to the same text to substantiate completely opposing views on a given issue.[24] Still, it is very easy to construct a hypothetical chart of ancient New Testament teaching that would seem to make matters easier for those who can only be secure with a "simple faith" in the pursuit of stable and decent households. But a quest for simple faith can lead to self-righteous dogma and condemnation, rather than the acceptance of the penitent, forgiveness, mercy, and love. I could offer, for example, the following composite of ten seemingly straightforward New Testament teachings:

Hypothetical New Testament "Ten Commandments" on the Family

1. Honor your parents (Mark 10:19; Matt. 19:19; Luke 18:20; Eph. 6:2).
2. Wives, be submissive to your husbands (Col. 3:18; Eph. 5:32; 1 Pet. 3:1).
3. Husbands, love your wives (Col. 3:20; Eph. 5:25, 28).
4. Children, obey your parents (Col. 3:20; Eph. 6:1-3; 1 Pet. 3:7).
5. Do not divorce (Mark 10:11, 12; Luke 16:18; Matt. 5:32; Luke 11:17).
6. Do not prevent the children from coming to Jesus (Mark 10:13-16; Matt. 19:13-15; Luke 18:15-17).
7. A divided household will not stand (Mark 3:24, 25; Matt. 12:25; Luke 11:17).
8. Love thy neighbor as thyself (Mark 12:32; Matt. 5:43; 19:19; 22:39; Luke 10:27; Rom. 13:8, 9; James 2:8).
9. Young men should control their passions (2 Tim. 2:22; Titus 2:6).
10. You are obligated to provide for your relatives, especially your own (nuclear) family (1 Tim. 5:8).

If we lived on an isolated island as part of a homogeneous network of families, these ten guidelines, all well-attested in the New Testament, could constitute a new Decalogue. We would need only add references regarding adultery, fornication, temptations, and coveting (desiring and trying to take fraudulently things that do not belong to you). However, we do *not* live on such an island. We exist in a modern, rather complex social milieu and technological market economy that intrudes on our daily living with a wide range of conflicts and pressures (media, outside peer or professional loyalties) that often are beyond parental or family control. To invoke some simplistic "new Decalogue" extracted from the New Testament is ultimately very inadequate and a most questionable procedure. Obviously, our listing of guidelines proceeds from the presumed traditional needs of the abstracted idea of an ideal family. As such, they are highly subjective and arbitrary. We arrive at them by editing out parts of the original text, ignoring the original intent or context of the passage, and minimizing the ways other New Testament passages might show a changed perspective that would require qualifications.

These inherent limitations require us to chart a different course in considering family teachings in the New Testament. It must be remembered that the earliest traditions in the New Testament—those of Jesus and Paul—do not contain much elaboration on families or households based on blood kinship. Neither Jesus nor the leaders of the early Christian missionary movement, especially Paul, expected the then-existing world structure to continue very long; they fully subscribed to apocalyptic eschatology.[25]

Particularly prior to A.D. 70, the churches expected the imminent return of Jesus, as well as a complete transformation of the created order. People did not spend much time devising detailed regulations for families or households. This observation should clarify why Jesus' teachings on the family, although a minor aspect of the gospel tradition, seems so strident and insensitive.[26]

Consider Matthew 10:34–36: "I have not come to bring peace, but a sword . . . to set a man against his father, and a daughter against her mother, and a daughter-in-law against her mother-in-law; and a man's foes will be those of his own household [*oikiakoi*])." Here Matthew depicts Jesus paraphrasing Micah 7:6, which alerts us to the manner in which Old Testament ideas were transposed into an eschatological setting in the New Testament at a time when it was believed that the end was at hand. Jesus was not so much concerned with traditional family arrangements as he was with the in-breaking of the Kingdom of God (*Basileia tou Theou*) and how this anticipation required a new kind of household.[27] *Blood relatives and language were no longer decisive criteria for the new Household that God and the ministry of Jesus make possible.* This fact helps us understand the gloomy prediction and seemingly harsh words in Mark 13:12: "And brother will deliver up brother to death, and the father his child, and children will rise against parents and have them to put death." Mark's "little apocalypse" (chapter 13) attempts to alert an ancient congregation to the ways the suffering witness of believers will disrupt traditional family loyalties and behavioral patterns. No longer are blood relations to be the people of God's decisive criterion for determining family relations. The classic formulation of this is "For whoever does the will of my Father in heaven is my brother, and sister, and mother" (Matt. 12:50; cf. Mark 3:35; Luke 8:21). The omission of any mention of an earthly father departs from the characteristic Old Testament and Greco-Roman emphasis.[28]

God is the pre-eminent parent and householder in the Jesus tradition and elsewhere in the New Testament. So impressed is Matthew with his idea that he compares his own interpretive task with the work of the Kingdom of God, which Jesus equated with that of a householder "who brings out of the treasury what is old and what is new (Matt. 13:52b). Likewise, the parable of the prodigal son, Luke's *old* treasure, can also obtain *new* pertinence. In Luke 15:11–32, we find a father and his two sons. These three are symbols of a new householder (God), the youthful sinner, and the rigidly loyal, mature brother who is consistent to a self-righteous fault. Of course, this parable is open to different interpretations. Is it a story about sinners, about two brothers, or a social drama?[29] Actually, this parable may be Luke's reinterpretation of Deuteronomy 21:18–21, where both parents are instructed to bring the stubborn and rebellious son to the elders of the city, to be stoned to death! In Luke's possible reinterpretation, capital punishment is replaced with God's mercy and compassion.

Irrespective of the interpretation, it seems inescapable that the parable of the prodigal son has something to say about the nature of family relations that should be practiced within new households. The younger son returns in a wretched condition to the household after squandering his inheritance in riotous living. By all conventional standards, he now merits nothing, and he knows this. Indeed, that is exactly what he would get, if the matter were left to his older brother. Yet the parent, who is also the householder, sees him from afar, rejoices, and begins to teach both sons the true power and meaning of extending undeserved love (*agapē*), forgiveness, mercy, and compassion. The parent here neither holds the younger son's irresponsibility nor the older son's anger and jealousy against him. Rather, he makes possible a reconciliation between brothers by taking action that has the potential of breaking down the walls between members of the household (cf. Eph. 2:13–22).

The stance of this householder epitomizes the work of Jesus, who — unlike many other ancient Jews — forgives and shows extraordinary compassion for all who languish in the margins of ancient Jewish society: women, children, slaves, outcasts, tax collectors, prostitutes, paralytics, the blind, epileptics, the mentally ill, and even Gentiles.[30] Nowhere is the bold precedent of "new household relations" shown more clearly than in Jesus' treatment of women and children. Women have a prominence in Jesus' ministry that is rather unusual in ancient Palestine. He engages women in public dialogue (John 4), heals them (Matt. 8:14, 15; 9:18–26; Luke 13:10–17), allows a woman to anoint his feet (Matt. 26:6–13; Mark 14:3–9; John 12:3–7), and prevents an adulteress from being stoned to death (John 7:53–8:11). Invariably, each responds to him with *exceptional new vistas of faith.*

Matthew stresses the decisive role of women who have had grave faults by traditional Jewish standards, but were used to further God's history of salvation. Matthew not only includes them in what would otherwise be a male-only genealogy (1:1–14), but calls attention to their plight and stresses their role in his version of the passion narrative. Luke offers the most sustained emphasis on the roles of women in his version of Jesus' story. He most frequently identifies these women by their names, and at one point castigated the apostles as "O foolish men" (24:25) for having disregarded the resurrection reports by women (24:11). At times John goes to great lengths to document Jesus' revolutionary openness in treating women — even a Samaritan woman and an adulteress — as members of his "*new* Household."

Although in Matthew, Mark, and Luke one receives the impression that Jesus so redefined the criteria for kinship with him that he minimized the role of parents, it should not be forgotten how frequently he quoted the fifth commandment, "Honor thy father and thy mother." His earthly parents, especially Joseph, may not have received much attention in his ministry, but it is clear that they took pains to provide Jesus with careful religious instruction (Luke 2:41–52) and were always ready to have him return home, no matter what the neighbors were saying (Mark 6:1–6). His mother remains near even at the end, and one suspects that Joseph had once again traveled with Mary to Judea. If one considers the portrayal of Joseph as a sensitive and protective father, willing to travel into Egypt to protect his son, it is scarcely thinkable that he changed for the worse later.[31] The only reason we hear so little about Joseph is that in the emerging new Household, the focus becomes fixed on God as a loving parent whose Household Jesus opens so widely.

Then too, the apocalyptic framework of many sections of the New Testament diverted attention away from the details of traditional parental functions and duties. The early Christian apocalyptic vision ushered in a new priority for actual and potential parents, one which (if accepted) would enable them to make the *agapē* normative for *living in the Household of God*. The result could be new family life-styles and parental understanding of their children and the neglected children of others ("neighbors"). We must also keep in mind that prior to A.D. 70, the Christian missionary movement consistently developed in dialogue with the synagogues of the diaspora. After all, most Christians during this period were not Gentiles, despite the misleading impression gained from the preponderance of Pauline epistles in the New Testament.

After A.D. 70, the specter of the impending end began to wane, both in Judaism and sectors of Christianity. Indeed, two distinct religions began to emerge as the Church developed its own literature, moved toward more institutionalized forms of worship or ministerial service, and saw the necessity of fashioning domestic rules for the households of the churches. Recent studies have shown that some of the early diaspora churches were losing women and slaves to Hellenistic cults such as those of Isis, Cybele, and Dionysus.[32] These cults allowed women and slaves greater measures of freedom and self-expression. Many of these women were also wives of Church men, and their free-lance participation in Hellenistic cults destabilized churches and families. Such circumstances meant that many parental functions and duties were also being abandoned: let the children come to Jesus (Mark 10:13–16), teach your children to love and fear God as well as heed his commandments (Deut. 6:1–6), or "Train up a child in the way he should go, and when he is old he will not depart from it" (Prov. 22:6).

Amid the uncertainty following the destruction of the second temple in A.D. 70 and the increased persecutions of Jews and Christians, leaders of the Church began adapting household codes or codes of subordination fashioned out of the Roman domestic tables. Christian leaders developed formulae for conduct within the Christian household in terms of a religion trying to survive. Typical are those formulae for wives to be subject to their husbands who, in turn, are to love their wives and not be harsh with them (Col. 3:18; Eph. 5:21, 22). Christian teachings on domestic relations now show a *changed perspective* reflecting *increased mutuality*. The domestic formulae make it clear that husbands have explicit obligations to love and not to brutalize their wives. In a similar manner, the developing parenesis instructs children to obey their parents (Col. 3:20; Eph. 6:1–3; 1 Pet. 3:7), but it also instructs parents not to provoke anger in their children and to raise them in the discipline and instruction of the Lord.

The pastoral epistles (First and Second Timothy and Titus) continue to set forth household codes. These early second-century epistles teach that women (mothers and wives) should love their children and husbands. Furthermore, women should give attention to raising their children as representing "good deeds" (1 Tim. 5:10).[33] Fathers also have a clear role, despite the fact that they are again referred to as managers of their children and households (see 1 Tim. 3:12). The pastorals give an extensive discourse on widows and call attention to the responsibility that adult offspring have in caring for their parents and grandparents (1 Tim. 5:3–16). Special provisions for widows and orphans are evident in the Old Testament and in traditions associated with Jewish Christianity (Exod. 22:22; Deut. 10:18; James 1:27).[34] That scarcely any mention of orphans appears in the pastorals perhaps indicates Christian care for them was presupposed in light of Paul's own "adoption terminology" (Rom. 8:23), or the welfare of orphans was no longer a priority matter in view of the other internal and external pressures on the churches (unless, of course, 1 Timothy 5:8 is intended to apply to orphans).

It may be that the lack of explicit interest in the welfare of orphans and the movement to re-establish forms of law and order in the pastorals marks the advance of a bourgeois Christianity more interested in protecting itself as an institution than caring for the oppressed within and outside its walls. During times of actual or impending socioreligious crisis and persecution, the Church tended to opt for a "civil religion," lest it incur the wrath of pagan officials and outsiders (1 Tim. 5:14).[35] By contrast to this dynamic in the pastorals, other "households of God" continued to be flexible and creatively prophetic in confronting the decadence and corruption of the values or practices that proceeded from the imperial cult and the evils of the secular order (Rev. 13, 18, 19).

SEXUAL CONDUCT AND THE HOUSEHOLD OF GOD

Determining the New Testament criteria for proper Christian sexual conduct is neither complex nor difficult. The background of Jesus, Peter, and Paul was Jewish. Their Scripture was the Old Testament, in some cases augmented by the *Halachah* (tradition of the elders). To some extent, the New Testament derives its stances on sexuality from these sources. In these stances, one finds *old* Scriptures tempered by *new* measures of compassion, forgiveness, and love on the part of the New Testament witnesses. Jesus' foremost concern is to foster quality relationships of wholeness between the believer and God and among believers as responsible partners in the new covenant and Household. Jesus' teachings on sexuality become profound and liberating when viewed in this light.

Both Jesus and Paul are explicit about two forms of acceptable sexual conduct: marriage[36] and voluntary celibacy.[37] Clearly, Jesus opposes unchastity or sexual promiscuity; he stands equally against adultery and even lustful thoughts (Matt. 5:27-32). While it is true that Jesus seems severe in his opposition to divorce, one must keep in view the abuses of the Law found among Jesus' contemporaries. Whimsical divorces and extreme forms of sexual indecency were common in his time, including the young Christian man who was "living with" his father's wife (1 Cor. 5:1) and adult men who were routinely sexually molesting young boys.[38] Such practices were abhorrent to Paul, as they doubtless would have been to Jesus, who sought to renew life's possibilities by returning to the original intent of *wholeness* and responsible mutual partnership behind the original Law or inherent in the earliest covenants. Their intent was not to re-codify the existing letter of the Law in more severe terms. For Jesus, Paul, and other New Testament witnesses, sexual relations were to be quality partnerships between responsible adults with mutual rights in the Household of God,[39] as paradigms for those who could benefit from this Household.

The New Testament disapproves of all sexual practices that are inconsistent with its own vision of the new Household. What is involved here is determining the usefulness of the New Testament's situational responses then in handling such matters today as prostitution, incestuous rape, various types of male and female homosexual patterns, teenage pregnancies, premarital, and extramarital sexual activity. These are all very much with us in Western society. Do the New Testament guidelines merely provide *condemnations* of such activities as sinful and disgraceful, holding the threat of hellfire over the heads of those who practice such sexual activity? For the answer, we can assess two dimensions of New Testament thought.

First, Jesus' teachings fundamentally center on the vision of the Kingdom of God as a new Household. As such, they accentuate disciplined, quality relationships based on a divine solidarity and kinship, not on traditional blood relation. The blood of Jesus Christ redefines what it means to be family members in the Household of God.

Second, Paul's thought resembles that of Jesus, insofar as Paul makes a theological priority out of the notion of *sōma* ("body"), which he contrasts with *sarx* ("flesh"). The former becomes the *household of life,* whereas the latter is the realm of sin and death. Although in different terms than Jesus, Paul also invites *all* into this household of new life. Furthermore, Paul may reject all forms of sexual promiscuity (1 Cor. 6:18, 19; Gal. 5:19; Rom. 1:24-27), but he neither dwells on the point nor otherwise attempts an analysis of the physiological, psychological or sociological factors that may cause such sexual practice.[40] By contrast, Paul does elaborate on the fruits of the Spirit and the spiritual gifts (*charismata*). These become part of the believers' lives when they identify with the new creation (2 Cor. 5:17). Believers thereby also claim membership in an expanding Household of that distinctive kind of love (*agapē*) that the Christ-event makes possible (1 Cor. 12–14; Rom. 12; Gal. 5:1–6:10).

By no means are the passions and desires of the flesh restricted to fornication (sexual promiscuity) in the New Testament. Paul uses the expression *sarkinos* (Rom. 7:14b) and *sarkikos* (1 Cor. 9:11; Rom. 15:27) interchangeably to mean "oriented to the material world" or "any human behavior that does not reflect God's spirit." *Paul, like other New Testament authors, seems to presuppose that people can and will change, if they are inspired and assisted in doing so.* The essence of Paul's "ministry of reconciliation" (2 Cor. 5:19–21) is the removal of barriers imposed by the world that alienate people from God. The ministry of reconciliation recruits persons from broken households and brings them into the Household of God. Thus, while Paul envisions God's reconciling activity as opening new possibilities for Jews and Gentiles as the people of God, the ministry of reconciliation has the wider purpose of reconciling humanity as a family in the Household of God.

The topic of reconciliation is the centerpiece of the Epistle to the Ephesians, which was written after A.D. 70 by one of Paul's younger co-workers or one of his students. There are differences between Paul's seven undisputed epistles and Ephesians with regard to ecclesiology, eschatology, and even theology.[41] The author of Ephesians transposes Pauls' theology (theocentric focus on God's salvific activity in the Christ-event) into a Christology (the elaboration of the person and expiational work of Christ). Still, the author of Ephesians represents accurately Paul's attitude about the scope of reconciliation and its significance regarding membership in the Household of God. I refer to Ephesians 2:11–22, which reads (emphasis mine):

[11]Therefore remember that at one time you Gentiles in the flesh, called the uncircumcision by what is called the circumcision, which is made in the flesh by hands— [12]remember that you were at that time separated from Christ, alienated from the commonwealth of Israel, and strangers to the covenants of promise, having no hope and without God in the world. [13]But now in Christ Jesus you who once were far off have been brought near *in the blood of Christ.* [14]For he is our peace, who has made us both one, and has broken down the dividing wall of hostility, [15]by abolishing *in his flesh* the law of commandments and ordinances, that he might create in himself one new man in place of the two, so making peace, [16]and might reconcile us both to God in one body through *the cross,* thereby bringing the hostility to an end. [17]And he came and preached peace to you who were far off and peace to those who were near; [18]for through [Christ] we both have access in one Spirit to the Father. [19]So then *you are no*

longer strangers and sojourners, but you are fellow citizens with the saints and members of the household of God, [20]built upon the foundation of the apostles and prophets, Christ Jesus himself being the cornerstone, [21]in whom the whole structure is joined together and grows into a holy temple in the Lord; [22]in whom you also are built into it for a dwelling place of God in the Spirit [emphasis mine].

For purposes of analysis, it is probably best to subdivide the pericope as follows: verses 11, 12, the former condition of the Gentiles (the past); verses 13-18, the reconciling work of Christ, a Christological hymn (the present); and verses 19-22, from strangers and sojourners to fellow citizens and members (the future). Many commentators agree on a threefold subdivision of Ephesians 2:11-22 but differ on the arrangement of verses. Markus Barth, for example, combines verses 11-13, explaining the grammatical difficulty in doing this as an inconsistency in Greek grammatical usage.[42] By grouping verses 11-13, Barth is able to highlight the Christological hymn that occurs in Ephesians 2:14-18. In my view, we can apprehend the significance of the hymm without obscuring the past–present–future sequence that the author of Ephesians may have had in mind.

The Christological hymn is thus at the pericope's center, detailing the present impact or effect of the work of Christ's *death* (blood, flesh, cross) and *resurrection* (the preaching of peace by the exalted Lord). The author clearly identifies the reconciling work as that of Christ, whereas Paul himself would have attributed the saving work to God. Preceding the hymn is a reflection on the former condition of the Gentiles (vv. 11, 12). In my view, the imagery of Israel ("circumcision, commonwealth, covenants, promise") intends to remind Gentile readers about the paradox that, although they once derided the Jews, the Gentiles were as alienated from the *new* Israel as the Jews. Ephesians 2:13 points out that Christ's blood has brought *both Jew and Gentile*—all of humanity—into a new level of being.

The second unit, verses 14-18, invokes a confessional hymn to accentuate the present effect of Christ's blood and message of reconciling peace. The final unit, verses 19-22, traces the implications of this for believers. In this new identity, they are no longer strangers (*xenos*) or sojourners (*paroikos*) in relation to each other, but fellow citizens (*sympolitai*) and members of the Household of God (*oikeioi tou theou*). Because of Christ's blood, all believers are supposed to be transported into a new Household of reconciliation and solidarity. In effect, the author of Ephesians invites his readers to a new kind of family relationship that exceeds the traditional obligations and debts between blood relatives. Beyond the ephemeral claims of human blood is the perennial claim by virtue of Christ's blood.

LISTEN TO THE BLOOD

The prolific Black philosopher and historian W. E. B. DuBois hardly qualifies as a commentator on the Epistle to the Ephesians, but he does offer a profound image that assists us in specifying the conceptual core of Ephesians. In the postscript of his *The Gift of Black Folk,* W. E. B. DuBois writes as follows (emphasis mine):

> Listen to the Winds, O God the Reader, that wail across the whip-cords stretched taut on broken human hearts; listen to the Bones, the bare bleached bones of the slaves, that line the lanes of Seven Seas and beat eternal tom-toms in the forests of the laboring deep; *listen to the Blood,* the cold thick blood that spills its filth across the fields and flowers of the Free; listen to the Souls that wing and thrill and weep and scream and sob and sing above it all. What shall these things mean, O God the Reader? You know. You know.[43]

It would be easy for activist Blacks, whether in Brazil, South Africa, or the United States, to find in DuBois's poetic invitation a clarion call to bitterness, cynicism, and social protest. The litany of historical atrocities against Blacks finds enough parallel among too many Blacks who show their marks of oppression by alarming rates of fratricide and other antisocial or countercultural activities that often account for the disproportional rate of incarcerating Blacks or committing them to mental hospitals. By listening only to the winds, bones, and blood invoked by DuBois, Blacks would only be listening with one ear. There is another blood for believers to hear with the other ear—the blood that symbolizes hope, new citizenship, and membership in the Household. Listening to the blood that the author of Ephesians has in mind can encourage a renewed, quality homecoming by the alienated, oppressed citizens who are so often treated as strangers in their native land.

Many New Testament authors give us a mandate to let Christian evangelical work enable others to enjoy a *constant "Homecoming"*— not only the one experienced by the prodigal son, but also the one experienced by the uncharitable, jealous, self-righteous older son. Today the institutional Church often seems casual, inept, or rigidly moralistic in relating to the needs and problems of Black families and households. Unfortunately, the Church in our time tends to adapt to the prevailing winds of the larger culture. She seems unlikely to accept the challenge of being a transformer of culture or a home for the homeless by making the Word genuinely adaptable for new life among *all* God's children—no matter how seemingly blemished or brutally oppressed. Such realities prompt us to explore how the theological process at work in the Bible impels the Black Church to new vistas of faith and a new listening to the blood in order to witness more effectively on behalf of the Household of God.

Theologian Matthew Lamb provides a sobering dictum in Latin—*Vox victimarum vox Dei.*[44] Translated, this means "the cry of the victims is the voice of God." If Black Church leaders have learned anything from the experience of Afro-Americans in the United States over the years, there should be no hesitance in admitting three things. First, racial hostilities and oppression, subtle and blatant, have made Afro-Americans one of the most victimized groups in American life. Second, these hostilities and oppression have allowed the Black Church to become the most significant institution of power in the Black community today. Almost inevitably, the first serious Black contender for the United States presidency had to be a minister! Third, white racism, whether "benign neglect" or manifest harassment, has, since slave days, had a deleterious impact on the stability of Black families and households, many of which *cry out,* not realizing their cries are the voice of God.

It is the task of the Bible scholar to examine and determine what the Bible, as the foundational document of the Church, says, particularly in light of its ancient context. The task of the Bible scholar becomes hermeneutics when he or she attempts to determine the text's meaning and relevance today. Here the exegete must learn from the theologian, even as the Black Church enters into a new dialogue with both. There is much to learn from recent developments in liberation theology, whether Black, Latin American, feminist, water buffalo, or African. All liberation theologies agree that one's own group's experience is a legitimate context for establishing categories and criteria for theological dialogue and a mode of extracting from and identifying with the theological process evident in the Bible.[45] For Cone, the Black experience finds its biblical parallels in the Exodus saga, the Old Testament prophets, and the liberating activity of Jesus in the New Testament.[46] I have tried to expand on these points.

Despite the consensus on this point among liberation theologians, one wonders how much Bible scholars or Church leaders have learned from it. To learn from the liberation theologians is for the Black Church to develop a new respect for and appreciation of *the hurts, needs, and hopes of Black families and households as loci for "doing theology."* Again, there is the challenge to *listen to the blood.* This means discarding the biblicist's simplicities of literalism and proof-texting. It also means discarding the other-worldly preoccupations of slave religion or the tendency to lord over as Ole Pharaohs in Black enclaves, and thus drain, in exploitative and self-aggrandizing ways, the limited resources of Blacks! In this, all are guilty to some extent, perhaps as unwitting proponents of a Black bourgeois Christianity imposed on Black families and households in need of vision, new listening, openness, and loving service *where the people are* so that they can arrive *where we want them to be.*

To hear the voice of God as the cries of our victimized Black families and households is *not* to present our faith as a religion of don'ts and moral condemnations. Rather, it becomes an agenda of presenting the faith in light of the contingencies of their situation. It means struggling to discern how the Church can become the healing, understanding, and loving agency of God's mercy to those who cry out, irrespective of how much those cries seem at times to be but a whisper from the churched and the unchurched in the Black community. The mandate and challenge is heightened all the more by the prospects of a nuclear apocalypse. Suddenly, traditional or conventional norms and approaches can dissipate, as we groan together and yet rejoice with new vistas of faith. By "listening to the blood" of Christ, believers can place themselves on the threshold of a new partnership between Bible, theology, Black Church, and Black families. We are called to witness again, in our time, as prophetic "Households of God." *Vox victimarum vox Dei.*[47]

CHAPTER TEN

The Things That Make for Peace:
New Testament Foundations
in the Nuclear Age

Wars, terrorism, and street violence are all too evident throughout the world today, but the ultimate threat to the human family is the prospect of nuclear war. All of humanity is hostage to nuclear weapons. Many of us consequently tend to live with a constant, quiet anxiety about nuclear arms, which epitomize violence in its most extreme form. Because of this, we conclude this book with reflections on biblical images of peace and hope that help us stave off any tendency to resign ourselves to the inevitability of nuclear destruction.

The Black Church has an important role to play in the task of peacemaking to prevent nuclear war, despite the fact that Blacks are most often merely the victims of white violence, and thus not highly visible in nuclear disarmament protests. James H. Cone offers a sobering, almost caustic, observation in this regard:

> Blacks and other victims of White violence are not surprised by the nuclear nightmare that has been created. That is why blacks, unfortunately, are seldom found in the crowds protesting nuclear arms. We have lived with White violence for nearly four hundred years, faced slave ships, auction blocks, lynchings, ghettos, inadequate education and medical care, indecent housing, chronic unemployment and constant police brutality. When physical survival is a daily task in which the odds are against you, because the nation in which you are a citizen has defined you as the enemy, there is little motivation to protest against a nuclear crisis that your enemies have created, especially when the people protesting look like your oppressors and do so little to connect justice with peace issues.[1]

Despite the manifest truth in Cone's insights, we need to thwart any perception that nuclear war lies outside the purview of the Black Church. It certainly was not outside the purview of Martin Luther King, Jr., who frequently opposed poverty, racism, and militarism and stressed their interrelatedness.[2] On the occasion of receiving the 1964 Nobel Peace Prize, King lectured at Oslo University on the subject of disarmament and world peace. Until the end of his life, he continued decrying "the triple evils of racism, materialism and militarism."[3] Recognizing that Blacks, too, had a vital stake in the peace movement, King showed how funds diverted to war efforts and nuclear arsenals only increased Black deprivation and oppression. Beyond that, one sadly notes today's concentration of Blacks in urban centers that would be the primary targets in any outbreak of nuclear war.

This chapter traces the relevance of the Bible for a witness for peacemaking that includes an expanded, distinctive role for the Black Church. We first identify aspects of the biblical view of creation and suggest that this correlates with biblical images of peace. Second is a discussion of obstacles that undermine the general Church's claims of endorsing peacemaking. Here the Church's own institutional self-interest becomes a factor, as it becomes possible to see that a Church tradition with less to lose materially may have the most to gain by taking up the cause of protecting the human family from the threat of nuclear extinction. Third is an exploration of New Testament apocalyptic as inconsistent with the nuclear "weapons of Armageddon" created by whites who alone cannot remove the threat posed by their creation.[4] Finally, we provide suggestions on the things that make for peace in light of the role envisioned for the Black Church.

The beginning of the Old Testament presents God's vision and promise of peace. They are part of the sixth century B.C. Priestly version ("P") of the creation myth (Gen. 1:1–2:4a). This version of the creation story precedes the older Jahwist ("J") version (Gen. 2:4b–3:24). Genesis 1:1–2:4a depicts the saga of God's creative activity over a period of six days.[5] Genesis 1:31 reads, "And God saw everything that he had made, and behold, it was very good." Once God establishes the goodness of creation, God can rest, and peace is the divinely intended norm for creation. Although the concluding unit of this Priestly version (Gen. 2:1–4a) makes no reference to *shalom* (lit. *šālōm:* "the peace that obtains when the demands of justice have been fully met"), it emphasizes the fact that the seventh day marks a time of completion and Sabbath rest.[6] In a sense, one can find here all the elements that make for the *shalom* of God: the goodness of the created order is established; the heavens and earth are completed; the progenitors of the human family are free to develop their potentials without predetermined restraints. God is at peace with creation, and divine rest is most appropriate. From the chaos evident in Genesis 1:2, the Priestly myth of creation moves to this primeval vision of peace. As Walter Brueggemann remarks, God resolves the problem of chaos by imposing order.[7] In this instance, order reflects the righteousness of God and the goodness that God intends for creation. The principal beneficiary is the primeval human family. There is no hatred, violence, and war in this biblical vision.

Later in the Book of Genesis, this vision of peace becomes a *promise* of peace, explicitly stated and associated with human faithfulness and justice (righteousness). Genesis 15:15 reads, "you shall go to your fathers in peace [*shalom*]; you shall be buried in a good old age." Here, God assures Abraham about the shalom that will constitute God's reward for demonstrating a faithful and righteous life. Abraham had developed a reputation as an obedient servant of God, at times shrewd, but not given to violence or hatred. In faithfulness to God, he was even willing to sacrifice his son, Isaac, if required (Gen. 22:1–19). Subsequent extrabiblical Jewish traditions virtually immortalized Abraham. For example, the Old Testament Pseudepigrapha elaborates the "trials of Abraham" in the Book of Jubilees.[8] The Old Testament's portrayal of Abraham adds substance and meaning to the vision and promise of peace. If Genesis 1:1–2:4a shows God working for a peace that makes Sabbath rest possible, then chapters 12–22 of Genesis show Abraham as the patriarch who, while receiving God's promise of peace, continues to work in obedience so his inheritance of peace would not seem taken for granted.

Toward the beginning of the New Testament, there are also striking reminders of the importance that early Christians and Jesus attached to the vision and promise of peace. In the so-called sermon on the mount skillfully arranged by Matthew, Jesus' seventh Beatitude is "Blessed are the peacemakers, for they shall be called sons of God" (Matt. 5:9). One commentator would have us accept a special interrelatedness between the fifth, sixth, and this seventh Beatitude, wherein the meek and merciful peacemaker renounces personal and material security.[9] Such an estimate leaves the impression that Jesus and Matthew envisioned peacemaking as reckless, passive nonresistance. The true sense of the seventh Beatitude finds better expression in Rudolph Bultmann's observation that all the Beatitudes are interrelated and "Whoever has his will set upon God's Reign also wills to fulfill the commandment of love."[10] The vision and promise of peace are calls to action on the part of persons seeking to participate in God's Kingdom (reign). The message is just as clear in Luke's gospel.

The Lukan infancy narrative lifts up the vision of peace (*eirēnē*) and reconfirms God's ancient promise of peace. Luke reports that at Jesus' birth, angels proclaimed, "Glory to God in the highest, and on earth *peace, goodwill toward humanity*" (*see* Luke 2:14). In my reading, I follow those ancient manuscripts that render the Greek word *eudokia* ("goodwill") as a nominative used in apposition with the subject, "peace."[11] This announcement thereby notifies all about what makes one a "son of peace" (Luke 10:6) or "makes for peace" in a substantial way (Luke 19:43; cf. v. 38). Willard Swartley, who elucidates the motif of peace as a redactional emphasis on the part of Luke, comments on the basis of the alternative version of Luke 2:14: "Glory to God in the highest, and on earth peace among men with whom he is pleased."

Heralding peace on earth because of God's limitless benevolence, this (2:14) sums up the divine commentary regarding the significance of

Jesus' birth. The preceding pericope of angelic announcement (vv.
10–12) clearly places the *eirēnē* ["peace"] texts within Israel's tradition—hope of a Messiah–Savior, a King par excellence who, like
Yahweh of old, will bring salvation to God's people. The text,
however, does not limit the Messiah's peace to Israel, but envisions
peace on earth among people everywhere.[12]

The missionary career of the apostle Paul falls between the times of Jesus
and Luke. At the beginning of Paul's epistles, there are variations of the
formula: "Grace to you and peace from God the Father and our Lord Jesus
Christ" (Gal. 1:3; 1 Thess. 1:1; 1 Cor. 1:3, 2 Cor. 1:2; Phil. 1:2; Philem.
1:3). The authors of Colossians and Ephesians so begin their epistles (Col.
1; 2; Eph. 1:2. Cf. 2 Thess. 1:2), as do the authors of the pastorals (1 Tim.
1:2; 2 Tim. 1:2; Titus 1:4). Doubtless, this reflects not only Paul's Jewish
background, so imbued with a consciousness of God's shalom, but also
reflects a lingering tutelage by Paul, even when he no longer labored in
mission. For Paul, peace, like ecumenical unity, was an important symbol
of solidarity for the Christian life. The author of Ephesians captures this
succinctly:

> For he is our peace, who has made us both one, and has broken down
> the dividing wall of hostility, by abolishing in his flesh the law of
> commandments and ordinances, that he might . . . reconcile us both
> to God in one body through the cross, thereby bringing the hostility to
> an end [Ephesians 2:14–16].

Nevertheless, the last reference to peace in the Bible seems, at first
glance, to withdraw God's divine promise of peace. In Revelation 6:4, John
the Divine reports that, when the second seal is broken, the rider on the red
horse is given the power to take peace from the earth. The impression that
remains is the horrible specter of utter destruction. However, the reader
should recognize that Revelation 6:4 is nothing but a warning. It is not
meant to undermine or obscure Christian hope. The breaking of seals is not
a profound theological disappointment; it is preparation for God's new
revelation of hope beyond the impact of the four horsemen, who epitomize
various human disasters. The message, as G. B. Caird adduces it, is that
Christians must always remember that Christ, by virtue of the victory on the
cross, is Lord of creation and controls world history:

> From one point of view the Cross was simply the product of the
> variegated turpitude of men: the bigotry of fanatics, the opportunism
> of corrupt priests, the moral astigmatism of lying witnesses, the
> vindictiveness of a national mob demanding that an innocent man
> suffer the death penalty for a crime precisely because he had refused
> to commit it for them, the vacillation of a governor yielding against

his judgment to popular frenzy, the treachery of one disciple, the denial of another, the cowardice of the rest, the taunts of callous by-standers. But because Jesus was content to accept the role of the Lamb assigned to him by his Father, he was able to transform all this into the signal triumph of divine love. He did not merely defeat the powers of evil; he made them agents of his own victory.[13]

Nearly two millennia ago, early Christian authors and editors began composing the little treatises and homilies that would become the New Testament. The homiletical proclamation of the gospel was vital in the life of the earliest Christian churches. It was unimaginable then that human beings would ever devise nuclear fission technology that would threaten the "eternal" rainbow covenant (Gen. 9:13–16) and pose a massive danger to all God's creation. While early Christian apocalyptic writers did envision God's sudden, even "imminent parousia"[14] (transformation of the created order), never was the prospect of global suicide envisioned. From beginning to end, the New Testament apocalyptic was a message of vindication and hope for Christians in a world that could be transformed. The thought was not of a kosmos that would be totally destroyed by either human beings or God. Yet, modern nuclear technology and space research have brought human existence far beyond the vistas of ancient biblical writers, to the brink of making earth little more than a burned-out cinder, like the planet Mars.

The frightful prospects of nuclear conflagration require religious leaders and their communities of faith to study, speak, and act boldly on behalf of world peace. But the Black Church in particular must redouble her efforts to reduce or remove the threat of nuclear war. Her voice and witness is needed to fill the moral void that appears to exist in the United States and the Soviet Union, despite governmental rhetoric about drastically reducing or eliminating nuclear weapons. The presence of the Black Church within a modern military-industrial "super power" is strategic, and her witness must be informed anew by New Testament foundations that make for peace. The Black Church, like the United Methodist Church, has no less a responsibility than the National Conference of Catholic Bishops, who issued their fairly comprehensive pastoral letter, *The Challenge of Peace: God's Promise and Our Response,* on May 3, 1983, or other ecclesiastical bodies.[15] An active witness by the Black church would help expand the discussion and recommendations for action.[16]

THE CHURCH'S CONFESSION OF PEACE AND SELF-INTEREST

One of the serious weaknesses of the pastoral letter issued by the National Conference of Catholic Bishops is that it does not confess those ways in which the modern-day Church's voice is muted by her own self-interest. As a result, that document, like so many other recent books on the subject from religious communities, does little more than sound the alarm and retrace the standard categories of the debate.[17] Prolonged attention focuses on the traditional debate regarding "just war" theories versus pacifism, the theological or moral viability of nuclear deterrence, and the values of nonviolence, without concern for related issues of a just world order. There is little evidence of a quest for the *new Word,* which is presumably always adaptable for new life in every age when illuminated by the ancient biblical text. The Black Church can become the vehicle for this new Word as she draws in the strength of a history of suffering. Leaders in the Black Church have the opportunity to move beyond parameters of institutional self-interest to reaffirm the biblical mandate for active peacemaking.

Despite the many impressive cathedrals of Europe and the highly visible, vocal, and commercial nature of so much of American religiosity, many people perceive the Church as irrelevant to the ongoing, vital concerns of daily life. For these, the Church has become too closely identified with national culture and the economic-political establishment. The realities of the Church's own institutional self-interest and role as a conservator of sociocultural values have, perhaps unwittingly, caused her to function almost as priest to the *status quo,* while tending to forget her call to prophetic witness. But most often the Black Church stands outside the mainline Church tradition and does not perceive herself principally as an extension of a nation's political economy. The Black Church's prophetic emphasis on social and racial justice qualifies her to address, in a unified and coherent manner, ideological tensions and trends that may portend global destruction.

Blacks are painfully reminded that their principal identity is not by virtue of nationality, but by virtue of race. Their Church extends beyond civil religion and becomes a paradigm for sharing, caring, and global hope. On the other hand, most members of white churches in the United States probably consider themselves to be first and foremost American. They are only "Christian" or "Methodist" as such religious labels conform to "American" values, whether economic (capitalism), political (republican democracy), or cultural (individualism, racism, sexism). American religion, including the electronic media biblicist religion, tends at times to degenerate into nothing more than a *civil* religion, a religion of nationalism with no substantive commitment to redistribution of wealth, sharing, and global hope. Within its diverse theological developments of the New Testament, we also find a movement toward civil religion as a form of passive peacemaking.

Toward the end of the first century, we find accommodationist patterns of ecclesiastic self-interest for institutional survival (notably the domestic codes of Colossians, Ephesians, the pastorals, and 1 Peter, together with various interpolations in other New Testament texts).[18] If institutional survival became a preoccupation within the Church so long ago, why should not the Church simply continue this comfortable tradition? Of course, the answer is that the unspeakable horrors posed by nuclear war demand a witnessing, active peacemaking. Inescapably, the Church is called to confession, to confront those aspects of secular ideologies that work against the purposes of God as revealed in the natural beauty of creation, in the biblical vision and promise of perfect peace (with justice), as revealed in the penultimate act of salvation in the Christ-event (death-resurrection) that gives rise to and sustains the Easter faith.

If people are unwilling to pray for the power to confess and to find appropriate opportunities to witness for peace and justice in the Church, all the rhetoric about a nuclear crisis is merely a public formality, if not a charade. The Church must set a bold example in our time as in the ancient context (Revelation 18). She must witness, even at the risk of her own so-called institutional self-interest, especially if any of us expect secular agencies (corporate or governmental) to do so. We may also need to confess that nuclear science and space technology become pejorative disciplines of "mammon," since they make the notion of progress meaningless by creating and sustaining atomic, hydrogen, and neutron bombs, missiles, or space-based laser systems. Progress has been eclipsed by the MADD philosophy of *M*utual *A*ssured *D*estruction *Deterrence* and by the Strategic Defense Initiative ("Star Wars"). J. Christiaan Beker sums the matter up nicely: "In the face of nuclear destruction . . . we are slowly but certainly forced to surrender the doctrine of progress that until now has constituted our version of the presence of the Kingdom of God in history ('realized eschatology')."[19]

PEACEMAKING AND APOCALYPTIC REDISCOVERY

Given the vast literature on the subject of nuclear war, the Three Mile Island scare, the ominous sight of missile silos and nuclear submarines, the general public in America seems to insulate itself from the possibility of *actual* nuclear war. Despite films such as *Testament, The Day After,* and most recently *Threads,* an astonishing degree of complacency, impotence, or resignation is found throughout America.

At least five different responses to the threat of nuclear war can be documented. First, a vast number of people remain ignorant about the size of existing nuclear arsenals, the types of weapons available, their costs, their deployment, and the "close calls" that we have already had. Some of these people consciously choose to escape from the reality of the problem, saying either that the topic is "too depressing" or that they are so desperate in trying to survive day-to-day as individuals that they do not have the time or energy to think about nuclear war. Another large group is somewhat aware of the dangers posed by sophisticated weapon systems, but they place considerable confidence in the fact that common sense will prevent such weapons from ever being used. Nevertheless, they insist that we must continue to stockpile these weapons. Third, a surprisingly large group of neoapocalypticists of the Hal Lindsay and biblicist variety subscribe to what may be called "the religiosity of doomsday." For them, the Bible predicts a fiery Armageddon. All the sanctimonious Christian needs to do is to wait passively for God's final judgment to condemn the sinful world in a nuclear fireball. These three groups would probably extol the value of peacemaking, but for them, it is a decidedly *passive* peacemaking that bespeaks the impotence of civil religion.

On the other hand, there are two more responses that share a commitment to *active* peacemaking. The fourth response is that of the military-industrial complex and their surrogates who derive large financial benefits from the defense industry or whose right-wing political ideology causes them to define "a strong America" by supporting a $316 billion 1986 defense budget. These people stand in combat-readiness, prepared to inflict *nuclear revenge* on the adversaries of the NATO Alliance. Fifth and finally, there is a woefully small group of "active peacemakers" who are the prophets and prophetesses of hope, engaging in the sincere quest for responsible Christian action and witness. Surely, these are they who Jesus has in mind in his "Sermon on the Mount": "Blessed are the peacemakers, for they shall see God" (*see* Matt. 5:9).

It is striking that Luke, who mentions the word *peace* more often than Mark, Matthew, and John combined (fourteen times by Luke in twelve passages) does not include the specific Beatitude regarding the peacemakers. This apparent discrepancy may be explained in various ways. Whether or not Luke was familiar with Matthew's arrangement of the Beatitudes, he may have adopted another tradition or stylized his blessings and woes after Old Testament formulae as found in Deuteronomy. Whatever the reason, the absence of any reference to peacemakers by the canonical evangelist who otherwise expressed the most sustained explicit interest in this subject merits further consideration. Does Luke's emphasis on peace give credence to Hans Conzelmann's view of Luke as political apologetic placating his patron, Theophilus, by representing the Jesus and early Church stories as in no sense a political threat to Rome? With attention to scholars who have sought to answer this question, Willard Swartley conducts an independent analysis of Lukan texts that mention peace. He concludes that Luke was *not* motivated by any political apologetic. Rather, Swartley insists that Luke strategically uses the idea of peace to accentuate a multiplicity of other themes:

> The themes connected to *eirēnē* in Luke's redactional purpose are many: redemption from oppression, light to the pagans, forgiveness of sins, blessings to the outsiders (Gentiles, a sinner, women), a "yes" to those of good will . . . affirming peace as the hallmark of the missionary growth of the Kingdom and the distinguishing character of the Jesus community, acceptance of God's purposes in the Messiah

Jesus (and conversely, judgement upon those who reject the peace of the Messiah), and receiving the peace of Christ's presence.[20]

Swartley highlights the normative nature and function of the Lukan Jesus' concern for peace or embodiment of peace. In Luke, the King of Peace (Luke 19:38; cf. "Prince of Peace," Isa. 9:6) becomes the model for the human family to engage in "the things that make for peace" (Luke 19:42). Indeed, as Stephen Mott has correctly noted, "the claim of justice is prior to that of peace" in the Bible.[21] Thus, Luke is far more concerned with salvation and claims of justice than a political apologetic that would compromise active peacemaking on behalf of the Kingdom of a just world order.

The relative paucity of committed, *active* peacemakers in today's nuclear age demands that New Testament foundations be examined afresh. I subscribe to the view of Professor Ernst Käsemann that apocalyptic is the mother of Christian theology. At the center of that apocalyptic is an *anthropology of hope*.[22] Beyond discrete notions of progress is the vision and promise of a transformed created order that anticipates the Kingdom of God *on earth*. "Thy will be done, on earth as it is in heaven," reads one of the petitions in the Lord's Prayer (Matt. 6:10) that is memorized by many and studied by few. Despite this, it seems that the hope that coheres in New Testament apocalypticism is central to any correct understanding of New Testament foundations. This hope is both a renewed promise and a call to faithful witness. In this light, the single most important challenge of New Testament sentences on peacemaking is assisting people to rediscover the New Testament apocalyptic, thereby symbolizing the imminence of God as they engage in active peacemaking in our nuclear age.

By New Testament apocalyptic, we mean an ethical eschatology in which God's power to sustain and transform becomes part of the Christian believer's practical life. This apocalyptic presupposes a radical disagreement between conventional wisdom and the wisdom of God. The author of the Epistle of James elaborates on the wisdom from above in James 3:17, 18, mentioning wisdom from above in relation to the peaceable, the good fruits, a harvest of righteousness (justice), and peacemaking. Likewise, the author of the Epistle to the Hebrews refers to righteousness (justice) as a peaceful fruit that requires training (Heb. 12:11) and then calls faint-hearted Christians to the task of peacemaking:

Therefore lift your drooping hands and strengthen your weak knees, and make straight paths for your feet, so that what is lame may not be put out of joint but rather be healed. Strive for peace with all men, and for the holiness without which no one will see the Lord [Hebrews 12:12–14].

The ancient biblical yearnings for justice, liberation, and peace remain elusive. The politico-military superpowers of our era—the United States of America and the Union of Soviet Socialist Republics—have divided the world into a Western block (NATO) and an Eastern block (Warsaw Pact). The rest of the world has become merely strategic spheres of influence, sources of raw mineral resources, cheap labor, and underdeveloped centers of poverty. It just so happens that most of the world's population resides in these regions which, like the oppressed racial and ethnic minority groups within the superpowers, have become both the tragic victims of international intrigue and a captive audience for the economic, political, and military war games of the superpowers. Worse still, racial, class, and family tensions or open conflict abound within many Third World nations. Even here, socioeconomic crises and cultural distortions fester, as the privileged within the ranks of the victimized seek to oppress their fellow citizens in a seemingly endless spiral of human degradation and social evil. In view of these grim realities, it could be easily concluded that the global situation today is hopeless. In too many ways, humanity seems to be on an irreversible collision course that will result in the nuclear destruction of all life forms on the planet earth.

Just as ancient New Testament authors struggled to discern the will of God beyond Jewish nationalism or the political economy of Rome (especially the Book of Revelation), Christians today must allow our visions for world peace to move beyond American or Soviet nationalisms and the competing political economies of East and West. We must ask why there are such huge stockpiles of instant mass murder in the world today. The answer is not as simple as "self-defense" or "national interest." We must inquire further: Whose defense; whose interest? The painful answer is: it is the *interest* of the wealthy and powerful; it is the *defense* of the elite group's turf and material possessions; it is sheer *greed* and the human need to impose one's will on others through economic and military power. In a world where no one wants to share his or her possessions, power, or turf, nuclear war becomes inevitable.

Perhaps the Black Church, with her long history of being regarded as the "least of these," may claim and exercise a leadership that can emerge only out of a commitment to the suffering witness of Jesus, who though poor, made many rich. We are at the curious juncture where the Black Church's vocation is no longer restricted to the poor and downtrodden, but includes a word of survival for the entire human family, one that seeks also to transform the rich and powerful. *The New Testament world and its apocalyptic is a world of hope—a life-affirming world for the powerless, the poor, the exploited; but it is also a world to which the wealthy and powerful are invited.* The experience of the Black Church enables it to be the bearer of this new Word because the wealthy and powerful have tended only to build great cathedrals for themselves and transpose the biblical world into their own luxurious settings of power and privilege. These patterns of power and privilege were evident in Palestinian Judaism of Jesus' Jerusalem and explain why he wept over the "holy" city that did not know the things that make for peace. It was in that city that he was crucified, and it may be through nuclear war that Christ will be crucified again. Yet, this need not be so! The hope resides in the collective witness of the human family, including the Black Church. We all must renew the quest for justice—the principle element that makes for peace.

Notes

INTRODUCTION

1. *See* Robin Scroggs, "Sociological Interpretation of the New Testament," in *The Bible and Liberation: Political and Social Hermeneutics,* Norman K. Gottwald, ed. (Maryknoll, N.Y.: Orbis Books, 1983), pp. 347–48. *See also* J. Deotis Roberts, *Black Theology in Dialogue* (Philadelphia, Pa.: Westminster Press, 1987), pp. 11–12.

2. R. A. Morrisey, *Colored People and Bible History* (Hammond, Ind.: W. B. Conkey Company, 1925), pp. 6–7.

3. Albert Cleage, *The Black Messiah* (Fairway, Kans.: Andrews & McMeel, Inc., 1969).

4. Alfred Dunston, *The Black Man in the Old Testament and its World* (Philadelphia, Pa.: Dorrance, 1974).

5. Latta Thomas, *Biblical Faith and the Black American* (Valley Forge, Pa.: Judson Press, 1986 [1976]).

6. Robert A. Bennett, Jr., "Africa and the Biblical Period," *Harvard Theological Review,* 64(1971):483–500.

7. Charles B. Copher, "The Black Man in the Biblical World," *The Journal of the Interdenominational Theological Center,* vol. 1, no. 2 (Spring, 1974):7–16; "3,000 Years of Biblical Interpretation with Reference to Black Peoples," *The Journal of the Interdenominational Theological Center,* vol. 13, no. 2 (Spring, 1986):225–46. *See also* Charles B. Copher, "Egypt and Ethiopia in the Old Testament," in *Nile Valley Civilizations,* Ivan Van Sertima, ed. (Journal of African Civilizations, Ltd., 1985):163–78.

8. Vincent Wimbush, "Biblical–Historical Study as Liberation: Toward an Afro-Christian Hermeneutic," *The Journal of Religious Thought,* vol. 42, no. 2 (Fall–Winter, 1985–1986):9–21.

9. Frank M. Snowden, Jr., *Blacks in Antiquity: Ethiopians in the Greco-Roman Experience* (Cambridge, Mass.: Harvard University Press, 1970).

10. *See* Charles H. Long, *Significations: Signs, Symbols, and Images in the Interpretation of Religion* (Philadelphia, Pa.: Fortress Press, 1986).

11. *See* J. Deotis Roberts, *Black Theology in Dialogue.*

12. "Wade in the Water," *Lift Every Voice and Sing: A Collection of Afro-American Spirituals and Other Songs* (New York: The Church Hymnal Corporation, 1981), no. 100.

13. Michel Foucault, *Power/Knowledge: Selected Interviews and Other Writings,* Colin Gordon, ed. (New York: Pantheon, 1980), cited by Lewis S. Mudge, "Thinking About the Church's Thinking: Toward a Theological Ethnography," *Theological Education* (Spring, 1984): 43, 54.

14. Snowden, *Blacks in Antiquity,* p. 114.

15. Cain H. Felder, "The Bible, Black Women and Ministry," *The Journal of Religious Thought,* vol. 41, no. 2 (Fall–Winter, 1984–1985); *Journal of the Interdenominational Theological Center,* vol. 12, nos. 1 and 2 (Fall–Spring, 1984–1985).

INTRODUCTION TO PART I

1. Mark Mathabane, *Kaffir Boy* (New York: New American Library, 1986), p. 58; cf. pp. 61, 76.

2. Ibid., p. 59.

3. Gayraud S. Wilmore, *Black Religion and Black Radicalism* (Maryknoll, N.Y.: Orbis Books, 1983), pp. 125, 257.

CHAPTER ONE

1. John S. Mbiti, *African Religions and Philosophies* (New York: Doubleday, 1970), pp. 62–76; Gayraud S. Wilmore, *Black Religion and Black Radicalism* (Maryknoll, N.Y.: Orbis Books, 1983), pp. 15–19.

2. Mbiti, *African Religions,* pp. 135–42, 208–16, 257–65; Aylward Shorter, *African Christian Spirituality* (Maryknoll, N.Y.: Orbis Books, 1980), pp. 15–19.

3. Latta Thomas, *Biblical Faith and the Black American* (Valley Forge, Pa.: Judson Press, 1986 [1976]), p. 18.

4. *See* Nlenanya Onwu, "The Current State of Biblical Studies in Africa," *The Journal of Religious Thought,* vol. 41, no. 2 (Fall–Winter, 1984–1985):35–46.

5. Vincent Wimbush, "Biblical-Historical Study as Liberation: Toward an Afro-Christian Hermeneutic," *The Journal of Religious Thought,* vol. 42, no. 2 (Fall–Winter, 1984–1985):10.

6. Ibid., pp. 10–11.

7. Julius Lester, ed., *The Seventh Son: The Thought and Writings of W. E. B. DuBois,* vol. 1 (New York: Random House, 1971), p. 78.

8. Ibid., p. 83.

9. *See* Amy Jacques-Garvey, ed., *Philosophy and Opinions of Marcus Garvey,* 2 vols. (New York: Atheneum, 1969); E. David Cronon, *Black Moses: The Story of Marcus Garvey* (Madison, Wisc.: The University of Wisconsin Press, 1969); Leonard Barrett, *The Rastafarians: Sounds of Cultural Dissonance* (Boston, Mass.: Beacon Press, 1977).

10. Charles H. Long, "Perspectives for a Study of Afro-American Religion in the United States," in *History of Religions,* vol. 2, no. 1 (August 1971):54–66, as cited by James H. Cone, *For My People* (Maryknoll, N.Y.: Orbis Books, 1984), p. 26.

11. Wilmore, *Black Religion,* p. 26.

12. Ibid., p. 235.

13. Cone, *For My People,* p. 83; cf. pp. 61–62, 72, and seriatim, chapters 7 and 8.

14. J. Deotis Roberts, *Black Theology Today: Liberation and Contextualization* (New York and Toronto: Edwin Mellen Press, 1984), pp. 179–87.

15. Cornel West, *Prophesy Deliverance* (Philadelphia, Pa.: Westminster Press, 1982), pp. 47–65.

16. Lewis S. Mudge, "Thinking About the Church's Thinking," *Theological Education* (Spring, 1984):43, 54.

17. Bruce Williams, "Lost Pharaohs of Nubia," in *Nile Valley Civilizations* (*Journal of African Civilizations,* Ltd., 1985), p. 35.

18. Ibid., pp. 29, 31.

19. Abbé Terrason, trans., *Histoire universelle,* (Paris, 1758), bk. 3, p. 341, cited by Cheikh Anta Diop, *The African Origin of Civilization: Myth or Reality?,* Mercer Cook, trans. (New York and Westport, Conn.: Lawrence Hill and Company, 1974 [1955]), pp. 2, 278; *see also* Brian M. F. Fagan, *Tomb Robbers, Tourists and Archeologists in Egypt* (New York: Charles Scribner's Sons, 1975), pp. 14–31.

20. Robert A. Bennett, Jr., "Africa and the Biblical Period," *Harvard Theological Review* 64(1971):485.

21. Diop, *African Origin,* p. 27.

22. *See* Bennett, "Africa and the Biblical Period," p. 489. On the dating of Isa. 11:11, *see* Otto Kaiser, *Isaiah 1-12: A Commentary,* 2d ed. (Philadelphia, Pa.: Westminster Press, 1983), p. 264; Raymond E. Brown, Joseph A. Fitzmyer, and Roland Murphy, eds., *The Jerome Biblical Commentary* (Englewood Cliffs, N.J.: Prentice-Hall, Inc., 1968), p. 273; Matthew Black, ed., *Peake's Commentary on the Bible* (London: Thomas Nelson and Sons Ltd., 1962), p. 499.

23. William Leo Hansberry, *Africa and Africans as Seen by Classical Writers,* Joseph E. Harris, ed. (Washington, D.C.: Howard University Press, 1977), pp. 9–13.

24. Sir Alan Gardiner, *Egypt of the Pharaohs* (New York: Oxford University Press, 1974 [1961]), p. 434; cf. Sergew Hable Sellassie, *Ancient and Medieval Ethiopian History to 1270* (Addis Ababa, United Printers, 1972), p. 21.

25. Hansberry, *Africa and Africans,* p. 12.

26. On the variety of local deities in Egypt, *see* Gardiner, *Egypt,* pp. 214–16. For the significance of Akhenaten's revolution in relation to the Bible, *see* Donald B. Redford, "The Monotheism of the Heretic Pharaoh: Monotheism or Egyptian Anomaly?, *Biblical Archaeology Review,* vol. 13, no. 3 (May/June, 1987):16–32.

27. Diop, *African Origin,* p. 43.

28. Ibid., p. 78.

29. Ibid., p. 19.

30. Ibid., pp. 11–21; Frank M. Snowden, Jr., *Blacks in Antiquity: Ethiopians in the Greco-Roman Experience* (Cambridge, Mass.: Harvard University Press, 1970), pp. 113–115.

31. Martin Bernal, *Black Athena: The Afroasiatic Roots of Classical Civilization,* vol. 1, *The Fabrication of Ancient Greece, 1785-1985* (London: Free Association Books, 1987), p. 18.

32. Diop, *African Origin,* p. 20.

33. Cone, *For My People,* pp. 99–121; James H. Cone, *Speaking the Truth* (Grand Rapids, Mich.: William B. Eerdmans Publishing Company, 1986), pp. 142–67; J. Deotis Roberts, *Black Theology,* pp. 115–18.

34. E. A. Wallis Budge, *The Egyptian Book of the Dead* (New York: Dover Publications, 1967); *also see* E. A. Wallis Budge, *Osiris and the Egyptian Resurrection,* 2 vols. (New York: Dover Publications, 1973).

35. Budge, *Book of the Dead,* pp. lxxxii–lxxxiii.

36. *See* George G. M. James, *Stolen Legacy* (New York: Philosophical Library, 1954; reprint San Francisco: Julian Richardson Associates, 1976), pp. 21–24.

37. Ephraim Isaac and Cain H. Felder, "Reflections on the Origins of the Ethiopian Civilization," International Congress of Ethiopian Studies (November, 1983), Addis Ababa, Ethiopia. *See* the extended discussion in chapter two.

38. Diop, *African Origin,* p. 73.

39. Gene Rice, "The Curse That Never Was (Genesis 9:18-27)," *The Journal of Religious Thought,* vol. 29 (1972):5-27; Gene Rice, "Two Black Contemporaries of Jeremiah," *The Journal of Religious Thought,* vol. 32 (1975):95-109; Gene Rice, "The African Roots of the Prophet Zephaniah," *The Journal of Religious Thought,* vol. 36, no. 1 (1979):21-31. *See* chapter three.

40. Rice, "Curse," p. 19.

41. Flavius Josephus, *Complete Works* (Grand Rapids, Mich.: Kregel Publications, 1960), p. 180; *Antiquities,* book 8, ch. 6, pp. 3, 5. Snowden, *Blacks in Antiquity,* p. 334, states that Josephus was probably acquainted with some native Egyptian or Ethiopian rendition that connected the Queen of "The Arabian Kingdom" (sic) with Egypt and Ethiopia. More likely, however, is the observation that Josephus merely reflects contemporary Jewish exegesis of the Old Testament episode. *See* Edward Ullendorff, *Ethiopia and the Bible* (London: Oxford University Press, 1968), p. 135.

42. Snowden, *Blacks in Antiquity,* pp. 202-204.

43. Martin Hengel, *Acts and the Ancient History of Earliest Christianity* (Philadelphia, Pa.: Fortress Press, 1980), p. 80: "As a result of the expulsion of the 'Hellenists' from Jerusalem the gospel was passed on to Samaria and finally in the figure of the Ethiopian on his way home, reached out to 'the ends of the earth' (cf. Zeph. 3:10; Ps., 68:32; Luke 11:31). In ancient geography, Ethiopia was the extreme boundary of the inhabited world in the hot south."

44. Ernst Haenchen, *The Acts of the Apostles: A Commentary* (Oxford, England: Basil Blackwell, 1971), p. 314.

45. Ibid., p. 315.

46. Hengel, *Acts,* pp. 79-80; cf. p. 75. In another vein, notice the extreme hesitancy of Wolf Leslau, *Falasha Anthology: The Black Jews of Ethiopia* (New York: Schocken Books, 1951), p. xliii to admit the possibility of black Jews in the biblical period.

47. *See* Cone, *For My People,* pp. 18-19, 65-67. *See also* Allan Boesak, *Black and Reformed* (Maryknoll, N.Y.: Orbis Books, 1984), pp. 10-15.

48. In Hebrew, *Tôrâ, Nebî'îm,* and *Kethubîm,* representing *TNK,* constitute the tripartite division of the Law ("instruction"), Prophets, and Writings. For a lucid overview of Old Testament canon formation, *see* Enid B. Mellor, *The Making of the Old Testament,* The Cambridge Bible Commentary (Cambridge, England: The University Press, 1972), pp. 108-28; James A. Sanders, *Torah and Canon* (Philadelphia, Pa.: Fortress Press, 1972).

49. *See* Georg Werner Kümmel, *Introduction to the New Testament,* 17th ed. (Nashville, Tenn.: Abingdon Press, 1973), pp. 478-501; Oscar Cullmann, *The Early Church,* ed. A. J. B. Higgins (Philadelphia, Pa.: Westminster Press, 1956), pp. 39-54; Bruce M. Metzger, *The Early Versions of the New Testament* (Oxford, England: Clarendon Press, 1977); O. Jessie Lace, *Understanding the New Testament,* The Cambridge Bible Commentary (Cambridge, England: University Press, 1965), p. 120.

50. Kümmel, *Introduction,* pp. 498-99.

51. Metzger, *Early Versions,* pp. 216, 251-56. My former colleague at Princeton

suggests, in an exploration of ancient Ethiopian manuscripts and other sources, that "Hamitic (Cushite) and Semitic invaders . . . subjugated the indigenous Negroid population." He is equally as arbitrary in claiming that "Semitic intruders from Southwest Arabia (Yemen) brought with them a more highly developed social organization, architecture and art as well as a system of writing."

52. Clement of Alexandria, *Stromata* I, 9, 44, and 63; III, 13, 93; V, 14, 96. Origen, *Commentary on John* 2, 12, 87 (IV, 67) as cited by Cullmann, *The Early Church,* p. 45, n. 12.

53. Hans Joachim Schoeps, *Jewish Christianity* (Philadelphia, Pa.: Fortress Press, 1969), pp. 136–40; *Theologie und Geschichte des Judenchristentums* (Tübingen: J. C. B. Mohr, 1949), pp. 334–42.

54. James W. Thompson, *The Middle Ages,* vol. 1 (New York: Alfred A. Knopf, 1931), p. 150; A. J. Arberry, in *History of the Middle East and Aegean Region, c. 1800–1350 B.C.,* Cambridge Ancient History Series, vol. 2 (Cambridge, England: Cambridge University Press, 1954), p. 312.

55. Snowden, *Blacks in Antiquity,* pp. 198, 331, identifies the problem in the "I am black and/but beautiful" (*melaina eimi kai kalē*) assertion in the Song of Songs. The Greek conjunctive particle *kai,* normally translated as "and" from the LXX, suddenly in Jerome's Vulgate is rendered in an adversative sense *sed* ("but") in the Latin. Augustine did not follow the Vulgate text; he restored the "and." *See also* Ephraim Isaac, "Genesis, Judaism and the 'Sons of Ham'," in *Slavery and Abolition: A Journal of Comparative Studies,* vol. 1, no. 1 (May, 1980), p. 8; *see also* chapter three.

56. J. Omosade Awolalu, "The Emergence and Interaction of Religions in Nigeria," *The Journal of Religious Thought,* vol. 41, no. 2 (Fall–Winter, 1984–1985):7–18.

57. Mbiti, *African Religions,* p. 245–52.

58. Wilmore, *Black Religion,* p. 27.

59. Nlenanya Onwu, "The Current State of Biblical Studies in Africa," *The Journal of Religious Thought,* vol. 41, no. 2 (Fall–Winter, 1984–1985):35–46; Mbiti, *African Religions,* pp. 36, 92, 119, 128; cf. Cone, *For My People,* pp. 72–73, 227.

60. Hansberry, *Africa,* pp. 29–36.

61. Ibid., p. 39; Diop, *African Origin,* pp. 179–203.

62. *See* Howard Thurman, *Jesus and the Disinherited* (Nashville, Tenn.: Abingdon Press, 1949), pp. 30–31; Amos N. Jones, Jr., *Paul's Message of Freedom: What Does it Mean for the Black Church?* (Valley Forge, Pa.: Judson Press, 1984), pp. 5–7, 17–18, 30, 38, 228.

63. Cone, *For My People,* p. 41; Robert McAfee Brown, *Unexpected News: Reading the Bible with Third World Eyes* (Philadelphia, Pa.: Westminster Press, 1984), p. 12.

64. Not to mention the passion narratives of the gospels and the call for radical spirituality, even martyrdom, in the apocalyptic segments of the New Testament, not least the Revelation.

65. Ernst Käsemann, *Perspectives on Paul* (Philadelphia, Pa.: Fortress Press, 1971), pp. 1–21. *See also,* J. Christiaan Beker, *Paul the Apostle: The Triumph of God in Life and Thought* (Philadelphia, Pa.: Fortress Press, 1980), and especially his *Paul's Apocalyptic Gospel: The Coming Triumph of God* (Philadelphia, Pa.: Fortress Press, 1982).

CHAPTER TWO

1. Bernhard W. Anderson, *Understanding the Old Testament* (Englewood Cliffs, N.J.: Prentice-Hall, Inc., 1974), p. 19. The full debate on the dating of the "J" source can be seen in Otto Eissfeldt, *The Old Testament: An Introduction* (New York: Harper & Row, 1965), pp. 164–70. While elements of Gen. 2:4b–3:24 (notably 2:10–14) are much older than 950 B.C., this dating shows that the first biblical reference to Cush in M.T./Hebrew Text (but, as "Ethiopia" in the Greek Old Testament [LXX]) occurs during the reign of King Solomon.

2. Claus Westermann, *Genesis 1–11: A Commentary* (Minneapolis, Minn.: Augsburg Publishing House, 1984 [1974]), p. 218.

3. Ibid., p. 184.

4. For summary listings of biblical passages that cite Cush/Ethiopia consult James Strong, *Strong's Exhaustive Concordance of the Bible* (Nashville, Tenn.: Thomas Nelson Publishers, 1979), pp. 230, 312.

5. Eissfeldt, *The Old Testament*, p. 184; Anderson, *Understanding the Old Testament*, pp. 423–24.

6. George A. Bottrick, "Sheba, Queen of," *Interpreter's Dictionary of the Bible*, vol. 4 (Nashville, Tenn.: Abingdon Press, 1962), p. 311.

7. Cf. Isa. 60:6, from Sheba.

8. Strabo, H. L. Jones, ed. and trans., *The Geography of Strabo*, the Loeb Classical Edition (Cambridge, Mass.: Harvard University Press, 1949), Book 15, 4:2.

9. This reference is to Homer's "the Ethiopians that are sundered in twain" (*aithiopas toi dichtha dedaistai*) in Od. 1:23.

10. Strabo, Book 1, 2:24.

11. Ibid., 2:25–28.

12. Ibid., 2:28.

13. Strabo, Book 2, 3:8.

14. Ibid.

15. Gus W. Van Beek, "Monuments of Axum in Light of South Arabian Archaeology," *Journal of the American Oriental Society*, vol. 87 (1967):14.

16. *See* Gregory of Nyssa, *Contra Eunomium* 1 (*Patristica Graeca* 45:264) and F. Cabrol and H. Leclerq, *Dictionnaire d'archeologie chretienne et du liturgie*, V (1), (Paris: Libraire Letouzey, 1922), pp. 590–92. Philostargius calls Theophilus "Indian" (*Historia ecclesiastica* 2:6; *Pat. Graec.* 65:469), but the word Indians was widely applied to Ethiopians in his time.

17. Carl Brockelmann, *History of the Islamic Peoples* (New York: Capricorn Books, 1960 [originally *Geschichte der Islamischen Völker und Staaten*, 1944]), pp. 3, 9.

18. Van Beek, "Monuments of Axum," p. 115.

19. Buttrick, "Sabeans," *Interpreter's Dictionary of the Bible*, vol. 4, p. 144.

20. Ibid., p. 145.

21. Thomas de Pinedo, *De Uribibus* (Graz, Switzerland: Akademische Druck V. Verlangsanstalt, 1958 [1678]); cf. Thomas de Pinedo, *Stephanus de Byzantinus cum Annotationibus*, 4:5: *"Populi Arabiae sunt Abadeni. . . ."* (Lipsiae, 1825).

22. Ludolphus Hiob, *Historia Aethiopica* (Frankfort, 1681) book 1, chapter 1: *"indigenae eneium non sunt sed venerunt ex ea Arabiae parte que felix vocatur. . . ."*

23. Eduard Glaser, *Abessinier in Arabien und Afrika*, (Munich, 1895); C. Conti

Rossini, *"Sugli Habasat,"* *Rendiconti, Regia Academi dei Lincei,* ser. 5 XV (1906), 39–59; *"Expeditions et possessions des Habasat en Arabie,"* *Journal Asiatique,* ser. 18 (1921), pp. 5ff.; *see also* his *Storia d'Etiopia* (Bergamo, 1928).

24. A. K. Irvine, "On the identity of the *Habashat* in the South Arabian Inscriptions," *Journal of Semitic Studies* vol. 10 (January–December, 1965), p. 181.

25. Ibid.

26. Cheikh Anta Diop, *The African Origin of Civilization: Myth or Reality?*, Mercer Cook, trans. (New York and Westport, Conn.: Lawrence Hill and Company, 1974 [1955]). Concerning the various theories about the origin of Zimbabwe, *see* G. Caton-Thompson, *Zimbabwe Culture* (Oxford, England: The Clarendon Press, 1931).

27. Edward Ullendorff, *The Ethiopians,* 2d ed. (New York: Oxford University Press, 1961), p. 51.

28. A. Murtonen, *Early Semitic: A Diachronical Inquiry into the Relationship of Ethiopic to the Other So-called South-east Semitic Languages* (Leiden: E. J. Brill, 1967).

29. George W. B. Huntington, ed. and trans., *The Periplus of the Erythraean Sea* (London: The Hakluyt Society, 1980).

30. As cited by E. Littmann, *Deutsche Aksum Expedition,* vol. 4 (Berlin: G. Reimer, 1913), pp. 4–17.

31. A. K. Irvine, "Identity of the *Habashat,*" pp. 178–96.

32. Ibid.

33. Ephraim Isaac and Cain H. Felder, "Reflections on the Origins of the Ethiopian Civilization," read in November, 1984, at the Congress of Ethiopian Studies, Addis Ababa, Ethiopia, pp. 10–13.

34. Eissfeldt, *The Old Testament,* pp. 287–90.

35. Norman Snaith, in George A. Buttrick, ed., *Interpreter's Bible,* 12 vols. (Nashville, Tenn.: Abingdon, 1957), vol. 3, pp. 10–11.

36. Ibid., p. 96; Edward Ullendorff, *Ethiopia and the Bible* (London: Oxford University Press, 1968), p. 142.

37. Ullendorff, *Ethiopia,* p. 134; cf. *Oxford Annotated Bible* (RSV), William Stinespring comments, 1 Kings 10 (note, p. 431), or Victor Gold's comment on Isa. 60:6 (note, p. 898); Buttrick, "Sabeans," *Interpreter's Dictionary,* vol. 4, p. 311.

38. Ullendorff, *Ethiopia,* p. 132.

39. Ibid., p. 134.

40. James B. Pritchard, *Ancient Near Eastern Texts,* vol. 1 (Princeton, N.J.: Princeton University Press, paperback ed., 1973), pp. 193–201.

41. Ibid.

42. Cf. Ullendorff, *Ethiopia,* p. 134.

43. Frank M. Snowden, Jr., *Blacks in Antiquity: Ethiopians in the Greco-Roman Experience* (Cambridge, Mass.: Harvard University Press, 1970), p. 113.

44. Cf. Tadesse Tamrat, *Church and State* (London: Oxford University Press, 1972), p. 9. According to J. Ryckmans, the title *mkrrb* designates *"Prere-Prince,"* (Prince-Priest) and *"Prince-Sacrificateur"* (prince-sacrificer).

45. Flavius Josephus, *Complete Works* (Grand Rapids, Mich.: Kregel Publications, 1960), p. 180; *Antiquities,* Book 8, Ch. 6, pp. 3, 5.

46. *See* Buttrick, *Interpreter's Bible,* 1 Kings, Introduction.

47. Josephus's translator's note cites 2 Kings 23:29, Jer. 44:30, plus general usage of the term *Pharaoh* by other prophets, p. 180. Also, Snowden, *Blacks in Antiquity,* p. 334, calls attention to the note in the Loeb edition of *Antiquities Judaicae*

which on pp. 660–61 states that Josephus was probably acquainted with some native Egyptian or Ethiopian tradition which connected the Queen of the Arabian Kingdom with Egypt and Ethiopia.

48. Ullendorff, *Ethiopia,* p. 135.

49. Snowden, *Blacks in Antiquity,* pp. 198, 331, notes that both the KJV and the Vulgate render the expression "I am black but beautiful." Cf. the *'Ebed-Melek* episode, Jer. 38:7, 10, 12.

50. Ullendorff, *Ethiopia,* p. 17.

51. Ibid., p. 9.

52. Ernst Haenchen, *Acts of the Apostles: A Commentary* (Oxford, England: Basil Blackwell, 1971), p. 310.

53. Snowden, *Blacks in Antiquity,* pp. 202–204, cites Origen's *Commentarius in Canticum Canticorum,* 2:367–70. Also, Jerome's *De Actibus Apostolorum,* 1:673–707.

54. Ullendorff, *Ethiopia,* pp. 9–10.

55. Ibid., p. 139.

56. Joseph R. Washington, Jr., *Black Sects and Cults* (New York: Doubleday, 1972), p. 134; *see* Elias Jones, "In Search of Zion: A Study of Three Religious Movements Related to Garveyism" (unpublished Ph.D. dissertation, University of Bern, Bern, Switzerland, 1986).

57. Dominique Torres, "Les Juifs Noirs de l'Oublie": "Ils sont issus de l'escorte juive que le roi Salomon donna a la reine de Saba lorsqu'elle repartit pour l'Ethiopie," Le Monde (Nov. 12, 1973), p. 11.

58. *See* Surah 27:22–23; cf. 34:15–20.

59. Abdullah Yusuf Ali, *The Holy Qur'an* (Washington, D.C.: American International Printing Co., 1946), p. 983; *see also* p. 1138. The Hoopoe "from Saba" reports of the woman ruler.

60. Surrah 105. For an elaborate tradition about Abraha's campaign at Mecca, consult Tor Andrae, *Mohammed: The Man and His Faith* (New York: Harper & Row, 1960), pp. 31–32.

61. R. A. Morrisey, *Colored People and Bible History* (Hammond, Ind.: W. B. Conkey Company, 1925), p. 20.

62. Ibid., p. 21.

63. Jeanne Noble, *Beautiful, Also, Are the Souls of My Black Sisters* (Englewood Cliffs, N.J.: Prentice-Hall, 1978), pp. 10 ff.

CHAPTER THREE

1. Ronald E. Clements, "Goy," in G. Johannes Botteryweck and Helmer Ringgren, eds., *Theological Dictionary of the Old Testament,* vol. 2 (Grand Rapids, Mich.: William B. Eerdmans Publishing Co., 1974–1984), pp. 426–29.

2. S. D. Goitein, *Jews and Arabs: Their Contacts Through the Ages* (New York: Schocken Books, 1964), p. 19–21.

3. Frank M. Snowden, Jr., *Blacks in Antiquity: Ethiopians in the Greco-Roman Experience* (Cambridge, Mass.: Harvard University Press, 1970), pp. 118–119: *"Aithiops* ('burnt-face'): the most frequent translation of CUSH found in the LXX, designating usually Africans of dark pigmentation and Negroid features, used as early as Homer [*Odyssey* 19. 246ff]. While *Aithiops* in ancient biblical and classical texts refers specifically to Ethiopians, the term also identifies Africans, regardless of race."

4. George A. Buttrick, ed., "Election," *Interpreter's Dictionary of the Bible,* vol. 2. (Nashville, Tenn.: Abingdon Press, 1962), p. 77. G. E. Mendenhall employs the term *secularization* in this sense.

5. Claus Westermann, *Genesis 1-11: A Commentary* (Minneapolis, Minn.: Augsburg Publishing House, 1984 [1974]), p. 459.

6. Ibid., p. 482.

7. Ibid., p. 486.

8. Gene Rice, "The Curse That Never Was (Genesis 9:18-27)," *The Journal of Religious Thought,* vol. 29 (1972), p. 13.

9. Westermann, *Genesis,* p. 47.

10. Ibid., p. 54.

11. Rice, "Curse," pp. 11-12; Westermann, *Genesis,* pp. 488-89; Isaac, " 'Sons of Ham'," pp. 4-5.

12. Rice, "Curse," pp. 7-8, suggests that the passage contains two parallel but different traditions — one universal (Gen. 9:18-19a; cf. 5:32; 6:10; 7:13; 10:1; 1 Chron. 1:4) and the other limited to Palestine and more parochial (Gen. 9:20-27, and seems presupposed in 10:21).

13. Westermann, *Genesis,* p. 484.

14. Rice, "Curse," pp. 17, 25.

15. *See* Ephraim Isaac, "Genesis, Judaism and the 'Sons of Ham'," *Slavery and Abolition: A Journal of Comparative Studies,* vol. 1, no. 1 (May 1980), p. 19.

16. Rice, "Curse," p. 26, n. 116.

17. Finis Jennings Dake, *Dake's Annotated Reference Bible* (Lawrenceville, Ga.: Dake Bible Sales, Inc., 1981 [1961]), pp. 8, 9, 36, 40. One of my African seminarians, who had been given *Dake's Annotated* by fundamentalist American missionaries, innocently presented me with a gift copy for study and comment!

18. Martin Noth, *A History of Pentateuchal Traditions,* Bernhard W. Anderson, trans. (Chico, Calif.: Scholars Press, 1981), pp. 21-23, 28 and the translator's supplement, pp. 262-63; Eissfeldt, *The Old Testament,* p. 184.

19. Buttrick, "Sabeans," *Interpreter's Dictionary,* vol. 4, p. 311.

20. The postexilic Priestly ("P") redaction accounts for the order Shem, Ham, Japheth (omitting Canaan) in Gen. 10:1 as well as for the inversion of this order in the subsequent verses, e.g., Gen. 10:2 the sons of Japheth, Gen. 10:6 the sons of Ham, and Gen. 10:21 "To Shem also, the father of all the children of Eber (Hebrew)."

21. Rice, "Curse," p. 16.

22. Contra B. W. Anderson's note in *The New Oxford Annotated Bible* (RSV), p. 179: "The term Cushite apparently [sic] includes Midianites and other Arabic peoples (Hab. 3:7)."

23. Isaac, " 'Sons of Ham'," pp. 3-17.

24. Sergew Hable Sellassie, *Ancient and Medieval Ethiopian History to 1270* (Addis Ababa: United Printers, 1972), p. 96; R. A. Morrisey, *Colored People and Bible History* (Hammond, Ind.: W. B. Conkey Company, 1925); Edward Ullendorff, *Ethiopia and the Bible* (London: Oxford University Press, 1968), pp. 6-8.

25. Snowden, *Blacks in Antiquity,* pp. 115-17; Cheikh Anta Diop, *African Origin of Civilization: Myth or Reality?,* Mercer Cook, trans. (New York and Westport, Conn.: Lawrence Hill and Company, 1974 [1955]), pp. 220-21; Sir Alan Gardiner, *Egypt of the Pharaohs* (New York: Oxford University Press, 1974 [1961]), p. 450.

26. Charles B. Copher, "3,000 Years of Biblical Interpretation with Reference to Black Peoples," *The Journal of the Interdenominational Theological Center,* vol. 13, no. 2 (Spring, 1986):225–46.

27. Gerhard von Rad, *Old Testament Theology,* 2 vol., D. M. G. Stalker, trans. (New York: Harper & Row, 1962), vol. 1, p. 7; vol. 2, p. 322.

28. Ibid., vol. 1, pp. 118, 178; Botterweck and Ringgren, eds., "Bāchar," *Theological Dictionary of the Old Testament,* vol. 2, p. 78; Buttrick, "Election," *Interpreter's Dictionary,* vol. 2, p. 76.

29. Botterweck and Ringgren, eds., "Bāchar," *Theological Dictionary of the Old Testament,* vol. 2, p. 82.

30. Ibid., p. 83.

31. Buttrick, ed., *Interpreter's Dictionary,* vol. 2, p. 79; George F. Moore, *Judaism,* vol. 2 (Cambridge, Mass.: Harvard University Press, 1932), p. 95; cf. Rashi's Commentary, *Deuteronomy,* pp. 56, 195.

32. von Rad, *Old Testament Theology,* vol. I, pp. 178, 223.

33. Botterweck and Ringgren, eds., "Bāchar," *Theological Dictionary of the Old Testament,* vol. 2, p. 78.

34. Moore, *Judaism,* p. 95.

35. Rudolf Bultmann, *Theology of the New Testament,* vol. 1 (London: SCM Press, Ltd., 1965 [1952] and New York: Charles Scribner's Sons, 1952), p. 97.

36. (LXX) Is. 43:20 *to genos mou to eklekton* = M.T. ʿammi běḥiri.

37. W. Bauer, *"Eklektos,"* *A Greek-English Lexicon of the New Testament,* W. E. Arndt and F. W. Gingrich, trans. and eds. (Chicago: University of Chicago Press, 1957), p. 242.

38. In 1 Clem. V.7, "the limits of the west" (*epi to terma tēs duseōs*) designates Spain (of Rome). Kirsopp Lake, trans., *Apostolic Fathers,* vol. I, Loeb Classical Library (Cambridge, Mass.: Harvard University Press, 1975), p. 16. Cf. Ernst Käsemann, *Commentary on Romans,* Geoffrey W. Bromiley trans. and ed. (Grand Rapids, Mich.: William B. Eerdmans Publishing Company, 1980), p. 402.

39. Luke's Acts of the Apostles outlines this scheme quite decidedly: Jerusalem (Acts 2), Antioch (Acts 12), Athens (Acts 17), and Rome (Acts 28). *See* Werner Georg Kümmel, *Introduction to the New Testament,* Rev. English Ed., Howard C. Kee, trans. (Nashville, Tenn.: Abingdon Press, 1973), pp. 164f.

40. Vincent Taylor, *The Gospel According to St. Mark* (New York: St. Martin's Press, 1966), p. 598; Werner H. Kelber, ed., *The Passion in Mark* (Philadelphia, Pa.: Fortress Press, 1976), pp. 120n., 155, 166.

41. The good reputations of the centurion in Luke 7:2ff and Cornelius the centurion in Acts 10:1, 22 are intentional designs by Luke. F. J. Foakes Jackson and Kirsopp Lake, *The Acts of the Apostles,* vol. 4 (Grand Rapids, Mich.: Baker Book House, 1979), p. 112; Ernst Haenchen, *Acts of the Apostles: A Commentary* (Oxford, England: Basil Blackwell, 1971), 346–349.

42. Haenchen, *Acts of the Apostles,* p. 309.

43. Ibid., p. 314.

44. Ibid., p. 315. Similarly: Martin Hengel, *Acts and the Ancient History of Earliest Christianity* (Philadelphia, Pa.: Fortress Press, 1980), p. 79.

45. Jackson and Lake, *Acts,* vol. 4, p. 98. Irenaeus (A.D. 120–202) reports that the Ethiopian became a missionary to "the regions of Ethiopia"; Epiphanius (A.D. 315–403) says that he preached in Arabia Felix and on the coasts of the Red Sea.

Unfortunately, there are no records of Ethiopian Christianity until the fourth century.

46. Irenaeus cites the text as if the variant reading is part of the text (*Adv. Haer.* iii.12.8). Alexander Roberts and James Donaldson, ed., *The Ante-Nicene Fathers* (Grand Rapids, Mich.: Wm. B. Eerdmans Publishing Co., 1981), vol. 1, p. 433. *See also, The Western Text, The Antiochian Text,* and *Textus Receptus*; the English A. V. includes v. 37. Jackson and Lake, *Acts,* vol. 4, p. 98, suggest that the principal significance of v. 37 is "perhaps the earliest form of the baptismal creed. It is also remarkable that it is an expansion of the baptismal formula 'in the name of Jesus Christ,' not of the trinitarian formula."

47. C. S. C. Williams, *The Acts of the Apostles* (New York: Harper & Row, 1957), p. 154. "Simeon the 'Black' may have come from Africa and may possibly be Simon of Cyrene." Haenchen, *Acts of the Apostles,* p. 395, n. 2, reminds us that 1 Cor. 12:28f lists first apostles, prophets, and teachers as persons endowed with *charismata,* and these constituted a charismatic office in Pauline churches.

48. Luke 1:3; Acts 1:1. See Hans Conzelmann, *The Theology of St. Luke,* Geoffrey Buswell, trans., (New York: Harper & Row, 1960), pp. 138–41; Richard J. Cassidy, *Jesus, Politics and Society* (Maryknoll, N.Y.: Orbis Books, 1978), pp. 128–30.

49. Notably the pastorals and 1 Peter; cf. Rom. 13:1–5.

50. It should be noted, however, that the extent of the political apologetic element in Luke–Acts continues to be at the storm center of New Testament debate. *See* Cassidy, *Jesus, Politics and Society*; Richard Cassidy, *Society and Politics in the Acts of the Apostles* (Maryknoll, N.Y.: Orbis Books, 1987); Donald Juel, *Luke–Acts: The Promise of History* (Atlanta, Ga.: John Knox Press, 1983); Jack T. Sanders, *The Jews in Luke–Acts* (Philadelphia, Pa.: Fortress Press, 1987).

CHAPTER FOUR

1. For example, H. H. Schrey, *The Biblical Doctrine of Justice and Law* (London: SCM Press, 1955); J. Arthur Baird, *The Justice of God in the Teaching of Jesus* (London: SCM Press, 1963); and Norman K. Gottwald, ed., *The Bible and Liberation: Political and Social Hermeneutics* (Maryknoll, N.Y.: Orbis Books, 1983).

2. A good illustration is Robert McAfee Brown, *Unexpected News: Reading the Bible with Third World Eyes* (Philadelphia, Pa.: Westminster Press, 1984).

3. *See* the classic historical work by John Hope Franklin, *From Slavery to Freedom* (New York: Alfred Knopf, 1987 3d ed. [1947]); Julius Lester, ed., *The Seventh Son: The Thought and Writings of W. E. B. DuBois,* vol. 1 (New York: Random House, 1971). *See also* Lerone Bennett, Jr., *Before the Mayflower: A History of the Negro in America* (Chicago: Johnson Publishing Co., 1962); Vincent Harding, *There Is a River: The Black Struggle for Freedom in America* (New York: Random House, 1983), pp. 385–401.

4. William Jones, *Is God a White Racist?: A Preamble to Black Theology* (Garden City, N.Y.: Anchor Books, 1973), p. 40-60.

5. Peter J. Paris, *The Social Teaching of the Black Church* (Philadelphia, Pa.: Fortress Press, 1985), pp. xiv–xv.

6. Ibid., p. 10.

7. Ibid., p. 11. Paris adds, ". . . or any other natural quality," but such a claim seems highly problematic, especially as applied to the natural quality of gender.

8. J. Deotis Roberts, *Black Theology in Dialogue* (Philadelphia, Pa.: Westminster Press, 1987), pp. 74–83.

9. Ibid., p. 80.

10. Ibid., p. 82.

11. James Cone, *For My People: Black Theology and the Black Church* (Maryknoll, N.Y.: Orbis Books, 1984), pp. 175–88.

12. Ibid., p. 181.

13. Ibid., p. 187.

14. Ibid., p. 188.

15. Robert S. Brumbaugh, *Plato for the Modern Age* (London: Collier-Macmillan, Ltd., 1962), p. 67.

16. Ibid., p. 66. *See* extended discussion of piety (*to eusebēs*) and religious duty (*to hosion*) as presented in a critique of "the Euthyphro" in A. E. Taylor, *Plato: The Man and His Work* (New York: The World Publishing Company, 1966 [1956]), pp. 148ff.

17. William Frankena, "The Concept of Social Justice," in Richard Brandt, ed., *Social Justice* (Englewood Cliffs, N.J.: Prentice-Hall, 1962), pp. 11, 19.

18. Gregory Vlastos, "Justice and Equality," in Brandt, *Social Justice*, p. 31. *See also* Carl J. Friedrich, *Transcendent Justice: The Religious Dimension of Constitutionalism* (Durham, N.C.: Duke University Press, 1964), p. 5.

19. Plato, *The Republic,* The Loeb Classical Library (New York: G. P. Putnam's Sons, 1930), p. 370 [translation mine].

20. As opposed to *dikē,* the term used by Plato in other contexts, at times with the manifest religious meaning. In *The Laws,* 874E, for example, Plato gives some credence to the existence of *Dikē* ("Justice the avenger of kindred blood") who as overseer employs a *lex talionis* to reprimand criminals. Similarly, in *The Laws,* 937E, Plato indicates that Herodotus's designation of *Dikē* as "the daughter of Reverence" is apt. It should be noted that *dikē* is also used in this latter context. It is used in the lower case to denote "a fair thing which has civilized the affairs of men." *See* Plato, *The Laws,* the Loeb Classical Library, R. G. Burg, trans. (New York: G. P. Putnam's Sons, 1926), pp. 263, 483.

21. Plato, *The Laws,* II, 858D.

22. John Gould, *The Development of Plato's Ethics* (Cambridge, England: The University Press, 1955), p. 123.

23. Plato, *The Laws,* II, 887A.

24. Ibid., 663B, D.; *The Republic,* 613A, as the just man practices virtue he is likened to God; *Theatetus,* 176A, to become like God (*homoiōsis theos*) one is to grow just, holy, and wise. Further on this, *see* Culbert Gerow Rutenber, *The Doctrine of the Imitation of God in Plato* (New York: King's Crown Press, 1946), pp. 2, 18, 67.

25. Plato, *The Laws,* I, 630D.

26. Ibid., II, 906B.

27. Gould, *Plato's Ethics,* p. 119.

28. Hence, J. Gould's assertion that Plato in *The Laws* abandoned Socratic moral idealism, replacing it with a "socialization of ethics" must be qualified. *See* Gould, *Plato's Ethics,* pp. 96ff.

29. Aristotle, *The Eudemian Ethics,* the Loeb Classical Library, H. Rackman, trans. (Cambridge, Mass.: Harvard University Press, 1935), I.viii.1–22.

30. Ibid., I. viii. 20.

31. Aristotle, *The Nichomachaean Ethics,* the Loeb Classical Library, H. Rackman, trans. (Cambridge, Mass.: Harvard University Press, 1962), I.iii.2. Here the English translation represents an adaptation of Philip Wheelwright, *Aristotle* (New York: The Odyssey Press, 1951), p. 159.

32. Aristotle, *The Politics,* The Loeb Classical Library, H. Rackman, trans. (New York: G. P. Putnam's Sons, 1932), I.i.12, p. 13.

33. Ibid., I.i.9 (1253A); cf. III.iv.2.

34. Aristotle, *The Politics,* III.vii.7–8; cf. *The Nichomachaean Ethics,* V.i.8: "The just is the lawful, equal and fair."

35. H. D. F. Kitto, *The Greeks* (Edinburgh: T. & T. Clark, Ltd., 1956), p. 75.

36. Friedrich, *Transcendent Justice,* p. 6.

37. H. J. Rose, *The Religion of Greece and Rome* (New York: Harper & Row, 1959), pp. 9, 15–16.

38. Kitto, *The Greeks,* p. 19.

39. Gerhard Kittel, et al, eds., *"dikē," Theological Dictionary of the New Testament,* 10 vols. (Grand Rapids, Mich.: William B. Eerdmans Publishing Company, 1973), vol. 3, pp. 178–79.

40. Acts 28:4.

41. Edith Hamilton, *Mythology* (New York: The New American Library, Inc., 1969), p. 37.

42. *See* Gerhard von Rad, *Wisdom in Israel* (New York: Abingdon Press, 1972), p. 91, especially n. 25. In Hesiod's *Works and Days,* Zeus is said to be "the giver and guardian of the law by which all human behavior has to be guided," but even here Zeus does not provide a moral code for social legislation.

43. George Foot Moore, *Judaism,* vol. 2 (Cambridge, Mass.: Harvard University Press, 1932), p. 7.

44. *See* I. Singer, ed., "Torah," vol. 12, *Jewish Encyclopedia* (New York: Gordon Press, 1964), p. 196. Ideas such as mercy, grace, redemption, and election in Judaism are important reminders that it should not be understood as a religion solely characterized by Law or strict justice (retribution/revenge).

45. Moore, *Judaism,* pp. 81–82.

46. David Daube, *Studies in Biblical Law* (Cambridge, England: The University Press, 1947), p. 2.

47. Ibid., p. 17.

48. Moore, *Judaism,* vol. 2, p. 180. This echoing the sentiments of Gerhard von Rad, *Old Testament Theology,* vol. 1, pp. 370–83; vol. 2, pp. 391–92. *See* Kittel, *"dikē," Theological Dictionary of the New Testament,* vol. 2, pp. 174–78; *"dikaios"* and *"dikaiosynē,"* pp. 189–96. *See also* John Donahue, "Biblical Perspectives on Justice," in John C. Haughey, ed., *The Faith That Does Justice* (New York: Paulist Press, 1977), pp. 66–78, 108–109.

49. Moore, *Judaism,* vol. 2, p. 84.

50. Daube, *Biblical Law,* pp. 105, 117–121: In this instance, The Hammurabi Code demanded that a man's own daughter be executed if that man has murdered another man's daughter; now, Exod. 21:23ff is seen as clarifying the matter—the wrongdoer himself must be executed.

51. He cites Exod. 21:31; Lev. 24:18ff; Deut. 19:21.

52. Daube, *Biblical Law,* p. 111.

53. Ibid., p. 128.

54. Ibid., p. 146.

55. Ibid., p. 39. As opposed to *pada* (the ransoming of the individual or thing to prevent destruction, slavery, doom).

56. Ibid., p. 40.

57. Ibid., p. 57.

58. Kittel, *"dikē, " Theological Dictionary of the New Testament,* vol. 2, p. 177; *"dikaios,"* p. 195.

59. George A. Buttrick, ed., "Righteousness," *The Interpreter's Dictionary of the Bible* (Nashville, Tenn.: Abingdon Press, 1962), vol. 4, p. 80.

60. von Rad, *Old Testament Theology,* vol. 1, pp. 370–71.

61. Singer, "Right and Righteousness," *Jewish Encyclopedia,* vol. 10, pp. 420–24.

62. Ibid.

63. Notably Gen. 15:6, which probably should be read vis-à-vis Gen. 26:5 as much as in terms of Gen. 22:1ff. Also pertinent would be such large sections of the Pentateuch as Lev. 19, which come to play such a seminal role in synagogal catechesis. *See* von Rad, *Old Testament Theology,* vol. 1, pp. 190–91.

64. Moore, *Judaism,* vol. 2, p. 182.

65. Daube, *Biblical Law,* pp. 155–60. Daube explores the possibility that by this question, Abraham recognizes the inherent evil of "communal responsibility," i.e., the righteous being expected to suffer with and for the evil. In other words, Abraham is seen as challenging God's notion of justice.

66. Singer, "Judgment, Divine," *Jewish Encyclopedia,* vol. 7, p. 385.

67. Ibid.

68. Ibid.

69. Robert Gnuse, *You Shall Not Steal* (Maryknoll, N.Y.: Orbis Books, 1985), pp. 36–47.

70. Daube, *Biblical Law,* p. 61.

71. Norman K. Gottwald, *All the Kingdoms of the Earth* (New York: Harper & Row, 1964), p. 116.

72. John R. Donahue, "Biblical Perspectives on Justice," in John C. Haughey, ed., *The Faith That Does Justice* (New York: Paulist Press, 1977), p. 74.

73. Sigmund Mowinckel, *The Psalms in Israel's Worship,* vol. 1, D. R. Thomas, trans. (Oxford, England: Basil Blackwell, 1962), p. 210.

74. For example, on the composite nature of Ps. 40, *see* Charles A. Briggs and Emile Grace Briggs, *The Book of Psalms,* vol. 1 (Edinburgh: T. & T. Clark, 1976 [1907]), p. 351.

75. Mowinckel, *The Psalms,* vol. 2, p. 114.

76. Ibid., vol. 2, p. 113.

77. W. Brugger and K. Baker, *Philosophical Dictionary* (Spokane, Wash.: Gonzaga University Press, 1972), pp. 412–13. Theodicy may be defined as a mode of thought which, given the existence of manifest evil and human suffering, set forth a defense of justice as a divine attribute (*theos, dikē*).

78. Mowinckel, *The Psalms,* vol. 1, pp. 208–209.

79. Roland E. Murphy, "Wisdom—Theses and Hypotheses," in John Gammie, et al., eds., *Israelite Wisdom: S. Terrien Festschrift* (New York: Scholars Press for UTS, 1978), p. 36.

80. Gerhard von Rad, *Wisdom in Israel,* p. 74.

81. Ibid., p. 76.

82. Ibid., pp. 78, 87, 92.

83. Ibid., p. 93.

84. Hans Jürgen Hermisson, "Observations on the Creation Theology in Wisdom," in Gammie, *Israelite Wisdom,* p. 45.

85. R. B. Y. Scott, *The Way of Wisdom* (New York: Macmillan Publishing Co., 1971), p. 118.

86. von Rad, *Wisdom in Israel,* pp. 54–55; cf., pp. 294–95.

87. *See* Samuel Terrien, "Amos and Wisdom," in Bernard W. Anderson and Walter Harrelson, eds., *Israel's Prophetic Heritage: Essays in Honor of James Muilenberg* (New York: Harper & Brothers, 1962), pp. 108–15.

88. Edmund Jacob, "Wisdom and Religion in Sirach," in Gammie, *Israelite Wisdom,* p. 250.

89. Presumably speaking of the canonical sapiential literature, Samuel Terrien has written, "The Sapiential literature assigned no role whatsoever to the motif, ritual or ideology of covenant." An unpublished paper cited by J. A. Sanders, "Comparative Wisdom: *L'Oeuvre Terrien,*" in Gammie, *Israelite Wisdom,* p. 11.

90. Jean Laporte, "Philo in the Tradition of Wisdom," in Robert L. Wilken, ed., *Aspects of Wisdom in Judaism and Early Christianity* (Notre Dame, Ind.: University of Notre Dame Press, 1975), pp. 122–23.

91. Sir. 5:5 ("Do not be so confident of atonement that you add sin to sin") is a helpful caution against works-righteousness casuistry. Here, one should not deduce that acts of justice *guarantee* salvation.

92. Edmund Jacob, "Wisdom and Religion in Sirach," in Gammie, *Israelite Wisdom,* p. 250: ". . . the entire sapiential literature is engulfed by a current which moves multiple elements and which are often found far from their original source."

93. Most notably William Frankena. Yet, others more accurately distinguish between distributive justice and social justice. Jean-Yves Calvez and Jacques Perin, *The Church and Social Justice* (London: Burns & Oats, English trans., 1961 [French ed., 1959]), pp. 146–47.

94. Typical of this view is Martin Dibelius, *James,* Hermeneia (Philadelphia, Pa.: Fortress Press, 1976), p. 43: "For Jesus and his followers expect everything to be accomplished by God. . . . The world is not going to be changed by humans. Rather, the Kingdom of God will come from heaven. The proclamation of the Kingdom of God is not revolutionary, because it is apocalyptic." Similarly, John Koenig, *Charismata: God's Gifts for God's People* (Philadelphia, Pa.: Westminster Press, 1978), pp. 154–55, says, "According to the Gospels, it is always God who brings in the Kingdom of God, not human beings who will build it."

95. Baird, *The Justice of God,* p. 14.

96. *See* Wayne A. Meeks, *The Moral World of the First Christians* (Philadelphia, Pa.: Westminster Press, 1986), pp. 104–105.

97. *See* John Reuman, *Righteousness in the New Testament* (Philadelphia, Pa.: Fortress Press, and New York: Paulist Press, 1982), pp. 16, 63, 125–26, 149. Consistent with frequent Old Testament usage of Hebrew words *sdq, ysr, Din, mspt,* even as intensified or otherwise refined in New Testament applications.

98. Matt. 5:4 (but without "as thyself"); 19:19; 22:39; Mark 12:31, 33 ("himself"), Luke, 10:29; Rom. 13:9; Gal. 5:14, James 2:8.

99. Pheme Perkins, *Love Commands in the New Testament* (New York: Paulist Press, 1982), pp. 12–13, 16. For Jubilees citation, *see*: R. H. Charles *A.P.O.T.,* vol. 2, p. 42.

100. Ibid., pp. 27–40, 60–65, 97–103.

101. *Skopeō* as a substantive participle ("interest") is vague. A literal translation of its usage here means "looking out for one's own 'things' " as the A. V. renders it;

194 *NOTES*

yet, the context permits 'interests' (R.S.V.) perhaps more than 'rights', contra F. W. Beare, *The Epistle to the Philippians* (London: Adams & Clark, 1959), pp. 72–73.

102. W. Bauer, *"Talanton," Greek-English Lexicon of the New Testament,* W. E. Arndt and F. W. Gingrich, trans. and ed. (Chicago: University of Chicago Press, 1957). p. 811. Only Matthew mentions the Talent as money in early Christian literature (q.v. 25:15–28); he probably has in mind the Syrian Talent (= $250.00 today). The denarius represents a day's pay for a laborer. Buttrick, *Interpreter's Dictionary,* vol. 1, p. 824.

103. *See* Joachim Jeremias, *The Parables of Jesus* (New York: Charles Scribner's Sons, 1972), p. 209.

104. Also, Rom. 2:3, 12:19–20; Matt. 18:8–9 and parallel; Matt. 11:20–24 and parallel; Matt. 12:41–42 and parallel; Mark 3:29; possibly, Heb. 6:4–6.

105. Further elaborated in chapter seven.

106. J. Massynbaerde Ford, "Reconciliation and Forgiveness in Luke's Gospel," in Richard J. Cassidy and Philip Sharper, eds., *Political Issues in Luke–Acts* (Maryknoll, N.Y.: Orbis Books, 1983), p. 81. *Also see* André Trochmé, *Jesus and the Non-violent Revolution* (Scottsdale, Pa.: Herald Press, 1973), pp. 27–40.

107. Roger Rustin, "Christian Views of Justice," *New Blackfriars,* vol. 59, no. 699 (August 1978): 344–45.

108. Joachim Jeremias, *Jerusalem in the Time of Jesus* (Philadelphia, Pa.: Fortress Press, 1977 [1962, 1967, 1969]), pp. 87–119.

109. Richard J. Cassidy, *Jesus, Politics and Society* (Maryknoll, N.Y.: Orbis Books, 1978), p. 31.

110. Karen Lebacqz, *Six Theories of Justice: Perspectives from Philosophical and Theological Ethics* (Minneapolis, Minn.: Augsburg Publishing House, 1986), pp. 61–62, 117.

111. Ernst Käsemann, "Ministry and Community in the New Testament," *Essays on New Testament Themes* (London: SCM Press, Ltd., 1964), p. 70.

112. John Koenig, *Charismata,* p. 94, warns against appealing to 1 Corinthians 12–14 for norms, especially "normative charismatic self-understanding and practice today."

113. On this formula, *see* Lebacqz, *Theories of Justice,* p. 118.

114. Elisabeth Schüssler Fiorenza, *In Memory of Her: A Feminist Theological Reconstruction of Christian Origins* (New York: Crossroad Publishing Company, 1984), pp. 100–103.

115. Mark 10:2–12; Matt. 5:21–32; 19:3–9; cf. 1 Cor. 7:39–40.

116. Schüssler Fiorenza, *In Memory of Her,* p. 213.

CHAPTER FIVE

1. Werner Georg Kümmel, *The New Testament: The History of the Investigation of Its Problems* (Nashville, Tenn. and New York: Abingdon, 1970), p. 3.

2. William E. Hatcher, *John Jasper: The Unmatched Negro Philosopher and Preacher* (New York: Fleming H. Revell Co., 1908), p. 108.

3. William A. Johnson, "Reflections on Preaching," *The Christian Ministry,* vol. 15, no. 6 (November 1984): 23–26.

4. Martin Dibelius, "Die Altestamentichen Motive in der Leidens-geschichte des Petrus – und des Johannes – Evangeliums," in *Botschaft und Geschichte,* vol. 1

(Tubingen, 1953), p. 242, as cited by J. Louis Martyn, *The Gospel of John in Christian History* (New York: Paulist Press, 1978), p. 93.

5. Martin Dibelius, *Jesus* (Philadelphia, Pa.: Westminster Press, 1949), pp. 34–35.

6. Septuagint (LXX): Gen. 41:43; Dan. 4:3.

7. Isa. 61:1.

8. Notice the editorial theological reshaping done by Matthew in order to make the kerygma of John the Baptist identical with that of Jesus (Matt. 3:2; 4:17). The greatly expanded kerygma of John the Baptist in Luke 3:3–18 in a similar way anticipates the Lukan inaugural sermon of Jesus (Luke 4:16–21). Such editorial work attests to the growing tendency within Christian communities of the first century to depict Jesus as supplanting the preaching of John the Baptist. For Matthew and Luke, this sets the stage for Jesus' preaching ministry to move completely beyond the kerygma of John the Baptist (cf. Matt. 11:12; Luke 16:16).

9. Ernst Fuchs, "Die Sprache in Neuen Testament," *Zur Frage nach dem Historischen Jesus* (Tubingen, 1960), p. 261, as cited in Amos N. Wilder, *Early Christian Rhetoric: The Language of The Gospel* (Cambridge, Mass.: Harvard University Press, 1971), p. 10.

10. Charles H. Dodd, *The Apostolic Preaching and Its Developments* (New York: Harper & Row, 1964), pp. 8, 9.

11. Gardner C. Taylor, *How Shall They Preach?* (Elgin, Ill.: Progressive Baptist Publishing House, 1977), p. 67.

12. Walter Brueggemann, *The Prophetic Imagination* (Philadelphia, Pa.: Fortress Press, 1978), p. 112.

13. Ivan Van Sertima, *They Came Before Columbus: The African Presence in Ancient America* (New York: Random House, 1977); Lerone A. Bennett, Jr., *Before the Mayflower: A History of the Negro in America* (Chicago: Johnson Publishing, 1962 [Revised ed., Baltimore, Md.: Penguin Books, 1970]), pp. 25–38.

14. Daniel A. Payne, *Sermons and Addresses, Bishop D. A. Payne, 1853–1891,* Charles Killian, ed. (New York: Arno Press, 1972), p. 10.

15. Ibid., p. 14.

16. Ibid., p. 15.

17. W. E. B. DuBois, *The Gift of Black Folk* (New York: AMS Press, 1971 [reprint of 1924 edition]), p. 322.

18. Ibid., p. 320.

19. E. Franklin Frazier, *The Negro Church in America* (New York: Schocken Books, 1974), p. 12.

20. James Weldon Johnson, *The Book of American Negro Spirituals* (New York: The Viking Press, 1925), pp. 20–21, as cited by Benjamin E. Mays, *The Negro's God as Reflected in His Literature* (New York: Atheneum, 1973 [1938]), p. 27.

21. Wilder, *Early Christian Rhetoric*, p. 27.

22. Carl Marbury, "Hebrews and Spirituals," in Henry J. Young, ed., *God and Human Freedom* (Richmond, Ind.: Friends United Press, 1983), p. 81.

23. Wayne A. Meeks, *The First Urban Christians* (New Haven, Conn.: Yale University Press, 1983), pp. 144, 174.

24. Col. 3:22–25; Eph. 6:5–8; 1 Tim. 6:1–2; Titus 2:9–10; and 1 Pet. 2:18–25.

25. Mays, *The Negro's God,* p. 30.

26. Marbury, "Hebrews and Spirituals," p. 92.

27. S. Scott Bartchy, *First Century Slavery and 1 Corinthians 7:21* (Missoula, Mont.: Scholars Press, 1973).

28. Mays, *The Negro's God,* p. 30.

29. James Weldon Johnson, *God's Trombones* (New York: The Viking Press, 1964 [1927]), pp. 17ff, 21ff.

30. Wilder, *Early Christian Rhetoric,* p. 56.

31. Walter H. Brooks, *The Pastor's Voice* (Washington, D.C.: The Associated Publishers, 1945), p. 113.

32. Ibid., p. 10.

33. George A. Singleton, *The Romance of African Methodism* (New York: Exposition Press, 1952).

34. Mays, *The Negro's God,* p. 88.

35. Ibid., pp. 90, 92.

36. *See* note 4 above.

37. W. E. B. DuBois, *The Souls of Black Folk* (New York: A. J. McClure, 1903; reprinted Greenwich, Conn.: Fawcett, 1961), pp. 190–91; Carter G. Woodson, *The History of the Negro Church* (Washington, D.C.: Associated Publishers, 1921), p. 281; and Robert S. Michaelson, "The Protestant Ministry in America," in H. Richard Niebuhr and Daniel Day Williams, eds., *The Ministry in Historical Perspective* (San Francisco: Harper & Row, 1983 [1956]), p. 268.

38. Robert A. Bennett, "Biblical Hermeneutics and the Black Preacher," *The Journal of the Interdenominational Theological Center,* vol. 1, no. 2 (Spring, 1974), pp. 45–46.

39. Ibid., p. 39.

40. Hatcher, *John Jasper,* pp. 141, 144.

41. Ibid., p. 39.

42. Taylor, *How Shall They Preach,* p. 31. *See*: Ralph G. Clingan, "Romans 3: The Preacher's Dilemma," *Journal of the International Theological Center,* vol. 9, no. 2 (Spring, 1982), esp. p. 150.

43. Useful resources for this endeavor would include Sandy F. Ray, "Elements in Black Preaching," *The Journal of Religious Thought,* vol. 30, no. 1 (Spring–Summer, 1973); James W. Cox, *Biblical Preaching: An Expositor's Treasury* (Philadelphia, Pa.: Westminster Press, 1983).

44. James Earl Massey, *Designing the Sermon: Order and Movement in Preaching* (Nashville, Tenn.: Abingdon, 1980); *The Sermon in Perspective* (Grand Rapids, Mich.: Baker Book House, 1976); *The Responsible Pulpit* (Anderson, Ind.: Wasner Press, 1974). Henry H. Mitchell, *The Recovery of Preaching* (San Francisco: Harper & Row, 1977); Don M. Wardlaw, ed., *Preaching Biblically* (Philadelphia, Pa.: Westminster Press, 1983), esp. chapter 6 by Gardner Taylor, "Shaping Sermons by the Shape of the Text and Preacher," pp. 137–52.

45. Roy C. Nichols, *Footsteps in the Sea* (Nashville, Tenn.: Abingdon Press, 1980); Sandy Ray, *Journeying Through A Jungle* (Nashville, Tenn.: Broadman Press, 1979); Robert T. Newbold, Jr., ed., *Black Preaching* (Philadelphia, Pa.: Geneva Press, 1977).

46. Howard Thurman, *The Growing Edge* (Richmond, Ind.: Friends United Press, 1956), pp. ix–x.

47. Cain H. Felder, delivered at Andrew Rankin Memorial Chapel, Howard University, Washington, D.C. (September, 1982).

48. Alain Locke, ed., *The New Negro* (New York: Atheneum, 1969), p. xvii.

49. Ibid., p. 8.

50. Omar Khayyam, *The Rubaiyat,* Edward Fitzgerald, ed. (New York: Walter J. Black, 1942 [1859]), pp. 19–20.

51. *See* G. B. Caird, *The Gospel of Saint Luke* (Middlesex, England, and New York: Penguin Books, 1963, 1965), pp. 140–41, on the significance of *analēmpsis* in Luke's theological horizon.

52. Hans Conzelmann, *The Theology of St. Luke* (New York: Harper & Row, 1960), p. 50.

53. *See* Edith Hamilton, *Mythology (New York: The New American Library,* 1969 [48th printing]), pp. 139–40.

54. Molière, "Act 1," *Eight Plays by Molière,* Morris Bishop, trans. (New York: The Modern Library, 1957), p. 155.

55. Alain Locke, "The New Negro," in James A. Emanuel and Theodore L. Gross, eds., *Dark Symphony: Negro Literature in America* (New York: The Free Press, 1968), p. 75.

56. Cain H. Felder, delivered at The Upper Room Baptist Church's Family Day, Washington, D.C. (October, 1983).

57. "Stress: Can We Cope?" *Time* (June 6, 1983), p. 50.

58. William Julius Wilson, *The Declining Significance of Race* (Chicago: University of Chicago Press, 1978), p. 154.

59. Ibid., p. 171.

60. James Gilchrist Lawson, ed., *The Best Loved Religious Poems* (Chicago: Fleming H. Revell Co., 1933), p. 115 [Edited for inclusive language by author].

61. "Runaway Children," *Life* (July, 1983), p.541.

CHAPTER SIX

1. Charles H. Long, *Significations: Signs, Symbols, and Images in the Interpretation of Religion* (Philadelphia, Pa.: Fortress Press, 1986), p. 133.

2. Ibid., pp. 133–34.

3. Ibid., p. 141.

4. Ibid., p. 186.

5. John P. Meier, *The Vision of Matthew: Christ, Church and Morality in the First Gospel* (New York: Paulist Press, 1979), p. 60.

6. George B. Caird, *The Gospel of Saint Luke* (Middlesex, England: Penguin Books, 1963 [New York: Penguin Books, 1965]), p. 79.

7. *See* Jacques Ellul, *The Ethics of Freedom* (Grand Rapids, Mich.: William B. Eerdmans Publishing Company, 1976), pp. 52–62.

8. Ernst Käsemann, *Jesus Means Freedom* (Philadelphia, Pa.: Fortress Press, 1969), p. 39.

9. Typical are Raymond T. Stamm or Oscar R. Blackwelder, "Galatians," in Buttrick, *The Interpreter's Bible* (Nashville, Tenn. and New York: Abingdon Press, 1953), p. 546.

10. Freedom from "social oppression and religious-cultural discrimination are inherently within Paul's purview in Galatians," according to Hans Deiter Betz, *Galatians: A Critical and Historical Commentary on the Bible,* Hermeneia (Philadelphia, Pa.: Fortress Press, 1979), p. 256.

11. Jacques Ellul, *The Ethics of Freedom* (Grand Rapids, Mich.: William B. Eerdmans Publishing Company, 1975), p. 35.

12. Erich Fromm, *Man for Himself* (Greenwich, Conn.: Fawcett, 1966), pp. 247–48.

13. *See* Erich Fromm, *Escape from Freedom* (New York: Holt, Rinehart & Winston, 1965), pp. 281–82 on the meaning for freedom and this modern dilemma.

14. Amos N. Jones, Jr., *Paul's Message of Freedom: What Does it Mean for the Black Church?* (Valley Forge, Pa.: Judson Press, 1984), pp. 18, 63.

15. Ibid., pp. 37–38, 48–55.

16. Ibid., p. 32.

17. Ibid., pp. 47–48, 64–66.

18. Ibid., pp. 69–71.

19. Gerd Leudemann, *Paul, Apostle to the Gentiles: Studies in Chronology* (Philadelphia, Pa.: Fortress Press, 1984), pp. 44–45.

20. Ibid., p. 45.

21. Betz, *Galatians,* p. 270.

22. C. K. Barrett, *Freedom & Obligation: A Study of the Epistle to the Galatians* (Philadelphia, Pa.: Fortress Press, 1985), p. 3.

23. Ernst Käsemann, *Commentary on Romans* (Grand Rapids, Mich.: William B. Eerdmans Publishing Company, 1980), pp. 60–61.

24. Betz, *Galatians,* pp. 60–61.

25. Ibid., pp. 93–94.

26. Jürgen Moltmann, "God Means Freedom," in Henry J. Young, ed., *God and Human Freedom* (Richmond, Ind.: Friends United Press, 1983), p. 19.

27. Luther E. Smith, "Community: Partnership of Freedom and Responsibility," in Young, *God and Human Freedom,* p. 27.

28. C. Eric Lincoln, *Race, Religion and the Continuing American Dilemma* (New York: Hill and Wang, 1984), p. 7.

29. Vincent Harding, *There Is a River* (New York: Vintage Books, 1983), p. 276.

30. James H. Cone, "Martin Luther King, Jr., Black Theology and the Black Church," *Theology Today* (January, 1984), vol. 40, no. 4, p. 41.

31. J. B. Phillips, trans., *The New Testament in Modern English* (New York: The Macmillan Company, 1958), pp. 408–409.

CHAPTER SEVEN

1. Gayraud S. Wilmore, *Black Religion and Black Radicalism* (Maryknoll, N.Y.: Orbis Books, 1983), p. 32.

2. By mentioning the African-American experience, we must also recognize that many people of color throughout the world have been and frequently still are victims of extreme forms of racial discrimination and disenfranchisement.

3. James H. Cone, *Speaking the Truth* (Grand Rapids, Mich.: William B. Eerdmans Publishing Company, 1986), p. 36.

4. *See* Gayraud S. Wilmore and James H. Cone, eds., *Black Theology: A Documentary History 1966-1979* (Maryknoll, N.Y.: Orbis Books, 1979), pp. 450, 452, 459. This observation is especially pertinent today in view of the internal debate between proponents of Black theology and Latin American Liberation Theology. The former focuses on racism (discrimination based on race/color); the latter focuses on class as the central analytical paradigm.

5. The guiding presumption for our analysis is that the author of the Epistle of James is a third- or fourth-generation Christian who writes ca. A.D. 100 in the tradition and name of James, the brother of Jesus (Mark 6:3; Matt. 13:52), who later becomes a pillar (Gal. 2:9) and the chief elder of the Jerusalem church (James

1:1; cf. Acts 15:13-29; 21:17-25).

6. James Hardy Ropes, *The Epistle of St. James,* International Critical Commentary (Edinburgh: T & T Clark, 1973; [1916]), pp. 28-33, 178-79; Arthur T. Cadoux, *The Thought of St. James* (London: James Clark, 1944), pp. 72-73; O. J. F. Seitz, "James and the Law," *Text und Untersuchen* 87 (1967):477.

7. Philip Carrington, *Primitive Christian Catechism* (Cambridge, England: University Press, 1949), p. 78.

8. Rudolf Obermüller, "Hermeneutischen Themen im Jakobusbrief," *Biblica* 53 (February, 1972): 235.

9. Martin Dibelius, *James,* Hermeneia (Philadelphia, Pa.: Fortress Press, 1976), p. 116.

10. Ropes, *James,* p. 201; Martin Dibelius, *James,* p. 124; C. L. Mitton, *The Epistle of James* (Grand Rapids, Mich.: William B. Eerdmans Publishing Company, 1966), p. 89; George A. Buttrick, ed., "The Epistle of James," *The Interpreter's Bible,* vol. 12, (New York: Abingdon Press, 1957), p. 24; Roy Bowen Ward, "The Communal Concern of the Epistle of James," Ph.D. dissertation, Harvard University, 1966, p. 21.

11. Sophie Laws, *The Epistle of James,* Harper's New Testament Commentaries (San Francisco: Harper & Row, 1981), p. 94; cf. Roy Bowen Ward, "Partiality in the Assembly: James 2:2-4," *Harvard Theological Review* 62 (1969):89.

12. A general reference condition: *ean* with subjunctive in the protasis (vv. 2, 3) and the indicative in the apodosis (v. 4).

13. Dibelius, *James,* p. 129.

14. Ibid., pp. 131-32.

15. Franz Mussner, *Der Brief des Jakobus* (Frieburg: Herders, 1967), p. 119.

16. Laws, *James,* p. 102; cf. W. Bauer, ed., *"dialogismos,"* A *Greek-English Lexicon of the New Testament,* W. E. Arndt and F. W. Gingrich, trans. and ed. (Chicago: University of Chicago Press, 1957), p. 185.

17. Dibelius, *James,* p. 129.

18. Bo Reicke, *Diakonie festreude und zelos* (1951), pp. 342-43, as cited by R. B. Ward, "Communal," p. 97.

19. Laws, *James,* p. 98.

20. Ward, "Communal," pp. 90-91. [See n. 10 above.]

21. Joseph B. Mayor, *The Epistle of James* (London: Macmillan and Co., Ltd., 1897), p. 81.

22. Dibelius, *James,* pp. 132-34; Laws, *James,* pp. 100-101.

23. Cf. Matt 15:19: *dialogismos ponēros*: there "evil thoughts," as included in a listing of the kind of behavior legislated against in the moral precepts of the Old Testament Decalogue.

24. Ward, "Partiality," p. 88.

25. Dative of respect. Blass, Debrunner, and Funk, *A Grammar of Greek Syntax* (Chicago: University of Chicago Press, 1961), p. 105.

26. Ward, "Partiality," p. 95.

27. Laws, *James,* p. 103.

28. Dibelius, *James,* pp. 39-45.

29. Gerhard Kittel, et al, eds., *"ptochos," Theological Dictionary of the New Testament,* vol. 6 (Grand Rapids, Mich.: William B. Eerdmans Publishing Company, 1973), pp. 888-902, 911; Dibelius, *James,* pp. 39-40; Louis Hartmann, trans. and ed., "Poverty," *Encyclopedic Dictionary of the Bible* (New York: McGraw Hill, 1963), pp. 1886-87.

200 *NOTES*

30. 1 Enoch 60:6; 94:4–9; 96:4; R. H. Charles, ed., *The Apocrypha and Pseudepigrapha of the Old Testament,* vol. 2 (Oxford, England: Clarendon Press, 1965 [1913]), pp. 22, 263–67.

31. Thomas Hoyt, Jr., "The Poor in Luke–Acts," Ph.D. dissertation, Duke University, 1975, pp. 111–112, 115; Raymond E. Brown, *The Birth of the Messiah* (Garden City, N.Y.: Doubleday, 1977), pp. 350–55, 363.

32. Laws, *James,* 103; Herman L. Strack, *Introduction to Talmud and Midrash* (Philadelphia, Pa.: Jewish Publication Society, 1931), p. 754: The expression of "rich in faith" occurs in rabbinic literature as a reference to "rich in Torah-knowledge" but dating such texts is highly problematic.

33. Ropes, *James,* p. 195.

34. Lit: *"Jacques s'efforce de nontrer que les cloisons sociales et singulierement le mépris du pauvre menacent l'unité des commaunautés, de la foi chrétienne":* Irénée Fransen, "Le premier examen de coinscience Chrétién: l'epître de Jacques" Bible et Vie Chretienne (1959): 33.

35. Bauer, *Greek-English Lexicon,* p. 411; Laws, *James,* pp. 104–5; George Moorish, *A Concordance of the Septuagint* (Grand Rapids, Mich.: Zondervan, 1976), p. 129.

36. Kittel, *"Blasphēmia," Theological Dictionary of the New Testment,* vol. 1, p. 624; Francis X. Kelly, "Poor and Rich in the Epistle of James," Ph.D. dissertation, Temple University, 1972, pp. 198, 200; "the rich are indicted because they have made a travesty of justice."

37. Seitz, "Law," p. 474.

38. Ibid., p. 476.

39. Laws, *James,* pp. 93, 110.

40. Dibelius, *James,* p. 142.

41. Jack P. Sanders, *Ethics in the New Testament* (Philadelphia: Fortress Press, 1975), p. 124.

42. Jacques Marty, *L'Epître de Jacques* (Paris: Felix Alcan, 1935), p. 81; Arnold Meyer, *Das Rästel des Jakobusbriefes* (Geissen: A. Topelmann, 1930), pp. 149–53.

43. Adolph Diessmann, *Light from the Ancient East* (London: Hodder and Stoughton, 1927), p. 362.

44. Dibelius, *James,* p. 142–43.

45. Laws, *James,* p. 110. On the influence of the Jesus tradition in Gal. 5:14 reference to the Lev. 19:18c quote, *see* Ernst Käsemann, *Commentary on Romans* (Grand Rapids, Mich.: William B. Eerdmans Publishing Co., 1980), p. 361.

46. Cf. Mark 10:19; 12:33; Matt. 19:18; 22:39 (q.v. 5:43, 7:12); and Luke 10:27.

47. Strack, *Introduction to the Talmud,* p. 755. Nevertheless, it is important to note that the language in James 2:9b and c is similar to that associated with the Jesus tradition. The sixth-century Codex Bezae text of Luke 6:5 adds, "On the same day, seeing someone working on the Sabbath, he [Jesus] said to him, 'Man, if indeed you know what you are doing, you are blessed, but if you do not know, *you are cursed and a transgressor of law"* [emphasis mine]. Cited by James L. Price, *The New Testament: Its History and Theology* (New York: Macmillan, 1987), p. 169. *See* S. G. Wilson, *Luke and the Law* (Cambridge, England: University Press, 1983), pp. 78, 125.

48. Kelly, "Poor and Rich," p. 138.

49. Hans Deiter Betz, *Galatians: A Critical and Historical Commentary on the Bible,* Hermeneia (Philadelphia, Pa.: Fortress Press, 1979), p. 261.

50. Ibid., pp. 274–75.

51. Ibid.

52. Seitz, "Law," p. 477.

53. Mark 12:31; Matt. 22:39; Luke 10:27; cf. John 13:34.

54. Kittell, *"entolē,"* *Theological Dictionary of the New Testament,* vol. 2, p. 549 asserts that Lev. 19:18 was a "common Rabbinic compendium of the second table." *See also* Kittel, *"nomos,"* *Theological Dictionary of the New Testament,* vol. 4, pp. 166–67.

55. Kelly, "Poor and Rich," p. 138.

56. Ibid., p. 475.

57. Seitz, "Law," p. 474.

58. Ibid., p. 475.

59. Kirsopp Lake, tr. *The Apostolic Fathers,* vol. 1 (Cambridge, Mass.: Harvard University Press, 1975 [1922]), p. 133.

60. Dan O. Via, "The Right Strawy Epistle Reconsidered: A Study in Biblical Ethics and Hermeneutics," *Journal of Religion,* vol. 49 (1969): 266.

61. Blass, Debrunner, and Funk, *A Grammar of Greek Syntax* (Chicago: University of Chicago Press, 1961), p. 119: *dia* with Genitive to denote agency.

62. Ropes, *James,* p. 201.

63. Via, "Reconsidered," p. 262.

64. Dibelius, *James,* p. 129.

65. Bauer, "krisis," *Greek-English Lexicon,* p. 454.

66. Ropes, *James,* pp. 275, 297; Dibelius, *James,* p. 229.

67. Cf. Luke 10:37: *ho poiēsas to eleos.*

68. Ward, "Communal," pp. 156–57.

69. Bauer, "katakauchaomai," *Greek-English Lexicon,* p. 412; cf. Blass, Debrunner, Funk, Grammar, pp. 97–98.

70. Laws, *James,* pp. 117–18.

71. Dibelius, *James,* p. 148.

72. Resembling the idea in Matt. 5:12, 14 in which R. E. Brown, "The *Pater Noster* as an Eschatological Prayer," *Theological Studies* 22 [1961]: 203 asserts, "Human forgiveness is the counterpart of the divine."

CHAPTER EIGHT

1. Krister Stendahl, *Bible and the Role of Women,* Facet Books Biblical Series, no. 15 (Philadelphia, Pa.: Fortress Press, 1966). Moshe Meidelman, *Jewish Women in Jewish Law,* vol. 6 (New York: KTAV, 1968). Joachim Jeremias, "Appendix: The Social Position of Women," *Jerusalem in the Time of Jesus* (Philadelphia, Pa.: Fortress Press, 1969), pp. 359–76. Robin Scroggs, "Paul and the Eschatological Woman," *Journal of the American Academy of Religion* 40 (1972): 283–303 and sequel article in *Journal of the American Academy of Religion* 42 (1974): 532–37. Raymond E. Brown, "Roles of Women in the Fourth Gospel," *Theological Studies* 36 (1975):688–99 and reprinted in his *Community of the Beloved Disciple* (New York: Paulist Press, 1979), pp. 183–98. Elizabeth S. Fiorenza, "Women in the Pre-Pauline Churches," *Union Theological Quarterly Review* 3 (1978):153–66 and *In Memory of Her: A Feminist Reconstruction of Christian Origins* (New York: Crossroad Publishing Company, 1984), esp. pp. 105–59. Jane Schaberg, *The Illegitimacy of Jesus: A Feminist Interpretation of the Infancy Narratives* (San Francisco: Harper & Row, 1987). Elaine Pagels, "God the Father/God the Mother,"

The Gnostic Gospels (New York: Random House, 1979) and the important review by Kathleen McVey, *Theology Today* 37 (January, 1981): 498–501. Phyllis Tribble, *God and the Rhetoric of Sexuality* (Philadelphia, Pa.: Fortress Press, 1978). Stephen B. Clark, *Man and Woman in Christ* (Ann Arbor, Mich.: Servant Books, 1980). Willard M. Swartley, *Slavery, Sabbath, War and Women: Case Issues in Biblical Interpretation* (Scottsdale, Pa. and Kitchener, Ontario: Herald Press, 1983), and Cain H. Felder's review in *Report from the Capitol* (October, 1983).

2. Elizabeth Cady Stanton, et al., *The Woman's Bible,* parts 1, 2 (New York: European Publishing Co., 1898); T. B. Allworthy, *Women in the Apostolic Church: A Critical Study of the Evidence in New Testament for the Prominence of Women in Early Christianity* (Cambridge, England: W. Heffer & Sons, Ltd., 1917); Charles Ryder Smith, *The Bible Doctrine of Womanhood and Its Historical Evolution* (London: The Epworth Press, 1923). *See* Swartley, *Women,* p. 313.

3. Primers in this area are such works as Jeanne Noble, *Beautiful Also, Are the Souls of My Black Sisters* (Englewood Cliffs, N.J.: Prentice-Hall, 1978); Robert A. Bennett, Jr., "Africa and the Biblical Period," *Harvard Theological Review* 64 (1971): 483–500; Snowden, *Blacks in Antiquity* (Cambridge, Mass.: Harvard University Press, 1970).

4. Cain H. Felder, "Racial Ambiguities in the Biblical Narratives," *Concilium,* vol. 51 (New York: Seabury Press, 1982): 17–24.

5. Phyllis A. Bird, *The Bible as the Church's Book* (Philadelphia, Pa.: Westminster Press, 1982), p. 91.

6. Phyllis Tribble attempts to provide correctives for such traditional evaluations of women and feminine images in the Old Testament. *See* "Depatriarchalizing in Biblical Interpretation," *Journal of the American Academy of Religion* 40 (March 1973) and *God and the Rhetoric of Sexuality,* pp. 16–17.

7. Robert A. Bennett, Jr., "Africa," pp. 497–98.

8. *See* Snowden, *Blacks in Antiquity,* p. 223 and Edward F. Ullendorff, *Ethiopia and the Bible* (London: Oxford University Press, 1968), p. 132. "The Story of the Queen of Sheba," based on the biblical account of the queen's visit to King Solomon, has undergone extensive Arabian, Ethiopian, Jewish, and other elaborations and has become the subject of one of the most ubiquitous and fertile cycles of legends in the Middle East. *See also* Joseph E. Harris, *Pillars in Ethiopian History* (Washington, D.C.: Howard University Press, 1974), pp. 35–42; Ivan Van Sertima, *Black Women in Antiquity* (New Brunswick, N.J.: Transaction Books, 1988).

9. Snowden, *Blacks in Antiquity,* p. 202, cites Origen's *Commentarius* in *Canticum Cantorum,* 2.367–70 and Jerome's *De Actibus Apostolorum,* 1. 673–707.

10. *"Makeda,"* *Dictionary of African Biography,* vol. 1 (New York: Rowman and Littlefield, 1970), pp. 97–99.

11. Abudullah Yusuf Ali, *The Holy Qur'an: Text, Translation and Commentary* (Washington, D.C.: American International Printing Co., 1946), Surah 27:22–23; 34:15–20; especially the comment on page 983.

12. Cf. "The Queen of the South" in Matt. 12:42 and Luke 11:31, where this Queen of Sheba legend has become reinterpreted by early Christians in such a manner as to transform her into an eschatological figure of judgment for the disbelieving Jews. *See* Chapter 2, above.

13. *See* Ernst Haenchen, *The Acts of the Apostles: A Commentary* (Oxford, England: Basil Blackwell, 1971 [1965]), pp. 309–17.

14. Joachim Jeremias, *Jerusalem,* p. 357, 363.

15. Ibid., pp. 371-73.

16. Swartley, *Women,* pp. 160-64, 235-49.

17. Raymond E. Brown, *The Birth of the Messiah* (Garden City, NY: Doubleday, 1980), pp. 73-74.

18. John P. Meier, *The Vision of Matthew* (New York: Paulist Press, 1979), pp. 54, 185.

19. Richard J. Cassidy, *Jesus, Politics and Society* (Maryknoll, N.Y.: Orbis Books, 1978), p. 21; R. E. Brown, *Birth,* p. 335; John Donahue, "Biblical Perspectives on Justice" in John C. Haughey, ed., *The Faith That Does Justice* (New York: Paulist Press, 1977), p. 106.

20. Raymond E. Brown, *The Gospel According to John, I-XII* (Garden City, N.Y.: Doubleday, 1966), p. 170 lists some of the religious and political reasons for antipathy between these two groups: the Samaritan refusal to worship at or recognize Jerusalem as the preeminent Holy City and lingering Jewish resentment against the Samaritans for having been accomplices with Syrian monarchs in 128 B.C.E. *See* R. J. Coggins, *Samaritans and Jews* (Atlanta, Ga.: John Knox Press, 1973), pp. 138-48.

21. *See* Marian Wright Edelman, *Families in Peril: An Agenda for Social Change* (Cambridge, Mass.: Harvard University Press, 1987), especially "The Black Family in America," pp. 1-22.

22. *Thaumazō* (lit. "amazed") is translated in this way by R. E. Brown, *John,* p. 173.

23. R. E. Brown, *The Community of the Beloved Disciple* (New York: Paulist Press, 1979), p. 188.

24. George A. Buttrick, ed., "Woman in the New Testament," *Interpreter's Dictionary of the Bible* (Nashville, Tenn.: Abingdon Press, 1962), *Supplement,* pp. 966-968; Leonard and Arlene Swidler, eds., *Women Priests: A Catholic Commentary on the Vatican Declaration* (New York: Paulist Press, 1977), especially Bernadette Brooten's entry "Junia . . . Outstanding Among the Apostles" (Rom. 16:7), pp. 141-43; Victor Paul Furnish, *The Moral Teachings of Paul* (Nashville, Tenn.: Abingdon Press, 1979), especially "Women in the Church," pp. 84-114.

25. *See* Swartley, *Women,* p. 318, n. 87 for a helpful listing of the recent debate on these passages.

26. Hans Deiter Betz, *Galatians: A Critical and Historical Commentary on the Bible,* Hermeneia (Philadelphia, Pa.: Fortress Press, 1979), p. 197.

27. Ernst Käsemann, *Commentary on Romans* (Grand Rapids, Mich.: William B. Eerdmans Publishing Company, 1980), p. 411. In 1. Tim. 3:11, criteria are stipulated for women to serve as "deacons."

28. *See* ibid., p. 413 for amplified comments on the early Christian practice of two "yoke-fellows" (1 Cor. 9:5).

29. Bernadette Brooden, "Junia," in Swidler, *Women Priests,* p. 141-143; Swartley, *Women,* p. 176-177.

30. J. Christiaan Beker, *Paul, the Apostle: The Triumph of God in Life and Thought* (Philadelphia, Pa.: Fortress Press, 1982), pp. 110-11; Cain H. Felder, "Paul's Reinterpretation of Jewish Apocalyptic," *The Journal of Religious Thought,* vol. 40, no. 1 (Spring-Summer, 1983): 18-23.

31. James D. G. Dunn, *Unity and Diversity in the New Testament: An Inquiry Into the Character of Earliest Christianity* (Philadelphia, Pa.: Westminster Press, 1977), pp. 341-59.

CHAPTER NINE

1. Walter Bruggemann, *In Man We Trust* (Atlanta, Ga.: John Knox Press, 1972), p. 72.

2. One must point out, however, that in 1974 only 37 percent of the United States household units were on the nuclear family model; 11 percent were couples with no children at home, 12 percent were single-parent families, 11 percent were remarried nuclear families, 4 percent were extended-kin networks, and 25 percent were simple or commune-type groupings. *See* Letty M. Russell, *The Future of Partnership* (Philadelphia, Pa.: Westminster Press, 1979), pp. 89, 94, 185.

3. For an exception, *see* Joanmarie Smith, "Grandmothers, Aunts, 'Aunts,' and Godmothers," in Gloria Durka and Joanmarie Smith, eds., *Family Ministry* (Oak Grove, Minn.: Winston Press, 1980), pp. 169–81.

4. The use of family terms to refer, in antiquity, to members of certain synagogues, churches, clubs and cults is noted by Wayne A. Meeks, *The First Urban Christians* (New Haven, Conn.: Yale University Press, 1983), pp. 87–89.

5. Herbert Anderson, *The Family and Pastoral Care,* Don S. Browning, ed. (Philadelphia, Pa.: Fairness Press, 1984); Thomas M. Martin, *Christian Family Values* (New York: Paulist Press, 1984); Elizabeth Achtemeier, *The Committed Marriage* (Philadelphia, Pa.: Westminster Press, 1976); Delores R. Leckey, *The Ordinary Way: A Family Spirituality* (New York: Crossroad, 1982); Theodore Mackin, *Divorce and Remarriage* (New York: Paulist Press, 1984).

6. John S. Mbiti, *African Religions and Philosophy* (Garden City, NY: Doubleday, 1970), pp. 138–40.

7. J. Deotis Roberts, *Roots of a Black Future: Family and Church* (Philadelphia, Pa.: Westminster Press, 1980), pp. 24–29, 39–44.

8. J. Deotis Roberts, *Liberation and Reconciliation: A Black Theology* (Philadelphia, Pa.: Westminster Press, 1971), p. 60. More recently, Amos N. Jones, Jr., has expressed concern about the Black family, but devotes hardly more than two pages to the topic in *Paul's Message of Freedom* (Valley Forge, Pa.: Judson Press, 1984), pp. 189–91.

9. Charles Wallace Smith, *The Church in the Life of the Black Family* (Valley Forge, Pa.: Judson Press, 1986).

10. Marian Wright Edelman, *Families in Peril: An Agenda for Social Change* (Cambridge, Mass.: Harvard University Press, 1987), pp. 51–94.

11. Martin, *Family Values,* pp. 24–33.

12. The bestowal of honor on one's parents continues to be a primary obligation in the Old Testament Pseudepigrapha and was paired with ancient Jewish teachings on the need to love one's brother, even Gentiles, in areas of the diaspora, according to Pheme Perkins, *Love Commands in the New Testament* (New York: Paulist Press, 1982), pp. 19–20.

13. George A. Buttrick, ed., "Family," *The Interpreter's Dictionary of the Bible,* vol. 2 (Nashville, Tenn.: Abingdon Press, 1962), p. 239.

14. Elisabeth Schüssler Fiorenza, in Judith L. Weidman, ed., *Christian Feminism: Visions of a New Humanity* (San Francisco: Harper & Row, 1984), p. 37. Further on her analysis of "Androcentrism" of the Bible, see Elisabeth Schüssler Fiorenza, *In Memory of Her* (New York: Crossroad, 1984), pp. 48–64.

15. Martin, *Family Values,* pp. 39–40; Achtemeier, *Marriage,* p. 114.

16. Joachim Jeremias, *Jerusalem in the Time of Jesus* (Philadelphia, Pa.: Fortress Press, 1975), pp. 271–272.

17. A full discussion appears in Raymond E. Brown, *The Birth of the Messiah* (Garden City, N.Y.: Doubleday, 1977); Jane Schaberg, *The Illegitimacy of Jesus: A Feminist Interpretation of the Infancy Narratives* (San Francisco: Harper & Row, 1987).

18. Hans Küng, *On Being a Christian* (Garden City, N.Y.: Doubleday, 1984 [1974]), p. 310.

19. *See* James Strong, *Strong's Exhaustive Concordance of the Bible* (Nashville, Tenn.: Thomas Nelson, 1979), pp. 340–345.

20. Salo Wittmayer Baron, *A Social and Religious History of the Jews,* vol. 2 (New York: Columbia University Press, 1952, 2d ed.), p. 23. One historian points out that for a lengthy period, some Jews in antiquity used the expression "God of Abraham, Isaac, and Jacob" as a magical invocation.

21. Normally, the first person plurals are taken as the "we of majesty" calling to mind "the heavenly council," but it may be merely a reference to divine parents.

22. Meeks, *Urban Christians,* pp. 23–25.

23. Gerd Theissen, *The Social Setting of Pauline Christianity* (Philadelphia, Pa.: Fortress Press, 1982), pp. 84–85.

24. Martin, *Family Values,* p. 110; Richard N. Longenecker, *New Testament Social Ethics for Today* (Grand Rapids, Mich.: William B. Eerdmans, 1984), pp. 14–15; Willard M. Swartley, *Slavery, Sabbath, War, and Women* (Scottsdale, Pa.: Herald Press, 1983), pp. 192–228.

25. Martin, *Family Values,* pp. 41, 42, 47; Fiorenza, *Memory,* pp. 110–118; cf. Jack T. Sanders, *Ethics in the New Testament* (Philadelphia, Pa.: Fortress Press, 1975).

26. *See* C. H. Felder, "Lessons from Jesus' Own Family," *The AME Zion Quarterly Review,* vol. 96, no. 1 (April, 1984): 34–38.

27. Schüssler Fiorenza, *Memory,* pp. 111, 126–27, 148, 151.

28. In Schüssler Fiorenza's desire to stress the newness of the "family" there is no room for "fathers" (patriarchal lords of the household): "Insofar as the new 'family' of Jesus has no room for 'fathers,' it implicitly rejects their power and status and thus claims that in the messianic community all patriarchal structures are abolished." Ibid., p. 147.

29. *See* Perkins, *Love Commands,* pp. 51–57.

30. Schüssler Fiorenza, *Memory,* p. 128 provides an amplified listing of the rejects and social outcasts of first-century Palestinian Judaism. *See also* Jeremias, *Jerusalem,* pp. 303–76.

31. Martin, *Family Values,* p. 44.

32. David L. Balch, *Let Wives Be Submissive: The Domestic Code in 1 Peter* (Chico, Calif.: Scholars Press, 1981), pp. 9, 85; John E. Elliott, *A Home for the Homeless: A Sociological Exegesis of 1 Peter, Its Situation and Strategy* (Philadelphia, Pa.: Fortress Press, 1981).

33. David C. Verner, *The Household of God: The Social World of the Pastoral Epistles* (Chico, Calif.: Scholars Press, 1983), pp. 134–139.

34. The author of James brings social concern for the orphan and widow to the center of his understanding about "pure religion" (James 1:27). *See* C. H. Felder, *Wisdom, Law, and Social Concern in the Epistle of James* (Ann Arbor, Mich.: University of Michigan microfilm, 1982), pp. 80–83.

35. Martin Dibelius and Hans Conzelmann, *The Pastoral Epistles* (Philadelphia, Pa.: Fortress Press, 1972), pp. 8–10, 39–41.

36. Mark 10:6–9; Matt. 19:4–6; 1 Cor. 7:1–5; cf. Gen. 2:24.

37. Matt. 19:12; 1 Cor. 7:7, 8, 38.

38. *See* Robin Scroggs, *The New Testament and Homosexuality: Contextual Background for Contemporary Debate* (Philadelphia, Pa.: Fortress Press, 1983), pp. 29–65; Furnish, *The Moral Teachings of Paul* (Nashville, Tenn.: Abingdon Press, 1979), pp. 68–82.

39. Russell, *The Future of Partnership,* pp. 81–100. An enlightening discussion on the New Testament notion of sexual partnership.

40. Paul's tendency is to group various "evils" in stock catalogues such as 1 Cor. 6:9–10; Rom. 1:26–32; Gal. 5:16–24. This practice is also evident in other New Testament authors: 2 Tim. 3:2; James 3:16, 4:3; cf. Jude 4, 6, 8, 18, 19.

41. For a summary of the critical problems in establishing Ephesians as an authentic epistle that Paul wrote from prison, *see* Werner Georg Kümmel, *Introduction to the New Testament* (Nashville, Tenn.: Abingdon Press, 1975), pp. 357–63. Some scholars nevertheless still insist that Paul is the author of Ephesians: Marcus Barth, *Ephesians 1–3,* Anchor Bible (Garden City, NY: Doubleday & Company, 1980), pp. 36–50; Arthur G. Patzia, *Colossians, Philemon, Ephesians* (San Francisco: Harper & Row, 1984), pp. 102–106.

42. Barth, *Ephesians,* p. 256.

43. W. E. Burghardt DuBois, *The Gift of Black Folk* (New York: AMS Press, 1971 [1924]), p. 341.

44. Matthew L. Lamb, *Solidarity with the Victims* (New York: Crossroads, 1982), p. 1. James H. Cone, *Speaking the Truth* (Grand Rapids, Mich.: William B. Eerdmans Publishing Co., 1986), p. 8, even insists that "there can be no Christian speech about God which does not represent the interests of the victims in our society."

45. James H. Cone, *God of the Oppressed* (New York: Seabury Press, 1975), pp. 16–38.

46. James H. Cone, *For My People: Black Theology and the Black Church* (Maryknoll, N.Y.: Orbis Books, 1984), pp. 63–68.

47. Küng, *Being,* p. 298. The following commentary on this "cry" is instructive: "When the earliest Gospel gives us Jesus' last words to his God in the form of an inarticulate cry, there is in it the echo of all the crying of a constantly suffering and oppressed and also guilt-laden people. They cried to God in Egypt when they scarcely knew him, and . . . in the promised land, then in the Babylonian exile and finally under the alien Roman power—in all possible situations of distress and sin."

CHAPTER TEN

1. James H. Cone, *Speaking the Truth* (Grand Rapids, Mich.: William B. Eerdmans Publishing Co., 1986), p. 66.

2. Martin Luther King, Jr., *Chaos or Community* (London: Hodder and Stoughton, Ltd., 1968 [1967]), p. 190. *See* William D. Watley, *Roots of Resistance: The Non-violent Ethic of Martin Luther King, Jr.* (Valley Forge, Pa.: Judson Press, 1985), pp. 101, 106; James M. Washington, ed., *A Testimony of Hope* (San Francisco: Harper & Row, 1986), p. 632.

3. David J. Garrow, *Bearing the Cross: Martin Luther King, Jr., and the Southern Leadership Conference* (New York: Random House, 1988), pp. 354–65, 545, 551.

4. Cone, *Speaking the Truth,* p. 74.

5. Otto Eissfeldt, *The Old Testament: An Introduction* (New York: Harper & Row, 1965), p. 36, points out that the Priestly version "has been completely transformed in the spirit of the supernatural and monolithic religion of Israel, though in poetic passages like Ps. civ, 6-9; Job xxxvii, 10-11, it has retained clear traces of its original nature. Also, since the Priestly Version depicts eight works distributed over six days, with two on each of the third and sixth days," scholars have come to agree that the seven day framework actually belongs to a later stage in the history of the text. On this, *see* Claus Westermann, *Genesis 1-11: A Commentary* (Minneapolis, Minn.: Augsburg Publishing House, 1984 [1974]), pp. 88-90.

6. Rashi, the medieval rabbinic scholar, considered "rest" itself to be a work as mentioned in Gen. 2:2. "Rest came; and the work was thus finished and completed." M. Rosenbaum and A. M. Silvermann, *Pentateuch with Targum Onkelos, Haphtaroth and Rashi's Commentary: Genesis* (New York: Hebrew Publishing Company, n.d.), pp. 8, 259.

7. Walter Brüeggemann, *Living Toward a Vision: Biblical Reflections on Shalom* (New York: United Church Press, 1984), p. 86.

8. On Abraham's Ten Trials, *see* Jubilees 15-18 in R. H. Charles, ed., *The Apocyrpha and Pseudepigrapha of the Old Testament,* vol. 2, Pseudepigrapha (Oxford, England: Clarendon Press, 1965 [1913]), pp. 34-40.

9. Andreij Kodjak, *A Structuralist Analysis of the Sermon on the Mount,* Religion and Reason 34 (Berlin; New York; Amsterdam: Mouton de Gruyter, 1986), pp. 54-56.

10. Rudolf Bultmann, *Theology of the New Testament,* 2 vols. (London: SCM Press, Ltd., 1965 [1952]), p. 21.

11. My reading is not only more consistent with Luke's theology, but is well attested in such ancient manuscripts as Sinaiticus and Vaticanus. Others prefer: "peace toward men of good will."

12. Willard M. Swartley, "Politics or Peace (*Eirēnē*) in Luke's Gospel," *Political Issues in Luke-Acts,* Richard J. Cassidy and Philip J. Scharper, eds. (Maryknoll, N.Y.: Orbis Books, 1983), pp. 25-26.

13. George B. Caird, *The Revelation of St. John the Divine* (London: Adam & Clark, 1966), p. 82.

14. Ernst Käsemann, "Primitive Christian Apocalyptic," *New Testament Questions of Today* (Philadelphia, Pa.: Fortress Press, 1979 [1969]), p. 109, n. 1.

15. Cynthia Ikuta, *A Just Peace* (New York: United Church of Christ, 1984); Joseph Fahey and Richard Armstrong, eds., *A Peace Reader: Essential Readings on War, Justice, Non-Violence and World Order* (New York: Paulist Press, 1987); Gray Cox, *The Ways of Peace: A Philosophy of Peace as Action* (New York: Paulist Press, 1986).

16. Now the United Methodist Council of Bishops have published *In Defense of Creation: The Nuclear Crisis and a Just Peace.* "A Pastoral Letter," "Foundation Document," and "Guide for Study and Action" (Nashville, Tenn.: Graded Press, 1986).

17. For a critical assessment of the logic and rhetoric of the Catholic Pastoral, *see* William E. Murnion, "The American Catholic Bishops' Peace Pastoral: A Critique of Its Logic," *Horizon,* vol. 13, no. 1 (Spring, 1986): 67-89. Murnion (p. 77), for example, suggests that the Pastoral focuses too narrowly on "the just war doctrine as an immutable principle of Catholic moral teaching" without sufficient attention to "the holy war ideology and millennial pacifism" which are also "sanctioned in the Bible and have precedents in Christian tradition." For a similar

observation, *see* Jaroslav Pelikan, *Jesus Through the Centuries: His Place in the History of Culture* (New Haven, Conn.: Yale University Press, 1985), p. 169: "The standard threefold typology of theories about 'Jesus and war' across that spectrum may conveniently serve to organize the variety: the doctrine of 'just war,' the theory of a 'crusade,' and the ideology of Christian pacifism. For each of these Jesus provided fundamental justification."

18. Martin Dibelius and Hans Conzelmann, *The Pastoral Epistles,* Hermencia (Philadelphia, Pa.: Fortress Press, 1972), pp. 39–41.

19. J. Christiaan Beker, *Paul's Apocalyptic Gospel: The Coming Triumph of God* (Philadelphia, Pa.: Fortress Press, 1984), p. 23.

20. Swartley, "Politics or Peace," pp. 29, 33.

21. Stephen Mott, *Biblical Ethics and Social Change* (New York: Oxford University Press, 1982), p. 168.

22. Ernst Käsemann, "On Paul's Anthropology," in *Perspectives on Paul* (Philadelphia, Pa.: Fortress Press, 1969), pp. 1–31. This is in no way to obscure Käsemann's earlier distinction that anthropology only becomes possible in the context of parenesis and ecclesiology but it is not evident in the earliest stratum of Christian Apocalyptic tradition. *See* Käsemann, "Primitive Christian Apocalyptic," *NT Questions,* pp. 116, 117.

Bibliography

Achtemeier, Elizabeth. *The Committed Marriage*. Philadelphia, Pa.: Westminster Press, 1976.

Ali, Abudullah Yusuf. *The Holy Qur'an: Text, Translation and Commentary*. Washington, D.C.: American International Printing Co., 1946.

Allworthy, T. B. *Women in the Apostolic Church: A Critical Study of the Evidence in New Testament for the Prominence of Women in Early Christianity*. Cambridge, England: W. Heffer & Sons, Ltd., 1917.

Anderson, Bernhard W. *Understanding the Old Testament*. Englewood Cliffs, N.J.: Prentice-Hall, Inc., 1974.

Anderson, Bernhard W., and Walter Harrelson, eds. *Israel's Prophetic Heritage: Essays in Honor of James Muilenberg*. New York: Harper & Brothers, 1962.

Anderson, Herbert. *The Family and Pastoral Care*. Don S. Browning, ed. Philadelphia, Pa.: Fairness Press, 1984.

Andrae, Tor. *Mohammed: The Man and His Faith*. New York: Harper & Row, 1960.

Arberry, A. J. *History of the Middle East and Aegean Region c. 1800–1350* B.C. Cambridge Ancient History Series, vol. 2. Cambridge, England: Cambridge University Press, 1954.

Aristotle. *The Eudemian Ethics*. The Loeb Classical Library. H. Rackman, trans. Cambridge, Mass.: Harvard University Press, 1935.

———. *The Nichomachaean Ethics*. The Loeb Classical Library. H. Rackman, trans. Cambridge, Mass.: Harvard University Press, 1962.

———. *The Politics*. Loeb Classical Library. H. Rackman, trans. New York: G. P. Putnam's Sons, 1932.

Awolalu, J. Omosade. "The Emergence and Interaction of Religions in Nigeria." *The Journal of Religious Thought,* vol. 41, no. 2 (Fall–Winter, 1984–1985).

Baird, J. Arthur. *The Justice of God in the Teaching of Jesus*. London: SCM Press, Ltd., 1963.

Balch, David L. *Let Wives Be Submissive: The Domestic Code in 1 Peter*. Chico, Calif.: Scholars Press, 1981.

Baron, Salo Wittmayer. *A Social and Religious History of the Jews,* 2d ed., vol. 2. New York: Columbia University Press, 1952.

Barrett, C. K. *Freedom & Obligation: A Study of the Epistle to the Galatians*. Philadelphia, Pa.: Fortress Press, 1985.

Barrett, Leonard. *The Rastafarians: Sounds of Cultural Dissonance*. Boston, Mass.: Beacon Press, 1977.

Bartchy, S. Scott. *First Century Slavery and 1 Corinthians 7:21*. Missoula, Mont.: Scholars Press, 1973.

Barth, Markus. *Ephesians 1–3,* Anchor Bible. Garden City, N.Y.: Doubleday & Company, 1980.

Bauer, W. *A Greek-English Lexicon of the New Testament.* W. E. Arndt and F. W. Gingrich, trans. and eds. Chicago: University of Chicago Press, 1957.

Beare, F. W. *The Epistle to the Philippians.* London: Adams & Clark, 1959.

Beker, J. Christiaan. *Paul the Apostle: The Triumph of God in Life and Thought.* Philadelphia, Pa.: Fortress Press, 1980.

_____ . *Paul's Apocalyptic Gospel: The Coming Triumph of God.* Philadelphia, Pa.: Fortress Press, 1982.

Bennett, Lerone, Jr. *Before the Mayflower: A History of the Negro in America.* Chicago: Johnson Publishing, 1962 [Revised: Baltimore, Md.: Penguin Books, 1970].

Bennett, Robert A., Jr. "Africa and the Biblical Period." *Harvard Theological Review* 64 (1971).

_____ . "Biblical Hermeneutics and the Black Preacher." *The Journal of the Interdenominational Theological Center,* vol. 1, no. 2 (Spring, 1974).

Bernal, Martin. *Black Athena: The Afroasiatic Roots of Classical Civilization.* Vol. 1, *The Fabrication of Ancient Greece 1785-1985.* London: Free Association Books, 1987.

Betz, Hans Dieter. *Galatians: A Critical and Historical Commentary on the Bible.* Hermeneia. Philadelphia, Pa.: Fortress Press, 1979.

Bird, Phyllis, A. *The Bible as the Church's Book.* Philadelphia, Pa.: Westminster Press, 1982.

Black, Matthew, ed. *Peake's Commentary on the Bible.* London: Thomas Nelson and Sons, Ltd., 1962.

Blass, Debrunner, and Funk. *A Grammar of Greek Syntax.* Chicago: University of Chicago Press, 1961.

Boesak, Allan. *Black and Reformed.* Maryknoll, N.Y.: Orbis Books, 1984.

Botterweck, G. Johannes, and Helmer Ringgren, ed. *Theological Dictionary of the Old Testament.* Davie E. Green, trans. Grand Rapids, Mich.: William B. Eerdmans Publishing Co., 1974-1984.

Bouyer, Louis. *A History of Christian Spirituality,* vol. 1. New York: Paulist Press, 1982.

Brandt, Richard, ed. *Social Justice.* Englewood Cliffs, N.J.: Prentice-Hall, Inc., 1962.

Briggs, Charles A., and Emile Grace Briggs. *The Book of Psalms.* International Critical Commentary, vol. 1. Edinburgh: T. & T. Clark, 1976 [1907].

Brockelmann, Carl. *History of the Islamic Peoples.* New York: Capricorn Books, 1960. [Originally, *Geschichte der Islamischen Völker und Staaten,* 1944.]

Brooks, Walter H. *The Pastor's Voice.* Washington, D.C.: The Associated Publishers, 1945.

Brown, Raymond, E. *The Birth of the Messiah.* Garden City, N.Y.: Doubleday and Co., 1977.

_____ . *The Community of the Beloved Disciple.* New York: Paulist Press, 1979.

_____ . *The Gospel According to John: I-XII.* Anchor Bible. Garden City, N.Y.: Doubleday, 1966.

_____ . "Roles of Women in the Fourth Gospel." *Theological Studies* 36 (1975).

_____ . "The Pater Noster as an Eschatological Prayer." *Theological Studies* 22 [1961].

Brown, Raymond E., Joseph A. Fitzmyer, and Roland Murphy, eds. *The Jerome Biblical Commentary.* Englewood Cliffs, N.J.: Prentice-Hall, Inc., 1968.

Brown, Robert McAfee. *Unexpected News: Reading the Bible with Third World Eyes.* Philadelphia, Pa.: Westminster Press, 1984.

Brueggemann, Walter. *In Man We Trust.* Atlanta, Ga: John Knox Press, 1972.

_____ . *Living Toward a Vision: Biblical Reflections on Shalom.* New York: United Church Press, 1984.

_____ . *The Prophetic Imagination.* Philadelphia, Pa.: Fortress Press, 1978.

Brugger, W., and K. Baker. *Philosophical Dictionary.* Spokane, Wash.: Gonzaga University Press, 1972.

Brumbaugh, Robert S. *Plato for the Modern Age.* London: Collier-Macmillan, Ltd., 1962.

Budge, E. A. Wallis. *The Egyptian Book of the Dead.* New York: Dover Publications, 1967.

_____ . *Osiris and the Egyptian Resurrection.* 2 vols. New York: Dover Publications, 1973.

Bultmann, Rudolf. *Theology of the New Testament.* 2 vols. London: SCM Press, Ltd., 1965 [52] and New York: Charles Scribner's Sons, 1952.

Burghardt, Walter, J., S.J. *Sir, We Would Like to See Jesus.* New York: Paulist Press, 1982.

Buttrick, George A., ed., *The Interpreter's Bible.* 12 volumes. New York: Abingdon Press, 1957.

_____ . ed. *Interpreter's Dictionary of the Bible.* 4 vols. Nashville, Tenn.: Abingdon Press, 1962.

Cabrol, F., and H. Leclerq. *Dictionnaire d'archeologie chretienne et du liturgie,* V (1). Paris: Libraire Letouzey, 1922.

Cadoux, Arthur T. *The Thought of St. James.* London: James Clark, 1944.

Caird, George B. *The Gospel of Saint Luke.* Middlesex, England: Penguin Books, 1963 [New York: Penguin Books, 1965].

_____ . *The Revelation of St. John the Divine.* London: Adam & Clark, 1966.

Calvez, Jean-Yves, and Jacques Perin. *The Church and Social Justice.* London: Burns & Oats, English translation, 1961 [French edition, 1959].

Carrington, Philip. *Primitive Christian Catechism.* Cambridge, England: University Press, 1949.

Cassidy, Richard J. *Jesus, Politics and Society.* Maryknoll, N.Y.: Orbis Books, 1978.

_____ . *Society and Politics in the Acts of the Apostles.* Maryknoll, N.Y.: Orbis Books, 1987.

Cassidy, Richard J., and Philip J. Scharper, ed. *Political Issues in Luke–Acts.* Maryknoll, N.Y.: Orbis Books, 1983.

Caton-Thompson, G. *Zimbabwe Culture.* Oxford, England: Clarendon Press, 1931.

Charles, R. H., ed. *The Apocrypha and Pseudepigrapha of the Old Testament.* Vol. 2, Pseudepigrapha. Oxford, England: Clarendon Press, 1965 [1913].

Clark, Stephen B. *Man and Woman in Christ.* Ann Arbor, Mich.: Servant Books, 1980.

Cleage, Albert. *The Black Messiah.* Fairway, Kans.: Andrews & McMeel, Inc., 1969.

Clement of Alexandria, *Stromata* I; III.

Clingan, Ralph G. "Romans 3: The Preacher's Dilemma." *The Journal of the Interdenominational Theological Center,* vol. 9, no. 2 (Spring, 1982).

Coggins, R. J. *Samaritans and Jews.* Atlanta, Ga: John Knox Press, 1973.

Cone, James. *For My People: Black Theology and the Black Church.* Maryknoll, N.Y.: Orbis Books, 1984.

_____. *God of the Oppressed.* New York: Seabury Press, 1975.

_____. "Martin Luther King, Jr., Black Theology and the Black Church." *Theology Today,* vol. 40, no. 4 (January, 1984).

_____. *Speaking the Truth.* Grand Rapids, Mich.: William B. Eerdmans Publishing Company, 1986.

Conzelmann, Hans. *The Theology of St. Luke.* Geoffrey Buswell, trans. New York: Harper & Row, 1960.

Copher, Charles B. "Bible Characteristics, Events, Places and Images Remembered and Celebrated in Black Worship." *The Journal of the Interdenominational Theological Center,* vol. 14, no. 1 and 2 (Fall, 1986/Spring, 1987): 75–86.

_____. "The Black Man in the Biblical World." *Journal of the Interdenominational Theological Center,* vol. 1, no. 2 (Spring, 1974): 7–16.

_____. "Egypt and Ethiopia in the Old Testament." *Nile Valley Civilization.* Ivan Van Sertima, ed. Journal of African Civilizations, Ltd., 1985.

_____. "3,000 Years of Biblical Interpretation with Reference to Black Peoples." *The Journal of the Interdenominational Theological Center,* vol. 13, no. 2 (Spring, 1986): 225–46.

The Council of Bishops, The United Methodist Church. *In Defense of Creation: The Nuclear Crisis and a Just Peace. "A Pastoral Letter," "Foundation Document,"* and *"Guide for Study and Action."* Nashville, Tenn.: Graded Press, 1986.

Cox, Gray. *The Ways of Peace.* New York: Paulist Press, 1986.

Cox, James W. *Biblical Preaching: An Expositor's Treasury.* Philadelphia, Pa.: Westminster Press, 1983.

Crim, Keith, gen. ed. *Interpreter's Dictionary of the Bible,* supplement. Nashville, Tenn.: Abingdon Press, 1976.

Cronon, E. David. *Black Moses: The Story of Marcus Garvey.* Madison, Wisc.: The University of Wisconsin Press, 1969.

Cullman, Oscar. *The Early Church.* Ed. A. J. B. Higgins. Philadelphia, Pa.: Westminster Press, 1956.

Dake, Finis Jennings. *Dake's Annotated Reference Bible.* Lawrenceville, Ga.: Dake Bible Sales, Inc., 1981 [1961].

Daube, David. *Studies in Biblical Law.* Cambridge, England: The University Press, 1947.

de Pinedo, Thomas. *De Uribibus.* Graz, Switzerland: Akademische Druck V. Verlangsanstalt, 1958 [1678].

_____. *Stephanus de Byzantinus cum Annotationibus.* Vol. 4:5. Lipsiae, 1825.

Dibelius, Martin. *Botschaft und Geschichte.* Vol. 1. Tübingen, 1953.

_____. *James.* Hermeneia. Philadelphia, Pa.: Fortress Press, 1976.

_____. *Jesus.* Philadelphia, Pa.: Westminster Press, 1949.

Dibelius, Martin, and Hans Conzelmann. *The Pastoral Epistles.* Hermeneia. Philadelphia, Pa.: Fortress Press, 1972.

Dictionary of African Biography. New York: Rowman and Littlefield, 1970.

Diessmann, Adolph. *Light from the Ancient East.* London: Hodder and Stoughton, 1927.

Diop, Cheikh Anta. *The African Origin of Civilization: Myth or Reality?* Mercer Cook, trans. New York and Westport: Lawrence Hill and Company, 1974 [1955].

Dodd, Charles H. *The Apostolic Preaching and Its Developments*. New York: Harper & Row, 1964.

DuBois, William E. B. *The Gift of Black Folk*. New York: AMS Press, 1971 [reprint of 1924 edition].

——— . *The Souls of Black Folk*. Greenwich, Conn.: Fawcett, 1961 [New York: A. J. McClure, 1903].

Dunn, James D. G. *Unity and Diversity in the New Testament: An Inquiry Into the Character of Earliest Christianity*. Philadelphia, Pa.: Westminster Press, 1977.

Dunston, Alfred. *The Black Man in the Old Testament and Its World*. Philadelphia, Pa.: Dorrance, 1974.

Durka, Gloria, and Joanmarie Smith, ed. *Family Ministry*. Oak Grove, Minn.: Winston Press, 1980.

Edelman, Marian Wright. *Families in Peril: An Agenda for Social Change*. Cambridge, Mass.: Harvard University Press, 1987.

Eissfeldt, Otto. *The Old Testament: An Introduction*. New York: Harper & Row, 1965.

Elliott, John E. *A Home for the Homeless: A Sociological Exegesis of 1 Peter, Its Situation and Strategy*. Philadelphia, Pa.: Fortress Press, 1981.

Ellul, Jacques. *The Ethics of Freedom*. Grand Rapids, Mich.: William B. Eerdmans Publishing Company, 1976.

Emanuel, James A., and Theodore L. Gross, ed. *Dark Symphony: Negro Literature in America*. New York: The Free Press, 1968.

Fagan, Brian M. F. *Tomb Robbers, Tourists and Archeologists in Egypt*. New York: Charles Scribner's Sons, 1975.

Fahey, Joseph, and Richard Armstrong, ed. *A Peace Reader*. New York: Paulist Press, 1987.

Felder, Cain H. "The Bible, Black Women and Ministry." *The Journal of Religious Thought,* vol. 41, no. 2 (Fall-Winter, 1984-1985); *Journal of the Interdenominational Theological Center* (July, 1985).

——— . "Lessons from Jesus' Own Family." *The AME Zion Quarterly Review,* vol. 96, no. 1 (April, 1984): 34–38.

——— . "Paul's Reinterpretation of Jewish Apocalyptic." *The Journal of Religious Thought,* vol. 40, no. 1 (Spring–Summer, 1983).

——— . "Racial Ambiguities in the Biblical Narratives." *Concilium,* vol. 51. New York: Seabury Press, 1982.

——— . Review of Willard Swartley, *Slavery, Sabbath, War and Women. Report from the Capitol* (October, 1983).

——— . *Wisdom, Law and Social Concern in the Epistle of James*. Ann Arbor, Mich.: University of Michigan microfilm, 1982.

Fiorenza, Elisabeth Schüssler. *In Memory of Her: A Feminist Theological Reconstruction of Christian Origins*. New York: Crossroad Publishing Company, 1984.

——— . "Women in the Pre-Pauline Churches." *Union Seminary Quarterly Review* 3 (1978).

Foucault, Michel. *Power/Knowledge: Selected Interviews and Other Writings*. Colin Gordon. ed. New York: Pantheon, 1980.

Franklin, John Hope. *From Slavery to Freedom*. 3d ed. New York: Alfred Knopf, 1987 [1947].

Fransen, Irénée. "Le premier examen de conscience chrétién: l'epître de Jacques."

Bible et Vie Chretienne (1959).

Frazier, E. Franklin. *The Negro Church in America*. New York: Schocken Books, 1974.

Friedrich, Carl J. *Transcendent Justice: The Religious Dimension of Constitutionalism*. Durham, N.C.: Duke University Press, 1964.

Fromm, Erich. *Escape from Freedom*. New York: Holt, Rinehart & Winston, 1965.
_____ . *Man for Himself*. Greenwich, Conn.: Fawcett, 1966.

Furnish, Victor Paul. *The Moral Teachings of Paul*. Nashville, Tenn.: Abingdon Press, 1979.

Gammie, John, et al, eds. *Israelite Wisdom: S. Terrien Festschrift*. New York: Scholars Press for UTS, 1978.

Gardiner, Sir Alan. *Egypt of the Pharaohs*. New York: Oxford University Press, 1974 [1961].

Garrow, David J. *Bearing the Cross: Martin Luther King, Jr., and the Southern Leadership Conference*. New York: Random House, 1988.

Glaser, Edward. *Abessinier in Arabien und Afrika*. Munich, 1895.

Gnuse, Robert. *You Shall Not Steal*. Maryknoll, N.Y.: Orbis Books, 1985.

Goitein, S. D. *Jews and Arabs: Their Contacts Through the Ages*. New York: Schocken Books, 1964.

Gottwald, Norman K. *All the Kingdoms of the Earth*. New York: Harper & Row, 1964.

Gottwald, Norman K., ed. *The Bible and Liberation: Political and Social Hermeneutics*. Maryknoll, N.Y.: Orbis Books, 1983.

Gould, John. *The Development of Plato's Ethics*. Cambridge, England: The University Press, 1955.

Gregory of Nyssa. *Contra Eunomium* 1. Patristica Graeca 45:264.

Haenchen, Ernst. *The Acts of the Apostles: A Commentary*. Oxford, England: Basil Blackwell, 1971 [1965].

Hamilton, Edith. *Mythology*. New York: The New American Library, Inc., 1969.

Hansberry, William Leo. *Africa and Africans as Seen by Classical Writers*. Joseph E. Harris, ed. Washington, D.C.: Howard University Press, 1977.

Harding, Vincent. *There Is a River: The Black Struggle for Freedom in America*. New York: Random House, 1983.

Harris, Joseph E. *Pillars in Ethiopian History*. Washington, D.C.: Howard University Press, 1974.

Hartmann, Louis. trans. and ed. *Encyclopedic Dictionary of the Bible*. New York: McGraw Hill, 1963.

Hatcher, William E. *John Jasper: The Unmatched Negro Philosopher and Preacher*. New York: Fleming H. Revell Co., 1908.

Haughey, John C. ed. *The Faith That Does Justice*. New York: Paulist Press, 1977.

Hengel, Martin. *Acts and the Ancient History of Earliest Christianity*. Philadelphia, Pa.: Fortress Press, 1980.

Hiob, Ludolphus. *Historia Aethiopica*. Book I. Frankfort, 1681.

Homer. *Odyssey*, 1:23.

Hoyt, Thomas, Jr. "The Poor in Luke–Acts." Ph.D. dissertation, Duke University, 1975.

Huntington, George W. B. ed. and trans. *The Periplus of the Erythraean Sea*. London: The Hakluyt Society, 1980.

Ikuta, Cynthia. *A Just Peace*. New York: United Church of Christ, 1984.

"Ils sont issus del" escorte juive que le roi Salomon donna a la reine de Saba lorsqu'elle repartit pour l'Ethiopie." *LeMonde* (Nov. 12, 1973).

Irvine, A. K. "On the identity of the *Habashat* in the South Arabian Inscriptions." *Journal of Semitic Studies,* vol. 10 (January–December, 1965).

Isaac, Ephraim. "Genesis, Judaism and the 'Sons of Ham'." *Slavery and Abolition: A Journal of Comparative Studies,* vol. 1, no. 1 (May, 1980).

Isaac, Ephraim, and Cain H. Felder. "Reflections on the Origins of the Ethiopian Civilization." Paper read at the International Congress of Ethiopian Studies, Addis Ababa, Ethiopia. November, 1983.

Jackson, F. J. Foakes, and Kirsopp Lake. *The Acts of the Apostles.* 4 vols. Grand Rapids, Mich.: Baker Book House, 1979.

Jacques-Garvey, Amy, ed. *Philosophy and Opinions of Marcus Garvey.* 2 vols. New York: Atheneum, 1969.

James, George G. M. *Stolen Legacy.* San Francisco: Julian Richardson Associates (New York: Philosophical Library, 1954).

Jeremias, Joachim. *Jerusalem in the Time of Jesus: An Investigation into Economic and Social Conditions during the New Testament Period.* Philadelphia, Pa.: Fortress Press, 1962, 1967, 1969, 1977.

_____ . *The Parables of Jesus.* New York: Charles Scribner's Sons, 1972.

Jerome. *De Actibus Apostolorum.*

Johnson, James Weldon. *The Book of American Negro Spirituals.* New York: The Viking Press, 1925.

_____ . *God's Trombones.* New York: The Viking Press, 1964 [1927].

Johnson, Paul. *A History of Christianity.* New York: Atheneum, 1976.

Johnson, William A. "Reflections on Preaching." *The Christian Ministry,* vol. 15, no. 6 (November, 1984).

Jones, Amos N., Jr. *Paul's Message of Freedom: What Does It Mean for the Black Church?* Valley Forge, Pa.: Judson Press, 1984.

Jones, Elias. "In Search of Zion: A Study of Three Religious Movements Related to Garveyism." Unpublished Ph.D. dissertation, University of Bern, Bern, Switzerland, 1986.

Jones, William. *Is God a White Racist? A Preamble to Black Theology.* Garden City, N.Y.: Anchor Books, 1973.

Josephus, Flavius. *Complete Works.* Grand Rapids, Mich.: Kregel Publications, 1960 [12th printing, 1974].

_____ . *Antiquities Judaicae.* Book 8, Loeb edition.

Juel, Donald. *Luke–Acts: The Promise of History.* Atlanta, Ga.: John Knox Press, 1983.

Kaiser, Otto. *Isaiah 1–12: A Commentary.* 2d ed. Philadelphia, Pa.: Westminster Press, 1983.

Käsemann, Ernst. *Commentary on Romans.* Trans. Geoffrey W. Bromiley. Grand Rapids, Mich.: William B. Eerdmans Publishing Company, 1980.

_____ . *Essays on New Testament Themes.* London: SCM Press, Ltd., 1964.

_____ . *Jesus Means Freedom.* Philadelphia, Pa.: Fortress Press, 1969.

_____ . *New Testament Questions of Today.* Philadelphia, Pa.: Fortress Press, 1979 [1969].

_____ . *Perspectives on Paul.* Philadelphia, Pa.: Fortress Press, 1971.

Kelber, Werner H., ed. *The Passion in Mark.* Philadelphia, Pa.: Fortress Press, 1976.

Kelly, Francis X. "Poor and Rich in the Epistle of James." Ph.D. dissertation, Temple University, 1972.

Khayyam, Omar. *The Rubaiyat.* (Ed. Edward Fitzgerald. New York: Walter J. Black, 1942 [1859].

King, Martin Luther. *Chaos or Community.* London: Hodder and Stoughton, Ltd., 1968 [1967].

Kittel, Gerhard, et al., ed. *Theological Dictionary of the New Testament.* 10 vols. Grand Rapids, Mich.: William B. Eerdmans Publishing Company, 1973.

Kitto, H. D. F. *The Greeks.* Edinburgh: T. & T. Clark, 1956.

Kodjak, Andreij. *A Structuralist Analysis of the Sermon on the Mount.* Religion and Reason 34. Berlin; New York; Amsterdam: Mouton de Gruyter, 1986.

Koenig, John. *Charismata: God's Gifts for God's People.* Philadelphia, Pa.: Westminster Press, 1978.

Kümmel, Werner Georg. *Introduction to the New Testament.* Revised English Ed. Howard C. Kee, trans. Nashville, Tenn.: Abingdon Press, 1973.

_____ . *The New Testament: The History of the Investigation of Its Problems.* Nashville and New York: Abingdon Press, 1970.

Küng, Hans. *On Being a Christian.* Garden City, N.Y.: Doubleday, 1984 [1974].

Lace. O. Jessie. *Understanding the New Testament.* The Cambridge Bible Commentary. Cambridge, England: University Press, 1965.

Lake, Kirsopp, trans. *Apostolic Fathers,* vol. 1. The Loeb Classical Library. Cambridge, Mass.: Harvard University Press, 1975 [1922].

Lamb, Matthew L. *Solidarity with the Victims.* New York: Crossroads, 1982.

Laws, Sophie. *The Epistle of James.* Harper's New Testament Commentaries. San Francisco: Harper & Row, 1981.

Lawson, James Gilchrist, ed. *The Best Loved Religious Poems.* Chicago: Fleming H. Revell Co., 1933.

Lebacqz, Karen. *Six Theories of Justice: Perspectives from Philosophical and Theological Ethics.* Minneapolis, Minn.: Augsburg Publishing House, 1986.

Leckey, Delores R. *The Ordinary Way: A Family Spirituality.* New York: Crossroads, 1982.

Leslau, Wolf. *Falasha Anthology: The Black Jews of Ethiopia.* New York: Schocken Books, 1951.

Lester, Julius, ed. *The Seventh Son: The Thought and Writings of W. E. B. DuBois,* vol. 1. New York: Random House, 1971.

Leudemann, Gerd. *Paul, Apostle to the Gentiles: Studies in Chronology.* Philadelphia, Pa.: Fortress Press, 1984.

Lift Every Voice and Sing: A Collection of Afro-American Spirituals and Other Songs. New York: The Church Hymnal Corporation, 1987.

Lincoln, C. Eric. *Race, Religion and the Continuing American Dilemma.* New York: Hill and Wang, 1984.

Littmann, E. *Deutsche Aksum Expedition,* vol. 4. Berlin: G. Reimer, 1913.

Locke, Alain, ed. *The New Negro.* New York: Atheneum, 1969.

Long, Charles H. "Perspectives for a Study of Afro-American Religion in the United States." *History of Religions,* vol. 2, no. 1 (August, 1971).

_____ . *Significations: Signs, Symbols, and Images in the Interpretation of Religion.* Philadelphia, Pa.: Fortress Press, 1986.

Longenecker, Richard N. *New Testament Social Ethics for Today.* Grand Rapids, Mich.: William B. Eerdmans Publishing Company, 1984.

Mackin, Theodore. *Divorce and Remarriage.* New York: Paulist Press, 1984.

McVey, Kathleen. "God the Father/God the Mother?" and "The Gnostic Gospels?" by Elaine Pagels. *Theology Today* 37 (January, 1981).

Martin, Thomas M. *Christian Family Values.* New York: Paulist Press, 1984.

Marty, Jacques. *L'Épître de Jacques.* Paris: Felix Alcan, 1935.

Martyn, J. Louis. *The Gospel of John in Christian History.* New York: Paulist Press, 1978.

Massey, James Earl. *Designing the Sermon: Order and Movement in Preaching.* Nashville, Tenn.: Abingdon Press, 1980.

———. *The Sermon in Perspective.* Grand Rapids, Mich.: Baker Book House, 1976.

———. *The Responsible Pulpit.* Anderson, Ind.: Wasner Press, 1974.

Mathabane, Mark. *Kaffir Boy.* New York: New American Library, 1986.

Mayor, Joseph B. *The Epistle of James.* London: Macmillan and Co., Ltd., 1897.

May, Herbert G., and Bruce M. Metzger, eds. *The New Oxford Annotated Bible* (RSV). New York: Oxford University Press, 1962, 1973.

Mays, Benjamin E. *The Negro's God as Reflected in His Literature.* New York: Atheneum, 1973 [reprint of 1938 edition].

Mbiti, John S. *African Religions and Philosophies.* New York: Doubleday, 1970.

Meeks, Wayne A. *The First Urban Christians.* New Haven, Conn.: Yale University Press, 1983.

———. *The Moral World of the First Christians.* Philadelphia, Pa.: Westminster Press, 1986.

Meidelman, Moshe. *Jewish Women in Jewish Law,* vol. 6. New York: KTAV, 1968.

Meier, John P. *The Vision of Matthew: Christ, Church and Morality in the First Gospel.* New York: Paulist Press, 1979.

Mellor, Enid B. *The Making of the Old Testament.* The Cambridge Bible Commentary. Cambridge, England: The University Press, 1972.

Metzger, Bruce M. *The Early Versions of the New Testament.* Oxford, England: Clarendon Press, 1977.

Meyer, Arnold. *Das Rästel des Jakobusbriefes.* Geissen: A. Topelmann, 1930.

Mitchell, Henry H. *The Recovery of Preaching.* San Francisco: Harper & Row, 1977.

Mitton, C. L. *The Epistle of James.* Grand Rapids, Mich.: William B. Eerdmans Publishing Company, 1966.

Molière. *Eight Plays by Molière.* Morris Bishop, trans. New York: The Modern Library, 1957.

Moore, George Foot. *Judaism,* vol. 2. Cambridge, Mass.: Harvard University Press, 1932.

Moorish, George. *A Concordance of the Septuagint.* Grand Rapids, Mich.: Zondervan, 1976.

Morrisey, R. A. *Colored People and Bible History.* Hammond, Ind.: W. B. Conkey Company, 1925.

Mott, Stephen. *Biblical Ethics and Social Change.* New York: Oxford University Press, 1982.

Mowinckel, Sigmund. *The Psalms in Israel's Worship.* 2 vols. D. R. Thomas, trans. Oxford, England: Basil Blackwell, 1962.

Mudge, Lewis S. "Thinking About the Church's Thinking: Toward a Theological Ethnography." *Theological Education* (Spring, 1984).

Murnion, William E. "The American Catholic Bishop's Peace Pastoral: A Critique of Its Logic." *Horizon,* vol. 13, no. 1 (Spring, 1986): 67–89.

Murtonen, A. *Early Semitic: A Diachronical Inquiry into the Relationship of Ethiopic to the Other So-called South-east Semitic Languages.* Leiden: E. J. Brill, 1967.

Mussner, Franz. *Der Brief des Jakobus.* Frieburg: Herders, 1967.

Newboldt, Robert T., Jr. *Black Preaching.* Philadelphia, Pa.: Geneva Press, 1977.

Nichols, Roy C. *Footsteps in the Sea.* Nashville, Tenn.: Abingdon Press, 1980.

Niebuhr, H. Richard, and Daniel Day Williams, ed. *The Ministry in Historical Perspective.* San Francisco: Harper & Row, 1983 [1956].

Noble, Jeanne. *Beautiful, Also, Are the Souls of My Black Sisters.* Englewood Cliffs, N.J.: Prentice-Hall, Inc., 1978.

Noth, Martin. *A History of Pentateuchal Traditions.* Trans. Bernhard W. Anderson. Chico, Calif.: Scholars Press, 1981.

Obermüller, Rudolph. *"Hermeneutischen Themen im Jakobusbrief,"* *Biblica* 53 (February, 1972).

Onwu, Nlenanya. "The Current State of Biblical Studies in Africa." *The Journal of Religious Thought,* vol. 41, no. 2 (Fall–Winter, 1984–1985).

Origen. *Commentarius in Canticum Canticorum.* 2:367–370.

_____ . *Commentary on John.* 2.12.87 (IV.67).

_____ . *Origen.* Classics of Western Spirituality. Introduction by Rowan A. Greer. New York: Paulist Press, 1976.

Pagels, Elaine. *The Gnostic Gospels.* New York: Random House, 1979.

Paris, Peter J. *The Social Teaching of the Black Church.* Philadelphia, Pa.: Fortress Press, 1985.

Patzia, Arthur G. *Colossians, Philemon, Ephesians.* San Francisco: Harper & Row, 1984.

Payne, Daniel A. *Sermons and Addresses, Bishop D. A. Payne, 1853–1891.* Charles Killian, ed. New York: Arno Press, 1972.

Pelikan, Jaroslav. *Jesus Through the Centuries: His Place in the History of Culture.* New Haven, Conn.: Yale University Press, 1985.

Perkins, Pheme. *Love Commands in the New Testament.* New York: Paulist Press, 1982.

Phillips, J. B., trans. *The New Testament in Modern English.* New York: Macmillan, 1958.

Philostargius. Historia ecclesiastica. Pat. Graec. 65:469.

Plato. *The Laws.* The Loeb Classical Library. R. G. Burg, trans. New York: G. P. Putnam's Sons, 1926.

_____ . *The Republic.* The Loeb Classical Library. New York: G. P. Putnam's Sons, 1930.

Price, James L. *The New Testament: Its History and Theology.* New York: Macmillan, 1987.

Pritchard, James B. *Ancient Near Eastern Texts,* vol. 1. Princeton, N.J.: Princeton University Press, 1973 (paperback ed.).

Ray, Sandy F. "Elements in Black Preaching." *The Journal of Religious Thought,* vol. 30, no. 1 (Spring–Summer, 1973).

_____ . *Journeying Through a Jungle.* Nashville, Tenn.: Broadman Press, 1979.

Redford, Donald B. "The Monotheism of the Heretic Pharaoh: Monotheism or Egyptian Anomaly?" *Biblical Archaeology Review,* vol. 13, no. 3 (May/June, 1987).

Reumann, John. *Righteousness in the New Testament.* Philadelphia, Pa.: Fortress Press; New York: Paulist Press, 1982.

Rice, Gene. "The African Roots of the Prophet Zephaniah." *The Journal of Religious Thought,* vol. 36, no. 1 (Spring–Summer, 1979).

_____ . "The Curse That Never Was (Genesis 9:18–27)." *The Journal of Religious Thought,* vol. 29 (1972).

_____ . "Two Black Contemporaries of Jeremiah." *The Journal of Religious Thought,* vol. 32 (1975).

Roberts, Alexander, and James Donaldson, ed. *The Ante-Nicene Fathers,* vol. 1. Grand Rapids, Mich.: William B. Eerdmans Publishing Company, 1981.

Roberts, J. Deotis. *Black Theology in Dialogue.* Philadelphia, Pa.: Westminster Press, 1987.

_____ . *Black Theology Today: Liberation and Contextualization.* New York and Toronto: The Edwin Mellen Press, 1984.

_____ . *Liberation and Reconciliation: A Black Theology.* Philadelphia, Pa.: Westminster Press, 1971.

_____ . *Roots of a Black Future: Family and Church.* Philadelphia, Pa.: Westminster Press, 1980.

Ropes, James Hardy. *The Epistle of St. James.* International Critical Commentary. Edinburgh: T. & T. Clark, 1973 [1916].

Rose, H. J. *The Religion of Greece and Rome.* New York: Harper & Row, 1959.

Rosenbaum, M., and A. M. Silvermann. *Pentateuch with Targum Onkelos, Haphtaroth and Rashi's Commentary: Genesis, Deuteronomy.* New York: Hebrew Publishing Company, n.d.

Rossini, C. Conti. "Expeditions et possessions des Habasat en Arabie." *Journal Asiatique,* ser. 18 (1921).

_____ . *Storia d'Ethiopia.* Bergamo, 1928.

_____ . "Sugli Habasat," *Rendiconti, Regia Academi dei Lincei,* ser. 5 XV (1906).

Russell, Letty M. *The Future of Partnership.* Philadelphia, Pa.: Westminster Press, 1979.

Rustin, Roger. "Christian Views of Justice." *New Blackfriars,* vol. 59, no. 699 (August 1978): 344–45.

Rutenber, Culbert Gerow. *The Doctrine of the Imitation of God in Plato.* New York: King's Crown Press, 1946.

Sanders, Jack T. *Ethics in the New Testament.* Philadelphia, Pa.: Fortress Press, 1975.

_____ . *The Jews in Luke–Acts.* Philadelphia, Pa.: Fortress Press, 1987.

Sanders, James A. *Torah and Canon.* Philadelphia, Pa.: Fortress Press, 1972.

Schaberg, Jane. *The Illegitimacy of Jesus: A Feminist Interpretation of the Infancy Narratives.* San Francisco: Harper and Row, 1987.

Schoeps, Hans Joachim. *Jewish Christianity.* Philadelphia, Pa.: Fortress Press, 1969.

_____ . *Theologie und Geschichte des Judenchristentums.* Tübingen: J. C. B. Mohr, 1949.

Schrey, H. H. *The Biblical Doctrine of Justice and Law.* London: SCM Press, 1955.

Scott, R. B. Y. *The Way of Wisdom.* New York: Macmillan, 1971.

Scroggs, Robin. *The New Testament and Homosexuality: Contextual Background for Contemporary Debate.* Philadelphia, Pa.: Fortress Press, 1983.

_____ . "Paul and the Eschatological Woman." *Journal of the American Academy of Religion,* vol. 40 (1972). *See also JAAR* vol. 42 (1974).

Seitz, O. J. F. "James and the Law." *Text und Untersuchen* 87 (1967).

Sellassie, Sergew Hable. *Ancient and Medieval Ethiopian History to 1270.* Addis Ababa: United Printers, 1972.

Shorter, Aylward. *African Christian Spirituality.* Maryknoll, N.Y.: Orbis Books, 1980.

Singer, I., ed. *Jewish Encyclopedia.* 12 vols. New York: Gordon Press, 1964.

Singleton, George A. *The Romance of African Methodism.* New York: Exposition Press, 1952.

Smith, Charles Ryder. *The Bible Doctrine of Womanhood and Its Historical Evolution.* London: The Epworth Press, 1923.

Smith, Charles Wallace. *The Church in the Life of the Black Family.* Valley Forge, Pa.: Judson Press, 1986.

Snowden, Frank M., Jr. *Blacks in Antiquity: Ethiopians in the Greco-Roman Experience.* Cambridge, Mass.: Harvard University Press, 1970.

Stanton, Elizabeth Cady, et al. *The Woman's Bible.* New York: European Publishing Co., 1898.

Stendahl, Krister. *The Bible and the Role of Women.* Facet Books. Biblical Series no. 15. Philadelphia, Pa.: Fortress Press, 1966.

Strabo. *The Geography of Strabo.* Loeb Classical Edition. H. L. Jones, ed. and trans. Cambridge, Mass.: Harvard University Press, 1949.

Strack, Herman L. *Introduction to Talmud and Midrash.* Philadelphia, Pa.: Jewish Publication Society, 1931.

"Stress: Can We Cope?" *Time* (June 6, 1983).

Strong, James. *Strong's Exhaustive Concordance of the Bible.* Nashville, Tenn.: Thomas Nelson Publishers, 1979.

Swartley, Willard M. *Slavery, Sabbath, War, and Women: Case Issues in Biblical Interpretation.* Scottsdale, Pa. and Kitchener, Ontario: Herald Press, 1983.

Swidler, Leonard and Arlene, ed. *Women Priests: A Catholic Commentary on the Vatican Declaration.* New York: Paulist Press, 1977.

Tamrat, Tadesse. *Church and State.* Cambridge, England: Oxford University Press, 1972.

Taylor, A. E. *Plato: The Man and His Work.* New York: The World Publishing Company, 1966 [1956].

Taylor, Gardner C. *How Shall They Preach?* Elgin, Ill: Progressive Baptist Publishing House, 1977.

Taylor, Vincent. *The Gospel According to St. Mark.* New York: St. Martin's Press, 1966.

Terrason, Abbé, trans. *Histoire universelle.* Bk. 3. Paris, 1758.

Theissen, Gerd. *The Social Setting of Pauline Christianity.* Philadelphia, Pa.: Fortress Press, 1982.

Thomas, Latta. *Biblical Faith and the Black American.* Valley Forge, Pa.: Judson Press, 1986 [1976].

Thompson, James W. *The Middle Ages,* vol. 1. New York: Alfred A. Knopf, 1931.

Thurman, Howard. *The Growing Edge.* Richmond, Ind.: Friends United Press, 1956.

_____ . *Jesus and the Disinherited.* Nashville, Tenn.: Abingdon Press, 1949.

Torres, Dominique. *"Les Juifs noir de l'Oublie."* *LeMonde* (November 12, 1973).

Tribble, Phyllis. "Depatriarchalizing in Biblical Interpretation." *Journal of the American Academy of Religion* 40 (March 1973).

_____ . *God and the Rhetoric of Sexuality.* Philadelphia, Pa.: Fortress Press, 1978.

Trocmé, André. *Jesus and the Non-violent Revolution*. Scottsdale, Pa.: Herald Press, 1973.

Ullendorff, Edward. *Ethiopia and the Bible*. London: Oxford University Press, 1968.

_____ . *The Ethiopians*. 2d ed. New York: Oxford University Press, 1961.

Van Beek, Gus W. "Monuments of Axum in Light of South Arabian Archeology." *Journal of the American Oriental Society,* vol. 87 (1967).

Van Sertima, Ivan. *Black Women in Antiquity*. New Brunswick, N.J.: Transaction Books, 1988. Reprinted from the *Journal of African Civilizations,* vol. 6, no. 1 (April, 1984).

_____ . *They Came Before Columbus: The African Presence in Ancient America*. New York: Random House, 1977.

_____ , ed. *Nile Valley Civilizations*. New Brunswick, N.J.: Journal of African Civilizations, Ltd., 1985.

Verner, David C. *The Household of God: The Social World of the Pastoral Epistles*. Chico, Calif.: Scholars Press, 1983.

Via, Dan O. "The Right Strawy Epistle Reconsidered: A Study in Biblical Ethics and Hermeneutics." *Journal of Religion* 49 (1969).

Von Balthasar, Hans Urs. *Spirit and Fire: A Thematic Anthology of his Writings*. Robert J. Daly, trans. Washington: Catholic University of America, 1984.

von Rad, Gerhard. *Old Testament Theology*. 2 vols. D. M. G. Stalker, trans. New York: Harper & Row, 1962.

_____ . *Wisdom in Israel*. New York: Abingdon Press, 1972.

Ward, Roy Bowen. *"The Communal Concern of the Epistle of James."* Ph.D. dissertation, Harvard University, 1966.

_____ . "Partiality in the Assembly: James 2:2–4." *Harvard Theological Review* 62 (1969).

Wardlaw, Don M., ed. *Preaching Biblically*. Philadelphia, Pa.: Westminster Press, 1983.

Washington, James M., ed. *A Testimony of Hope*. San Francisco: Harper & Row, 1986.

Washington, Joseph R., Jr. *Black Sects and Cults*. New York: Doubleday, 1972.

Watley, William D. *Roots of Resistance: The Nonviolent Ethic of Martin Luther King, Jr*. Valley Forge, Pa.: Judson Press, 1985.

Weidman, Judith L., ed. *Christian Feminism: Visions of a New Humanity*. San Francisco: Harper & Row, 1984.

West, Cornel. *Prophesy Deliverance*. Philadelphia, Pa.: Westminster Press, 1982.

Westermann, Claus. *Genesis 1–11: A Commentary*. Minneapolis, Minn.: Augsburg Publishing House, 1984 [1974].

Wheelwright, Philip. *Aristotle*. New York: The Odyssey Press, 1951.

Wilder, Amos N. *Early Christian Rhetoric: The Language of the Gospel*. Cambridge, Mass.: Harvard University Press, 1971.

Wilken, Robert L., ed. *Aspects of Wisdom in Judaism and Early Christianity*. Notre Dame, Ind.: University of Notre Dame Press, 1975.

Williams, Bruce. "Lost Pharaohs of Nubia." In *Nile Valley Civilizations,* Ivan Van Sertima, ed. *Journal of African Civilizations, Ltd.,* 1985.

Williams, C. S. C. *The Acts of the Apostles*. New York: Harper & Row, 1957.

Wilmore, Gayraud S. *Black Religion and Black Radicalism*. Maryknoll, N.Y.: Orbis Books, 1983.

Wilmore, Gayraud S., and James H. Cone, ed. *Black Theology: A Documentary History 1966-1979,* Maryknoll, N.Y.: Orbis Books, 1979.

Wilson, S. G. *Luke and the Law.* Cambridge, England: University Press, 1983.

Wilson, William Julius. *The Declining Significance of Race.* Chicago: University of Chicago Press, 1978.

Wimbush, Vincent. "Biblical-Historical Study as Liberation: Toward an Afro-Christian Hermeneutic." *The Journal of Religious Thought,* vol. 42, no. 2 (Fall-Winter, 1985-1986).

Woodson, Carter G. *The History of the Negro Church.* Washington, D.C.: Associated Publishers, 1921.

Young, Henry J., ed. *God and Human Freedom.* Richmond, Ind.: Friends United Press, 1983.

CHAPTERS IN BOOKS CITED

Brooten, Bernadette. "Junia." In Leonard Swidler and Arlene Swidler, eds., *Women Priests: A Catholic Commentary on the Vatican Declaration.* New York: Paulist Press, 1977.

Donahue, John. "Biblical Perspectives on Justice." In John C. Haughey, ed., *The Faith That Does Justice.* New York: Paulist Press, 1977.

Frankena, William. "The Concept of Social Justice." In Richard Brandt, ed., *Social Justice.* Englewood Cliffs, N.J.: Prentice-Hall, Inc., 1962.

Jacob, Edmund. "Wisdom and Religion in Sirach." In John Gammie et al. eds., *Israelite Wisdom: S. Terrien Festschrift.* New York: Scholars Press for UTS, 1978.

Laporte, Jean. "Philo in the Tradition of Wisdom." In Robert L. Wilken, ed., *Aspects of Wisdom in Judaism and Early Christianity.* Notre Dame, Ind.: University of Notre Dame Press, 1975.

Marbury, Carl. "Hebrews and Spirituals." In Henry J. Young, ed., *God and Human Freedom.* Richmond, Ind.: Friends United Press, 1983.

Moltmann, Jürgen. "God Means Freedom." In Henry J. Young, ed., *God and Human Freedom.* Richmond, Ind.: Friends United Press, 1983.

Murphy, Roland. "Wisdom-Theses and Hypotheses." In John Gammie et al. eds., *Israelite Wisdom: S. Terrien Festschrift.* New York: Scholars Press for UTS, 1978.

Scroggs, Robin. "Sociological Interpretation of the New Testament." In Norman K. Gottwald, ed., *The Bible and Liberation: Political and Social Hermeneutics.* Maryknoll, N.Y.: Orbis Books, 1983.

Smith, Luther E. "Community: Partnership of Friendship and Responsibility." In Henry J. Young, ed., *God and Human Freedom.* Richmond, Ind.: Friends United Press, 1983.

Vlastos, Gregory. "Justice and Equality." In Richard Brandt, ed., *Social Justice.* Englewood Cliffs, N.J.: Prentice-Hall, Inc., 1962.

General Index

Aaron, 42, 141
Abraham, 169
Achtemeier, Elizabeth, R., 61–62
Aquinas, St. Thomas, 75
Aeschylus, 25
Africa and Africans as Seen by Classical Writers (Hansberry), 7
African American Church: and justice, 78
Agapē, 71, 76, 158, 159, 162
Agatharchides, 24
Akhenaton, 10
Albright, W. F., 23
Ali, Abdullah Yusef, 35
Amos of Tekoa, 63
Aristarchus, 25
Aristotle, 75; and distributive justice, 56–59; *Nichomachaean Ethics, The,* 57, 58
Athanasius, 15
Baird, J. Arthur, 68
Barrett, C. K., 110
Barth, Karl, 18, 103, 104
Barth, Markus, 163
Bathsheba, 140, 143
Beker, J. Christiaan, 173
Ben-Jochannan, Yosef: *The Black Man's Religion,* 7
Bennett, Robert A., xii, 9, 88
Bereshit Rabbah, 15
Betz, Hans, 110, 111, 128
Bible: and Black experience, 6–7; and Black families, 150–66; election and sacralization in, 43–46; roles of women in, 140–42; women in, 139–49; women in ministry in, 142–45
Biblical: literalism, 89; mandates on justice and social class, 53–78;

meaning and the Black religious experience, 5–21; narratives, racial motifs in, 37–48; scholarship: Black, 7–8; Eurocentric, xi–xviii; modern, 53
Biblical usage: in American Black churches, 79–191; in Black church art and education, 86–88; guidelines for, 88–90; and Negro spirituals, 85–86
Bilqis, 31, 35, 141
Bird, Phyllis A., 140
Black: Africa and Egypt, relationship of, 9–11; families, the Bible and, 150–66; preachers, challenges to, 88; religious experience, early, 8–11; theology, xiii, 16–17; women and ministry, 139–49
Black church: American, 54–55, 79–191; ancient, 78; art and education in, 86–88; biblical usage in, 79; challenges facing, 164–65; mission and outreach of, 137; and peacemaking, 167–77; preaching in, 81–85
Black Religion and Black Radicalism (Wilmore), 7, 118
Blacks: in the biblical tradition, xi–xviii, 12–14; and Israel, 43
Blood kinship, New Testament, 155–60
Boesak, Allan, 14
Book of Jubilees, 70
Borders, William Holmes, 90
Brooks, Walter L., 87
Brown, Raymond E., 143
Brueggeman, Walter, 82, 168
Brumbaugh, Robert S., 56
Bultmann, Rudolf, 45, 68, 169

223

Cadoux, A. T., 120
Caird, G. B., 105, 170–71
Canaan, 39, 40
Candace, 34
Canon formation, 14–15
Carrington, Philip, 120
Cassidy, Richard, 74
Charismata, 76
Charismatic justice, 75–78
Christian freedom, politics of, 113–17
Christian worldview, early, 46
Church, and peace, 171–73
Class: 50–134; and God's law, 118–34; stratification, Old Testament, 153
Cone, James H.: on the Bible, 165; on the Black church, 115; Black Power and Black Theology, xiii; on church discrimination, 119; For My People, 7, 14, 81; on Marxism, 55; on peace making, 167
Congress of Ethiopian Studies, xv
Congress of National Black Churches, xvi
Contextualization, 16
Conzelman, Hans, 174
Copher, Charles B., xii
Cornelius, 13, 47
Crates, 25
Crummell, Alexander, 83
Daube, David, 60, 61, 63
Decalogue, 128–29, 152
Deissmann, Adolph, 126
de Volney, Constantin, 9
Diaspora, Black, xi, 5
Dibelius, Martin, 80, 88; on law, 120, 126, 131; on mercy, 133; on New Testament social reform, 68
Diop, Cheikh Anta, 7, 10, 12, 17; The African Origin of Civilization, 7
Discrimination, in James, 120–34
Divine call to freedom, 106–9
Dodd, C. H., 81
Donahue, John, 64
Drewes, A. I., 29
Du Bois, W. E. B., 163–64
Edict of Toleration, 15
Eisegesis, 89
Egypt, 40; and Black Africa, 13–14; dynasties of, 10–11; religious beliefs in, 11; sources of culture of, 9–11

Egyptian Book of the Dead (Budge), 11
Election, 43–46
Ellul, Jacques, 107
Ephorus, 25
Epistle of James, 118–34
Epistle to the Galatians, 102–17
Eratosthenes, 24
Eschatological justice, 72–73
Ethiopia: ancient, 22–36; canon formation in, 15; civilization of, 28; conversion of official of, 47; Ethiopian-Semitic relationship, 28; Ethiopians in the Old Testament, 43
Euripides, 25
Eurocentric biblical scholarship, xi, xiv, 13–14, 16, 22, 53
Eusebius, 14–15
Evans, Arthur, 17
Family, 136–66; Black, and the Bible, 150–66; and the church, 159–60; definition of, 137; Jesus and, 156–157; in New Testament, 155–60; in Old Testament, 151–55
Farmer, William, xi
Fauntroy, Walter, 84
Fiorenza, Elisabeth Schüssler, xi, 77, 78, 152
First Urban Christians, The (Meeks), 85
Floyd, John, 118
Foucault, Michel, xiv, 8
Frazier, E. Franklin, 85
Freedom: American, 103–4; and the Bible, 104–9; Christians and, 113–17; and class, 102–17; cost of, 113–17
Friedrich, Carl J., 58
Fromm, Erich, 107–8
Galatians, background and structure of, 109–13
Garnet, Henry Highland, 83
Garvey, Marcus, 7
Gifts, spiritual, 75
Gilkes, Cheryl Townsend, 16
Glaser, E., 27
God's Trombones (Johnson), 86–87
Gorapor, H., 23
Gould, John, 57
Grimes, Leonard A., 83

Grimke, Francis J., 84
Gunkel, Hermann, 23
Haenchen, Ernst, 13, 47
Ham, 23, 26, 36; curse of, 38-41
Hamito-Semitic language family, 28-30
Hannah, 140, 143
Hammon, Jupiter, 90
Hansberry, William Leo, 10, 17; *Africa and Africans as Seen by Classical Writers,* 7; *The African Presence in Asia,* 7; *Africans and Their History,* 7; *Pillars in Ethiopian History,* 7
Harding, Vincent, 115
Healy, James, 83
Hedgeman, Anna Arnold, 84
Hengel, Martin, 13
Herodotus, 9
Hiob, Ludolphus, 27
Hirsch, E. G., 62
Historical-critical Bible study, 6-8, 79
Holly, James T., 83
Homer, 25
Household of God, 137, 159-63
Humanity, origin of, 38-39, 40
Ikenga-Metuh, Emefie, 16
Irvine, A. K., 27, 29
Isaac, Ephraim, xv, 12, 30
Isaiah, Book of, 64
Jahwist, 38, 41, 61, 141; redactor, 23; version of creation, 153
James, Book of, and discrimination, 120-25
Japeth, 38, 39, 40
Jasper, John, 79, 89
Jeremiah, 64
Jeremias, Joachim, 153
Jesus: on the family, 156-57; on sexual conduct, 161; and women, 158-59
Jones, Amos, 108-9
Johnson, James Weldon, 85; *God's Trombones,* 86-87
Johnson, William A., 79
Josephus, Flavius, 12-13; on the Queen of Sheba, 32-33, 34, 36
Journal of Religious Thought, The, xii, xvi, 16
Judah, descendants of, 42
Judaism and justice, 59-63
Junias (Junia), 146

Justice: American Black church and, 54-55, 78-101; ancient Black church and, 78; Aristotle and, 57-58; biblical mandates on, 53-78; charismatic, 75-78; classical theory of social, 68; commutative, 75; compensatory, 73-74; definition of, 56; distributive, 56-59, 75-78; eschatological, 72-73; Greco-Roman, 56-59; and love, 69-71; New Testament, 68-78; Old Testament, 59-63; Pentateuchal, 60-63; Plato and, 56-57; in prophetic literature, 63-64; in Psalms and wisdom literature, 63-68; reciprocal, 71-72
Kaffir Boy (Mathabane), 3
Kandakē, 13, 139, 141-42
Kelly, Leontine T. C., 90
Kesh, 10
Käsemann, Ernst, 75-76, 128, 175
Kaufman, Kohler, 62-63
King, Martin Luther, Jr., 84, 90, 115, 168
King, Willis J., 90
Kitto, H. D. F., 58, 59
Koinōnia, 18
Küng, Hans, 153
Kush, 26
Lamb, Matthew, 164
Laporte, Jean, 67
Latin American Liberation Theology, 55
Law, The (Plato), 56-57
Law of love, 69-71
Laws, Sophie: on James, 121, 122, 124; on mercy, 133; on royal law, 126-127
Lebacqz, Karen, 75
Legalism and James, 130-31
Leudemann, Gerd, 109-10
Lincoln, C. Eric, 114
Lock, Alain, 92, 93
Long, Charles, 7, 103
Love: agapē, 71; and justice, New Testament, 69-71
Luke, attitude toward Blacks, 47-48
Magnificat, 143
Makeda, 31, 141
Marbury, Carl, 85
Marxist thought and justice, 55

Matthew, Wentworth A., 35

Mays, Benjamin, 87–88; *The Negro's God,* 85

Mbiti, John, 16; *African Religions and Philosophy,* 151

Menes, 11

Menthoteps, 11

Mercy, reciprocity of, 132

Ministry, women and, 139–49

Miranda, Jose, xi

Miriam, 42, 140, 141

Moltmann, Jürgen, 113

Moore, George Foot, 45, 59, 60, 62

Moral action, New Testament, 155–60

Moral obligations in James, 130–31

Morrisey, R. A., xi; *Colored People and Bible History,* 35–36

Moses, marriage of, 42, 139

Mott, Stephen, 175

Mowinckel, Sigmund, 64, 65

Muratorian canon, 14

Murtonen, A., 28–29

Mussneer, Franz, 121

Narmer (Menes), 11

National Conference of Catholic Bishops: *The Challenge of Peace: God's Promise and Our Response,* 171

Negro spirituals and biblical usage, 85–86

New Testament: blood kinship and, 155–60; freedom and, 104–9; justice and, 68–78; moral action and, 155–60; nuclear age and, 167–77; peacemaking and, 169–71; preaching from, 90–101; radicalism and, 17–21; secularization in, 46–48; sexual conduct and, 160–63

Noah, 23, 39, 40–42

Nubia, 15, 23

Nuclear age, 167–77

Obermüller, Rudolf, 120

Oikos tou theou, 18, 19

Old Testament: and Blacks, 17–18; class stratification in, 153; and families, 151–55; and freedom, 104; and peacemaking, 168–69; race sacralization in, 38–43; and women, 140–42

Origin of post-diluvial humanity, 38–39

Onwu, Nlenanya, 16

Origen, 13 and

Pan-African Congress, 7

Paris, Peter J., 54

Paul, the apostle, 18, 45; on distributive justice, 75–76; on the divine call to freedom, 106–9; on sexual conduct, 161–62; on slavery, 86; on women in the ministry, 145–48

Payne, Daniel Alexander, 83

Peace, 167–77

Peacemaking, 173–77; and the Black church, 167–77; in New Testament, 169–71; in Old Testament, 168–69

Pentateuchal justice, 60–63

Pharaohs, Black, 8, 10–11

Phoebe, 146

Plato, 17; and justice, 56–59

Posnansky, Merrick, 9

Powell, Adam Clayton, 84

Preaching: Black, 88; etymology of, 80–81; history of, 81–85; from New Testament, 90–101

Priestly redactor, 23, 38, 41, 61, 152, 154

Prophets, justice and, 63–64

Psalms, justice and, 64–68

Queen of Nubia, 13

"The Queen of the South," 12, 139

Queen of Sheba *(see* Sheba, Queen of)

Rahab, 140, 143

Race, 2–48; Old Testament, 38–43

Races of Africa, and Egypt and Negro Africa (Seligman), 9

Racial motifs, biblical, 37–48

Racial prejudice, Old Testament, 42

Racism in ancient times, 37–38

Radicalism, New Testament, 17–21

Ramses II, 10, 11

Ransom, Reverdy, 84

Ray, Charles Bennett, 83

Reciprocal justice, 71–72

Reconciliation and the Household of God, 162–63

Recontextualization, 16–17, 19, 20

Reicke, Bo, 122

Religious beliefs, Egyptian, 11

Republic, The (Plato), 5

Revels, Hiram R., 84

Rice, Gene, 42

Roberts, J. Deotis, 54–55; *Black Theology Today* 7; *Roots of a Black Future: Family and Church,* 151

Robinson, J. A. T., xi

Romance of African Methodism, The, (Singleton), 87

Ropes, J. H., 120, 131

Rose, H. J., 58, 59

Rossini, Conti, 26, 27

Sabaeans, 24–27, 30, 32

Sacralization: biblical, 43–46; of the "curse of Ham," 38–40; definition of, 38; of Israel's election, 44–46; of Noah's descendants, 40–42; in Old Testament, 38–43

Salome Alexandra, 140

Samaritan woman, the, 144–45

Sargon II, 32

Schliemann, Heinrick, 17

Scott, R. B. Y., 66

Seba, 23, 26, 41

Secularization: definition of, 38; in New Testament, 46–48

Seebass, Horst, 44

Seitz, O. J. F., 120, 125–26, 129

Selassie, Haile, 34

Semitic languages, 28–30

Sexual conduct, 160–63

Sheba, Queen of: 12–13, 37, 41, 139; as a Black, 22–36, 141; interpretations regarding, 30–32

Shem, 23–24, 38–42

Siculus, Diodorus, 17

Smith, Luther E., 114

Snowden, Frank, xii

Social class, biblical mandates on, 53–78

Social stratification in the church, 133–34

Solomon, 31, 32

South Arabian-Ethiopian relations, 28–30

Stephanus of Byzantium, 27

Strabo, 9, 24, 25

Subjugated knowledges, 8, 16

Supernatural, the, 5

Swartley, Willard, 169–70, 174–75

Symeon, 47–48

Syrophoenician woman, 143

Table of Nations, 41

Tahargua, xiv

Tamar, 140, 143

Tanak, 14, 15

Taylor, Gardner, 81, 89

Temptation narratives, 105–6

Tewoflos, 26

Theodicy, 17–18, 54–55

Theology, political, xii–xiii

Thomas, Latta, 5–6; *Biblical Faith and the Black American,* xii

Thrauō, 19

Thurman, Howard, 90, 91, 116

Thutmose III, 11

Tiglath-pileser III, 32

Tirhaka, 43

Torres, Dominique, 35

Triumphalism, 15

Truth, Sojourner, 83

Turner, Henry McNeal, 3–4, 83

Turner, Nat, 83, 118

Ullendorff, 33–34

United Methodist Council of Bishops, xvii

Van Beek, Gus, 26

Varick, James, 83

Via, Don O., 130

Victoria, Francisco Xavier de Luna, 83

Vivian, C. T., 84

von Rad, Gerhard, 44, 62, 66

"Wade in the Water," xiii–xiv

Walker, Wyatt T., 84

Waters, Alexander, 84

West, Cornel: *Prophesy Deliverance,* 8

Westermann, Claus, 23, 38–39, 40

Wilder, Amos N., 85, 87

Williams, Bruce, 8–9

Williams, Henry Sylvester, 7

Wilmore, Gayraud, 16; *Black Religion and Black Radicalism,* 7, 118

Wilson, William Julius, 98

Wimbush, Vincent, xii, 6

Wink, Walter, xi

Wisdom literature and justice, 64–68

Women: and the Bible, 139–49; and Jesus, 158–59; New Testament status of, 77–78

Young, Andrew, 84

Scripture Index

GENESIS

1–11	39
1:1–2:4	152, 168
1:26, 27	61
2:4–3:24	23, 153, 168
2:13	23
3:4–6	140
4	152
5:1, 2	61
8:20–22	38
9:1–17	38
9:6	60, 72
9:13–16	171
9:18–27	38, 39
9:20–27	39
9:28	38
9:29	38
10	12, 41
10:6	23, 40
10:7	23, 26, 41
10:21–31	42
10:28	23, 26, 41
10:29	23
15:15	169
16	140
16:1	12
17:16–19	140
18:25	62
19:36	152
21	140
22	152
22:1–19	169
25	140
25:3	27

25:21–26	140
27	152
29:31	140
30	152
37	152
37:1–36	17
38	152

EXODUS

3:7–9	104
5:10–21	104
6:25	12
14:13	113
14:21	xiv
15:20	140
21	104
21:7–8	61
21:20	61
21:21	61
22:22	160
22:24	127
23:2	62
23:3	62
23:6	123
23:11	123

LEVITICUS

19:9	123
19:10	123
19:15	62, 111, 121, 122, 127
19:18	69, 70, 72, 128
25:10	73

NUMBERS

12	139, 141
12:1	12, 42
12:1–16	38
12:10	141
25:7	12

DEUTERONOMY

6:1–6	159
10:18	160
15	104
15:7–11	123
16:18	62
16:18–20	111
19:21	72
21:18–21	157
24:1–4	152

JOSHUA

10:13	89

1 SAMUEL

1:5	140
1:30	12
2:1–10	143
2:34	12

2 SAMUEL

11	140
18:21–32	43

1 KINGS

3:1	141

10	*30, 33, 139, 141*	
10:1–10	*12, 31, 33*	
10:9	*141*	
10:13	*31, 33*	
10:14	*15, 31*	
10:15	*32*	
11:41	*33*	
21:1–5	140	

2 KINGS

19:9	*43*

1 CHRONICLES

1:1–2:55	*41*
1:9	*23*
1:17–34	*41*
1:23	*23*
2:1–55	*42*

2 CHRONICLES

9	*33, 139, 141*
19:7	*111*

EZRA

6:1	*153*

NEHEMIAH

10:28–30	*153*

PSALMS

1:5	*131*
9:19	*123*
22:1	*65*
38:28	*65*
49:6	*65*
49:16	*65*
61:13	*132*
62	*65*
68:31	*15*
71:4	*124*
81:4	*124*
85:1	*124*
85:2	*124*
87:4	*15*
99:4	*65*
103:10	*65*

106:30	*12*

PROVERBS

22:6	*159*
29:13	*66*

SIRACH

3:3	*67*
3:14b	*67*
3:30	*67*
4:11	*124*
7:3	*67*
7:32	*124*
10:15	*67*
14:9	*67*
15:14	*68*
15:15	*68*
17:22	*67*
18:3	*68*
27:8	*67*
35:17	*67, 124*
35:18	*67*
40:12	*67*
40:13	*67*
40:17	*67*
42:1b	*127*
50:27	*67*
51:23	*67*

ISAIAH

1:17	*63*
11:11	*9*
20:3–6	*23*
29:19	*123*
34:8	*131*
37:9	*12, 43*
43:3	*24*
45:14	*23, 24*
53:7	*13, 78*
53:8	*13, 78*
56:6	*73*
58:7	*123*
61:1	*73, 123*
64:8	*154*

JEREMIAH

7:5–7	*64*

25:24	*32*
27:12	*132*
27:38	*132*
38:7	*12*
38:7–13	*43*
39:15–18	*43*
39:16	*12*
46:9	*43*

EZEKIEL

33:1–6	*81*

HOSEA

11:1	*13*

AMOS

2:4	*64*
2:7	*123*
4:1	*63, 123*
4:12	*64*
5:15	*64*
5:24	*64*
8:4–6	*64*

MICAH

7:6	*157*

NAHUM

3:8	*23*
3:9	*23*

HABAKKUK

2:2	*69*

ZEPHANIAH

1:1	*12, 43*
2:12	*12*
3:10	*12*

ZECHARIAH

10:12	*132*

MALACHI

1:11	*89*

2:13–16	*152*	

MATTHEW

1:1–14	*158*
1:3	*143*
1:5	*143*
1:6	*143*
1:16	*153*
1:19	*69*
2:13–22	*13*
3:17	*105*
5:3	*124*
5:9	*169*
5:12	*73*
5:21	*131*
5:22	*131*
5:27–32	*161*
5:43	*71*
6:10	*175*
7:18	*74*
8:11	*13*
8:12	*13*
8:14	*158*
8:15	*158*
9:18–26	*158*
10:1–16	*73*
10:34–36	*157*
10:42	*73*
11:4–6	*73*
11:29	*74*
12:4–21	*139*
12:18	*131*
12:36	*72*
12:42	*12, 34*
12:50	*19, 157*
13:52b	*157*
14:21	*77, 142*
15:21–28	*143*
15:38	*77, 142*
16:27	*132*
18:15–20	*74*
18:23–25	*72*
19:16–22	*129*
19:18	*129*
19:19	*129*
22:14	*45*
22:16	*106*
22:39	*129*

23:23	*131*
23:27	*119*
23:28	*119*
25:14–20	*76*
25:31–41	*73*
25:31–46	*72*
26:6–13	*158*
27:19–24	*69*

MARK

1:4	*80*
1:12	*105*
1:13	*105*
1:14	*80*
1:15	*80*
6:1–6	*159*
6:20	*69*
6:30–44	*142*
7:26–30	*143*
8:1–10	*142*
10:13–16	*159*
12:14	*106*
13:12	*157*

LUKE

1:36	*143*
2:14	*169*
2:25	*69*
2:36	*143*
2:41–52	*158*
3:22	*105*
3:23	*153*
4:16–30	*73, 106*
4:18	*19*
4:23–38	*143*
5:20	*70*
5:43	*71*
6:20	*124*
6:33	*71*
8:21	*143*
10:6	*169*
10:25–28	*70*
10:29–37	*70*
10:36	*70*
10:37	*70*
10:37	*74*
11:31	*12, 34, 139*

11:42	*70, 131*
12:48	*74*
13:10–17	*158*
13:29	*13*
14:14	*72*
15:11–32	*157*
18:1–8	*143*
18:20	*129*
19:1–10	*74*
19:38	*175*
19:42	*175*
19:43	*169*
20:21	*106*
23:39–43	*106*
23:50	*69*
24:11	*158*
24:25	*144, 158*
27:3	*71*
27:5	*71*

JOHN

3:1–23	*144*
4	*158*
4:4–42	*144*
4:42	*77*
7:24	*131*
12:3–7	*158*
12:47	*74*
15:6	*74*
17:25	*69*
20:4	*144*
20:5	*144*

ACTS

1:8	*13*
5:14	*77*
6:2	*74*
8:26–40	*13, 47, 78, 142*
8:27	*13, 139*
8:27–39	*34*
8:32	*13*
8:33	*13*
8:36	*78*
8:37	*47*
9	*107*
9:1–22	*106*

10:12–48	*47*	3:13	*72*	1:9	*109*
10:22	*69*	5	*152*	1:10, 11	*111*
10:34–43	*47*	5:1	*161*	1:11–2:14	*111*
10:36	*143*	5:17	*162*	1:11–24	*106*
10:38	*125*	6:1–8	*74*	1:18	*112*
11:28	*48*	6:18	*161*	2:2	*112*
13:1	*18, 47–48*	7:21–24	*86*	2:6	*111, 112*
15:5	*112*	9:9	*75*	2:9	*112*
16:3	*112*	9:11	*162*	2:10	*19*
16:6	*109*	9:15	*75*	2:18–21	*112*
18:2	*146*	9:16	*91, 106*	2:30	*112*
18:18	*146*	9:19	*75*	3:1	*109, 110*
20:35	*19*	9:27	*73*	3:1–4:31	*112*
21:8	*143*	10:18	*45*	3:10	*110*
21:9	*143*	11:1	*112*	3:19–29	*112*
		11:7	*145, 147*	3:28	*45, 114, 146*
ROMANS		11:13	*87*	4:10	*107*
1:24–27	*161*	11:14	*87*	4:21–31	*112*
2:11	*106, 111*	11:22	*87*	5:1	*106, 112,*
2:13	*69*	12:4–8	*75*		*113*
3:25	*xvi*	12:11	*76*	5:1–6:10	*162*
3:25–29	*128*	12:13	*45, 75*	5:3	*128*
5:7	*113*	12:14	*162*	5:6	*112*
5:9	*xvi*	12:14–20	*76*	5:12	*109, 110*
7:12	*69*	12:28	*76*	5:14	*70, 72, 114,*
7:14b	*162*	13:1	*21*		*128*
8:23	*160*	14:4	*76*	5:15	*114*
8:31–39	*21*	14:5	*76*	5:19	*161*
9:11	*74*	14:15	*86*	5:22–6:6	*117*
11:18	*132*	14:18	*76*	5:25	*112*
11:29	*107*	14:19	*76*	6:10	*19, 70, 115*
12	*162*	14:34	*145, 147*	6:16	*45*
12:3	*75*	14:35	*145, 147*		
12:6	*75*	15:1	*81*	**EPHESIANS**	
12:4–8	*76*	15:12–58	*18*	2:11–22	*162–163*
13:8	*72*	15:31	*79*	2:13	*163*
13:8–10	*128*	16:19	*146*	2:14–16	*170*
13:9	*128, 129*			4:7	*76*
14	*19*	**2 CORINTHIANS**		5:21	*159*
14:10–12	*72*	3:17	*116*	5:22	*159*
15	*19*	4:5	*88*	6:1–3	*160*
15:25–29	*19*	5:17	*162*	6:5–8	*105*
15:27	*162*	5:19–21	*162*		
15:28	*46*	8	*19*	**PHILIPPIANS**	
16:1–16	*146*	8:4–14	*19*	2:3	*71*
16:3–5	*146*	8:14	*19*	2:4	*71*
		9:1	*19*	2:5–9	*19*
1 CORINTHIANS		**GALATIANS**		3:12–16	*18*
1:27–28	*45*	1	*107*		

3:13	73
3:14	73
4:8	69

COLOSSIANS

3:9	81
3:11	45
3:12	45
3:18	159
3:20	160
3:22–25	105

2 THESSALONIANS

1:6–9	72

1 TIMOTHY

1	87, 107
1:12–17	106
2:11	147
2:12	147
5:3–16	160
5:8	74
5:10	160
5:14	160
5:19	74

2 TIMOTHY

2	87
2:15	91
3:6	147
3:7	147
3:16	83
4:19	146

HEBREWS

12:11	175
12:12–14	175
13:1–3	72

JAMES

1:10	123
1:19–25	120
1:19–27	132
1:22–25	130
1:25	120
1:26	120
1:27	120, 160
2:1	121
2:1–6	125
2:1–7	120–125
2:1–13	119, 120, 132
2:2	122
2:2–4	121
2:3	122
2:5	45, 124
2:5–7	125
2:6	19, 123, 124, 134
2:8	72
2:8–11	128
2:8–12	120, 128
2:8–13	120, 125–134
2:8–14	126
2:9	127
2:9–12	128
2:10	127, 128, 130
2:11	127, 129, 130
2:12	130, 131
2:13	73, 131, 132, 133
2:14–17	19, 130
3:17	175
3:18	175
4:11	120
4:12	120
5:1	123
5:9	131
5:20	75

1 PETER

2:9	45
2:18–25	105
3:7	147, 160
4:9	72
4:10	76

2 PETER

2:13	87

JUDE

12	87

REVELATION

2:18–29	148
6:4	170
7:1	89
7:9	48
13	160
18	160, 173
19	160

BARNABAS

4:2	132
4:12	132

1 CLEMENT

5:7	46

2 CLEMENT

4:3	129
4:33	129
10:6	132
18:2	131

1 ENOCH

93:1	124
93:2	124

JUBILEES

15:30	124
20:2	70

at a sit-down Chinese restaurant, with those silver pots of tea and orange slices when they bring the bill." The life they had was perfect.

Clay imagined the end of summer city: the shimmer of heat, the drip from window units overhead, the chorus of ice cream trucks, office buildings leaking air-conditioning onto the humid sidewalks where fat tourists were wandering dumbstruck. It would be enough for him. Marble countertops and this perfect swimming pool and the touch-responsive light switches were all well and good, but be it ever so humble, etc.

"You don't think anything's wrong with Rose, do you?" A briefer moment of surrender than orgasm.

Clay began reflexively to say that everything was fine, but he did not believe it, and anyway, in matters of fact, belief was not salient. "She seemed okay to me. Did you notice something?"

"No." Amanda swallowed, a hand at her throat. Was something wrong with *her*? "Do you feel okay?"

"I feel normal. I feel like myself." Clay had never been the most observant of men.

Amanda stood. She wiped her stomach with a pair of his folded boxer shorts. Her arms, her legs, her waist— they showed her forty-three years. There was that sway, the gentle ripple of the excess flesh, the subtle give, though it felt nice in your hand, soft to the touch.

Naturally, there were days she rounded her shoulders, wanted not to be seen. Mostly she was the kind of woman interested in blending in. The way she wore her hair, the kinds of clothes she favored. Amanda was a type. She was not ashamed of that. But there were moments—this was one—where she felt individual and perfect. Maybe it was just the barely perceptible reverberations of the orgasm. She was a thing beautiful to behold. Stained and sweaty and sagging, also smooth and ripe and desired. Humans were monsters but also perfect creations. She felt what is termed sexy but is really just an animal's satisfaction in being an animal. Had she been a deer, she'd have leaped over a branch. Had she been a bird, she'd have lifted into the sky. Had she been a house cat, she'd have run her own tongue over herself. She was a woman, so she stretched and shifted the weight from one leg to the other like a statue from antiquity.

"Let's go smoke." Clay, adolescent, was proud of his performance, like he'd heaved a shot put or sunk a basketball. She'd soiled his underwear, so he stalked to the door naked. There was no grace to it; his dick disrupted symmetry, an insult to beauty.

"Put on your clothes."

"What's wrong with sitting naked in the night air and smoking?"

"Well . . . Ruth and G. H."

"Who cares?"

Clay pulled open the door, but it was Amanda who noticed: interruption in the pane of glass. A crack that was more than a flaw. It was thin but deep, stretched for inches, a slash, a rent. "Look at that."

Clay peered at the glass. He put his hand in hers.

"This wasn't here before." She dropped her voice, not wanting to be overheard.

"You're sure?" A mumble, lips puckered around the cigarette.

Amanda traced the crack with her finger. It was from the noise. A noise big enough to crack glass. Noise as a tangible thing. She shivered from the cool air and the reminder too. She closed the door behind her, stood naked in the chill air, unprotected by clothes, a dare to the night and whatever else was out there.

30

Still naked, Neanderthal, essential, Clay went to fix them drinks. They'd finish packing later. They'd finish packing in the morning. They'd skip packing, go directly to Target for new toothbrushes and bathing suits and books and lotion and pajamas and earbuds and socks. Or they wouldn't! They didn't need things. Things would not keep them safe from power outages or sudden noises loud enough to crack glass or any other unexplained phenomena. They were extraneous; things did not matter.

Amanda flipped open the heavy cover of the hot tub. The steam was waiting for her, vanished into the dark. There was light illuminating the trees, which made the view more satisfying. You could feel you owned them, though no one could ever claim to own a

tree. She couldn't see. She pressed where she knew buttons were, kept at it until the machine whirred into life. The thing bubbled like the Weird Sisters' cauldron. If only it had been. Amanda would have bargained for the health of her poor feverish son, of both her children, of course, even though she had nothing to offer a witch, just the same desire as every human alive. She should, she realized, get up, pull on a robe, tiptoe into the dark room and gauge Archie's temperature with a touch of her hand.

It was G. H., answering the dare of her nudity. He wore his swimsuit, trim and conservative, the kind of thing white sons named for their great-grandfathers wore in Nantucket. There was not a trace of anything untoward in his smile, as though it were precisely what he expected, to find this woman he barely knew nude and obviously postcoital on his deck. "I see we both had the same idea."

It would have been disingenuous to feign shame. She was released from that. Didn't even blush. "Turned out to be a nice night, I guess."

He gestured toward the tub. "After you, please. If you don't mind the company." Nothing felt strange to him anymore. "We had the same idea. Ruth didn't want to join me, but I'm glad not to be alone out here." As close as he could come to admitting fear.

The water was very hot, but the bubbles the tub was frantic with were cold, popped against her skin, staccato relief. G. H. sat across from her, a decorous enough distance, though what did that matter? She might have been his daughter. They were nothing to each other, naked strangers. "There's a crack in the door." She gestured toward it. "I noticed it just now. I think it must be—"

He had done his own investigation. "There's one in the door downstairs. They call that a hairline crack, right? A nice turn of phrase. The shape of the letter Y. If I push, really push, I bet I can break the thing." He would not push on the glass. He would not break it. He needed it, though glass provided only the illusion of safety.

"Do you think it was from—"

He let his face say it. Why were they still debating this? "I have always thought of myself as a sophisticated man. Someone who had seen the world as it was. But I have never seen anything like this, so now I wonder if this thing I have always thought about myself was a delusion."

Their silence was not unfriendly. They had said everything there was to be said. It was like a love affair ended amicably. They needed only to wait for the sun to rise and the whole thing would be over, relief and re-

gret. In the house, Ruth lay on the bed, thinking of her daughter, and Archie slept dreamless, and Rose slept dreamful, and Clay filled glasses with ice, thinking of nothing.

"I just want everything to be okay."

G. H. looked up at the stars. It was dark enough there that you could truly see them. It never made him feel any which way. He liked being in the country, but not because it was good for his soul. Did the stars make him feel small? They did not. He already knew he was small. That's how he'd got rich. He just said her name, nothing more.

"I didn't believe you. I was wrong. Something is happening, something bad is happening." She could not stand it.

"The quiet is so noisy. That was one of the first things I noticed, when we started spending nights out here. I found it hard to sleep. At home, we can't hear anything. We're high up. Sometimes a siren, but even then, the wind kind of carries that away." The world from their apartment looked like a silent film.

"We still have power." She could see the steam, a veil over the dark.

"I was telling you, earlier, that with information anything is possible. I owe my fortune, humble as it is, to information." He paused. The tub burbled. "I saw

it, you know. Before the lights went out. I looked at the market and knew something was coming."

"How is that possible?" This sounded not financial but spiritual.

Clay opened the door. "Are you okay?"

"We're just talking." G. H. waved at Clay.

He walked toward the tub as though it were not odd, to be seen naked like this, to find his wife naked with a stranger. Clay would pretend.

"You learn how to read the curve. You spend as long as I have doing it, and you understand. It tells you the future. It holds steady and promises harmony. It inches up or down, and you know that means something. You look more closely, and try to understand just what it means. If you're good at it, you get rich. If you're not, you lose everything."

"And you're good at it?" Amanda took the glass her husband was offering her.

Clay slipped into the water, making too big a splash. "What are you talking about?"

"Information." G. H. said it like it was simple.

"He says he knew something was coming—," Amanda explained. She believed him. She needed to believe something.

"You saw—what? What's happened, anyway? The power went out. Amanda got some push notifications

from the *New York Times*. We heard a loud noise."
Hearing himself enumerate it, Clay realized it was
enough.

"Did you see the end of the world?" Could numbers
really predict that? The glass in her hand was cold and
perfect.

"It's not the end of the world," G. H. said. "It's a
market event."

"What are you talking about?" Clay thought G. H.
sounded like a madman with a placard marching
around the financial district. You saw that, often, on
Wall Street, the actual street, which was closed off by
bombproof bollards.

"I think I know so much." G. H. was apologetic.
"Maybe not everything can be known." The steam
clouded his glasses. He could neither see nor be seen.
Every day was a gamble.

"Maybe everything is fine," Clay said. They were
getting carried away. They were saying things they
shouldn't say.

"I hope for our sake that it is." G. H. didn't like to
have nothing but hope. That was something he'd dis-
liked in Obama; the nebulous, almost religious promise. He preferred a plan.

There was, below them, a loud splash.

Amanda was afraid, immediately. She sat up in the

center of the tub, turned to the yard behind them. "What was that?"

G. H. reached out of the tub to silence the jets. The machine responded immediately, a low hum instead of that laundry churn. The silence made it seem more dark, somehow. There was a splash, a definite, deliberate splash in the pool. Yards away, but it could not be seen.

It was one of the children, sleepwalking to their drowning. It was a watcher from the woods come to kill them. It was a zombie, it was an animal, it was a monster, it was a ghost, it was an alien. "What was—"

George shushed her. He was still capable of fear.

"What is that?" She was not whispering, and she was panicking. "Maybe it's a deer." She remembered the fence. What would a deer in distress sound like, what would a deer's tears sound like?

"A frog." Clay thought this was obvious. "A squirrel. They can swim."

G. H. pushed up out of the tub and walked toward the house, where there was a switch to light the pool from within. It was a nice touch when they had a party. The abstraction of light through water dancing in the treetops. They both saw, there in the pool below them, a flamingo, pink and absurd, elegantly splashing. It beat its wings, impatient, on the surface of the pool.

"That's a flamingo." She said it even though it was obvious. A pink bird was a flamingo. It was so specific—the comma of its beak, the forte mark of its illogical neck—that a toddler would know it. "That's a flamingo?"

"That's a flamingo." With his fingertips, G. H. rubbed the steam from his glasses. They did not know what was happening in the world, but they knew that.

The flamingo beat its wings more. They let their eyes adjust, and they could see another flamingo, no, two, no, three, no, four, no, five, no, six. Strutting on the lawn with their backward gait. Bobbing and sinewy. Two of the birds took flight as birds do: balletic. Lift over the fence, touch down in the water. They dipped their heads below the surface. Did they imagine it held food? There was a disarming intelligence in their eyes. Their wings were wider than you'd think. At rest, they held those so close to the sack of their bodies. Unfurled, though: they were majestic. Their beauty was astonishing. Logic fell away.

"Why—" *Why* didn't matter. Did *how* or did *is this real* or anything else matter? Amanda could see that George Washington could see these birds too, but there was documented evidence that delusion could be shared. She got out of the tub, rubbery with the absorbed heat. She stood naked as the day she appeared

on this planet. She watched three flamingos cavorting happily in the swimming pool, their compatriots on the grass beyond. "Just tell me you see this."

George nodded. He didn't know this woman at all. But he knew his mind and his eyes. "I see it."

Clay went cold, deep inside himself. Tomorrow they'd set sail in their car, and here was an omen. Their trip would displease the gods. They were being given a sign. Whisky sloshed into the tub as he stood. The birds started.

Three flamingos lifted out off the pool's surface with a masculine flaunting of wings. Any flamingo, seeing this, would have wanted to incubate their issue. These were flamingos, the best of flamingos, hale and powerful. They rose into the air, a simple trick, and above the trees. The flamingos on the grass followed, seven human-sized pink birds, twisty and strange, ascending into the Long Island night, beautiful and terrifying in equal measure.

They were silent for a while. Good old-fashioned awe. Religious feeling. The stars above didn't cow them, but these strange birds did. Amanda shivered. George blinked behind his glasses. Clay held on to the glass in his hand because it was cold and reminded him that he was alive.

31

G. H.'s familiar old fridge yielded nothing but surprise. He'd not have filled it with such things: cold cuts in folded paper, the curls of leftover grilled zucchini, hard white cheese in greasy cellophane, a Pyrex mixing bowl of strawberries some- one had thoughtfully hulled. He felt insane with hunger, or maybe only insane. He found a box of crackers, an open bag of chips, a cardboard tube of cookies. He put everything on the counter. Someone else would have arranged this bounty, complementary items together, but he didn't bother.

Clay did not ask if he wanted a drink. He pressed one into the man's black hands: "George." He'd found his swim trunks, drying on the railing. He'd found Ar-

chie's hacked-at T-shirt, and it revealed his subdued middle-aged muscles.

"We all saw that." Amanda had put on a robe. She had no idea whose it was, and forgot to pull the thing closed over her lap.

George thanked him through a mouthful of gummy cheese. He coughed a little. "I saw it."

"We're all hallucinating?" It was appealing to pretend that you were exempt from what was happening.

"They're from a zoo. The electrical grid failed and couldn't keep them in captivity." George hacked at the cheese with a steak knife. "They must be tagged, you know, like those invisible fences that keep dogs on your property."

"Zoos clip wings, don't they?" Amanda had read this in *The Trumpet of the Swan*. She wasn't sure it was true. "Those birds could fly. Those birds were *wild*."

Clay took up George's steak knife and sliced into the salami. "There has to be a logical explanation."

"They weren't wearing bands or anything." Amanda closed her eyes to return to the scene. "I looked. I looked for them."

George thought it hardly needed saying. "There are no wild flamingos in New York."

"We all just saw it. What the fuck is actually hap-

pening?" The vulgarity didn't possess the power she wanted. She wanted to run into the yard screaming at the birds to come back, to show themselves, to explain.

Ruth had showered and changed into the shapeless, expensive things she wore at home, freshly laundered. She emerged from downstairs and didn't even feel un-defended, as she would have if she'd encountered the doorman while dressed thus. She was at peace with these people. They knew one another now. Downstairs, she had tried to use her phone to be sure. Yes, she had flipped through the pictures in her album, out-of-focus shots because toddlers never stopped darting, giggling, squirming. She noticed that Amanda's robe was parted so you could see her mons.

George had turned on all the lights, prophylactic against fear. "We're having a midnight snack."

"You missed something." Amanda was not being sardonic but sincere.

"Sit down, darling." G. H. was filled with affection for Ruth. G. H. was reportorial. He stuck to the facts. He mentioned even Amanda's nakedness. Seven fla-mingos. If he'd been asked to draw a flamingo, he'd have come up with a triangle for the bill, and he'd have been wrong.

"I thought flamingos were flightless," Ruth said. "I assumed. Maybe I never gave it a thought before."

"They were the same size as Rose." Amanda could see them, ascending like Christ was said to have.

"I knew they were pink, but I didn't know they were pink like that. It doesn't seem like a natural color." G. H. made his wife a drink.

"You're sure." Ruth didn't doubt them, though. There was nothing they might have mistaken for a flamingo. She'd abandoned her expectations.

"A flamingo is a flamingo." Amanda wanted to be clear. "The question isn't if we're sure, but why—"

"You've got rich people out here." Clay was inspired. "They're someone's private collection. A miniature zoo. Some Hamptons estate that's actually an ark. Those billionaires are survivalists. They all have compounds in New Zealand where they plan to go when the shit hits the fan."

"Is there something sweet?" Ruth sipped the drink. She didn't really want it.

Amanda pushed the cookies across the island to her. "Maybe the noise we heard *was* thunder. Some kind of mega storm. I've heard of birds being blown off their migratory paths. There was that hurricane in the Atlantic, and the birds got lost."

Clay tried to remember what he had never known. "Are they migratory birds? And if so, do they cross the ocean? Maybe that's possible."

"Don't they congregate in lakes? Don't they eat some kind of shrimp, hence their pink feathers? I think that's true," Ruth said.

"We're just a bunch of adults who don't know anything about birds," said George. He was used to being able to explain everything. Could the curve explain the birds? There was a relationship, but he'd need days to work it out. He'd need a pencil, a newspaper, some quiet. "We don't know anything about noises loud enough to crack glass. We don't know anything about a blackout in New York City. We're four adults who don't know how to get a cell-phone signal or make the television work or do much of anything at all."

The room filled with chewing, ice running up against glass.

"Funny how I was telling you about *Swan Lake*." Ruth smiled. "Swans, flamingos. The same, but not."

"I need it to be tomorrow." Clay consulted the digital clock on the microwave's face. "We should sleep."

"You want to go home," G. H. said. "We're lucky to be already home."

"Unless." Ruth had no interest in dispensing platitude and comfort. She could not see a bright side. "This was a sign. You shouldn't go. We can't go with you."

"You said you'd show us the way," Amanda said.

"It's not safe. Out there," Ruth said. What if Rosa

didn't come on Thursday? What if something out there was coming for them?

"We have to take Archie to the doctor!" Amanda felt it in her body like a bird's urge to migrate.

"What do you think is going to happen to us?" Clay wasn't looking for reassurance, just an honest guess. "We're leaving—you said you'd help us find the way."

George had never believed in unknowns. Algebra showed that they were easy to figure out. Math didn't pertain anymore, or it was a math he could barely work. "Nothing will happen to us if we just drive down the road," he told his wife.

"You think traffic will flow. That there's food. Water? I don't trust people. I don't trust the system." Ruth was sure. "Maybe Archie will get better if we stay put. Maybe tomorrow he'll wake up, fever gone, and want to eat everything in the house."

"Maybe he just needs antibiotics or something?" Clay didn't want to go now. He was terrified.

"I feel safe here." Ruth knew that this family's safety was not truly her problem. "All I want is to feel safe."

"You could stay," George said.

"We can't do that." Amanda was decisive.

Could they not, though? Clay was not so sure. "We could—we could go downstairs. You could have your bedroom."

They were quiet, like they knew it was coming. It came. The same noise? Sure. Yes. Probably. Why not. Who knew. Once, twice, three times. The window over the sink cracked. The pendant light over the counter did too. The electricity probably should have turned off, but it didn't. No one would ever be able to answer precisely why. The noises overlapped, but were discrete, the sound—they didn't know this—of American planes, in the American sky, speeding toward the American future. A plane most people didn't know existed. A plane designed to do unspeakable things, heading off to do them. Every action had an equal and opposite reaction, and there were more actions and reactions than could be counted on the party's eight hands. What their government was up to, what other governments were up to; just an abstract way of talking about the choices of a handful of men. Lemmings were not suicidal, they were driven to migrate and overconfident about their ability. The leader of the pack was not to blame. They all plunged into the sea, thinking it easy to traverse as a puddle; so human an instinct in a bunch of rodents. Millions of Americans huddled at home in the dark, but only thousands of them heard these noises, and comforted children and one another, and wondered just what they were. Some people got sick, because that was just their constitution. Others

listened and realized how little they understood about the world.

Ruth did not cry out. There was no sense in that. Tears welled, but she blinked them back. Hands on the edge of the countertop, she crouched down, as maybe, decades ago, she'd been taught to, in case of nuclear annihilation. She just hovered there in a half squat, the pull of her muscles not an unpleasant thing.

Amanda screamed. Clay screamed. G. H. screamed. Rose screamed. The children threw themselves from their beds and found the adults, and it was their mother they ran to—always was, in these situations—and they pressed their faces against the foreign robe that covered her nakedness and she held them tight to her body, trying to cover their ears with her hands, but they had four ears between them and she had only two hands. She was not enough.

That noise again. It was the final one. It was one of the last planes. The insects outside fell silent, baffled. The bats that hadn't succumbed to white-nose syndrome fell from the sky. The flamingos barely paid it mind. They had enough to worry about.

32

They did the sensible thing. They huddled together in that big king. Family bed—Amanda hated the idea. Thought it was for antivaxxers and mothers who breastfed their five-year-olds, but she couldn't bear Archie and Rose being away from her. They turned the lights off because the children were exhausted, but privately wished to leave them burning to keep the night away.

"You can—" Clay wanted to invite Ruth and G. H. to bed with them! It almost made sense.

"Try to sleep." G. H. held his wife's hand, and they descended the kitchen steps once more.

Neither adult could sleep. Soon, though, the children began to snore. The curve of Rose's body made Clay think of those natural bridges on the California

coast, hollowed out by the ocean over millennia. Eventually, though, those collapsed. They said the ocean was coming for them all. He appreciated the persistence of her lungs. It was incredible that you didn't need to tell yourself to breathe or walk or think or swallow. They had asked themselves questions when they decided to have children—do we have the money, do we have the space, do we have what it takes—but they didn't ask what the world would be when their children grew. Clay felt blameless. It was George Washington and the men of his generation, their mania for plastic and petroleum and money. It was a hell of a thing to not be able to keep your kid safe. Was this how everyone felt? Was this, finally, what it was to be a human?

He kissed the worn cotton on Rose's shoulder and regretted that he did not believe in prayer. God, she looked like her mother. Nature was fond of repetition. Did one flamingo know another from yet another?

Amanda kept reaching for Archie's arm. He flinched a little, each time, but did not wake. She wanted to ask her husband something but couldn't think of the right words. Was this it? Was this the end? Was she supposed to be valiant?

Clay couldn't see his son in the dark. He thought of how he still sometimes crept into the children's rooms. They never woke during these nocturnal visits. You

told yourself there was an end to the worry. You told yourself it was sleeping through the night, then weaning from the breast, then walking then shoelaces then reading then algebra then sex then college admissions then you would be liberated, but this was a lie. Worry was infinite. A parent's only task was to protect his child.

He couldn't imagine his own mother anymore; she'd been dead most of his life. His father must have performed this office. It did not square with what he knew of the man, but that was how a parent loved.

Amanda touched the boy's cheek and found it was hot. She tried to distinguish between fever and summer, mammalian adolescence and illness. She touched the boy's forehead, throat, his shoulder, pushed away blankets to cool his body. She touched his chest, the steady drumbeat. Archie's skin was soft and dry, warm like a machine left on too long. She knew that fever was the body's distress signal, a pulse from its emergency broadcast system. But the boy was sick. Maybe they were all sick. Maybe this was a plague. He was her *baby*. He was their *baby*. She couldn't imagine a world indifferent to that.

Theirs was a failure of imagination, though, two overlapping but private delusions. G. H. would have pointed out that the information had always been there

waiting for them, in the gradual death of Lebanon's cedars, in the disappearance of the river dolphin, in the renaissance of cold-war hatred, in the discovery of fission, in the capsizing vessels crowded with Africans. No one could plead ignorance that was not willful. You didn't have to scrutinize the curve to know; you didn't even have to read the papers, because our phones reminded us many times daily precisely how bad things had got. How easy to pretend otherwise. Amanda whispered her husband's name.

"I'm awake." He could not see her, then he could. He needed only to look more closely.

"Should we still go?"

He pretended to be thinking this over, but the dilemma was already plain to him: no, they shouldn't, yes, they must. "I don't know."

"We have to get Archie to a doctor."

"We do."

"And Rosie. What if the same thing—" To say it would have been to risk it. She didn't bother. Rose would have loved the flamingos. Maybe they should feel only awe at life's mysteries, as children did.

"She's fine. She seems okay." She did; same old Rose. Reliable, implacable, really, that strength of the second-born. He wasn't even thinking wishfully. Clay had faith in his daughter.

"She seems okay. I seem okay. Everything seems okay. But it also seems like a disaster. It also seems like the end of the world. We need a plan. We need to know what we're going to do. We can't just stay here forever."

"We can stay here for now. They said so." Clay had heard the offer.

"You want to stay here?" Amanda wanted him to say it first.

He tried to think how many cigarettes he had left. He did want to stay. Despite the sick teen, despite the nicotine withdrawal, despite the fact that this was not their beautiful house. Clay was afraid, but maybe they could pool courage between all of them and find enough to do something, anything, whatever that was. "It's safe here. We have power. We have water."

"I told you to fill the bathtub."

"We have food, and a roof, and G. H. has some money, and we have one another. We're not alone."

They both were and were not alone. Fate was collective but the rest of it was always individual, a thing impossible to escape. They lay that way for a long time. They didn't talk because there was nothing to discuss. The sounds of their sleeping children were relentless as the ocean.

A dry heaviness on the tongue and in the throat, a wince that made it hard to see, the brute stupidity of hangover, and God they were too old for this. When would they learn not to be this way? Amanda hurried from the bed to drink at the bathroom sink, accidentally licking the metal faucet. She knew she'd vomit, in that way you always do. Sometimes you just need to admit to yourself what you know. Salt on the tongue. She bent at the waist like a yogi contemplating the toilet, then something that felt like a belch but burned in the back of the throat, and the release. The vomit was thin and pink as a flamingo (get it?). She let it leave her. Her eyes watered, but she did not look away from it. Her stomach contracted once, twice, three times, and the vomit leaped from stomach to throat to water, and

once that was done she flushed it down and rinsed her mouth and felt ashamed. That was how all people the world over ought to have felt that morning.

Clay heard her terrible retch. You couldn't just doze through something like that. The room was too warm from too many bodies. At some point in the night, the air-conditioning had switched off. The kind of hangover where you yearn to throw open windows, strip the beds, clean your way back into virtue. A noisy, wet revolution inside his stomach. It would not be pretty.

Archie sat up and looked at his dad. He mumbled like his mouth was full of something. "What's happening?"

"I'm going to get us some water." Did he notice that Rose was not there? It seemed to make sense in that moment.

Clay filled glasses. He sipped his, relieved, then refilled it. "Rosie." He called out to the empty house. There was no answer. The refrigerator's icemaker made its periodic whirr. There was a trick to carrying three, but he managed it.

Pallid Amanda sat on the edge of the bed. Archie had pulled a pillow over his head. "Drink up." Clay put the glasses on the table. Whenever you were sick with something undetermined, you were supposed to drink water. Water was the first line of defense. If there

was something in the air—if the storm had blown in more than just tropical birds—and that something was in the water, the whole system a closed loop, he didn't know it.

"Thanks, honey," his wife said.

Clay moved urgently, trot down the hall, quick slam of the door. The bathroom redolent of Amanda's vomit and his own shit, that postmidnight binge pouring out of him in seconds. He stood in the shower as penance, asshole burning, rinsing his mouth over and over again, spitting the water against the tile wall, angry. Did he know if this was hangover or a symptom of something worse? He did not.

On the other side of the wall, Amanda opened the door to the backyard—ugh, the smell of their bodies— where the sweet air was alive with light. She wanted to undo the bed, but her boy still lazed. "How are you feeling, baby?" She thought he looked more himself.

Archie tried to come up with the right answer. He felt strange or weird or sleepy or whatever, but that was how he felt whenever he woke up before noon or so. He was mad or something in that moment, turned away from his mother and pulled the covers over his head.

"I should check your temperature. We were so worried, I was planning on taking you to see Dr. Wilcox

this afternoon, after we get back, but maybe we don't need to."

Archie made an irritated little groan. "We're going back?"

"Come on. I know you're sleepy, but sit up, let Mom look at you." Amanda sat on the bed beside her son.

He pulled himself up to sitting, but slowly, his way of protest and his way of showing off the elastic efficiency of his adolescent body, an angled line morphing gradually from obtuse to acute.

The back of her hand against his forehead, Amanda looked in her son's eyes, bottomlessly beautiful to she who had made them, even when crusted and shrunken by sleep. "You don't feel so warm anymore." She put her palm against his forehead, his neck, his shoulder, his chest. "Does your throat hurt?"

He didn't know if his throat hurt. He hadn't thought about it. His mother would not leave him to sleep until he cooperated, so he did, opening his mouth wide as though to yawn as a way of gauging the health of his throat. Seemed fine. "No."

Good mother, she ignored the boy's sour breath. She looked into the pink recesses of his body as though she knew what she was looking for, or as though what was in there could be seen.

Archie closed his mouth and then his tongue tapped

a tooth, a tic, a test, and the salt of blood flowed over his taste buds. Familiar, but you remembered that, no matter what, the taste of blood. Curious, he ran his tongue over enamel again and the tooth yielded to that gentlest nudge. His mouth filled with saliva.

Archie opened his mouth wider, and it spilled out, now, onto his neck, dribbled down his chest, saliva, drool, like a baby's, cut with crimson that didn't quite mix into it, like salad dressing insufficiently shaken. Blood was usually a surprise. His mouth continued to water, and to bleed. He put a finger to it, probing into the problem, and touched the tooth, and it fell over with a fleshy pop, down like a domino, onto his tongue and then, horribly, back into his mouth like a cherry pit almost swallowed. He spit it out, and the tooth landed in his palm. He stared at it. It was bigger than he'd have guessed.

"Archie!" Amanda thought at first the boy was vomiting. That would have made more sense. But this was so controlled, so understated. He'd just leaned forward over his hand and dripped blood onto his bare chest.

"Mom?" He was confused.

"Are you going to be sick, honey? Get out of the bed!"

Archie stood up and walked to mirror. "I'm not

sick!" He held the tooth out in his palm, sticky and pink with blood.

She did not understand.

Archie looked at himself in the mirror. He opened his mouth and willed himself to confront the wet dark of it. He swooned a little, because it was disgusting. With his finger, he touched another tooth, a bottom one, and it, too, gave, then he grabbed onto it and pulled it right out of his gums, now near black with blood. Then another. Then another. Four teeth, tapered at the root, solid and white, four little pieces of evidence, four little proofs of life. Was he meant to scream? He closed his mouth and let the liquid gather there for a second, then spit it out onto the ground, not caring if he soiled the rug because what did that matter, really? Another of his teeth fell out and dropped onto the ground, where of course it did not make a sound. In the vast universe, it was too small to matter.

"Archie!" Amanda did not know what was happening. Of course she didn't.

He crouched to the ground to pick up his tooth. It was bigger than the hollow little shells that he'd left under his pillow until he turned ten. It tapered at the root, animal and menacing. He held them in his palm like a diver proud of his pearls. "My teeth!"

Amanda looked at her boy, slender and pathetic in his ticking-stripe boxer shorts. "What is it?"

The boy did not weep because he was too baffled to. "Mom. Mom. My teeth." He held his hand out for them to see.

"Clay!" She didn't know what to do but appeal to a second opinion. "My god, your teeth!"

"What's happening to me?" His voice was ridiculous because he couldn't talk properly without the percussion of tongue against tooth.

Amanda took the boy by the shoulders, steered him back to the bed. He was too tall otherwise. She pressed palm, then back of hand, to his forehead. "You're not hot? I don't understand—"

Clay came as beckoned, towel at his waist, irritation on his face. "What's happening?"

"There's something wrong with Archie!" Amanda thought it was evident.

"What is it?"

The boy held his hand out toward his father.

Clay did not understand. Who would? "Honey, what happened?"

"I was just—my tooth felt weird, and I touched it, and it fell out."

This was the moment. This was the ravine. Clay was going to lay his body down. "How is this—does he

still have a fever?" Clay reached out to touch the boy's arm, his neck, his back. "You're warm—does he feel warm?"

"I don't know. I thought it wasn't so bad, but I don't know." Amanda could not remember having said those words so many times. She didn't know, she didn't know, she didn't know anything.

Clay looked from the child to his wife, baffled. Maybe the boy was sick, maybe he was contagious? "It's okay. You're okay."

"I don't feel okay!" But this wasn't true. Archie felt . . . fine? As normal as possible. His body was working to keep it together. It would shed what was extraneous to preserve the whole.

In some private part of himself, Clay stopped to see if all was well with his body. He did not know that it was not. Then he came awake, more truly, and looked at his son, bloody and toothless, and tried to think of what to do next.

"Did you fill the bathtub?" Amanda was doing what she was able to. "It's an emergency! We'll need water!"

34

It was Clay's instinct to consult the Washingtons. Put four heads together. A conference, strength in numbers, the wisdom of their more advanced age, but none of them had ever seen anything like this. They huddled and inspected like Caravaggio's Thomas and friends. Incredulity was about right.

"You're feeling all right, though?" Ruth didn't see how that was possible.

Archie just shrugged. He'd said it over and over again already.

"Well. This is something. We need to think about getting him to the doctor." G. H. felt this clear. "Not back in Brooklyn. Here."

"We have that pediatrician's number." Ruth had done her research for when Maya and Clara and the

boys came to visit. They'd never had to use the information, but they had it.

"He needs the emergency room," G. H. said.

Clay nodded, grave. Been there, done that, like any parent worth his salt. A glob of peanut butter lurking in a berry smoothie. An overconfident leap from the jungle gym. Labored breath one terrible winter night. "You're right. This shouldn't wait." How he wished it could.

"Where's the hospital?" Amanda was unsure what to do with her body. She walked in circles, she stood and sat like a dog that can't get comfortable. "Is it far?"

"Maybe fifteen minutes—" G. H. looked to his wife for confirmation.

"Farther, I think. You know these roads—it's probably closer to twenty, maybe longer? I think it depends on if you take Abbott or cut over to the highway—" Ruth didn't want to care. She didn't want what it would entail. She couldn't help herself. She was human. "Do you want some water or something?"

Archie shook his head. "I don't need to go to the hospital. I feel okay, I really do."

"We just need to be certain, honey." Amanda actually wrung her hands like an amateur character actor. "You'll give us directions? Unless someone's phone has suddenly started working? No?"

"I can give you directions," G. H. said.

"You'll draw us a map. The GPS is no good. You'll make us a map. And we'll go." Amanda went to the desk. Of course Ruth kept a cup of sharpened pencils, a pad of blank paper.

"I can draw you a map. But it's very simple once you get back to the main road—"

"I got lost." Clay put a hand on his son's shoulder. He could barely look at them. "I got lost. Before."

"What do you mean?" Amanda asked. "Lost?"

"It's not simple at all! I went out. To go and find out what was happening. To get to the bottom of— whatever. And I drove down the lane and I passed that egg stand and I thought I knew where I was going, and I was wrong. I drove around, then I turned around, then I was really lost. I don't know how I found my way back. I heard that noise and I thought I was going to lose my mind and then there it was, the turn I had been looking for, the road up to the lane up to the house. It was just right there."

"So you didn't see anyone. Or anything. You didn't go anywhere." Amanda sounded accusatory, but this was a relief: he hadn't even had the chance to look! They were all overreacting. There was nothing. An industrial accident, those noises four consecutive con-

trolled explosions, the power loss easily explained. Not great! But not the worst.

"I could show you the way. We'll go too. All of us."

"No." Ruth was firm. Her whole body shook. "We're not leaving. We're not doing that. We're waiting here. Until we hear something. Until we know something." She would let them stay, but she wasn't risking her life for them.

"There's nothing to worry about. We'll drive them. We'll talk to someone, find out what people know, maybe we'll fill up the car, come right back here."

"You can stay. All of you. You can stay here, in this house, with us." This was as far as Ruth could go. "Just stay here."

"Stay here." Clay thought about it. He'd been thinking about it. "Until—until what?"

"But George, you can't leave. You can't leave me here, and I can't leave, and that's where we are," Ruth said.

"What if it's forever?" Amanda could not wait. Her son was sick. "What if the cell phones never come back—I mean, they barely worked out here before, when everything was normal. What if the power goes out, what if Archie is truly sick, what if we're all sick, what if that noise made us sick?"

"I'm not sick, Mom." Why wasn't anyone listening to him? He felt fine! Yes, it was weird his teeth had fallen out. But what was the doctor going to do—glue them back in? Something (his own instinct? some other very quiet voice?) told him to stay where they were.

Ruth wondered what Maya was doing. She wondered why it seemed perfectly viable to her that her grandsons had heard that noise in Amherst, Massachusetts. They had only milk teeth, barely held in place at all. Maybe the noise had knocked those loose, and reduced their mothers to hysterics. If you couldn't save your child, what were you doing? She knew they could not choose to stay with her, not when their child was sick. "I don't think I can go out there."

"It will be fine." G. H. couldn't promise that. They'd all been waiting for some decisive moment. Some corner being turned. Perhaps this was it, the gradual descent into illogic, the frog finding that the water is at last too much to bear. The hottest year in recorded history, hadn't he read that once? But the boy was sick, or something was wrong with him, and that was the only information they had. "You can wait here."

"I can't stay here alone."

"We'll pack up, we'll go to the hospital, and then we'll go back to Brooklyn," Clay thought aloud. "You don't need to drive us there. A map should be fine."

G. H. began to draw.

"Or we could come back. We could leave Rose here with Ruth, and we can come back for her." Amanda didn't want the girl to have to see what was happening to her brother. She thought this might be less worrisome.

"I can stay with Rose. I can even pack your things, you can go right now." Ruth liked a project.

"Fine." Clay stood. That made more sense. Let the adults do what was needed. They'd come back for Rose.

It was Amanda who realized, or Amanda who said it. The five of them had been so preoccupied by the situation. A shame: the perfect day. The light playing prettily across the pool, its reflection dancing across the back of the house, the green more lush from the rain, and not a cloud to be seen. "Where's Rose?"

35

S he was watching that one movie she'd forgotten
she'd downloaded. Amanda looked in the girl's
bedroom, but the girl was not there. She was in the
bathroom. Amanda went to look, but the girl was not
there. Back to the living room. "I can't find Rose?"

They all agreed this made no sense. Clay went back
to the master bedroom, which was empty. Amanda
looked out the back door at the perfect day then in
progress. Amanda looked into the laundry room, then
went back to the master bedroom herself, not trusting
Clay to be thorough. She looked in the walk-in closet,
she looked under the bed, as though Rose were a house
cat. She looked in the master bathroom, which still
smelled of the violent rejections of their bodies.

Clay found his wife in the hallway. "I don't understand. Where is she?"

Amanda returned to the girl's room and peeled back the covers to see the foot of the bed, not sure, exactly, what she expected to find there. She hesitated before the bedroom closet like someone in a movie. Did the director intend a feint (Rose curled up with a book), or a shock (a stranger wielding a knife), or a puzzle (nothing at all)? There was just the smell of the cedar balls left to dissuade moths with a taste for cashmere. Now, then: panic, and at last, a concrete target upon which it could fix.

Back to the living room, where Rose was not watching television or sitting with a book, to the kitchen, where Rose was not eating or working the too-hard Oriental-rug jigsaw puzzle, to the door overlooking the pool, but no, Rose had been forbidden to swim alone (just sensible). Amanda opened the front door as though she'd find the girl there, *Trick or treat!* Nope, just the grass, darkened by the fallen rain, and the chatter of birds.

The girl was downstairs in the part of the house that most belonged to the Washingtons. She'd gone out to the garage to see what diversions it might hold. She was sitting in the car's back seat, obedient as a certain

kind of dog, ready for the trip home. Okay, louder: "Rosie!"

"Rosie, Rosie." Amanda said it to herself. She went back into the bathroom. Once the girl had loved to hide and surprise them. Amanda pulled back the shower curtain to find only the tub full of an inch of water. She'd told Clay to fill the tub, and this was what he'd come up with? She went back to the living room. "I can't find Rose."

Clay wanted another glass of water. "Well, she has to be here somewhere." He gestured toward the bedrooms.

"She's not there—" Why wasn't he listening?

"She's taking a shower?"

"She's not—" She was not stupid!

"She's in the—" He didn't know what he meant any longer.

"She's not, she's not, I looked, she's not anywhere, where is she?" Amanda was not yelling, but she was not whispering.

"Did you look downstairs?" Archie's tone was withering.

"I'll look downstairs." G. H. stood. "She's probably just exploring the house."

"I can't find her?" Amanda put it as a question because it seemed so silly—*I can't find her! I can't find*

my child! Like saying you couldn't find your earlobes or your clitoris.

Amanda went and stood in the kitchen, unsure what to do next. Ruth followed because she was moved to reassure her. That damnable instinct. She had to help. They were colleagues not as mothers but humans. This—all this—was a problem to be shared. "She must be outside." Ruth could picture the girl, watching monarchs flex their wings on the milkweed. "She's gone to play."

"I looked out front."

"Let's go outside."

Clay sat beside his son again. "Amanda. Calm down. Let's think. She could be in the garage, or out past the hedge, let's just go find her—"

"What the fuck do you think I'm doing, Clay? I'm going to get my shoes to go *find* her." Amanda rushed toward the bedroom.

"Archie, do you know where your sister went?" Clay was patient.

Archie spoke softly. Did he? He had an instinct, but it didn't make sense. "No."

Amanda came back in her slip-on Keds. She didn't even have tears in her anymore. "I feel insane. Where is Rose?"

"I'm sure she's just outside." Ruth wasn't all that sure of anything.

Amanda should have screamed, but there was no scream. The fact that she was so quiet was somehow more unsettling. "Get your shoes on and help me fucking look for her."

Through the door, Clay could see his rubber thongs by the hot tub. "I'll go out front, by the herb garden. I'll look past the hedge."

"She's just wandered somewhere." Ruth tried to convince. "There's no television, so she's playing the way we used to, just wandering about. There's nothing to worry about here." She meant: there was no traffic, there were no kidnappers. There were no bears or mountain lions. There were no rapists or perverts, no people at all. They were equipped to handle certain fears. This was something else. It was hard to remind yourself to be rational in a world where that seemed not to matter as much, but maybe it never had.

Downstairs, G. H. found his closet, packed with supplies, his bed, tidily made, his bathroom, the mute and useless television, the broken back door, his cell phone plugged into its optimistic white cables. He put the phone into his pocket.

In the living room, Archie stuffed his feet into his Vans and used his tongue to contemplate the tender

empty pockets in his gums. They were soft and pleasant, like the recesses of the human body his own was designed to fit into, something he'd never know firsthand. Could he forgive the universe that denial of his own particular purpose? He wouldn't get the chance. He opened the back door and went to join his father, went to find his sister.

"There's nothing to worry about?" Amanda's imagination, exhausted, had given up. She went outside with the rest of her family, into that beautiful day, too distracted to notice if it was different from the thousands of other days of her life thus far. Her "Rose! Rose!" was loud and impassioned enough to startle animals she couldn't see and would never know were there.

Amanda had theories. A mother always did. An errant step into an unused well, a hundred feet deep, disguised by the fulsome St. Augustine grass. A bough, sundered by that noise, falling from overhead. A snake bite, a twisted ankle, a bee sting, maybe she simply got turned around. They couldn't call 911! Who would save them?

G. H. took the downstairs door, closed it gingerly. The grass was damp and thick.

"I'm going up front." Clay did just that.

Ruth was afraid; once you had a kid, you knew to

be afraid. "We should look in the garage." Ruth led the way.

Amanda followed her.

Archie walked past the yard to the little shed. He knew his sister wasn't in there, but he had to look. The door stood open, and Archie leaned against the structure, looked back at the house. *Stupid little kid.* He knew she'd gone back into the woods. Why wasn't he able to say this out loud? And how did he know it? It didn't matter. Archie shivered the way you might when you walk into a spiderweb, the way you might if you saw a spider dart from beneath your pillow and lose itself in your mosaic-printed bedsheets, the way you might if a spider crept from your shoulder up your neck and nestled into the comforting cave of your ear, the way you might if a spider dropped from the ceiling and landed on your hair and then picked its way forward carefully down the slope of your nose so you could barely see it with your wide-set eyes, the way you might if a spider started and bit you and its poison dripped into your bloodstream and then became a part of you, inextricable as your DNA, the thing that made you. His left knee felt funny, then gave out beneath him, and Archie doubled over, and he started to vomit but it wasn't vomit, just water, a bit of blood. Guess what? It was pink like—

36

C lay could feel the gravel through his flip-flops. They were almost worn out, at the end of their life. If you wanted to mitigate your guilt over making garbage, you could mail them back to the manufacturer, gratis, who would dump them in Ecuador, Guatemala, Colombia, some place like that where NGOs taught people to snip them into pieces and stitch them into rubber mats for white people to buy. There was nothing out front, there was nothing past the hedge, just the very same view that had taunted him the day before. Was that only yesterday? "Rose!" His voice didn't carry. It didn't go anywhere. It fell to the verdant ground.

In the garage Ruth pointed out the ladder up to the loft. A girl might want to play up there! Ruth had half-plans to someday turn it into a guest apartment.

Amanda scooted up the ladder, but there was nothing up there.

The women came out of the garage as Clay rounded the corner and G. H. completed a circuit of the house. The four of them looked at one another.

"She's gone?" Amanda didn't know what else to say.

"She can't be gone—" Ruth meant gone, finality, disappearance.

Whatever this was, it wasn't the rapture. Rose definitely would have been saved, but Clay knew they couldn't yield to pure myth. "She must have just—gone somewhere."

"She was so curious about other houses. And the eggs! Maybe she went to the egg stand." Ruth had her doubts.

"Where's Archie?" Clay looked toward the back-yard.

"He was right there." Amanda could hold only one thing in her head at that moment.

"He seems better." Such optimism! It only worked if he excused the fact of the boy's missing teeth, but parenthood meant occasional magical flights of fancy.

Ruth nodded. "One of us should go down to the egg stand."

Amanda strode away, impatient. "I'll go. Clay, go to the back. Look in the woods. But don't go far—"

"I'll look inside again." Ruth dismissed the two men. "You go out back."

He and G. H. cut through the front door, and from the back deck Clay saw his son, prone, in the grass. He called his name. He ran toward him. He could no longer remember what he was supposed to be doing.

The boy was on his knees and his chest like a Muslim in prayer. Clay slipped a hand into his armpit and pulled him back.

"Dad." Archie looked at him, then leaned forward and vomited once more, a beautiful plash of liquid onto earth.

"What's happened?" G. H. was demanding an explanation. "You're all right, you're all right."

Ruth saw this from the deck. She hurried, knowing she was needed. They braced the boy's body between theirs and walked at the deliberate pace of the elderly. The boy kept choking, or seizing, but there was nothing left in him to escape his mouth. His eyes were almost but not exactly closed, fluttering like the eyes of a kind of now-antiquated camera, but did they see? Did they capture anything?

Ruth was cataloging. They had old antibiotics. They had a hot water bottle. They had that powdered drink for when you were down with flu. You dissolved it in hot water and slept for hours. They had sea salt and

olive oil and basil and laundry detergent and Band-Aids and a huge package of those little travel packages of tissues that were so handy to have in your purse. George had ten thousand dollars in cash tucked away for emergencies. They were rich! Would any of that be a salve to whatever this was?

"Let's get him inside." G. H. captained this endeavor. They proceeded, awkward, up the wide wooden steps. The pool's filtration system began its scheduled cycle, which told him that it was 10:00 a.m. It whirred and gurgled joyfully.

They laid the boy's body on the sofa. "Archie, honey are you okay? Can you tell me?"

Archie looked up at the trio. "I don't know."

Clay looked at the other adults. "Where's Rose?"

"I think she's probably playing down the road. She borrowed one of the bikes. I know she's been bored. She's just having—she's playing." G. H. tried to make this sound inevitable. "Let's get Archie some water. We can't have him dehydrating."

Clay did know that Rose loved to *do*. She was always with a book, and in her books, girls her age had big hearts and appetites for adventure. They did unlikely, brave things, facing down private fears, then chastely held hands with boys with beautiful eyelashes. These books had given her a sense of the world as

something to be conquered with derring-do. Books ruined everyone—wasn't that what his academic work was meant to show? "Water. Right."

Ruth had already filled another glass. "Drink this up."

"Sit up, easy now." Clay's body remembered the pose of early parenthood, ready to leap and right your toddler's toppling body.

"We have to go to the hospital." George had decided. "We have to go now."

"You can't leave me." Ruth unfolded the blanket on the sofa's back and draped it over the boy's body.

"He's sick. You see that."

"We can't go without my daughter—"

"We'll go. You and me. We'll take Archie."

"No. You can't, George, you can't leave."

"Ruth. You find Amanda. You two find Rose. You stay here."

Did she have it in her to do this? Wasn't she bored with having to be strong and noble and competent, best supporting actress? Wasn't she allowed to be hysterical and afraid? "George, please."

He looked into his wife's eyes. "We'll come back. We'll come right back."

"You'll never come back. Don't you see that something is happening? It's happening right now. What-

ever it is, it's happening to Archie, it's happening to all of us, we can't leave." Ruth was not crying or hysterical, which made what she said more unsettling.

Clay did not notice the tingle in his knees, his elbows, or he did and took it for fear. "Ruth, please. We need help."

This was his moment. Men of his generation made decisions, they waged wars, they made fortunes, they acted with conviction. "We're going. Clay, take Archie to the car. Bring that blanket. Ruth, get him a bottle of water. Archie, you lie down in the back seat."

"George. I won't let you do this. I can't let you do this. I can't."

"This is the only thing we can do. This is the thing that I have to do." George held the keys in his hand. He didn't spell it out for her because he knew Ruth and knew she'd understand: if they weren't human, in this moment, then they were nothing.

Ruth didn't know how to enumerate the things she could not do. She could not do any of this. "You're coming back to me. You're coming back for us."

"Set a timer. Get your phone. Set the alarm. One hour." G. H. was sure he could do this.

"You can't make promises you can't keep!" Ruth fumbled with her phone.

"It will take one hour. Less. I'll drive to the hospi-

tal. I'll leave them and turn around and come back for you and Amanda and Rose. You'll find Rose. Do you understand? I'll set a timer too."

"It won't work. It won't work out."

"It will. There is no choice. Look." He pressed the digital display, and the seconds began counting down. "I'm going to leave Clay and Archie there, and then I'll be back for the three of you by the time this goes off."

"How do you know the hospital will be—" Clay faltered.

"Clay." George did not think it worth discussing. He knew what was supposed to happen. "We're going. Get him into the car."

"Come on, honey." Clay helped his son to his feet and remembered his hands at the toddler's waist. So skinny he could circle it, fingertips touching.

Ruth draped the blanket around Archie's shoulders again. "One hour." She pressed the button on her phone, and the seconds started ticking. "That's what you get. You've promised."

"It's nothing to worry about." George gripped his keys, heavy to connote luxury. Was he lying? Was he hopeful?

Ruth didn't believe in prayer, so she thought of nothing.

37

G. H. knew they would find Rose. That was what mothers did. Some secret sonar, like those birds that hide a hundred thousand seeds in October and stay fat all winter. The car came to life like the reliable, expensive machine that it was.

Archie shivered on the leather back seat.

"You tell me if you need to stop and be sick." The way he said it, it sounded like George was thinking of his car, but a parent was versed in vomit and worse, baptized in it, able, for the rest of life, to find not horror but pity. Seven-year-old Maya on the corner of Lex and Seventy-Fourth, vomiting whole flakes of white fish into his outstretched hands. Just another memory, just another moment, but he'd do it again if it had been

his adult daughter in the back seat, toothless and in the grip of some ailment for which they had no noun. You were a father forever.

Clay shifted to the left to retrieve his wallet from his right back pocket. Incredible he'd remembered it, some secret instinct. He thumbed through plastic chits in search of their insurance card. They used Amanda's plan; it was better than the one at the college. An exhale upon finding it, the relief of something, finally, going right.

"We're going to get you to a doctor." Clay turned around to look at his son. Was he thinner, was he paler, was he frailer, was he smaller? "You're okay. You're okay."

"I'm okay." Obedient Archie was determined to take this like a man. Archie was a man now.

The car turned from driveway to access road to main road. George drove more slowly than normal, despite the quickened heartbeat, the sense of rush, the seconds accruing on the timer. None of the men in the car noticed the little egg shack, none of them knew that Amanda was inside it, finding, instead of Rosie, only the goodly scent of farm labor. The Mudds, whose land that was, would never again bring fresh-laid eggs back to that little shed.

It all swam before Clay, green, green, rich, wet, thick, menacing, useless, impotent, angry, indifferent green. "I saw someone. When I went out before."

George did not mark this. "You said you got lost. Pay attention. There's pencil and paper in the glove box. Draw a map. We turned right from the driveway, and I turned left back there. We go over this hill and make another right." He was planning for contingencies. What if they were separated? What if—there were endless scenarios.

Clay opened the glove box, where there was a pad and a pencil, the owner's manual, the insurance and registration information, a package of tissues, a slender first aid kit. Order, preparation, tidiness. Everything about G. H. and Ruth's life was orderly, prepared, tidy. Rich people were so lucky. "There was a woman. On the road. She flagged me down. She was speaking Spanish."

"You saw someone—yesterday, when you went out?" Absurd that was yesterday! G. H. tried but could not answer what day of the week it was. "Why didn't you say?"

"She was—she was standing on the side of the road. She flagged me down. I talked to her. Well, I tried to." He knew his son was listening. It was terrible to be ashamed in front of your own child.

"We asked you what you had seen." George was irritated. He needed all the information before he could decide what to do next.

"She was dressed like a maid. I guess? In a polo shirt. A white polo shirt. I thought—I don't know. I couldn't understand her. She was speaking in Spanish, and I don't know what she was saying, and I would have used Google Translate but I couldn't and then I just—" He didn't know if he could say it in front of Archie.

G. H. thought of Rosa, who kept their own house in order, whose husband sculpted and tended the hedge, whose children played quietly, sometimes, as their parents worked in the summer heat, pretending not to see the swimming pool, though Ruth had once told Rosa the children were welcome to swim. They never would. It was not in them. Had it been her? "A Hispanic woman?"

Archie was listening, but Archie understood. He didn't know what he would have done; he knew that it was foolishness to pretend that anyone would know what they might do in such a moment.

"I left her there. I didn't know what else to do. I didn't know what was happening. I didn't know *something* was happening." Clay could never have imagined anything so specific as the unexplained birds, the lost

teeth. What if Rose, right then, was wandering on the side of the road, and sought help from some passing motorist? Why would she? He had no idea what she thought, his daughter.

"Never mind." G. H. didn't think morality was a test. It was an ever-shifting set of concerns. "Pay attention. Draw a map that you'll be able to read. Write down what we do."

"I left her. She needed help. We need help." It was karma, was that it? Clay thought the universe didn't care. He was probably right. But maybe it did; maybe it was math.

"We're going for help. You see this bend in the road? There's a farm just past there, McKinnon Farms. It's a landmark." It was odd to try to see the whole thing with fresh eyes. G. H. never thought about these roads. He possessed them without having to see them. This was their place, but it was also not their place. He didn't know who the McKinnons were, if they still had anything to do with the farm that bore their name. He and Ruth hadn't gone round to shake hands when they closed on the house. How would the locals take that, the black strangers in the eighty-thousand-dollar car? They holed up. They didn't even like to stop at the grocery or the gas station, conspicuous and tense. Would he need a gun, in the days to come? G. H. had never

believed in the things. Would the cash in the safe in the master bedroom closet do anything to help them?

Clay drew some lines on the paper. They were inscrutable the second he removed the pencil. His heart was not in it. His heart was in the back seat; his heart was wherever Rose was. "You don't understand." The sight lines were unobstructed, and the fields rolled away in their irritating and persistent way. "I didn't know what to do. I can't do anything without my phone. I'm a useless man. My son is sick and my daughter is missing and I don't know what I'm supposed to do right now in this moment right here, I have no idea what to do." His eyes horribly damp, Clay tried for composure. He swallowed the sob like it was a burp. He was so small.

George did not trust the place. If he'd had a cardiac event, he'd have paid the three thousand dollars for a helicopter lift back to Manhattan, where people took on faith the humanity of black people. This place was not good enough for him, beautiful as it was. Here, people were suspicious, resentful of and beholden to the rich, the outsiders. Here, people prayed that Mike Pence was an agent of the godly in the imminent end. All that research that doctors and nurses thought black people could *take it*, and withheld the palliative opioids. "I know what to do."

Clay couldn't say out loud that he didn't think the doctor would have anything for them. He had put the child's teeth into a Ziploc bag. It was in his left pocket, and he worried it like some gruesome rosary. "Maybe they'll be able to explain everything at the hospital."

"Before that. We need to stop. We're going to Danny's house."

"Whose house?"

George couldn't explain his faith that Danny, of all people, would understand what was happening, and have, if not a solution, a strategy. That's the kind of man he was. They could go to Danny and say the girl was missing or the boy was sick or they were all afraid of the noises in the night, and Danny, like the Wizard of Oz, could grant good health and safe passage. "Danny was our contractor. He's a neighbor. He's a friend."

The day outside seemed so normal. "We have to get Archie to the hospital."

"We will. Ten minutes. We'll stop for ten minutes. I'm telling you, Danny will help, he'll have an idea."

Clay was supposed to fight, he felt sure, but he only shrugged. "If you think so."

"I do." George had made his life this way. Problems had solutions, and Danny would have information and also might lead by example. He and Clay could come

back, roll up the sleeves of a chambray shirt, and protect the people they loved.

"There's no one around." Clay wondered if they'd see that woman again. He'd huddled with his family in the comfort of the king-size bed with its lovely semen-stained sheets, and that Mexican woman—but maybe she wasn't Mexican—had passed the night . . . he had no idea where.

"Too far from the beach to be a beach house. Not actually on a farm, so not a farmhouse. Not especially old, so not an historic house. Not brand-new and tricked out, so not a luxury house. Just a quiet place, the ends of the earth, somewhere to be alone and quiet and comfortable." Hadn't they earned the luxury of a little remove from the poor, the ignorant, the worse? "But it's an illusion, really. It's just a few minutes. A couple of miles this way. Stores, a movie theater, the highway, people. A movie theater, a mall. The ocean."

"We went there."

"A Starbucks."

"We stopped there."

"The conveniences. Alone but not really alone. It's just the idea. It's the best of both worlds."

"No cars. Have you heard a plane?" Clay stopped expecting to recognize the trees, the bends, the turns, the rises. "A helicopter? A siren?"

It was clear they'd have to learn a new way through a new world. "I haven't heard anything."

From the back seat, Archie listened. He watched out of the window, but he could only see the sky. He thought of Rose, and the deer she'd seen, but didn't know that they'd all got quite far away, in the night.

There was meaning in G. H.'s exhalation. Age made you more patient. "Everything is different. Are you writing this down?"

Clay looked at the map he'd made. It was illegible, useless. So he'd failed as a cartographer too. You told yourself you'd be attuned to a holocaust unfolding a world away, but you weren't. It was immaterial, thanks to distance. People weren't that connected to one another. Terrible things happened constantly and never prevented you from going out for ice cream or celebrating birthdays or going to the movies or paying your taxes or fucking your wife or worrying about the mortgage. "I'm writing it down."

G. H. was sure of it. "Danny will know something."

38

Ruth pulled open the door to the little shed. The hinge complained, but Amanda did not respond.

"Come on, now." Ruth didn't want to be this person. The helpmeet; the supporting player. Her daughter was also lost to her. Who would help her find her grandsons? Who would hold her up?

"Where's Rose, where's Rosie. What are we going to do?" Amanda was sitting on an upturned bucket.

"Come on. Stand up. Come out of here. Into the light." The little building smelled.

The women went outside. The sun asserted itself. Ruth checked the timer on the phone. It had been eleven minutes. George would be back in forty-nine. This was not so long. You could reduce it down to seconds and keep vigil, count it out loud. She'd hear

the approach of the car on the gravel. She'd see him again. "That's better," she said, and it was. The fresh air made some kind of promise. "They took Archie. He was sick again."

Amanda couldn't think about this too.

"We made a plan. One hour. They'll take him. George will be back for you and me and Rose."

"Should we go to the woods in the back? Should we walk to the road? How far is it? Is it this way?" Amanda pointed, but she wasn't sure where.

"The road is down that way. Would she go down there?" This didn't make any sense to Ruth. She couldn't imagine why the girl would forsake the safety of the little brick house.

"I don't know! I don't know why she'd leave. I don't know where she'd go." Amanda couldn't say it, but what if the girl hadn't left at all, was already dead, somewhere in the house? That thing with JonBenét Ramsey had begun as the search for a missing child, but her corpse had been in the basement all the while. Who killed JonBenét Ramsey, anyway? Amanda couldn't remember.

"Let's go back inside. Let's walk through the house once more." Ruth had a terrible vision—the girl in the powder room by the side entrance, toothless and faint?

"Rose!" Amanda screamed it. The day was silent in response. There was nothing out there for them.

"Let's look inside. Let's be methodical." Ruth needed them to make sense of things.

They hurried up the driveway, the gravel shifting under their steps. Amanda could feel every rock through the thin rubber soles of her shoes. Ruth could not move quite as fast as the younger woman, but she did. There was an urgent matter to attend to. "Let's go inside." Amanda said it like it had been her idea. "Maybe she's hiding." There was no reason for the girl to hide, but maybe she was? She was jealous of the attention her brother had earned. She was lost in a book. She didn't want to go home. "Do you think they've got to the hospital yet?"

"It's too soon. But they're on their way." Ruth went into the house by the side door. She opened the little closet where they had some waterproof boots, the chemical ice melt for the steps, one of the two broad plastic snow shovels, an old canvas tote bag stuffed with other canvas tote bags. No Rose.

"They're going. They'll be safe." Amanda was convincing herself.

"George will leave Clay and Archie. They can see the doctor. Then he'll come right back for us."

"I'm not leaving without Rosie!" Amanda opened the powder room door. Nothing.

"Of course. That's the plan. He'll come back for the three of us." It was just sensible.

"And what? We'll leave? We didn't finish packing!" They needed their things.

"We'll go back. We'll see to Clay and Archie. Then I don't know what." Ruth wanted to say: You don't need your things. You have us. We have one another.

"Rose!" The name just fell into the empty house. There was only the exhalation of all those appliances, but neither woman heard that anymore. "Then what? What's the doctor going to say? What's the doctor going to do? Did Clay even take the teeth with him?" They'd put them into a plastic baggie. Macabre. Would a doctor screw them back into his head?

"I don't know then what."

"We'll go home? We'll come back here?" Neither made any sense.

Ruth opened the pantry door. No thirteen-year-old girl would hide there. "I don't know!" She was, in fact, yelling. Ruth was mad too. "I don't know what we'll do, don't ask me as though I have some answer at my disposal that you don't. I don't know what we'll do."

"I just want to know what the fuck is going to happen. What the fuck is the plan. I want to know that

we're going to find my kid and all three of us are going to get in your fucking expensive car and drive to the hospital and the doctor is going to tell me that my baby is okay, and that we're all okay, and that we can all go back to our house."

"I know that. But what if that's not possible?"

"I just want to get the fuck away from here and you and whatever is happening—" Amanda hated her.

"It's happening to all of us!" Ruth was furious.

"I know that it's happening to all of us!"

"You don't care, do you, that I'm here and my daughter is in Massachusetts—" She could feel the ghost embrace, her grandsons' four sweet hands.

"I care, I don't know what I'm supposed to do about it. My daughter is in— I don't know where my daughter is!"

"Stop yelling at me." Ruth sat down at the kitchen island. Ruth looked up at the glass globe of the pendant light, the one that had shattered when the planes—she didn't know those were planes—had flown overhead. Why did this woman not understand that however unlucky they were, they were also lucky? Ruth wanted to sleep in her own bed. But she wanted these people to stay.

"I'm sorry." Did she mean it? It didn't matter. "Rose!" Amanda looked at the woman and under-

stood. They could not leave this house. They could not go back to Brooklyn. They could see the doctor and maybe stop at the store and come back here and hide and wait for whatever was coming. This woman was not a stranger at all; she was their salvation. "I'm sorry. I just want my daughter."

"I want my daughter too." Ruth could hear Maya's voice, the sweet register of her girlhood. Ruth could not make peace with whatever was required. She wanted to know that her child and her grandchildren were safe, but of course, Ruth would never know that. You never know that. You demanded answers, but the universe refused. Comfort and safety were just an illusion. Money meant nothing. All that meant anything was this—people, in the same place, together. This was what was left to them.

"Rose!" Amanda did not sit because she could not. She went back through the living room, into the bedroom that was Archie's, through the bathroom where the tub was now empty, to the bedroom that had been Rose's. Amanda knelt on the floor and looked under the bed, where there was nothing, not even dust. She went back to the bathroom and plugged the drain properly and began filling the tub with water.

She emerged into the living room. "I'm sorry. I'm sorry I yelled. I'm sorry I'm terrible. I want my daugh-

ter, I don't know why I yelled at you. I know you understand, but I want my daughter. She was just right here.
I don't understand what's happening." She wanted to
hug Ruth, but she could not.

Ruth did understand. Everyone understood. This
was what everyone wanted, to be safe. This was the
thing that eluded every single one of them. Ruth stood
up. So, she'd look for the girl, or her corpse, if she was
dead. She'd do what was required, she'd do what was
human.

Amanda pushed open the doors to the back porch
and looked down at the pool. She screamed her daughter's name at the woods. The trees moved a little in the
wind, but that was the only thing that happened.

39

It didn't even look like a driveway, but through a little copse, the way widened, and then was paved. There was a lawn that seemed manicured from a distance but was actually wild, feverish. From afar the green was so dazzling, you assumed it had to be the work of man. There was a fence, and there was the house, colonial, an ersatz echo of the original American ideal, with seven bedrooms, whirlpool tubs, granite countertops, central air.

George saw the silver Range Rover and was reassured. Danny was in residence. They'd been right to come. He'd only begun to say "Let's go," but Clay's need was as urgent as his, because he was already out of the car. "Archie. You stay there. You lie down."

The boy looked up at the older man. He could see

that the sky was more blue now, that it would be a perfect day for lunch outside, though what he could eat with his toothless mouth he wasn't sure. "Okay. I'll wait."

The front door was a slick and jolly yellow, something Danny's wife, Karen, had seen in a magazine. G. H. rang the doorbell. He almost knocked and then told himself to be more patient. It wouldn't do to turn up like a lunatic. The world might have gone mad, but they had not.

Danny and Karen had passed the night as uneasily as the rest of them. The family bed, four-year-old Emma between them as the boom died out overhead. Karen almost catatonic, thinking of her son, Henry, at his father's place in Rockville Center. Their phones hadn't worked, and the boy was deeply attached to his mother, and she knew, they both knew, he was probably even then calling out for her, fruitless. Would his father bundle him into the car and drive him home? Karen tried to will it to be so, but among their irreconcilable differences was his inability to understand what she wanted. Danny was in the kitchen, taking stock of what they had on hand, and was irritated by the interruption. This was evident as he opened the door.

"George," he said, recognition but not warmth. Danny was very handsome. This was always the first

impression he made. Regular exposure to the sun had rendered his skin golden. Genetic predisposition had salted his brown hair. His stance was wide as his shoulders, his posture confident, because he knew that he was handsome and therefore he stood like he knew it. He offered himself to the world, and the world said its thanks. He was surprised but also not that surprised.

"Danny." G. H. hadn't planned what would happen next. But there was some relief in just seeing another human being. It seemed it had been so long since that night at the concert, shaking hands and praising the performers.

The sight of the man reminded Danny of work. That was just a matter of putting on a smile, reassuring people, barking orders, collecting a check; it had nothing to do with his real life—the woman upstairs reading a book about dragons to a frightened but also indifferent little girl. Once he'd seen the news alert, Danny had gone out for supplies, for news. He'd come home with groceries but little else. "This is a surprise."

G. H. could see he'd miscalculated. He understood the man's posture. He should have known that what he'd always believed of people was true; that social order had allowed most of them to believe themselves not social animals. "I'm sorry to bother you at home like this."

Danny looked from George to the stranger beside him. Had he ever liked George? Not really. It didn't matter; that was not the question. There was nothing to it. So he didn't like Obama, either. It had to do only with the presumption of it, the fist bumping, the joviality. It insulted him, a mockery of the world as he understood it. "What—what can I do for you?" He made it clear that he was off the clock, not interested in doing anything for the many.

G. H. felt the beginning of a smile, a salesman's tactic. "Well, something is happening." He was not stupid. "We were driving by, and I thought I would check in on you. See if you're here. If you're okay. If you'd heard anything."

Danny looked over his shoulder, back into the house, past the curlicue of the banister. He saw motes dancing in the morning light from the living room's double-height windows. He saw everything as it ought to have been, but he didn't trust it. He didn't trust anything. He stepped toward the men and closed the door behind them. "Heard anything? You mean, besides what we heard yesterday?"

"I'm Clay." He didn't know what else to say. Clay wondered if this man would walk the woods with them until they met Rose. Would he have medicine for Archie? Would he have an internet connection? Would

he welcome them into this handsome house, the size of a hotel, and would it be like a party, and if so did they have a swimming pool? He imagined the women had recovered Rose, playing in the shade of the woods. He imagined that Archie was feeling better, a temporary stomach bug. Maybe they didn't need anything from this man and all was well, maybe they'd just say hello, commiserate, ask whether the noise—when had that been?—had cracked any of his windows.

Danny went on. "I'm surprised you guys are out."

"What do you mean?" G. H. was trying to get something, anything.

"What do I mean?" Danny's laugh was hard, angry. "There's some real shit going on out there, George. You don't know that? You can't hear it from that nice house of yours? My guys did a good job, but I know you heard that last night."

"My family is renting George's house. We're here from the city." Clay didn't know why he was trying to explain himself; he couldn't understand how little Danny was interested.

"That's a lucky break for your family." Danny knew the man was from the city. It was clear. He did not care. "Can you imagine what a shitshow that must be?"

"What do you know? Have you heard anything?" George asked.

"I know what you probably know." Danny sighed, impatient. "Apple News says there's a blackout. I think, okay, we're safe out here. I've got no service. I've got no cable. But I've got power. So I drive into town for some stuff. I think the store's going to be mobbed, right? Nope. Quiet. Not like before a snowstorm, more like after a foot has fallen. No one knows what's going on. It's just another day. I come home, hear that noise, and think, That's it, we're not leaving. Then last night— the noise again. Three times. Bombs? Missiles? I don't know, but I'm staying put until I hear that I shouldn't."

"You went to the store." George wanted to be clear.

"Stocked up. Came home. It just doesn't feel like out there is the place to be."

"My son is sick." Clay didn't know how to explain that something had knocked the teeth from Archie's sixteen-year-old mouth. It made no sense. "He was vomiting. He seems okay, now." Clay was still hopeful.

G. H. interjected. "He lost his teeth. Five of them. They just fell out. We can't explain it."

"His teeth." Danny was quiet for a while. "You think it had something to do with that noise?" Danny didn't know that the teeth in Karen's mouth were themselves loose, would soon fall out.

"Did your windows crack?" George asked.

"The shower door. The master bath." Danny

thought it was obvious. "It's something. Had to be a plane. I don't think there's any information getting out, so I assume it's a war. The beginning of a war."

"War?" Somehow this had not occurred to Clay. This seemed almost disappointing, a letdown.

"Has to be an attack I think? They were talking about the super hurricane on CNN. The Iranians or whoever—they planned it right. The perfect shit-show." Danny had seen a broadcast of a local Washington anchor in a boat to show the water standing inside the Jefferson Memorial.

"You think we're under attack?" G. H. didn't, but he wanted to hear.

"They've been saying there was chatter, this has to be what they were chattering about." Danny pitied anyone who couldn't see how obvious it was.

This man was a conspiracy theorist. He was crazy. Clay was a professor. "Chatter? What happened at the store? We need to go to the hospital."

"You've got to read the papers. Deeper than page one. The Russians recalled their staff from Washington, did you notice that? That was in bold print, that got a 'breaking.' Something's afoot, man." Danny coughed and put his hands in his pockets.

"We're going to the hospital." Clay said it again, but he was less certain.

"What you do is your business. What I'm doing is staying right here." Danny wanted them gone.

"This is what you think, Danny?" G. H. turned it around on him.

"Nothing is making a whole lot of sense at the moment. If the world doesn't make sense, I can still do what's rational. It's not safe out there." Danny nodded toward the expanse of nothing, which did not look any different, but he wasn't fooled.

"Archie is sick." Clay needed an answer.

George understood why Danny had closed the door at his back. George had expected human communion, but he forgot what humans were actually like. "I thought it was the right thing to do. Seek medical attention."

Danny was not smiling. "That's the old way, George. You're not thinking clearly."

"My daughter is missing. We woke up this morning, and she was gone. She was in the woods with her brother, playing, when we heard that noise. Then last night, his teeth." Clay didn't know how to finish so absurd a story. "I don't know what to do." It came out of him as a confession.

It wasn't that Danny didn't feel bad. There was only so much he could think about. "He's your son. You have a difficult choice."

308 · RUMAAN ALAM

"He's sixteen." Help us, Clay was saying, in his way.

There is no help, Danny was saying. They had misunderstood what kind of person he was. They had misunderstood people. "I don't know what you're going to do. I'd do anything I had to for my daughter. So that's what I'm doing. I'm locking the doors. I'm getting out my gun. I'm waiting. I'm watching."

Was the mention of a gun a threat? G. H. understood it as one. "We shouldn't go to the hospital."

"I don't have any answers for you guys. I'm sorry." This apology was mostly a remembered instinct. But Danny was sorry, for all of them. He shared what information he had. "Yesterday, I saw deer from the kitchen."

G. H. nodded. Deer were everywhere out there.

Danny clarified. "Not deer, not a *family* of deer. A migration. I've never seen so many in my life. A hundred? Two hundred? I couldn't even guess." There were more than that. The eye couldn't take them all in, couldn't find them in the shadows of the trees. Only the people who knew such things knew there were around thirty-six thousand deer in the county. They were not the deer Rose had seen but were on their way to join those. A mass migration. A disaster response. A disaster indicator. A disaster unfolding.

Clay wanted to tell him that the night before they'd seen a flock of flamingos, but it would have seemed like one-upmanship.

"The animals," Danny continued. "They know something. They're spooked. I don't know what's happening, and I don't know when we're going to figure out what is. Maybe this is it. Maybe this is as much as we'll ever know. Maybe we just need to sit tight and be safe and pray or whatever works for you." They were animals too. This was their animal response.

Clay felt they'd been talking for an hour. "You told Ruth you'd be back."

"We have time." G. H. would keep his promise.

Danny felt there was little point going on like this. "Guys, I'm going to go inside now. I'm going to say goodbye and good luck." He meant that last bit. They'd all require it. "If you go back out. If you—well, you can stop by. But I can't offer you much more than just conversation. You understand."

George felt foolish. Of course this was how Danny would be. All business. They were not friends, and even if they had been, these were extraordinary circumstances. "I guess that's it then."

Danny offered some advice. "I think you should get back in your car and drive to your house." Leave, also

leave me alone. "That's the only thing I've got for you. Hunker down, lock the door, and—" He didn't have a plan beyond that. "Fill the bathtub. Store water. Take stock of your food. See what supplies you have."

"I think we'll do that." G. H. wanted to be back among his things.

Danny nodded, kind of tossing his chin forward, authoritative. He extended a handshake. His grip was firm as it always was. He didn't say anything more, went back inside. He didn't lock the door. But he stood just inside to listen to the men walk away.

In the car, Archie sat up. He looked better or the same. He seemed weak or strong. That moment was what counted the most.

They sat in the idling car for a minute. Maybe two. Maybe three. It was Clay who broke the silence. "George. What are we doing?"

G. H. had been foolish. People disappointed. He would do better. They would still be good, kind, human, decent, together, safe. "I don't think we can go to the hospital, gentlemen. Do we agree? I don't think we can go."

Archie understood. Archie had been listening. "I'll be fine. I don't think we should go."

Clay said it. "I want to go home. Can we go home?

Let's go home. It's not far. We're so close. Let's go."
He meant George's house, of course, and so they went,
were back well before the alarm on Ruth's phone told
them that it had been an hour. Less than an hour, and
everything was changed.

40

Rose had woken with conviction. That's what it was to be a kid, but also she had a mission. Her eyes sharpened their focus: bedside table, green porcelain lamp, a framed photo she hadn't even bothered looking at yet, her own pale foot poking out of the bed linens, sherbet light melting onto the wall. Slack, damp mouths, pink shoulders, tangled hair. Another day, and those were a gift. Rose scooted free of her family and onto the carpet. The youngest child was used to not being noticed.

She left the suite because she didn't want to wake them. No one took her seriously because she was a kid, but Rose was not an idiot. That noise last night was the answer her parents had been pretending not to wait for. But Rose had read books, Rose had seen movies, Rose

knew how this story would end, and Rose knew they shouldn't panic, but prepare. In the bath off her bedroom, she peed, and it took a long time. Rose washed her hands and face. Though Rose wasn't particularly quiet—letting the toilet seat bang, running the water, closing the door more noisily than was necessary—this all felt furtive.

Shoes tied, a spritz of Off! on the ankle where the mosquitoes were most merciless, water. She pushed her refillable plastic bottle into the refrigerator's built-in dispenser. Rose unwrapped a banana and listened to the wet sound of her own chewing. The garbage was overflowing: crinkled cellophane, stained paper towels, used-up hunks of lemon no one had thought to compost. They had almost nothing left to eat. Rose knew they needed things, but more than that, they needed people. She would find both, in the house in the woods. Rose put a nectarine into her bag, where it would knock around in the cheap nylon, be bruised and leaking by the time she got around to it. She packed a book, as you never knew when you'd need a book.

Rose remembered. Into the woods and just in that direction, over there, that way, right there, kind of to the left, straight, under trees and over that little hill. She had an instinct that city living hadn't dulled. An animal, damp on canvas toes, her steps barely regis-

tered on the leaves, just the tiniest protest amid bird-song and breeze. Her body knew there was no predator nearby.

Rose and Archie had only been improvising, but maybe they hadn't. Kids knew something, and the knowledge that they had was tacit or unspeakable. Rose recognized every marker: the swell of the earth, the moldering log, certain fallen limbs. If she had looked back, Lot's wife, Rose might have seen a flamingo, pink and furious, flying through the air. The truth: they'd blown in on the winds. One of evolution's old tricks. Stowaway lizards on a log, swept to sea like Noah and Emzara, might make landfall on some new shore, and get busy getting busy, their descendants devastating native foliage. The flamingos were as angry as the humans to find themselves there. But they'd have to make do. They'd have to suss out some algae. They nested once a year, but that was all it took, and maybe a thousand generations from then they'd be inbred and some other crazy color (antifreeze blue from sipping from swimming pools?), some new species. Maybe they'd be all that was left.

Rose sang to herself, in her head first, and then she felt bold, or different, or fine, or happy, and sang out loud, a One Direction song, the kind of thing Archie would have mocked her for liking but secretly enjoyed.

Rose felt a clarity that was hers by rights. She understood. Once she got to that other house, she'd be able to answer the questions that seemed to matter to everyone. There would be people there and they would have an answer, or at least her family would not feel so alone.

The morning was cool, but you could tell the day would be hot. The leaves underfoot were barely damp: the tops of the trees were that thick. A time zone away, it was still dark, but then it was dark in so many places. Some people were committing suicide. Some people were packing things up in cars and hoping they'd be able to get a mile or two or ten or whatever it would take to reach wherever safety endured. Some people thought they'd cross the border, not realizing that such lines were imaginary. Some people didn't know anything was amiss. There were towns in New Mexico and Idaho where nothing had happened yet, though it was odd how no one could seem to talk to the satellites overhead. People still went to jobs that in time they would see were wholly useless, selling potted plants or making up hotel beds. Governors declared states of emergency but couldn't figure out how to tell anyone. Stay-at-home mothers were irritated that Daniel Tiger was not available. Some people started to realize they'd had a naive faith in the system. Some people tried to maintain that system. Some people were vindicated

that they'd stockpiled guns and those filter straws that made any water safe to drink. However much had happened, so much more would happen. The leader of the free world was sequestered beneath the White House, but no one cared about him, certainly not a little girl tripping through the woods and thinking about Harry Styles.

Rose wasn't brave. Kids were merely too young to know to look away from the inexplicable. Kids stared at the raving schizophrenic on the subway while adults cast eyes down and thought about podcasts. Kids asked questions they didn't know were deemed impolite: why do you have that bump on your neck, is there a baby growing in your tummy, did you always have no hair, why are your teeth silver, will there still be elephants when I'm all grown up? Rose knew what the noise was, but no one had asked her. It was the sound of fact. It was the change they'd pretended not to know was coming. It was the end of one kind of life, but it was also the beginning of another kind of life. Rose kept walking.

Rose was a survivor and would survive. She knew, by some instinct (maybe just the human connection), that she was in the minority. Somewhere south, levees had ceded to the river. Waters rose into second-story bedrooms and people made their way to attics and rooftops. In Philadelphia, a woman delivering for the third

LEAVE THE WORLD BEHIND · 317

time—a son, to be named for her brother, killed while deployed in Tehran—felt the baby on her chest just as the hospital lost power, so it was like the blackout was due to the shock of his skin on hers. All the babies in the neonatal intensive care unit died within hours. Christians gathered in their churches, but so did nonbelievers, thinking their devout neighbors might be better prepared. (Not so, alas.) In some places people were panicking about food, in others they were pretending not to. The staff at a Salvadoran restaurant in Harlem grilled food in the street, handing it out for free. Only twenty-four hours in, most people stopped listening to archaic radios and expecting to understand. Was this a test of faith? It affirmed only their faith in their ignorance. People locked doors and windows and played board games with their families, though a mother in St. Charles, Maryland, drowned her two daughters in the bathtub, which struck her as far more sensible than a round of Chutes and Ladders. That game required neither skill nor strategy; all it had to teach was that life was mostly unearned advantage or devastating fall. It took unimaginable courage to kill your children. Few people could manage it.

Damp at her neck, her forehead, her upper lip with its nascent mustache, Rose marched on. A few miles away, the herd of deer that Danny had seen had found

another, strength in numbers, and were walking in the direction that instinct told them, an astonishing sight, like the buffalo on the plains before white people killed them all. People in nearby houses couldn't exactly believe it, but were more credulous than they'd been a week ago. The next generation of these deer would be born white as the unicorn in those Flemish tapestries that Rose and her family would never see. Not albinism, the one geneticist who worked it out would discover, but intergenerational trauma. Life was like that; life was about change.

Some of the nearby locals got into their cars and drove toward the city. There were no police, so they sped. Brooklyn smelled: spoilage in refrigerated cases gone warm, garbage accreting on corners or wherever, plus the trapped commuters—the bipolar homeless man, the press secretary to the mayor, the optimists who'd been heading to job interviews at Google— slowly becoming unclaimed corpses.

There, in the woods, the air was sweet and rotten, as summer air tended to be. Rose wondered: Would they be a mother and father and one or two children? Would they be white like her family, or black like the Washingtons, or Indian like Sabeena's family, or from Saudi Arabia or Taipei or the Maldives? Did they know, in Saudi Arabia and Taipei and the Maldives, what was

happening in Waycross, Georgia, where the staff of forty jailers had left fifteen hundred men to the elements? Unexpected liberty: the sodden ceiling yielding, trapping bodies in the rubble, forever behind bars, but maybe their souls got out? None of those forty believed wind and rain could undo the work of man. None of those forty mourned those dead even one bit. They were bad men, they told themselves, not knowing how little it mattered whether you'd spent your life being good or bad.

Rose had been walking for an hour or her entire life. She unzipped her bag and bit into the bruised nectarine. Some flying insect, sensing the sweetness, hovered nearby. She ate the white flesh in one, two, seven, fourteen bites. The fruit pulled away so neatly from the stone at its center. A fruit's stone was something like a miracle, rutted and rough. She let it fall to the ground, hoping that, years from now, it might yield a tree.

She was not dumb. She did not expect salvation. She understood that alone, they had nothing. Now they would have something, and it would be thanks to Rose. She saw the roof through the woods, just where she knew it was going to be.

But the house was just like theirs! That seemed to mean something, even if, in a way, all houses looked

the same. Rose was heartened by this, the echo of the Washingtons' house, the way a baby's babble sounds like reassuring speech. Brave, she made her way around to the front door. Rose walked right up the brick path meant for visitors. She knocked firmly, fist tight and confident.

Careful not to crush the plantings, she stood in the mulch and pressed her face against the windows. A field of flowery wallpaper, an oil painting of a brown horse, a brass sconce, a closed door, a mirror reflecting back only her own face—her face, resolute and optimistic. She couldn't know, would never know, that the Thornes, the family who lived there, were at the airport in San Diego, unable to make arrangements since there were no flights operating domestically because of a nationwide emergency without precedent, as though precedent were required. The Thornes would never see this house again in their lives, though Nadine, the matriarch, would sometimes dream of it before she succumbed to cancer in one of the tent camps the army managed to erect outside the airport. They'd burn her body, before they stopped bothering with that, as the bodies outnumbered the people left to do the burning.

Rose walked to the back of the house and knocked on the sliding glass door. The room was different from the Washington's: the furniture heavier, the walls

darker. The house was not made to welcome vacation-
ers but appointed according to the tastes of the people
who lived there. Maybe those people were huddled in
the basement, waiting with guns; maybe those people
had heard the sound and got into their car and driven
as fast as possible. Rose went to the detached garage
and found cardboard boxes and pegboards hung with
tools but no car. There was, though, a boat, sheathed in
dirty canvas.

"You're not home." She said it out loud, but was
talking to herself. She rang the doorbell, and heard the
tinkle of it through the cheap, hollow door. She was
not going back without what she had come for.

There were ornamental stones marking the flower
bed alongside the house. Rose weighed tossing one
against the back door, then noticed that the panes bedside the front door were already cracked. She stood
back and threw it. The glass spilled into the house, the
stone fell back at her feet. The noise was brief; there
was just the sound of nothing. Rose pulled the sleeve of
her hoodie over her hand, held a smaller rock like it
was a hot pan, and banged into the points of glass that
clung to the frame. She reached inside, and the dead
bolt was right there. It was that simple.

The house smelled of cat. She'd find the cat food
and the litter box, but never the animal itself, which

had gone off to do whatever the animals were doing. She turned on the lights as a concession to her own fear. Rose knew, in that way you do, that she was alone. But she went into every room, opened every closet, pulled back the shower curtains, knelt to look beneath the beds. There was a pink-carpeted bedroom, the wooden bed with its floral spread angled to catch the full view of the treetops. There was a den, cabinets full of board games and puzzles, wide sectional in a standoff with the biggest television Rose had ever seen. There was a dining room, the vacuum cleaner's path marked on the immaculate blue carpet, the table polished and lustrous.

The refrigerator was a cacophony of magnets and notes and recipes and holiday cards, smiling families barefoot at the shore or posed against autumn foliage. Rose opened the door, and there was more there than at the Washingtons': salad dressings, ketchup, a glass jar of cornichons, soy sauce, one of those cardboard cans you pop to reveal biscuit dough. There were little plastic bottles of some medicine, an open stick of butter, some white cranberry juice. There were clean glasses in the dish rack, and she helped herself.

Sitting at the kitchen island, Rose saw the telephone, the fruit bowl with two lemons in it, the jumble of papers and mail. She opened a drawer in the kitchen,

and it was that drawer: rubber bands, dimes, an old battery, a pair of scissors, some coupons, a wrench. In the powder room off the hallway, Rose admired the little dish of soaps molded to look like seashells.

She went back to the den and switched on the television. The screen was blue. Rose opened the cabinet beneath it and found the PlayStation, the dozens of plastic boxes holding the various games, and dozens of DVDs. They didn't have a player at their house, but there was one in the classroom, and she was not stupid. She decided on *Friends*; they had the whole box set. It was the episode where Ross fantasized about Princess Leia.

The sound of the television made her feel so much better. She turned the volume loud to keep her company as she ransacked. Band-Aids, Advil, a package of batteries. These were treasure but meant as proof. There was a blue-walled bedroom, sparsely filled; clearly its teenage inhabitant had left home. This, Rose thought, this could be Archie's. She wouldn't mind the guest room, its staid oval rug, its fussy, frilly curtains. Home was just where you were, in the end. It was just the place where you found yourself.

She didn't know that her mother was, at that moment, sitting in quiet in the empty, bird-smelling egg shack. When Amanda saw her son again, it would take

her some time to find her voice. A shock. Then, later, she'd see her daughter again, and still be unable to speak. She'd just shiver.

Rose knew the way back—over that rise, then down it, carefully, correcting for gravity—past this familiar tree and that familiar tree and the little clearing with its sacred beam of light. She'd seen once, on the internet, that trees knew not to grow into one another, held themselves at some remove from their neighbors. Trees knew to occupy only their given patch of earth and sky. Trees were generous and careful, and maybe that would be their salvation.

She'd go back. She'd probably been missed, already, and felt a little guilty over not leaving a note. But she'd show them her bag, the things she'd found, tell them about the house in the woods with the DVD player and the three nice bedrooms and the camping supplies in the basement and the pantry lined with cans. She was only a girl, but the world still held something, and that mattered. Maybe her parents would cry over what they didn't know and what they did, which was that they were together. Maybe Ruth would empty the dishwasher and G. H. would take out the garbage, and maybe the day would truly begin, and if the rest of it—something for lunch, a relaxing swim, those pool floats, catching up on a magazine, attempting that jig-

saw puzzle?—was unclear, so be it. If they didn't know how it would end—with night, with more terrible noise from the top of Olympus, with bombs, with disease, with blood, with happiness, with deer or something else watching them from the darkened woods—well, wasn't that true of every day?

Acknowledgments

I'm deeply indebted to this book's editors—Helen Atsma, Sara Birmingham, and Megan Lynch—as well as to all their colleagues at Ecco, and, as always, to Julie Barer and Nicole Cunningham. I am very thankful for the generosity of Laura Lippman, Dan Chaon, Jessica Winter, Meaghan O'Connell, and Lynn Steger Strong. It is not an exaggeration to say this book would not exist without David Land; David, I hope for many more years of vacations (crumb-topped doughnuts, swimming pools, cake from a box on rainy days) with you.